The Nature of Learning

USING RESEARCH TO INSPIRE PRACTICE

Edited by Hanna Dumont, David Istance and
Francisco Benavides

OECD

ORGANISATION FOR ECONOMIC CO-OPERATION AND DEVELOPMENT

The OECD is a unique forum where governments work together to address the economic, social and environmental challenges of globalisation. The OECD is also at the forefront of efforts to understand and to help governments respond to new developments and concerns, such as corporate governance, the information economy and the challenges of an ageing population. The Organisation provides a setting where governments can compare policy experiences, seek answers to common problems, identify good practice and work to co-ordinate domestic and international policies.

The OECD member countries are: Australia, Austria, Belgium, Canada, Chile, the Czech Republic, Denmark, Finland, France, Germany, Greece, Hungary, Iceland, Ireland, Italy, Japan, Korea, Luxembourg, Mexico, the Netherlands, New Zealand, Norway, Poland, Portugal, the Slovak Republic, Slovenia, Spain, Sweden, Switzerland, Turkey, the United Kingdom and the United States. The Commission of the European Communities takes part in the work of the OECD.

OECD Publishing disseminates widely the results of the Organisation's statistics gathering and research on economic, social and environmental issues, as well as the conventions, guidelines and standards agreed by its members.

This work is published on the responsibility of the Secretary-General of the OECD. The opinions expressed and arguments employed herein do not necessarily reflect the official views of the Organisation or of the governments of its member countries.

ISBN 978-92-64-08647-0 (print)
ISBN 978-92-64-08648-7 (PDF)

Series: Educational Research and Innovation
ISSN 2076-9660 (print)
ISSN 2076-9679 (online)

Also available in French: *Comment apprend-on ? La recherche au service de la pratique*

Photo credits: Cover © Cultura Royalty-Free/Inmagine.com.

Corrigenda to OECD publications may be found on line at: *www.oecd.org/publishing/corrigenda*
© OECD 2010

Foreword

There is intense interest today in the nature of learning and creating the environments for it to flourish. Global drivers are pushing all countries to give priority to generating high levels of knowledge and skills with attention increasingly to more demanding forms of "21ˢᵗ century competences". The corollary concern is that traditional educational approaches are not adequately delivering on such demanding agendas. There have been major strides in measuring learning outcomes – of which our own PISA surveys are a prime example – which turns the spotlight onto how those outcomes can actually be changed. Meanwhile, despite high levels of educational investment (including in educational technology) and extensive educational reforms in our different countries, we know how difficult it is to make an impact on the "black box" of teaching and learning.

At OECD, we have developed an impressive battery of studies and surveys to address these different priorities. The PISA surveys are now prominently established on the world scene since the first survey took place a decade ago, with the initial results from the latest 2009 wave of student measurement covering 65 countries becoming available at the end of this year. The recent Teaching and Learning International Survey (TALIS) gathered data from over 70 000 teachers and school principals in lower secondary education in 23 countries to provide a detailed international picture on the conditions of teaching and learning, with main results published in 2009 and further work planned. Our Centre for Effective Learning Environments (CELE) looks at these questions from the perspective of the facilities and buildings for learning to ask what designs and facilities management are appropriate for the 21ˢᵗ century.

The OECD Centre for Educational Research and Innovation (CERI) is making its own very important contribution through wide-ranging analysis of learning and innovation, including by the "Innovative Learning Environments" project (ILE) which has produced this volume. CERI combines the forward-looking study of innovation with research-informed analysis to bring the different options for policy and practice into sharper relief. In recent years, CERI has worked intensively on a number of related key themes: how countries can make innovation more system-wide and sustainable, the nature of 21st century skills, how technologies can be used to reshape learning environments and the characteristics of "new millennium learners", exemplary formative assessment practices in schools and for low-skill adults, neuro-science and learning. CERI organised a major conference in Paris in May 2008 on all these themes to celebrate its 40th anniversary – "Learning in the 21st Century: Research, Innovation and Policy".

This book is a milestone in ILE work to follow the first project publication (*Innovating to Learn, Learning to Innovate*) in 2008. As the title *The Nature of Learning: Using Research to Inspire Practice* suggests, it aims to inform educational policy and practice via evidence-based reflection on how learning environments should be designed. Leading educational researchers and learning specialists were invited to review relevant research findings on a particular slice of the overall picture and to present their key implications in an understandable, accessible way. We are delighted that such eminent contributors from North America and Europe have agreed to take part. It is a most impressive line-up of authors providing very high quality chapters.

These chapters range over both the current understanding of the nature of learning and different educational applications. They cover the development of how learning has come to be understood, and key insights from the cognitive, emotional and biological perspectives. They look at approaches using, and evidence about, group work, technology, formative feedback and project-based learning, as well as what takes place beyond school settings in families and communities. They consider not only directions to follow but also how change might best be implemented. The volume concludes with a synthesis of the main findings, drawing all into seven key concluding principles and discussing their implications. We see it as invaluable reading for all those interested in knowing what research has to say about how to optimise learning for young people which we hope will inspire changes in practice.

This volume has been designed and edited by Hanna Dumont, of the University of Tübingen Germany, David Istance of the CERI Secretariat, and Francisco Benavides, formerly of CERI. It greatly benefited from seminar discussions in 2009 in Weimar in Germany (May), Oslo in Norway (August/ September) and at the CERI Governing Board meeting in Paris (November).

Barbara Ischinger

Director, Directorate for Education

OECD

Acknowledgements

We owe a large debt of thanks to the chapter authors, who accepted our initial invitation to join this venture and then responded to our many requests with so much patience: Brigid Barron, Monique Boekaerts, Erik De Corte, Linda Darling-Hammond, Kurt Fischer, Andrew Furco, Pam Goldman, Cristina Hinton, Venessa Keesler, Richard E. Mayer, Larissa Morlock, Elizabeth S. Rangel, Lauren B. Resnick, Barbara Schneider, Michael Schneider, Robert E. Slavin, James P. Spillane, Elsbeth Stern and Dylan Wiliam.

We extend a special word of gratitude to Monique Boekaerts, Erik De Corte and Michael Schneider who have played crucial additional roles in the design and the dissemination of this study. For the OECD, we wish to record our indebtedness to Hanna Dumont, of the University of Tuebingen Germany, who worked ceaselessly on all aspects of the volume from conception to completion as editor and author.

This book would not have been possible without the Directorate for Education and Training (Utdanningsdirektoratet) in Norway, which provided essential financial support. The Norwegian Directorate for Education and Training also generously hosted a key event in Oslo, 31 August and 1 September 2009, bringing together the authors and the participating ILE system representatives to discuss the contents in detail and to help shape the conclusions of this volume. We would particularly like to extend our thanks to Per Tronsmo, Katrine Stegenborg Teigen and to the former and current Norwegian CERI Board members Petter Skarheim and Hege Nilssen and to the rest of the conference team.

We thank the Thuringian Ministry of Culture and Education in Germany for hosting a seminar in Weimar on 14-15 May 2009 which brought key authors and experts together at a critical point in the study. We would particularly like to thank Rupert Deppe (also CERI Board member), Christine Minkus-Zipfel and Christina Kindervater for their most valuable support of this work.

We acknowledge the input made by all the participants at these events, as well as that of the CERI Governing Board made collectively and individually since the beginning of this study.

Within the OECD very special thanks are due to Taeyeon Lee for her dedicated hard work on this volume in the first half of 2010 during her traineeship with CERI from Kyung Hee University, Korea. Francesc Pedró contributed his expertise on technology issues in Chapter 1. We are grateful that Francisco Benavides was able to remain connected with the work after his transfer within the Education Directorate. OECD's Public Affairs and Communications Directorate (PAC) gave valuable detailed editorial advice. James Bouch looked after the logistics throughout much of the preparation of this report and Lynda Hawe, Peter Vogelpoel and Florence Wojtasinski contributed to the finalisation process prior to publication. CERI colleagues in general contributed in innumerable ways (including to the selection of an appropriate title).

Table of contents

Chapter 4. **The crucial role of motivation and emotion in classroom learning**. . . 91
— *Monique Boekaerts*

Chapter 5. **Learning from the developmental and biological perspective** 113
— *Christina Hinton and Kurt W. Fischer*

Chapter 6. **The role of formative assessment in effective learning
environments** 135
— *Dylan Wiliam*

Figures

Tables

Boxes

Executive summary

Why such interest in learning?

Over recent years, learning has moved increasingly centre stage for a range of powerful reasons that resonate politically as well as educationally across many countries, as outlined by Dumont and Istance (Chapter 1). These define the aims of this important volume from the work on Innovative Learning Environments produced by OECD's Centre for Educational Research and Innovation (CERI).

OECD societies and economies have experienced **a profound transformation from reliance on an industrial to a knowledge base**. Global drivers increasingly bring to the fore what some call "21st century competences". The quantity and quality of learning thus become central, with the accompanying concern that traditional educational approaches are insufficient.

Similar factors help to explain the **strong focus on measuring learning outcomes** (including the Programme for International Student Assessment [PISA]) over the past couple of decades, which in turn generates still greater attention on learning. To move beyond the diagnosis of achievement levels and shortcomings to desirable change then needs a deeper understanding of how people learn most effectively.

The rapid development and ubiquity of ICT are re-setting the boundaries of educational possibilities. Yet, significant investments in digital resources have not revolutionised learning environments; to understand how they might requires attention to the nature of learning.

The sense of reaching the limits of educational reform invites a fresh focus on learning itself: education has been reformed and reformed again in most OECD countries, leading many to wonder whether we need new ways to influence the very interface of learning and teaching.

The research base on learning has grown enormously but many researchers observe how inadequately schools tend to exemplify the conclusions of the learning sciences. At the same time, far too much research on learning is disconnected from the realities of educational practice and policy making. Can the bridges be made to inform practice by this growing evidence base?

The coverage of *The Nature of Learning*

This volume aims to help build the bridges, "using research to inspire practice". Leading researchers from Europe and North America were invited to take different perspectives on learning, summarising large bodies of research and identifying their significance for the design of learning environments, in such a way as to be relevant to educational leaders and policy makers.

The early chapters address the nature of learning, including through the cognitive, emotional and biological perspectives. The contributions that follow review approaches and evidence for different types of application: formative assessment, co-operative and inquiry-based forms of learning, technology-based applications – as well as learning beyond classroom environments in communities and families. The penultimate chapter considers strategies to refocus educational organisations with their in-built resistance to innovation and change.

The chapters do not offer exhaustive coverage of all the relevant research findings but together they provide a powerful knowledge base for the design of learning environments for the 21st century. As summarised by De Corte (Chapter 2), many scholars now agree on the key importance for organisations and policy to develop in learners "adaptive expertise" or "adaptive competence", *i.e.* the ability to apply meaningfully-learned knowledge and skills flexibly and creatively in different situations.

Transversal conclusions on learning

The transversal conclusions, recasting the evidence reviewed in the different chapters more holistically, are synthesised by Istance and Dumont in the final chapter together with discussion of the challenge posed by their implementation. The conclusions are presented below with a small selection of the key arguments made by the different authors.

> The learning environment recognises the learners as its core participants, encourages their active engagement and develops in them an understanding of their own activity as learners.

The learning environment recognises that the learners in them are the core participants. A learning environment oriented around the centrality of learning encourages students to become "self-regulated learners". This means developing the "meta-cognitive skills" for learners to monitor, evaluate and optimise their acquisition and use of knowledge (De Corte, Chapter 2; Schneider and Stern, Chapter 3). It also means to be able to regulate one's emotions and motivations during the learning process (Boekaerts, Chapter 4; Hinton and Fischer, Chapter 5).

Wiliam (Chapter 6) notes that many have called for a shift in the role of the teacher from the "sage on the stage" to the "guide on the side." He warns against this characterisation if it is interpreted as relieving the teacher, individually and collectively, of responsibility for the learning that takes place.

Resnick, Spillane, Goldman and Rangel (Chapter 12) identify as critical the gap between the "technical core" (*i.e.* classroom teaching) and the formal organisation in which it is located and the wider policy environment, a gap which reduces learning effectiveness and innovative capacity.

> The learning environment is founded on the social nature of learning and actively encourages well-organised co-operative learning.

"Effective learning is not purely a 'solo' activity but essentially a 'distributed' one: individual knowledge construction occurs throughout processes of interaction, negotiation and co-operation" (De Corte, Chapter 2). Neuroscience shows that the human brain is primed for interaction (Hinton and Fischer, Chapter 5). However valuable that self-study and personal discovery may be, learning depends on interacting with others.

There are robust measured effects of co-operative forms of classroom learning when it is done properly as described by Slavin (Chapter 7). Despite this, such approaches still remain on the margins of much school activity. The ability to co-operate and learn together should be fostered as a "21st century competence", quite apart from its demonstrated impact on measured learning outcomes.

> The learning professionals within the learning environment are highly attuned to the learners' motivations and the key role of emotions in achievement.

The emotional and cognitive dimensions of learning are inextricably entwined. It is therefore important to understand not just learners' cognitive development but their motivations and emotional characteristics as well. Yet, attention to learner beliefs and motivations is much further away from standard educational thinking than goals framed in terms of cognitive development (Boekaerts, Chapter 4).

Being highly attuned to learners' motivations and the key role of emotions is not an exhortation to be "nice" – misplaced encouragement will anyway do more harm than good – but is first and foremost about making learning more effective, not more enjoyable.

Powerful reasons for the success of many approaches using technology (Mayer, Chapter 8), co-operative learning (Slavin, Chapter 7), inquiry-based learning (Barron and Darling-Hammond, Chapter 9) and service learning (Furco, Chapter 10) lie in their capacity to motivate and engage learners.

> The learning environment is acutely sensitive to the individual differences among the learners in it, including their prior knowledge.

Students differ in many ways fundamental to learning: prior knowledge, ability, conceptions of learning, learning styles and strategies, interest, motivation, self-efficacy beliefs and emotion, as well in socio-environmental terms such as linguistic, cultural and social background. A fundamental challenge is to manage such differences, while at the same time ensuring that young people learn together within a shared education and culture.

Prior knowledge is one of the most important resources on which to build current learning as well as one of the most marked individual difference among learners: "…perhaps the single most important individual differences dimension concerns the prior knowledge of the learner" (Mayer, Chapter 8). Understanding these differences is an integral element of understanding the strengths and limitations of individuals and groups of learners, as well as the motivations that so shape the learning process.

"Families serve as the major conduit by which young children acquire fundamental cognitive and social skills" (Schneider, Keesler and Morlock, Chapter 11), meaning that prior knowledge is critically dependent on the family and background sources of learning and not only what the school or learning environment has sought to impart.

> The learning environment devises programmes that demand hard work and challenge from all without excessive overload.

That learning environments are more effective when they are sensitive to individual differences stems also from the findings stressed by several authors that each learner needs to be sufficiently challenged to reach just above their existing level and capacity. The corollary is that no-one should be allowed to coast for any significant amounts of time on work that does not stretch them.

Learning environments should demand hard work and effort from all involved. But the findings reported in this volume also show that overload and de-motivating regimes based on excessive pressure do not work because they do not make for effective learning. For Schneider and Stern (Chapter 3), a fundamental cornerstone is that "learning is constrained by capacity limitations of the human information-processing architecture" (also stressed by Mayer, Chapter 8).

> The learning environment operates with clarity of expectations and deploys assessment strategies consistent with these expectations; there is strong emphasis on formative feedback to support learning.

Assessment is critical for learning. "The nature of assessments defines the cognitive demands of the work students are asked to undertake" (Barron and Darling-Hammond, Chapter 9). It provides "the bridge between teaching and learning" (Wiliam, Chapter 6). When assessment is authentic and in line with educational goals it is a powerful tool in support of learning; otherwise it can be a serious distraction.

Formative assessment is a central feature of the learning environment of the 21st century. Learners need substantial, regular and meaningful feedback; teachers need it in order to understand who is learning and how to orchestrate the learning process.

The research shows strong links between formative assessment practices and successful student learning. Such approaches need to be integrated into classroom practice to have such benefits (Wiliam, Chapter 6).

> The learning environment strongly promotes "horizontal connectedness" across areas of knowledge and subjects as well as to the community and the wider world.

Complex knowledge structures are built up by organising more basic pieces of knowledge in a hierarchical way; discrete objects of learning need to be integrated into larger frameworks, understandings and concepts. (Schneider and Stern, Chapter 3).

The connectedness that comes through developing the larger frameworks so that knowledge can be transferred and used across different contexts and to address unfamiliar problems is one of the defining features of the 21st century competences. Learners are often poor at transferring understanding of the same idea or relationship in one domain to another.

Meaningful real-life problems have a key role to play in bolstering the relevance of the learning being undertaken, supporting both engagement and motivation. Inquiry- and community-based approaches to learning offer extensive examples of how this can be done (Barron and Darling-Hammond, Chapter 9; Furco, Chapter 10). An effective learning environment will at the least not be at odds with the influences and expectations from home; better still, it will work in tandem with them (Schneider, Keesler and Morlock, Chapter 11).

A demanding educational agenda

The force and relevance of these transversal conclusions or "principles" do not reside in each one taken in isolation from the others. Instead, they provide a demanding framework and all should be present in a learning environment for it to be judged truly effective. The educational agenda they define may be characterised as:

- **Learner-centred**: the environment needs to be highly focused on learning as the principal activity, not as an alternative to the critical role of teachers and learning professionals but dependent on them.

- **Structured and well-designed:** to be "learner-centred" requires careful design and high levels of professionalism. This still leaves ample room for inquiry and autonomous learning.

- **Profoundly personalised**: the learning environment is acutely sensitive to individual and group differences in background, prior knowledge, motivation and abilities, and offers tailored and detailed feedback.

- **Inclusive:** sensitivity to individual and group differences, including of the weakest learners, defines an educational agenda that is fundamentally inclusive.

- **Social:** The principles assume that learning is effective when it takes place in group settings, when learners collaborate as an explicit part of the learning environment and when there is a connection to community.

The final discussion of the volume addresses the challenge of implementation. While many suggestions for change relate to teacher skills and professional development, the implications extend deeply into the "routines" of schools (Resnick, Spillane, Goldman and Rangel, Chapter 12), raising the importance but also the difficulty of sustained innovation.

Chapter 1

Analysing and designing learning environments for the 21st century

Hanna Dumont and David Istance

University of Tübingen Germany and OECD, Paris

Hanna Dumont and David Istance set out the reasons why, over recent years, learning has moved increasingly centre stage politically. These include the nature of knowledge economies and societies, the demands of 21st century competences, the ubiquity of ICT, frustration with the lack of success of repeated education reforms and the burgeoning learning research base. They call for harnessing knowledge about learning and applying it more systematically to education. The chapter argues why these developments call for a particular focus on innovative "micro" arrangements – "learning environments" – which are conceptualised in this OECD work at a level between individual learners and conventional educational parameters. The chapter locates the book as seeking to address the "great disconnect" (as it has been called) between research, on the one hand, and policy and practice, on the other.

Introduction

Over recent years, learning has moved increasingly centre stage politically for a range of powerful reasons. This volume – which is both a collection of research reviews and an analysis of the implications of learning science research for educational design – is closely defined by these changes. This chapter elaborates on these contemporary developments that set the stage for the chapters to follow. These developments call for harnessing knowledge about learning and applying it more systematically to education. The chapter elaborates why these developments argue for a particular focus on the "micro" level of learning environments and why this needs to be forward-looking with a strong focus on innovation.

Learning moves centre stage

Key developments that we have summarised with the phrase "learning moves centre stage" can be grouped into five important currents of change. These are described briefly below and then core themes are elaborated in more detail.

Our societies and economies have experienced a profound transformation from reliance on an industrial to a knowledge base. Global drivers increasingly bring to the fore what some call "21st century competences" – including deep understanding, flexibility and the capacity to make creative connections, a range of so-called "soft skills" including good team-working. The quantity and quality of learning thus become central, with the accompanying concern that traditional educational approaches are insufficient.

There has been a strong focus and advance in measuring learning outcomes, including through the OECD's own PISA surveys, which in turn generates still greater public and political attention on learning. But there is no consensus about which outcomes matter most, and educational debates have swirled around opposing poles – between talk of "basics" and demanding "21st century skills", between "standards" and citizenship. Moreover, to move from charting levels, patterns and shortcomings in learning outcomes to making desirable change happen requires a major step including through posing the question: "how can we foster effective learning and what inspiring models exist from which others might learn?"

Education has been reformed and reformed again – **the sense of reaching the limits of educational reform invites a fresh focus on learning** itself. Reforms tend to rely particularly on manipulation of the institutional variables most amenable to policy influence or most in the public eye. Often, educational policy is driven by short-term considerations which, however unavoidable, are unlikely to form a convincing basis for profound change in educational practice. This leads many to wonder whether we need new ways to influence the very interface of learning and teachings rather than to treat it as a "black box".

The rapid development and ubiquity of ICT, and its importance especially in the lives of young people, are re-setting the boundaries of educational possibilities and augmenting the role of non-formal learning. There is widespread disappointment, however, that heavy investments in computers and digital connections have not revolutionised learning environments whether because the investments have focused too much on technology and not enough on enhancing learning opportunities, or because critical thresholds of ICT use for education have not been reached.

The research base on learning grows but, rather than guiding change, learning scientists lament that too many schools do not exemplify their conclusions. At the same time, far too much research on learning is disconnected from the realities of educational practice and policy making. There is, as it has been called, a "great disconnect".

The global knowledge society

One of the most fundamental of the changes of recent decades in OECD countries in particular is their transformation from an industrial to a knowledge base. Knowledge is now a central driving force for economic activity, and the prosperity of individuals, companies and nations depends increasingly on human and intellectual capital. Innovation is becoming the dominant driving force in our economy and society (Florida, 2001; OECD, 2004; Brown, Lauder and Ashton, 2008). Education and learning systems, for which knowledge is their core business, are clearly right at the heart of such a mega-trend.

We are living in a "global village". Through the process of globalisation, economies are closely linked to each other and the recent crisis has only emphasised just how inter-dependent are the prospects of different countries and populations. A different set of economies has emerged to claim their place in the front ranks, notably but not only China and India. The relocation of industrial activities to countries with lower labour costs brings its own challenges for "re-skilling" and learning in those from which activities are being lost.

There have come important shifts of population, bringing together culturally different beliefs, views and habits in life. Globalisation is manifest in international travel and contact with cultures and people from other countries. All this raises profound questions about how well education is preparing students for openness to others, cultural diversity and providing equality of educational opportunity for all its citizens (OECD, 2010a).

The shift to the global knowledge economy has been driven *inter alia* by the advances in science and technology, in particular in information and communication technologies. The widespread dissemination and use of the Internet and other advanced forms of media touches our everyday lives in manifold ways. Some may stress the liberating potential this represents as the barriers of time and distance are lowered; others draw attention instead to the information overload and the international digital divides that they bring. Education and learning are caught right in the middle of these very diverse developments, being driven to accommodate rapid change and overload but also to provide the bedrock foundations with which to cope with such change.

We are facing major challenges of sustainability. In part this is about the environment and ecology which are fundamentally related to individuals' values and habits and to wider corporate and political cultures. In part, this is the issue of the sustainability of OECD societies in which birth rates are low and populations are ageing, and of welfare societies and pension systems forged under the markedly different conditions of the post-WWII 20th century. There is also the issue of the sustainability of any society in which a shared sense of cohesion, equity and solidarity is needed when individualism becomes so dominant (OECD, 2008a). Learning values and attitudes, not just knowledge in a narrower sense, is fundamental but such learning is notoriously difficult to organise into an educational project, still more to teach.

As knowledge has become so fundamental then so has learning – how and how well that knowledge is acquired become uppermost. But attention to even this rapid summary of some of the major developments confronting early 21st century societies emphasises that the trends themselves and the knowledge, values and attitudes to be learned are complex and multi-faceted.

Laying foundations for lifelong learning

These powerful economic and social drivers, and the concern that initial formal education by itself is inadequate to respond to them, have underpinned the emergence of the broader concept of "lifelong learning" (*e.g.* OECD, 1996). This concept recognises that learning is not exclusive to the early years but continues throughout the lifespan; it acknowledges that learning takes place not only in schools and universities, but in many different formal, non formal and informal learning environments.

Different rationales can be forwarded for lifelong learning (Istance *et al.*, 2002). For some commentators, the economic and instrumental arguments have excessively dominated the political discourse and they remind us that lifelong learning should equally recognise "that each individual has a learning potential" (Longworth and Davis, 1996, p. 21) and is "an essential ingredient to the growth and development of the human person" (Jarvis, 2009). In this spirit, thorough-going lifelong learning should not only be viewed as a means to a dynamic economy, but also for effective community and social engagement, participatory democracy and for living fulfilling and meaningful lives.

The broad sweep of lifelong learning notwithstanding, the extent and quality of initial schooling during the formative years are crucial for learning later in life (Gorard, 2009; Hargreaves, 2003). The knowledge, skills, values and attitudes acquired during this early life-stage provide the foundation for the lifelong learning habit. Therefore, schools are pivotal organisations of the learning society yet their contribution in laying the foundation for lifelong learning has tended to be neglected. An important reason for this is because so much educational discourse is already dominated by a schools focus that lifelong learning proponents have been eager to concentrate instead on what takes place at later ages and stages. But, the paradoxical result is to strip the concept of its cradle-to-grave ambition by equating it implicitly with extended tertiary education and training (OECD, 2005).

What does laying the foundation for lifelong learning mean? One key measure of the success of schools in achieving this is the extent to which they equip young people both with a meaningful knowledge base and with the 21st century competences outlined next.

21st century competences

The major trends in societies and economies sketched above have focused attention increasingly on the demanding kinds of learning that may be summarised as "21st century skills or competences". These give content to the focus on "outcomes" that too often has not been sufficiently concerned with the question of **which** outcomes to prioritise. Higher-order thinking skills are increasingly integral to the workplace of today and tomorrow. We need to learn to generate, process and sort complex information; to think systematically and critically; to take decisions weighing different forms of evidence; to ask meaningful questions about different subjects; to be adaptable and flexible to new information; to be creative; and to be able to identify and solve real-world problems (Bransford *et al.*, 2000; Darling-Hammond, Barron, Pearson, Schoenfeld and Elizabeth, 2008; Fullan, Hill and Crevola, 2006; Green, 2002; OECD, 2008b).

Young people should ideally acquire a deep understanding of complex concepts and gain media literacy and the ability to use advanced information technologies (Sawyer, 2008; Darling-Hammond *et al.*, 2008; MacDonald, 2005). Teamwork, social and communication skills are integral to work and social life in the knowledge society. Students should develop into self-directed, lifelong learners, especially when education needs to prepare students "for jobs that do not yet exist, to use technologies that have not yet been invented, and to solve problems that we don't even know are problems yet" (Darling-Hammond *et al.*, 2008).

This does not mean that in future all will be moving into intellectual or technical occupations. The complex knowledge society has led in general to "up-skilling" but it has not evaporated the need for manual or service occupations and the creative fields are likely to be important sources of employment in the future. Young people may expect to operate in very diverse professional situations, including manual and artistic fields.

To draw attention to the skills used in contemporary and future workplaces is not to privilege only the economic demands over the competences called for to be effective in communities, social and personal life: the 21st century competences are relevant to all these domains. So, as expressed by de Corte (this volume), a core goal of education should be the acquisition of "adaptive competence, *i.e.* the ability to apply meaningfully learned knowledge and skills flexibly and creatively in a variety of contexts and situations".

Given their central role in the learning society, how are today's schools facing up to these 21st century demands? Practice varies widely, of course, within and across different OECD systems. We can say nevertheless that the pedagogic model underlying too many schools is still aimed at preparing students for the industrial economy, sometimes dubbed "instructionism" What goes on in many classrooms and schools is very different from the activities that are at the heart of knowledge-based enterprises in the knowledge economy. The implicit "mind-as-container metaphor" (Bereiter, 2002, p. 20) of schools does not reflect the productive, creative side of working with knowledge. This raises profound questions about whether the learning models and environments in the core of schooling are equipping students with the skills that are key to knowledge-based 21st century societies. Our report aims to clarify how learning might be organised so that they achieve this more effectively.

New Millennium Learners

The rapid development and ubiquity of ICT are changing the nature of socialisation, connecting to others, as well as augmenting the role of non-formal learning. More and more children and young people in OECD societies grow up with ready availability to Internet connections, mobile phones and videogame consoles. It has become typical for teenagers to connect to the Internet on a daily basis at home: as many as 95% or more 15-year-olds do so in the Nordic countries, the Netherlands, England and Austria (OECD, 2010b). They are so connected on average for two hours a day, mostly engaged in social interactions and the consumption of digital content but sometimes on school-related tasks.

The identities of young "new millennium learners" (the title of the relevant OECD project) are shaped by their interactions with other young people in an enlarged digital landscape of opportunities. This is also about how they learn: access to digital media is changing the way learners acquire information and elaborate knowledge. Indeed, young people's use of digital media is consistent with forms of learning that are well-aligned with the 21st century competences discussed above and with established principles of learning. It tends to be highly social, involves a good deal of experimentation and "tinkering", and encourages the production and sharing of knowledge; digital media facilitate learning that is more about interaction and participation rather than the passive consumption of information or knowledge (Ananiadou and Claro, 2009).

Understanding how young people learn, play and socialise outside the classroom may thus prove to be a useful inspiration for educational innovation. Digital media have the potential to transform learning environments permitting intensive networking and access anywhere and at anytime, thus helping to solder connections in the fragmented worlds and experiences of young people in school and outside. Technology can help empower learners to become active in shaping their own learning environments.

How far such potential and forms of learning carry over into explicitly educational activities at present is altogether another question. Traditional learning environments tend to be "low-tech" and in many schools there is not the intensity of technology use to reap its benefits. There needs to be a critical threshold of technology use attained or surpassed before measurable gains in educational results become visible, as recently charted using PISA evidence (OECD, 2010b). Today's estimated use of technology in compulsory education in the European Union countries, averaged across schools in general as opposed to innovative and technology-rich learning environments, falls far short of such threshold levels at less than one hour per week (Empirica, 2007). This pales compared with the 14 hours or so weekly connection average at home mentioned above. And, as Mayer also reminds us (this volume), the presence of technology itself is no guarantee that its particular benefits will be exploited for learning.

The limits of educational reform

In recent decades, there have been many educational reforms in OECD and other countries, implemented with the view of improving school quality and raising achievement, especially among the low-achievers. These reforms have included, among other things: major teacher training programmes, provision and use of new technologies, curriculum changes and system restructuring to give more autonomy to schools. Significant amounts of resources have been allocated to facilities and equipment, reducing class size and improving teacher qualifications.

Reforms are constantly impacting on the surface structures and institutional parameters of schools but it is far harder to reshape the core activities and dynamics of learning in the classroom. There is a tendency to focus on variables that are visible and relatively easy to change, resources permitting: it is altogether simpler, if expensive, to reduce class size and raise the numbers of computers in schools than it is, for instance, sustainably to improve teachers' capacities to respond to individual student differences. But approaches to improving educational quality via resourcing tend to be very indirect and succeed only to the extent that they change teaching and learning in classrooms and other settings.

Fullan and colleagues (2006) argue that "very few policy makers, or practitioners for that matter, really understand what quality means on a daily basis". Bereiter (2002) calls the disengagement from the core activity of instruction the "fundamental malady" of school reform. It is far from obvious, however, what instruments of policy would realise the difficult balance of understanding the classroom in all its richness while extending professional autonomy.

All this adds up to a daunting challenge, and not one that will be addressed at all adequately if it is assumed to be just a matter of policy makers becoming more enlightened. It calls for much greater transparency of what takes place in organised learning in countless settings, done in a way that is supportive of professionalism rather than intrusive or divisive. Such an opening of classroom doors (and windows and walls) to sympathetic scrutiny would by itself be a major shift of practice, and one that many within education would find discomfiting. It is to recognise that some of the primary sources of influence that policy reform can exercise will be through the powerful but largely intangible factors of shaping school cultures and climates: not only are these notoriously difficult to influence but they scarcely add up to a media-friendly policy programme defined around a small number of succinct punchy messages.

Hence, the reform challenge calls for a refocusing on the nature of learning and the means to best promote it but the mechanisms to do so are often far-removed from the realities of contemporary educational systems and politics. It will also need to bring researchers and practitioners squarely into the picture, rather than assume that these matters are primarily for educational policy makers to sort out for themselves. This in turn raises profound issues of knowledge management, which typically is seriously under-developed in education (OECD, 2000; OECD, 2004), and of addressing the "great disconnect" (Berliner, 2008) between educational research, on the one hand, and policy and practice, on the other.

Burgeoning research on learning – an evidence base for policy and practice?

Empirical evidence about how the mind works, how the brain develops, how interests form, how people differ, and, most importantly, how people learn has expanded tremendously over recent decades (Olson, 2003; Sawyer, 2006). Many different fields are now contributing to the understanding of learning and instruction: cognitive science, educational psychology, computer science, anthropology, sociology, information studies, neurosciences, education, design studies and instructional design (Sawyer 2008). A powerful knowledge base on how people learn has been accumulated and "the story we can now tell about learning is far richer than ever before" (Bransford *et al.*, 2000, p. 3). De Corte (this volume) also charts how this research has increasingly shifted from artificial laboratory exercises and situations to real-life classroom activity and hence to become much more relevant for education.

With the burgeoning of research has come the claim that practice and indeed educational policy can become genuinely "evidence-based" (OECD, 2007). This science of learning "underscores the importance of rethinking what is taught, how it is taught, and how learning is assessed" (Bransford *et al.*, 2000) and can guide the design of new and more powerful learning environments (De Corte, 2000). Raudenbush (2008) even goes so far as to conclude that "knowledge about the impact of instruction supplies a scientific basis for policy concerning resources. The study of classroom instruction therefore plays a role in educational policy that is similar to the study of clinical practice in health policy."

This optimistic claim for the potency and significance of the knowledge base contrasts markedly with the viewpoints described in the previous section lamenting the widespread lack of understanding of what goes on in classrooms – at the least it suggests that the terrain is unfavourable for the research messages to take root. We can question whether, from the research side, a common distrust of policy makers is the attitude most likely to convince them to sit up and take notice. Indeed, if the expectation is that it is up to others to digest the lessons of the learning sciences rather than to engage in genuine dialogue and educational design, the enterprise of shaping policy and practice is likely to fail.

In part, the problem stems from the sheer impenetrability of so much research, written by researchers for researchers and often only for the sub-set of those sharing a particular specialised interest. As well as inaccessibility, therefore, the fragmentation of the knowledge base is another barrier to be crossed: if those working within the learning sciences fail to make the bridges between the different sub-disciplines and specialisms it is scarcely surprising if others are unable to do so. Hence, there is the need for a major endeavour if the value of the knowledge base is to start to be realised: to synthesise and make accessible and relevant an often fragmented and difficult knowledge base. The dissemination of research results in an accessible and easily understood manner through reviews can mediate the communication of research evidence to policy makers and practitioners (Harlen and Crick, 2004) and there exist good examples of this worthwhile enterprise (*e.g.* APA Work Group of the Board of Educational Affairs, 1997; Bransford *et al.*, 2000; Vosniadou, 2001). Our book makes its own contribution to this cause.

Yet, the hopes that this might open the way to the widespread adoption of the conclusions from the learning sciences may still be overly optimistic, quite apart from whether the political will and conditions are there to do so. A fundamental problem lies in the contemporary understanding of learning, as outlined by de Corte in the next chapter, as essentially "contextualised". To the extent that the nature and outcomes of learning depend critically on context, it raises questions about the very enterprise of developing generalised conclusions for widespread adoption.

A second fundamental problem is the one outlined by Resnick and her colleagues in Chapter 12. Learning scientists know a lot about the nature of learning and instruction but tend to know less about the organisations and cultures in which these routinely play out. It follows that their explicit or implicit agendas for influencing change tend to fall short. If this insufficiency is to be overcome, the insights from different branches of organisational and sociological research need to be absorbed, addressing directly the beliefs of teachers and the contexts in which they work. In other words, understanding how individuals learn is not a sufficient basis for designing the environments in which they might learn better – this requires attention at the least to the other half of the equation, the environments themselves.

Why learning environments?

The different factors moving learning "centre stage" underpin the approach taken by the Innovative Learning Environments (ILE) project, to which this volume contributes. They argue for a powerful focus on learning itself and for integrating the "micro" level strongly into the frame rather than to treat the teaching/learning interface as a "black box" as so much educational policy thinking tends to do.

The term "micro level" itself is imprecise and depends on whether education and learning are being looked at through a telescope or under a microscope. "The classroom" and "the classroom level" offer summary short-hand terms that suggest organised learning activities involving groupings larger than the single learner. But, they automatically turn attention away from the learning located in workshops or the sports field, at a distance, and in communities and a variety of non-formal settings, even if this is not the intention.

They may be misleading if they suggest that we are only interested in what takes place within a particular institutional and/or physical unit as education is currently organised, not by learning in different configurations and contexts. The "classroom level" may be acceptable simplification for many purposes, but not when the very diversity of learning settings and approaches is at issue.

We refer instead to "learning environments". This is inside the "black box" but is more aggregated than the individual or particular learning episodes taken in isolation from the learning context – "environment" – in which learners and lessons are located. A "learning environment" thus understood is crucially focused on the dynamics and interactions between four dimensions – the **learner** (who?), **teachers and other learning professionals** (with whom?), **content** (learning what?) and **facilities and technologies** (where? with what?). Such dynamics and interactions include the different pedagogical approaches and learning activities in the learning week or term or year. Time is thus fundamental as any sets of relationships or mix of activities only make sense in how they unfold over time, not as snapshots. Assessment is integral both through the way that assessment objectives shape content and through the role it plays in the interactions and dynamics of teaching and learning. This is a more holistic understanding of "environment" than when it denotes – as it commonly does – the physical or technological settings of learning (though facilities and technological infrastructure certainly contribute to it; see *e.g.* Manninen *et al.*, 2007).

This conceptualisation builds on the insight into the nature of learning outlined by de Corte in the next chapter: that learning should be understood as "contextualised". The immediate context for any particular learning episode is precisely the" learning environment" as we understand it. Social, family and community influences – the core subject matter in Chapters 10 and 11 – are included in this framework especially through the learner dimension: this refers not only to learner numbers and demographic profiles (age, gender etc.) but to their social backgrounds, attitudes, family environments and so forth. This conceptualisation also accords with the insights developed by Resnick and her colleagues in Chapter 12 as mentioned above: much learning research is limited through underemphasis on the organisational and cultural routines in which learning is taking place.

The ILE project is primarily interested among all learning environments in those that are aimed at young people – at least in part – and are innovative in approach. We have deliberately avoided referring to them as "innovative schools" as what interests us are the ways that learning is organised and configured not the institutions themselves and not all such environments will be found in schools *per se* (though many will be). The focus on innovation stems from the starting point of this chapter – the powerful reasons moving learning centre stage call for new approaches and configurations, not a return to the comfort zone of the tried and tested. Meeting the principles of learning effectiveness as developed in this report and synthesised in Chapter 13 will require significant change from established practice in the majority of educational settings available for young people in most of our systems.

The aims of this book

The aim of this book is to provide our own contribution to bridging the "great disconnect" between research on student learning, on the one hand, and the worlds of policy and practice, on the other. Obviously, the latter cover a wide range – from the classroom teacher or school leader to the adviser, administrator or politician – with different roles and needs. Such range notwithstanding, the strong focus in the following chapters on marshalling the evidence from the learning sciences and what it says about the design of learning environments should offer insights that are relevant to all of them in different ways.

Leading educational researchers and learning specialists were each asked to review research findings from different countries from a particular perspective with the target audience of policy makers and practitioners explicitly in mind. The chapters cover both theoretical reviews about the nature of learning (cognitive science, motivation and emotions, neuroscience etc.) through more educational perspectives (inquiry-based and co-operative approaches, formative assessment, technology applications), through to evidence regarding learning in the non-formal settings of communities and families. The penultimate chapter reflects on implementing innovation, while our own final chapter seeks to draw all these diverse threads together into new synthesis.

Although ambitious in scope and rich in detail, neither we nor the chapter authors claim to offer anything like exhaustive coverage of the relevant research findings on learning. There are research traditions and corners of the world that are not well represented, still more so as this volume has deliberately eschewed the "handbook" approach that has been followed far more effectively by leading researchers themselves (*e.g.* Bransford *et al.*, 2000; Sawyer, 2006).

It instead profits from its OECD origins in three distinct ways. First, being produced by the OECD it is naturally international in scope. Second, the position of OECD as an inter-governmental organisation producing analyses and absorbing research means that the reform and policy agendas always provide the larger framework in ways that is not automatically the case in the research community. And third, as part of a larger project (Innovative Learning Environments), as well as connecting up to parallel work on innovation, this volume is helping to inform endeavours to innovate in OECD education systems rather than standing alone as a state-of-the-art review.

The report is based on the belief that the transformation of our schools into learning environments for the 21st century should be informed by the available evidence. Such evidence is not itself a sufficient basis to redesign schools and school policy but it does provide powerful messages about what encourages learning and what inhibits it. In an era of such enthusiasm for "evidence-based" policies (OECD, 2007) it is only appropriate that these insights should be brought to bear to inform and influence change. Thus, the aim of the book is to inform educational policy and practice and to help shape the reform agenda appropriate for the 21st century.

References

Ananiadou, K. and M. Claro (2009), "21st Century Skills and Competences for New Millennium Learners in OECD Countries", OECD Publishing, Paris; EDU Working Paper No. 41.

APA Work Group of the Board of Educational Affairs (1997), *Learner-centred Psychological Principles: A Framework for School Reform and Redesign*, American Psychological Association, Washington, DC.

Bereiter, C. (2002), *Education and Mind in the Knowledge Age*, Lawrence Erlbaum, Mahwah, N.J.

Berliner, D.C. (2008), "Research, Policy, and Practice: the Great Disconnect" in S.D. Lapan and M.T. Quartaroli (eds.), *Research Essentials: An Introduction to Designs and Practices,* Jossey-Bass, Hoboken, N.J., pp. 295-325.

Bransford, J.D., A.L. Brown and R.R. Cocking (eds.) (2000), *How People Learn: Brain, Mind, Experience, and School*, National Academy Press, Washington, DC.

Brown, P., H. Lauder and D. Ashton (2008), "Education, Globalisation and the Future of the Knowledge Economy", *European Educational Research Journal,* Vol. 7, No.2, pp. 131-156.

Corte, E. de (2000), "Marrying Theory Building and the Improvement of School Practice: A Permanent Challenge for Instructional Psychology", *Learning and Instruction*, Vol. 10, No. 3, pp. 249-266.

Darling-Hammond, L., B. Barron, D.P. Pearson, A.H. Schoenfeld, E.K. Stage, T.D. Zimmerman, G.N. Cervetti and J.L. Tilson (2008), *Powerful Learning: What We Know about Teaching for Understanding*, Wiley.

Empirica (2007), *Benchmarking Access and Use of ICT in European Schools 2006 – Results from Headteacher and Classroom Teacher Surveys in 27 European Countries*, European Commission, Brussels.

Florida, R. (2001), *The Rise of the Creative Class: And How It's Transforming Work, Leisure, Community and Everyday Life*, Basic Books, New York, NY.

Fullan, M., P. Hill and C. Crevola (2006), *Breakthrough*, SAGE, London.

Gorard, S. (2009), "The Potential Lifelong Impact of Schooling", in P. Jarvis (ed.), *The Routledge International Handbook of Lifelong Learning* (pp. 91-101), London: Routledge.

Green, A. (2002), "The Many Faces of Lifelong Learning: Recent Education Policy Trends in Europe", *Journal of Education Policy*, Vol. 17, No. 6, pp. 611-626.

Hargreaves, A. (2003), *Teaching in the Knowledge Society: Education in the Age of Insecurity,* Teacher's College Press, New York.

Harlen, W. and R.D. Crick (2004), "Opportunities and Challenges of Using Systematic Reviews of Research for Evidence-Based Policy in Education", *Evaluation and Research in Education*, Vol. 18, No. 1-2, pp. 54-71.

Istance, D.H., H.G. Schuetze and T. Schuller (2002), *International Perspectives on Lifelong Learning: from Recurrent Education to the Knowledge Society,* Open University Press, Buckingham UK.

Jarvis, P. (ed.) (2009), *The Routledge International Handbook of Lifelong Learning,* Routledge, London.

Longworth, N. and W.K. Davis (1996), *Lifelong Learning: New Vision, New Implications, New Roles for People, Organisations, Nations and Communities in the 21st Century,* Kogan Page, London.

MacDonald, G. (2005), "Schools for a Knowledge Economy", *Policy Futures in Education, 3*(1), pp. 38-49.

Manninen, J., A. Burman, A. Koivunen, E. Kuittinen, S. Luukanne, S. Passi, H. Särkkä (2007), *Environments that Support Learning: An Introduction to the Learning Environments Approach*, Finnish National Board of Education, Helsinki.

OECD (1996), *Lifelong Learning for All*, OECD Publishing, Paris.

OECD (2000), *Knowledge Management in the Learning Society,* OECD Publishing, Paris.

OECD (2004), *Innovation in the Knowledge Economy: Implications for Education and Learning*, OECD Publishing, Paris.

OECD (2005), "How Well Do Schools Contribute to Lifelong Learning?", *Education Policy Analysis 2004 Edition*, Chapter 3, OECD Publishing, Paris.

OECD (2007), *Evidence in Education: Linking Research and Policy*, OECD Publishing, Paris.

OECD (2008a), *Trends Shaping Education*, OECD Publishing, Paris.

OECD (2008b), *Innovating to Learn, Learning to Innovate*, OECD Publishing, Paris.

OECD (2010a), *Educating Teachers for Diversity: Meeting the Challenge*, OECD Publishing, Paris.

OECD (2010b), *Are the New Millennium Learners Making the Grade? Technology Use and Educational Performance in PISA 2006*, OECD Publishing, Paris.

Olson, D.R. (2003), *Psychological Theory and Educational Reform: How School Remakes Mind and Society*, Cambridge University Press, Cambridge.

Raudenbush, S.W. (2008), "Advancing Educational Policy by Advancing Research on Instruction", *American Educational Research Journal*, Vol. 45, No. 1, pp. 206-230.

Sawyer, R.K. (2006), *The Cambridge Handbook of the Learning Sciences*, Cambridge: Cambridge University Press, London.

Sawyer, R.K. (2008), "Optimising Learning: Implications of Learning Sciences Research", in OECD (2008b), pp.45-65.

Vosniadou, S. (2001), *How Children Learn*, The International Academy of Education (IAE) and the International Bureau of Education (UNESCO).

Chapter 2

Historical developments in the understanding of learning

Erik de Corte
University of Leuven

Erik de Corte describes a progression in which earlier behaviourism gave way increasingly to cognitive psychology with learning understood as information processing rather than as responding to stimuli. More active concepts of learning took hold ("constructivism"), and with "social constructivism" the terrain is not restricted to what takes place within individual minds but as the interaction between learners and their contextual situation. There has been a parallel move for research to shift from artificial exercises/situations to real-life learning in classrooms and hence to become much more relevant for education. The current understanding of learning, aimed at promoting 21st century or "adaptive" competence, is characterised as "CSSC learning": "constructive" as learners actively construct their knowledge and skills; "self-regulated" with people actively using strategies to learn; "situated" and best understood in context rather than abstracted from environment; and "collaborative" not a solo activity.

Introduction

The interest in learning and how to influence it have been around throughout history. Already in ancient Greece, Socrates (fifth century B.C.) and in Rome Seneca (first century A.D.) wrote about the nature of learning. At the dawn of the modern era, Juan Luis Vives (1492-1540) and Comenius (1592-1671) formulated influential ideas about learning and teaching (see *e.g.* Berliner, 2006). In the less distant past, Johann Friedrich Herbart (1776-1841) and his followers can be considered as the precursors of the scientific study of learning and teaching. They stressed, for instance, the important role in learning of prior knowledge consisting of mental states or ideas (*Vorstellungen*); new ideas are learned by relating them to already existing mental states by a process of "apperception" (see *e.g.* Bigge, 1971).

The scientific study of learning began in earnest, however, at the beginning of the 20th century. The first section of this chapter presents an overview of the major concepts and theories of learning over that century in the Western world: behaviourism, Gestalt psychology and the Würzburg School of *Denkpsychologie*, cognitive psychology, constructivism and socio-constructivism.

The scientific study of learning encouraged high expectations concerning its potential to improve educational practice. However, as argued in the next section, throughout the 20th century the relationship between research and practice has instead been an awkward and not very productive one. The chapter continues with a review of the dominant current perspective on learning in educational settings that can guide the design of innovative learning environments, including as illustration an example for mathematical problem-solving in an upper primary school. I conclude with some final comments and implications of the review for policy.

Major concepts of learning throughout the 20th century

Behaviourism

The behaviourist understanding of learning originated in the United States in the early 1900s, where it came to dominate during the first part of the 20th century. The basic idea of the behaviourist perspective is that learning consists of a change in behaviour based on the acquisition, strengthening and application of associations between stimuli from the environment (*e.g.* the presentation of "3 + 3") and observable responses of the individual (the answer "6"), so-called "S–R bonds" or connections. This view underlies a family of behaviourist learning theories that vary especially in the mechanisms seen to be influential in determining the S-R bonds. For education, the two most important behaviourists were Thorndike and Skinner.

Thorndike's variant of behaviourism dominated the early decades of the 20th century and is usually called "connectionism". For Thorndike, the connections between stimuli and responses are controlled by different laws of learning, the most important being the "law of effect": a response to a stimulus is strengthened or reinforced when it is followed by a positive rewarding effect, and this occurs automatically without the intervention of any conscious activity. For example: "How much is 16 + 9?" Pete answers: "25". Reinforcement by the teacher: "That is correct, Pete". The second major law – S-R connections become stronger by exercise and repetition – is the "law of exercise". It is not hard to see the direct connection between this view of learning and the so-called "drill-and-practice" programmes. In this era, Thorndike had a substantial impact on education, especially with his 1922 book *The Psychology of Arithmetic*.

Skinner (1953) developed his variant of behaviourism known as "operant conditioning" towards the middle of the century. In contrast to Thorndike, Skinner distinguished between behaviour elicited by external stimuli and operant behaviour initiated by the individual (for instance, spontaneously assuming the right body position to perform a correct serve in tennis). Rewarding (the coach says "excellent") the correct parts (the right body position) of the more complex behaviour taken as a whole (performing a correct serve), reinforces it and makes it more likely to recur. Reinforcers thus control the occurrence of the desired partial behaviours and this is called "operant conditioning".

Skinner argued that his operant conditioning was immediately applicable to classroom learning even though it was based on experiments with pigeons and other animals. Learning is considered as the stepwise or successive approximation of the intended complex behaviour such as the correct serve in tennis. It is guided by reinforcement of appropriate contributing but partial behaviour produced by the individual or elicited by different situational arrangements organised by the teacher to facilitate their appearance. The best-known application of Skinner's theory to education is in "programmed instruction", in which the correct sequence of the partial behaviours to be learned is determined by detailed task analysis.

Gestalt psychology and the Würzburg School of "Denkpyschologie"

The European counterparts of the behaviourist theories in the first part of the 20th century were Gestalt psychology and the Würzburg School of the psychology of thinking. Both schools strongly disagreed with psychology as the science of behaviour, a view which they considered too mechanistic. Although behaviourism was quite well known in Europe, it never became as dominant as in the United States.

The key idea of Gestalt psychology is expressed in the German word *Gestalt* which means a "configuration" – an organised whole as opposed to a collection of parts. Exponents such as Wertheimer and Köhler argued that human behaviour cannot be fully understood by the behaviourist approach of breaking it down into its constituent parts. On the contrary, it has to be studied as a whole (Bigge, 1971). The mind interprets sensory data according to organising principles whereby humans perceive whole forms – "gestalts" – rather than atomistic perceptions (De Corte, Greer and Verschaffel, 1996): the spontaneously-observed whole (*e.g.* Rembrandt's painting Night Watch) comes first and is afterwards gradually given structure. The whole is more than the composite parts. For learning and thinking, the major contribution of Gestalt psychology is their study of insight: learning consists of gaining insight, discovering a structure, and hence of acquiring understanding. Insightful learning occurs as the sudden solution to a problem. But because the Gestalt approach to learning remained rather global, it had little to say about instruction (Knoers, 1996).

The Würzburg School led by Külpe, focused on the study of thinking, especially problem solving. A basic idea of the Würzburgers was that a problem-solving process is guided by a determining tendency, *i.e.* the thinking process is goal-oriented and controlled by the task (*Aufgabe*). Building on this idea, Selz (1913) studied thinking processes and discovered that good thinking depends on using appropriate solution methods, and that there are specific methods for solving particular problems (see also Frijda and De Groot, 1981).

Cognitive psychology

An important development in American psychology was initiated in the late 1950s and has become known as the "cognitive revolution"; this resulted in the shift from behaviourism to cognitive psychology (Gardner, 1985). People are no longer conceived as collections of responses towards external stimuli but essentially as information processors. One reason for this shift was growing dissatisfaction in psychology with the ability of behaviouristic theories to explain complex mental phenomena. But also, according to Simon (1979) who was a pioneer of cognitive psychology, this development was strongly influenced by the ideas of Würzburg and Gestalt psychology, and by the emergence of the computer as an information-processing device that became a metaphor for the human mind.

The so-called "information-processing" approach became increasingly dominant in instructional psychology in the 1970s and, in contrast to behaviourism, strongly influenced European research. Instead of being satisfied with studying externally-observable behaviour, the aim was to analyse and understand the internal mental processes and the knowledge structures that underlie human behaviour. So, the interest for education is, for instance, in grasping the strategies involved in competent mathematical problem-solving or unravelling the conceptual structure of a students' knowledge of the French Revolution.

This new perspective was accompanied by a fundamentally different understanding of the nature of human cognition, namely a shift from an atomistic toward a Gestalt view. This considered the organisation of knowledge as the central characteristic of cognition (Greeno, Collins and Resnick, 1996). The behaviouristic, response-strengthening metaphor of learning was replaced by the knowledge-acquisition metaphor (Mayer, 1996; see also Sfard, 1998). Learning is seen as the acquisition of knowledge: the learner is an information-processor who absorbs information, performs cognitive operations on it and stores it in memory. Accordingly, lecturing and reading textbooks are the preferred methods of instruction; at its most extreme, the learner is the passive recipient of knowledge seen as a commodity dispensed by the teacher (Mayer, 1996; Sfard, 1998).

Constructivism

To unravel internal mental processes and knowledge structures in their studies of human learning and thinking, cognitive psychologists had to administer more complex assignments than the simple laboratory tasks used by the behaviourists. Out of this research work emerged the idea during the 1970s and 1980s that learners are not passive recipients of information; rather, they actively construct their knowledge and skills through interaction with the environment and through reorganisation of their own mental structures. As argued by Resnick (1989): "Learning occurs not by recording information but by interpreting it" (p. 2). Learners are thus seen as sense-makers. Stated differently, the knowledge-acquisition metaphor had to be replaced by the knowledge-construction metaphor (Mayer, 1996). For instance, De Corte and Verschaffel (1987) found evidence supporting this constructive view of children's learning even in the simple domain of solving one-step addition and subtraction word problems. Indeed, they observed in first-graders a large variety of solution strategies, many of them not taught in school – in other words, they were constructed by the children themselves. For example, to solve the problem "Pete had some apples; he gave 5 apples to Ann and now he still has 7 apples; how many apples did he have initially?" a number of children estimated the size of the initial amount and checked their guess by reducing it by 5 to see if there were 7 elements left, a kind of trial-and-error approach that they invented themselves. The accumulating evidence in favour of the constructive nature of learning was also in line with and supported by the earlier work of influential scholars like Piaget (1955) (see Annex) and Bruner (1961) (see Annex).

There are many different versions of constructivism (Phillips, 1995; Steffe and Gale, 1995). One of the distinctions relevant for education is between radical and moderate constructivism. Radical constructivists claim that all knowledge is purely an idiosyncratic cognitive construction and not at all the reflection of a reality "out there". For moderate (or realist) constructivists, learners arrive at cognitive structures that eventually correspond to external realities in the environment, and this construction process can be mediated by instruction. But common to all constructivist perspectives is the learner-centred approach whereby the teacher becomes a cognitive guide of student learning instead of a knowledge transmitter.

Socio-constructivism

In the late 20th century, the constructivist understanding of learning was further amended by the emergence of the "situated cognition and learning" perspective that stresses the important role of context, especially social interaction (Brown, Collins and Duguid, 1989; Greeno, 1989). Strongly influenced by the landmark work of Vygotsky (see Annex) (1978), but also by anthropological and ethnographic research (*e.g.* Rogoff and Lave, 1984; Nunes, Schliemann and Carraher, 1993), the information-processing constructivist approach to cognition and learning came in for increasing criticism. The major objection was that it considers cognition and learning as processes taking place encapsulated within the mind, with knowledge as something self-sufficient and independent of the situations in which it unfolds. In the new paradigm, cognition and learning are conceived of as interactive activities between the individual and a situation, and knowledge is understood as situated, "being in part a product of the activity, context, and culture in which it is developed and used" (Brown *et al.*, 1989, p. 32).

Cognition is thus considered as a relation involving an interactive agent in a context, rather than as an activity in an individual's mind (Greeno, 1989). This led to new metaphors for learning as "participation" (Sfard, 1998) and "social negotiation" (Mayer, 1996). One of many examples that illustrate this situated nature of cognition comes from the work of Lave, Murthaugh and de la Rocha (1984); they studied recruits to a Weight Watchers dieting programme carrying out shopping and planning and preparing diet meals. A major outcome of the study was the virtually error-free mathematics problem-solving observed in dieting shoppers in the supermarket whereas they made frequent errors with parallel problems using paper- and-pencil methods in a formal test situation.

The evolving concept of learning

During the 20th century the concept of learning has thus undergone important developments. For behaviourists, it was conceived of as response-strengthening through reinforcements. The advent of cognitive psychology brought fundamental change by putting the focus on the central role of information processing which led to the view of learning as the acquisition of knowledge in rather passive ways. With the focus on the active role of the learner as a sense-maker came a new metaphor for learning as "knowledge construction". Near the end of the century this constructivist view was amended by highlighting the important role of the situation in which cognition and learning occur and the socio-constructivist understanding of learning is seen as "participation" or "social negotiation". The latter constitutes the current dominant view of learning. In this approach the psychological processes evolving in the learner, on the one hand, and the social and situational aspects impacting learning, on the other hand, are considered to be reflexively related, with neither having priority over the other (Cobb and Yackel, 1998). This distinguishes the socio-constructivist standpoint from the socio-cultural approach that accords precedence to the social and cultural processes.

Theories of learning and educational practice: an awkward relationship

The major aim of education is to promote student learning. Therefore, with the emergence of the scientific study of learning, expectations grew that this would yield principles and guidelines to improve classroom practice and learning materials. We can now examine whether and to what degree the different concepts of learning reviewed in the previous section have met these expectations.

De Corte, Verschaffel and Masui (2004) have argued that what has been called an "educational learning theory" (Bereiter, 1990) should involve the following four components:

1. Aspects of competence that need to be acquired.

2. The learning processes required to pursue and attain competence.

3. Principles and guidelines to initiate and support those learning processes.

4. Assessment methods for monitoring and improving learning processes.

A condition for any learning theory to be potentially relevant for classroom practice, therefore, is that it should address those components. Thorndike's connectionism as well as Skinner's operant conditioning met to a large degree such requirements: they provided a coherent theory with methods for specifying aspects of competence to be learned, a theory of how such learning takes place and methods and conditions for instruction and intervention (Resnick, 1983).

Nevertheless, these behaviourist theories failed to influence educational practices in any substantial way. A large body of research was carried out under both approaches, but mainly in controlled laboratory situations using non-academic, often artificial and even meaningless learning tasks and materials (such as nonsense words or syllables). Consequently, there was a large gap between the tasks and situations covered by the research, on the one hand, and the complex realities of classrooms, on the other. Neither connectionism nor operant conditioning had anything substantial to offer, for instance, about teaching and learning deep conceptual knowledge or thinking and reasoning skills. As observed by Berliner (2006) about connectionism: "Thorndike's contributions were both monumental and misleading. While he brought rigour to educational research and gained a respected place for educational psychology in the colleges of education of the last century, he led us to irrelevance as well."

In contrast to behaviourism, Gestalt psychology and the Würzburg School made interesting contributions to better understanding the thinking skills that education should foster in students, as illustrated by the work of Wertheimer (1945) on productive thinking or the studies of Selz (1913) on problem solving. Selz, for instance, focused on unravelling methods that are suitable and efficient for solving particular problems. Once such methods have been uncovered, they can be learned by individuals and teachers can and should help students to acquire such solution methods. But this promising idea has not led to much evaluative research and implementation. This observation applies generally to the application of Gestalt psychology and the Würzburg School to education: major components of an educational learning theory (namely, aspects of competence, effective learning processes, guidelines to support those processes and assessment methods) are largely missing or at best very sketchy, and this holds especially for the learning to facilitate the acquisition of thinking skills and for the intervention methods to initiate and support such learning (Resnick, 1983).

There are parallels with the early days of cognitive psychology in the United States. While in the behaviouristic era the study of learning was prominent in psychological research, the focus shifted with the advent of cognitive psychology. The information-processing approach aimed at understanding the internal processes and knowledge structures underlying human competence and to do this it was necessary to confront people with sufficiently complex tasks so as to elicit the intended information-processing activities. As a consequence, the tasks and problems used in research became more similar to those involved in the subject-matter domains of school curricula (Resnick, 1983). But, due to the primary interest in unpacking mental processes and knowledge structures, the study of the learning needed to acquire competence was pushed into the background (Glaser and Bassok, 1989).

Towards the end of the 20th century, however, this situation began to change. First, with the substantial progress that was made in the 1970s and

1980s in understanding knowledge structures, skills and the processes underlying expert performance, there re-emerged an interest in the learning processes required to acquire such competence, and consequently in the instructional arrangements that can support this acquisition. Second, the rise of the socio-constructivist perspective that stresses the importance of context and especially social interaction, stimulated interest in studying learning in the complex reality of classrooms (Greeno *et al.*, 1996).

In line with these developments, research on learning in education has thus undergone tremendous changes over the past two decades. With the focus on learning and teaching tasks in real classrooms, using a variety of quantitative as well as qualitative research methods, this work has much greater relevance for education compared with behaviourist studies. Indeed, it has substantially contributed to our understanding of student learning in the different subject-matter domains of the school curriculum, as well as of the teaching methods that facilitate productive learning. This is well illustrated and documented in the two volumes of the *Handbook of Educational Psychology* that were published in 1996 (Berliner and Calfee) and 2006 (Alexander and Winne), as well as in the *Cambridge Handbook of the Learning Sciences* (Sawyer, 2006). For instance, research on mathematics learning has yielded a great deal of insight into the knowledge and skills involved in successful problem-solving and into students' difficulties with mathematical problems. This work has resulted in guidelines for designing innovative learning environments for problem solving and for the development of assessment instruments for monitoring learning and teaching (De Corte and Verschaffel, 2006).

These positive developments notwithstanding, complaints about what Berliner (2008) has recently called "the great disconnect" between research and practice are still the order of the day. Leading researchers are themselves very well aware of this situation. For instance, in her 1994 Presidential Address to the Annual Meeting of the American Educational Research Association, the late Ann Brown argued: "Enormous advances have been made in this century in our understanding of learning and development. School practices in the main have not changed to reflect these advances." (1994, p.4; see also Weinert and De Corte, 1996). And very recently Berliner (2008) stated: "Toward the end of the 20th century, learning in real-world contexts began to be studied more earnestly (Greeno, Collins and Resnick, 1996), but, sadly, such research still appears not to be affecting practice very much." (p. 306)

Consistent with these assertions, in our own research we have recently observed that the new insights about learning and teaching mathematical problem-solving are not easily implemented in classroom practice, even when they have been translated into a reform-based textbook (Depaepe, De Corte and Verschaffel, 2007). This should not be considered as a failing on the practitioner side to adapt to and apply our research; bridging the research/

practice gap will require all stakeholders in the school system – researchers, policy makers and practitioners – to work on this as a joint endeavour (see also De Corte, 2000).

What are the causes of this enduring awkward relationship between research and practice? Berliner (2008) provides an enlightening analysis of the "great disconnect". Looking over the history of education, the general understanding of what constitutes the act of teaching is relatively fixed and stable, making it difficult to change teaching behaviour. Classrooms are diverse and complex settings, making it unlikely that research findings can be translated into teaching "recipes" that fit all classrooms and are generally applicable in practice. William James, one of the founders of educational psychology, already remarked in 1899 that psychology is a science while teaching is an art and that sciences do not generate arts directly out of themselves. As argued much more recently by Eisner (1994), teaching is an art in the sense that it is not dominated by prescriptions and routines, but is influenced and guided by qualities and contingencies that are unanticipated and unfold during the course of action.

But although good teaching is an art in the sense described by Eisner, this does not prevent a well-grounded theory of learning from being relevant for educational practice (National Research Council, 2005). It can provide teachers with a useful framework for analysis of and reflection on the curriculum, textbooks and other materials, and their own practice. While even a good theory cannot yield concrete prescriptions for classroom application, its principles can be used flexibly and creatively by teachers as guidelines in planning and performing their educational practice, taking into account the specific characteristics of their student population and classroom setting.

Bridging the gap between theory/research on learning and educational practice constitutes a major joint challenge for educational researchers and professionals, but also for policy makers who can help create the conditions to reduce this "great disconnect". This is an important issue and I discuss it further in the final section of this chapter.

Current understandings of learning

Bransford *et al.* (2006) distinguish between three major strands in research on learning:

- Implicit learning and the brain.
- Informal learning.
- Designs for formal learning and beyond.

In **implicit learning**, information is acquired effortlessly and some-times without someone being aware of having acquired it – language learn-ing in young children is a good example. **Informal learning** takes place in homes, playgrounds, museums, among peers and in other settings "where a designed and planned educational agenda is not authoritatively sustained over time" (Bransford *et al.*, 2006, p. 216). Examples include the everyday learning in non-Western cultures that lack formal schooling as documented in ethnographic studies (*e.g.* Luria, 1976), but also in the informal learning of mathematics in Western cultures, for instance, as illustrated by the study of the shopping and cooking activities of dieters referred to above (Lave *et al.*, 1984). **Designs for formal learning and beyond** corresponds largely with learning from teaching in educational settings. According to Bransford *et al.*, this strand involves "the use of knowledge about learning to create designs for formal learning and beyond (where 'beyond' includes ideas for school redesign and connections to informal learning activities) and to study the effects of these designs to further inform theoretical development." (2006, p. 221)

It follows from this perspective on formal learning that: (1) systemising and advancing knowledge about learning is crucial (the main focus of this section); (2) design-based research (see Annex) is an appropriate avenue for advancing this knowledge; and (3) it is important to stimulate synergies between formal and informal learning.

On the latter point, according to the U.S. National Research Council (2000), students spend only 21% of their waking time in school, against 79% in non-school activities where informal learning is taking place in interaction with adults, peers and multiple sources of stimuli and information. Formal schooling is thus far from the only opportunity for and source of learning in our modern society in which ICT and media have become so ubiquitous and influential. No wonder that the motivation of youngsters for school learning has to compete with the seduction to engage in other activities that are often perceived as more interesting. Therefore, it is critically important to enhance cross-fertilisation between formal innovative learning environments and stu-dents' informal learning. One way of doing this is by linking new informa-tion to students' prior formal as well as informal knowledge.

Adaptive competence as the ultimate goal of education and learning

Many scholars in the field of education now agree that the ultimate goal of learning and instruction in different subjects consists in acquiring "adap-tive expertise" (Hatano and Inagaki, 1986; see also Bransford *et al.*, 2006) or "adaptive competence", *i.e.* the ability to apply meaningfully-learned knowl-edge and skills flexibly and creatively in different situations. This is opposed to "routine expertise", *i.e.* being able to complete typical school tasks quickly and accurately but without understanding.

Building adaptive competence in a domain requires the acquisition of several cognitive, affective and motivational components (De Corte, 2007; De Corte, Verschaffel and Masui, 2004):

1. **A well-organised and flexibly accessible domain-specific knowledge base** involving the facts, symbols, concepts and rules that constitute the contents of a subject-matter field.

2. **Heuristics methods**, *i.e.* search strategies for problem analysis and transformation (*e.g.* decomposing a problem into sub-goals, making a graphic representation of a problem) which do not guarantee but significantly increase the probability of finding the correct solution through a systematic approach to the task.

3. **Meta-knowledge** involving, on the one hand, knowledge about one's cognitive functioning or "meta-cognitive knowledge" (*e.g.* believing that one's cognitive potential can be developed through learning and effort); and, on the other hand, knowledge about one's motivation and emotions that can be actively used to improve learning (*e.g.* becoming aware of one's fear of failure in mathematics).

4. **Self-regulatory skills**, regulating one's cognitive processes/activities ("meta-cognitive skills" or "cognitive self-regulation"; *e.g.* planning and monitoring one's problem-solving processes); and skills regulating one's volitional processes/activities ("motivational self-regulation", *e.g.* maintaining attention and motivation to solve a given problem).

5. **Positive beliefs** about oneself as a learner in general and in a particular subject, about the classroom or other context in which learning take place, and about the more specific content within the domain.

Prioritising adaptive competence does not mean that routine expertise becomes unimportant: it is obvious that mastering certain skills routinely (*e.g.* basic arithmetic, spelling, technical skills) is crucial to efficient functioning in all kinds of different situations. If certain aspects of solving a complex problem can be performed more or less mechanically, it creates room to focus on the higher-order cognitive activities that are needed to reach the solution. People can also learn to use their routine competences more efficiently with passing years.

But adaptive competence is so important because it goes beyond that – it "…involves the willingness and ability to change core competencies and continually expand the breadth and depth of one's expertise" (Bransford *et al.*, 2006, p. 223). It is fundamental, indeed necessary, to acquiring the ability to transfer one's knowledge and skills to new learning tasks and contexts (De Corte, 2007; Hatano and Oura, 2003). It follows that adaptive competence is central to lifelong learning.

Considering adaptive competence as such a key goal has important implications for the learning processes to best acquire it. The traditional dominant form of school learning has been teacher-directed or – as termed by Simons, van der Linden and Duffy (2000b) – "guided learning" – "a trainer or teacher takes all the relevant decisions and the learner can and should follow him or her. He decides about the goals of learning, the learning strategies, the way to measure outcomes and he takes care of feedback, judgments, and rewards". (p. 4)

As an important component of adaptive competence consists of skills in self-regulating one's own learning and thinking, it is obvious that such teacher-directed or guided learning is certainly not the only appropriate way to achieve it. Simons *et al.* distinguish in addition two other ways of learning, namely "experiential" and "action learning". Experiential learning is not controlled by the teacher and has no pre-determined objectives. What is learned is determined by the context, the learner's motivation, others with whom the learner in contact, discoveries made, etc. What is acquired is a by-product of the activities in which one is involved. Action learning is not a by-product but, unlike guided learning, the learner plays a much more active role in determining the objectives of the learning and it is largely self-organised and self-planned.

In line with Simons *et al.* (2000b), I argue that novel classroom practices and cultures are needed to create the conditions for a substantial shift from guided learning towards action and experiential learning, resulting in a balanced, integrated use of these three ways of learning in order to support the progressive acquisition of adaptive competence. Such a balance should allow for structure and guidance by the teacher where and when needed and it should create space for substantial self-regulated and self-determined student learning. It should also leave open opportunities for what Eisner (1994) has called "expressive outcomes", *i.e.* unanticipated results from incidental learning in a variety of situations such as a museum, a forest, etc.

School learning needs to be more ambitious than was traditionally the case in taking on additional objectives: it should be active/constructive, cumulative, self-regulated, goal-directed, situated, collaborative, and permit individually different processes of meaning construction and knowledge building (De Corte, 1995; 2007). This takes into account Shuell's (1988) view of good learning (see also Mayer, 2001; National Research Council, 2000).

Simons *et al.* (2000b) identify an even more extended list: the shift towards action learning, on the one hand, requires more active, more cumulative, more constructive, more goal-directed, more diagnostic and more reflective learning; the shift towards experiential learning, on the other hand, requires more discovery-oriented, more contextual, more problem-oriented, more case-based, more social and more intrinsically-motivated learning. In a booklet in the "Educational Practices Series" of the International Academy of Education entitled *How Children Learn*, Vosniadou (2001) summarised the empirical evidence which supports most of these characteristics. She presents the research findings as underlying twelve "principles of learning" and argues their relevance for educational practice: (1) active involvement; (2) social participation; (3) meaningful activities; (4) relating new information to prior knowledge; (5) being strategic; (6) engaging in self-regulation and being reflective; (7) restructuring prior knowledge; (8) aiming towards understanding rather than memorisation; (9) helping students learn to transfer; (10) taking time to practice; (11) developmental and individual differences; and (12) creating motivated learners.

Effective learning: constructive, self-regulated, situated and collaborative (CSSC learning)

It is not possible to review here all the features and principles to guide and support students in acquiring adaptive competence, and I focus on the four key characteristics, namely that learning is constructive, self-regulated, situated and collaborative. The four vignettes in Box 2.1 describe concrete examples illustrating them.

Box 2.1. **Four vignettes illustrating characteristics of effective learning**

Vignette 1

Solution of a simple subtraction by a primary school pupil: 543-175 = 432. How did this pupil arrive at making this incorrect subtraction?

Vignette 2

Someone buys from a 12-year-old street vendor in Recife, Brazil, 10 coconuts at 35 cruzeiros a piece. The boy figures out quickly and accurately the price in the following way: "3 nuts is 105; 3 more makes 210; … I have to add 4. That makes … 315 … It is 350 cruzeiros."

When the boy had to solve traditional textbook problems in school, he did much less well than while doing his business on the street. In the class he did not use the procedures that he applied so readily on the street, but he tried to apply the formal algorithms learned in school which he did not master very well (From Nunes, Schliemann and Carraher, 1993)

Box 2.1. **Four vignettes illustrating characteristics of effective learning** *(continued)*

Vignette 3

To foster fifth-graders' competence in reading comprehension a teacher decides – in line with the new standards for language teaching – to teach four reading strategies: activating prior knowledge, clarifying difficult words, making a schematic representation of the text, and formulating the main idea of the text. The teacher's aim is not only that the pupils can execute these strategies but also that they will themselves be able to regulate their use, *i.e.* that they will autonomously and spontaneously apply the strategies whenever appropriate.

In the initial stage of learning a strategy, the teacher models extensively in front of the class how the strategy works and how it has to be applied. Thereafter, the strategy is practised in a discussion format with the whole class using short texts. In this stage, strategy use is still mainly regulated by the teacher through asking questions such as "Are there any difficult words in the text?" but the learners have to execute the strategies themselves.

In the next phase, the learners – split into small groups of three to four pupils – are given the opportunity to apply the strategies under the guidance of the teacher. This takes place in the form of dialogues during which the members in each group take turns in leading the discussion: the learners take responsibility not only for executing but also for regulating the strategies. The teacher remains available to give support and help as far as necessary, but focuses on stimulating discussion and reflection about strategy use.

Vignette 4

In connection with the events in Kosovo a project focusing on studying the situation in the Balkans was set up in a class of 25 students of the third year of secondary school. One pupil in the class had an ethnic Albanian background with parents who had emigrated a few years before from Kosovo to Belgium.

The class was divided into five "research groups" of five pupils. Each group studied the Balkans from a different perspective: (i) political, (ii) social, (iii) economic, (iv) cultural and (v) religious.

When the research groups were ready with their study work after several lesson times, the class was reorganised into "learning groups". In each learning group there was a representative of the different research groups. By combining and discussing their knowledge about the five perspectives in each learning group, all pupils were now learning about the global situation and problems of the Balkans.

Learning is constructive

The constructivist view of learning has nowadays become more or less common ground among educational psychologists (see *e.g.* Phillips, 2000; Simons *et al.*, 2000a; Steffe and Gale, 1995). But, what does this mean exactly? There is strong evidence now that learning is in some sense always constructive, even in environments with a predominantly guided learning approach. This is convincingly demonstrated by the research showing the occurrence of misconceptions (such as "multiplication makes bigger") and defective procedural skills (as illustrated in Vignette 1) among students in traditional mathematics classrooms. As expressed pithily by Hatano: "it is very unlikely that students have acquired them by being taught" (1996, p. 201).

What is essential in the constructivist perspective is the mindful and effortful involvement of students in the processes of knowledge and skills acquisition in interaction with the environment. This is illustrated nicely by the rather cumbersome but accurate calculation procedure invented by the Brazilian street vendor in Vignette 2, and also by the solution strategy of first graders for one-step word problems mentioned in the earlier short description of constructivism.

There are, however, many versions of constructivism in the literature spanning a wide variety of theoretical and epistemological perspectives, as described by Phillips (1995) in his article *The good, the bad, and the ugly: The many faces of constructivism*. This characterisation still holds true today, so that at present we cannot yet claim to have a fully-fledged, research-based constructivist learning theory. The present state of the art thus calls for continued theoretical and empirical research to give a deeper understanding and a more fine-grained analysis of constructive learning processes that promote the acquisition of worthwhile knowledge, cognitive and self-regulation skills, and the affective components of adaptive competence. We need more research into the role and nature of teaching to foster such learning.

Learning is self-regulated

Constructive learning, being about the process rather than the product, is also "self-regulated". This captures the fact that "individuals are meta-cognitively, motivationally and behaviourally active participants in their own learning process" (Zimmerman, 1994, p. 3). Although research on self-regulation in education began only about 25 years ago, a substantial amount of empirical and theoretical work has already been carried out with interesting results (for a detailed overview see Boekaerts, Pintrich and Zeidner, 2000; see also National Research Council, 2000; National Research Council, 2005; Simons *et al.*, 2000a).

First, we now know the major characteristics of self-regulated learners: they manage study time well, set higher immediate learning targets than others which they monitor more frequently and accurately, they set a higher standard before they are satisfied, with more self-efficacy and persistence despite obstacles. Second, self-regulation correlates strongly with academic achievement, and this has been found in different subject areas (Zimmerman and Risemberg, 1997). Third, recent meta-analyses of teaching experiments show convincingly that self-regulation can be enhanced through appropriate guidance among primary and secondary school students in the way illustrated in Vignette 3 in Box 2.1 (Dignath and Büttner, 2008; Dignath, Buettner and Langfeldt, 2008; see also Boekaerts *et al.*, 2000). Important recent research by Anderson (2008) shows that the learning and achievement of disadvantaged students can be improved significantly by teaching self-regulatory skills.

There is still need for continued research in order to gain a better understanding of the key processes involved in effective self-regulation in school learning, tracing the development of students' regulatory skills, and unravelling how and under what classroom conditions students become self-regulated learners. That is, there is much still to be understood about how students learn to manage and monitor their own capacities of knowledge-building and skill acquisition and about how to enhance the transition from external regulation (by a teacher) to self-regulation.

Learning is situated or contextual

It is also widely held in the educational research community that constructive and self-regulated learning occurs and should preferably be studied in context, *i.e.* in relation to the social, contextual and cultural environment in which these processes are embedded (for a thorough overview see Kirschner and Whitson, 1997; see also National Research Council, 2000; National Research Council, 2005). In the late 1980s, the importance of context came into focus with the situated cognition and learning paradigm. This, as described above, emerged in reaction to the view of learning and thinking as highly individual and involving purely cognitive processes occurring in the head, and resulting in the construction of encapsulated mental representations (Brown *et al.*, 1989). The situated view rightly stresses that learning is enacted essentially in interaction with, and especially through participation in, the social and cultural context (see also Bruner, 1996; Greeno *et al.*, 1996). This is also well illustrated in Vignette 2 by the calculation procedures invented by the Brazilian street vendor in the real-world context of his business. In mathematics, the situational perspective has stimulated the movement toward more authentic and realistic mathematics education (De Corte *et al.*, 1996).

The "situated cognition" perspective has nevertheless also come in for criticism. It has been criticised for being only "a 'loosely coupled' school of thought" (Gruber, Law, Mandl and Renkl, 1995), for making inaccurate and exaggerated claims from which inappropriate educational lessons might be drawn (Anderson, Reder and Simon, 1996) and for downgrading or at least not appropriately addressing the role of knowledge in learning (Vosniadou, 2005; Vosniadou and Vamvakoussi, 2006). There is therefore a need for further theoretical inquiry and empirical research to better integrate the positive aspects of both cognitive psychology and situativity theory (see also Vosniadou, 1996).

Learning is collaborative

The collaborative nature of learning is closely related to the situated perspective that stresses the social character of learning. Effective learning is not a purely solo activity but essentially a distributed one, involving the individual student, others in the learning environment and the resources, technologies and tools that are available (Salomon, 1993). The understanding of learning as a social process is also central to socio-constructivism, and despite the almost idiosyncratic processes of knowledge building, it means that individuals nevertheless acquire shared concepts and skills (Ernest, 1996). Some consider social interaction essential, for instance, for mathematics learning as individual knowledge construction occurs through interaction, negotiation and co-operation (see Wood, Cobb and Yackel, 1991).

The available literature provides substantial evidence supporting the positive effects of collaborative learning on academic achievement (Slavin, this volume; see also Lehtinen, 2003; Salomon, 1993; van der Linden, Erkens, Schmidt and Renshaw, 2000). It suggests that a shift toward more social interaction in classrooms would represent a worthwhile move away from the traditional emphasis on individual learning. It is important to avoid going too far to the opposite extreme, however: the value for learning of collaboration and interaction does not at all exclude that students develop new knowledge individually. Distributed and individual cognitions interact during productive learning (Salomon and Perkins, 1998; see also Sfard, 1998), and there remain numerous unanswered questions relating to collaborative learning in small groups (Webb and Palincsar, 1996). For instance, we need a better understanding of the ways in which small-group activities influence students' learning and thinking, of the role of individual differences on group work and of the mechanisms at work during group processes (van der Linden *et al.*, 2000).

In addition to the four main characteristics of the CSSC conception of learning, two other aspects can be mentioned briefly: learning is **cumulative** and **individually different**. That it is cumulative is implied in it being constructive – students develop and build new knowledge and skills on the basis of what they already know and can do. Ausubel argued already in 1968 that the most important single factor influencing learning is the learner's prior knowledge. That claim has been vindicated by the studies showing that prior knowledge explains between 30 and 60% of the variance in learning results (Dochy, 1996). The importance of prior knowledge clearly also underscores the value of linking formal to informal learning.

Learning is also individually different, which means that its processes and outcomes vary among students on a variety of pertinent variables. Prior knowledge is one of these variables, but so are ability, students' conceptions of learning, learning styles and strategies, their interest, motivation, self-efficacy beliefs and emotions. Encouraging and sustaining effective learning therefore means that school should provide as much as possible adaptive education (Glaser, 1977) to take account of these differences.

Meeting criticism of constructivist approaches

The understanding of learning described above is broadly the socio-constructivist view, albeit combining and integrating the **acquisition** and the **participation**, *i.e.* the individual and social aspects of learning. However, although the available literature provides fairly good support for CSSC learning (more extensive overviews can be found in Bransford *et al.*, 2006; National Research Council, 2000; 2005), the constructivist perspective has also come in for criticism. Kirschner, Sweller and Clark (2006) argue that approaches based on constructivism rely excessively on discovery learning and provide minimal guidance to students, ignoring the structure of human cognitive architecture and resulting in cognitive overload of working memory. These authors plea for a return to direct instruction.

The critics are correct in concluding that pure discovery does not yield the best learning gains as has been shown by Mayer (2004) in an overview of the literature of the past fifty years. But, they mistakenly equate constructive learning with discovery learning. Learning as an active and constructive process does not at all imply that students' construction of their knowledge and skills should not be guided and mediated through appropriate modelling, coaching and scaffolding by teachers, peers and educational media (Collins, Brown and Newman, 1989). Indeed, Mayer's extensive review (2004) shows that guided discovery learning leads to better learning outcomes than direct instruction. He concludes that:

> A powerful innovative learning environment is characterised by a good balance between discovery and personal exploration, on the one hand, and systematic instruction and guidance, on the other hand, while being sensitive to individual differences in abilities, needs, and motivations among learners.

> The balance between external regulation by the teacher and self-regulation by the learner will vary during the student's learning history

– as competence increases the share of self-regulation can also grow and explicit instructional support correspondingly fall. Following these principles for the design of learning environments will at the same time prevent cognitive overload and induce so-called "germane cognitive load" that facilitates effective learning. (Schmidt, Loyens, van Gog and Paas, 2007)

Box 2.2 presents a brief overview of a learning environment at the classroom level that embeds this CSSC learning concept.

Box 2.2. **A CSSC classroom learning environment for mathematics problem-solving in a primary school**

Goal of the project: design and evaluation of an innovative learning environment to foster CSSC learning processes for adaptive competence in mathematics among fifth graders. The "CLIA model" (Competence; Learning; Intervention; Assessment) (see De Corte *et al.*, 2004) was used as the guiding framework. This project was to design a learning environment (LE) in close collaboration with four participating teachers covering a series of 20 lessons to be taught by those teachers over a four-month period (Competence: the LE focused on the acquisition by students of a self-regulation strategy for solving maths problems. It consisted of five stages: i) build a mental representation of the problem; ii) decide how to solve it; iii) execute the necessary calculations; iv) interpret the outcome and formulate an answer; v) evaluate the solution. A set of eight heuristic strategies (including draw a picture; distinguish relevant from irrelevant data) was embedded in the strategy.

Learning and intervention: to elicit and support CSSC learning processes in all pupils, the learning environment was designed with the following three basic features embodying the CSSC view of learning.

1. A set of carefully-designed situated, complex and open problems was used that differ substantially from traditional textbook tasks as illustrated by the following example.

    The teacher told the children about a plan for a school trip to Efteling, a well-known amusement park in the Netherlands; were that to turn out to be too expensive, one of the other amusement parks might be an alternative. Each group of four pupils received copies of folders with entrance prices for the different parks. The lists mentioned distinct prices depending on the period of the year, the age of the visitors and the kind of party (individuals, families, groups). In addition, each group received a copy of a fax from a local bus company addressed to the school principal giving information about the prices for buses.

    The first task of the groups was to check whether it was possible to make the school trip to the Efteling given that the maximum price per child was limited to 12.50 euro. After finding out that this was not possible, the groups received a second task: they had to find out which of the other parks could be visited.

Box 2.2. **A CSSC classroom learning environment for mathematics problem-solving in a primary school** (continued)

2. A learning community was created through the application of a varied set of activating and interactive instructional techniques, especially small-group work and whole-class discussion. Throughout the lessons the teacher encouraged students to reflect on the cognitive and self-regulation activities involved in the five-stage strategy of skilled problem-solving. These instructional supports were gradually faded out as students became more competent and self-regulated in their problem-solving activities.

3. A novel classroom culture was created through the new social norms about learning and teaching problem-solving, such as: discussing about what counts as a good response (e.g. often an estimation is a better answer to a problem than an exact number); reconsidering the role of the teacher and the students in the mathematics classroom (e.g. the class as a whole, under the guidance of the teacher, will decide which of the generated solutions by the small groups is the optimal one after evaluation of the pros and cons of the alternatives).

Assessment: students' progress toward the goals of the learning environment was assessed summatively using a variety of instruments. Formative assessment was substantially built in, resulting in diagnostic feedback facilitating informed decision-making about further learning and teaching. This was obtained as a result of discussions and reflection on articulated problem-solving strategies in small groups and in the whole class.

Results:

The LE had a significant and stable positive effect on students' competence in solving maths problems.

In parallel to these improved results was a substantial increase in the spontaneous use of the heuristic strategies taught.

Results on a standardized achievement test covering the entire math curriculum showed a significant transfer effect to other parts of the curriculum such as geometry and measurement

The low-ability students, and not only those with high and medium ability, also benefited significantly from this LE.

A new CSSC-oriented learning environment, combining a set of complex and realistic problems with highly interactive teaching methods and a new classroom culture, can thus significantly boost students' competency in solving mathematical problems.

(For a detailed report of the study see Verschaffel, De Corte, Lasure, Van Vaerenbergh, Bogaerts and Ratinckx, 1999)

Concluding remarks and implications for policy

The CSSC learning concept is nowadays well supported by research evidence. It can, as illustrated by the study summarised in Box 2.2, be implemented as the framework for the design of innovative learning environments at all levels of the educational system, and for classrooms as well as for whole schools. This positive conclusion should not lead to complacency among scholars in the field of learning and teaching. It should rather stimulate and challenge the research community to continue its endeavours as even the brief review contained in this chapter reveals the many complex issues remaining to be studied and clarified, the marked progress notwithstanding. The aim should be to elaborate a more thorough explanatory theory of the learning processes that facilitate and enhance the acquisition of adaptive competence.

In view of implementation of the CSSC concept, it is interesting to ask whether teachers' and students' ideas and beliefs about learning converge with this approach. Taking as a starting point De Corte's (1995) concept of effective learning as a constructive, cumulative, self-regulated, goal-oriented, situated and collaborative process of knowledge and meaning building, Berry and Salhberg (1996) developed an instrument to measure and analyse ideas about learning of 15-year-old students in five schools in England and Finland. A major conclusion of the study was that most students adhere to the knowledge transmission model that is difficult to fit with the CSSC concept. They conclude: "…our pupils' ideas of learning and schooling reflect the static and closed practices of the school" (p. 33).

Berry and Sahlberg add that this conclusion is mirrored by similar findings from other studies for teachers and adult students. So, we should be concerned that students' and teachers' beliefs about learning can be a serious obstacle for the implementation of CSSC learning approaches, the more because, as already mentioned, of the deeply entrenched stability of teaching behaviour (Berliner, 2008). Changing beliefs constitutes in itself a major challenge.

Reducing the "great disconnect" and addressing the awkward relationship between learning research, on the one hand, and educational practices, on the other, with the sustained implementation of innovative CSSC learning environments confronts education professionals, leaders and policy makers with major challenges. First, curricula and textbooks would need to be revised or re-designed. Challenging though this is it is certainly not enough – integrating new ideas in textbooks does not guarantee that they will appropriately be used in practice (Depaepe *et al.*, 2007). Indeed, research shows that teachers interpret the new ideas through their past experiences (Remillard, 2005) and their often traditional beliefs about learning and teaching. This easily results in absorption of the innovating ideas into the existing traditional classroom practices. Moreover, as argued by the Cognition and Technology Group at Vanderbilt (1997), the changes implied for teachers are "much too complex to be communicated succinctly in a workshop and then enacted in isolation once the teachers returned to their schools" (p. 116).

There is therefore strong need for intensive professional learning and development of school leaders and teachers, aiming at the "high fidelity" application of innovative learning environments and materials, while focusing on changing predominant perceptions and beliefs about learning. Such changes in teachers can be facilitated by an iterative process in which their current views are challenged by being confronted with successful alternative practices (Timperley, 2008; see also National Research Council, 2000).

Finally, the sustainable implementation of the CSSC learning concept requires that it is appropriately communicated to and supported by the broader community around the school (Stokes, Sato, McLaughlin and Talbert, 1997). This is necessary to avoid what Dewey called already in 1916 "the isolation of the school" but it is of the utmost importance if we are to foster synergies between formal learning in the classroom and informal learning outside the school (National Research Council, 2000).

Annex

The Swiss epistemologist and psychologist **Jean Piaget** (1896-1980) proposed one of the most influential theories of cognitive development based on his observations of and interviews with children solving intellectual tasks. According to his theory cognitive development has four stages that all people pass through in the same order: sensorimotor (birth to age 2), preoperational (ages 2 to 7), concrete operational (ages 7 to 11) and formal operational (ages 11 to 14). Of special importance in the context of this chapter is Piaget's recognition that children's knowledge is not a mere copy of the external reality; on the contrary, children build their knowledge themselves through action on physical, social and conceptual objects (de Ribeaupierre and Rieben, 1996).

Jerome Bruner (1915–) is one of the most influential American educational psychologists of the 20th century. He was very instrumental in the move in the USA from behaviourism to cognitive psychology. Influenced by Piaget, he distinguished three modes of thinking: enactive, iconic and symbolic. In contrast to Piaget he did not link each mode to a specific period in children's development, but considered each mode as present and accessible throughout, but dominant during a developmental stage. His view of knowledge as a constructed entity and his advocacy of discovery learning have contributed to the emergence of constructivism. Later on he became more and more influenced by Vygotsky's cultural-historical perspective on development resulting in the viewpoint that the full development of the mind's potential requires the participation in social and cultural activities (Bruner, 1996).

Lev Vygotsky (1896-1934) was a Russian psychologist, a contemporary of Piaget but who died far too prematurely at the age of 38. Since his cultural-historical (also called "socio-historical") theory became known in the USA and Europe in the 1970s, he has been very influential in Western developmental and educational psychology. The focus of his work was the development of higher psychological processes such as thinking, reasoning and problem-solving. His basic idea is that cognitive development can be understood only in terms of the historical and cultural contexts and settings that children experience and participate in. In contrast to Piaget, he thus attributes an important role in cognitive development to the social environment of the child, especially through face-to-face interactions and language (Vygotsky, 1978).

In contrast to experiments that aim to describe how learning occurs under given conditions of instruction, **design-based research** focuses on designing, implementing and evaluating new instructional interventions. Design-based research aims at contributing to the innovation of school practices and so goes beyond merely developing and testing particular interventions. This approach seeks to contribute to theory-building about learning from instruction and the design of learning environments based on theoretical notions of what the optimal course of a learning process should be to attain a certain educational objective. In a recursive cycle of analysis and theory reformulation, examination of learning activities and student outcomes either support the initial theoretical notions or are used to revise them (De Corte, Verschaffel and Depaepe, in press; The Design-Based Research Collective, 2003).

References

Alexander, P.A. and P.H. Winne (eds.) (2006), *Handbook of Educational Psychology, Second Edition,* Mahwah, NJ: Lawrence Erlbaum Associates.

Anderson, J.R., L.M. Reder and H.A. Simon (1996), "Situated Learning and Education", *Educational Researcher*, Vol. 25, No. 4, pp. 5-11.

Anderson, L. (2008), "Successful School Programs for Disadvantaged Students", paper presented at a meeting of the International Academy of Education organized at the University of Athens, Athens, Greece, September.

Ausubel, D.P. (1968), *Educational Psychology: A Cognitive View,* New York: Holt, Rinehart and Winston.

Bereiter, C. (1990), "Aspects of an Educational Learning Theory", *Review of Educational Research,* Vol. 60, No. 4, pp. 603-624.

Berliner, D.C. (2006), "Educational Psychology: Searching for Essence throughout a Century of Influence", in P.A. Alexander and P.H. Winne (eds.), *Handbook of Educational Psychology, Second Editio*n, Mahwah, NJ: Lawrence Erlbaum Associates.

Berliner, D.C. (2008), "Research, Policy, and Practice: The Great Disconnect", in S.D. Lapan and M.T. Quartaroli (eds.), *Research Essentials: An Introduction to Designs and Practices*, Hoboken, NJ: Jossey-Bass, pp. 295-325.

Berliner, D.C. and R.C. Calfee (eds.) (1996), *Handbook of Educational Psychology,* New York: Macmillan.

Berry, J. and P. Sahlberg (1996), "Investigating Pupils' Ideas of Learning", *Journal of Learning and Instruction*, Vol. 1, No. 6, pp. 19-36.

Bigge, M.L. (1971), *Learning Theories for Teachers (Second edition),* New York: Harper and Row.

Boekaerts, M., P.R. Pintrich and M. Zeidner (2000), *Handbook of Self-Regulation,* San Diego: Academic Press.

Bransford, J., N. Vye, R. Stevens, P. Kuhl, D. Schwartz, P. Bell, A. Meltzoff, B. Barron, R. Pea, B. Reeves, J. Roschelle and N. Sabelli (2006), "Learning Theories and Education: Toward a Decade of Synergy", in P.A. Alexander and P.H. Winne (eds.), *Handbook of Educational Psychology Second edition*, Mahwah, NJ: Lawrence Erlbaum Associates, pp. 209-244.

Brown, A. (1994), "The Advancement of Learning", *Educational Researcher*, Vol. 28, No. 8, pp. 4-12.

Brown, J.S., A. Collins and P. Duguid (1989), "Situated Cognition and the Culture of Learning", *Educational Researcher*, Vol. 18, No. 1, pp. 32-42.

Bruner, J.S. (1961), "The Act of Discovery", *Harvard Educational Review*, Vol. 31, No. 1, pp. 21-32.

Bruner, J.S. (1996), *The Culture of Education*, Cambridge, MA: Harvard University Press.

Cobb, P. and E. Yackel (1998), "A Constructivist Perspective on the Culture of the Mathematics Classroom", in F. Seeger, J. Voigt and U. Waschescio (eds.), *The Culture of the Mathematics Classroom*, Cambridge, UK: Cambridge University Press, pp. 158-190.

Cognition and Technology Group at Vanderbilt (1997), *The Jasper Project: Lessons in Curriculum, Instruction, Assessment, and Professional Development*, Mahwah, NJ: Lawrence Erlbaum Associates.

Collins, A., J.S. Brown and S.E. Newman (1989), "Cognitive Apprenticeship: Teaching the Crafts of Reading, Writing, and Mathematics", in L. Resnick (eds.), *Knowing, learning, and Instruction: Essays in Honour of Robert Glaser*, Hillsdale, NJ: Lawrence Erlbaum Associates, pp. 453-494.

Corte, E. de (1995), "Learning Theory and Instructional Science", in P. Reiman and H. Spada (eds.), *Learning in Humans and Machines: Towards an Interdisciplinary Learning Science*, Oxford: Elsevier Science, pp. 97-108.

Corte, E. de (2000), "Marrying Theory Building and the Improvement of School Practice: A Permanent Challenge for Instructional Psychology", *Learning and Instruction,* Vol. 10, No. 3, pp. 249-266.

Corte, E. de (2007), "Learning from Instruction: The Case of Mathematics", *Learning Inquiry,* Vol. 1, No. 1, pp. 19-30.

Corte, E. de, B. Greer and L. Verschaffel (1996), "Mathematics Teaching and Learning" in D.C. Berliner and R.C. Calfee (eds.), *Handbook of Educational Psychology*, New York: Macmillan, pp. 491-549.

Corte, E. de and L. Verschaffel (1987), "The Effect of Semantic Structure on 1st-graders Strategies for Solving Addition and Subtraction Word Problems", *Journal for Research in Mathematics Education*, Vol. 18, No. 5, pp. 363-381.

Corte, E. de and L. Verschaffel (2006), "Mathematical Thinking and Learning", in K.A. Renninger and I.E. Sigel (Series Eds), W. Damon, R.M. Lerner (Eds-in-Chief.), *Handbook of Child Psychology, Volume 4: Child Psychology and Practice (6th ed.)*, Hoboken, NJ: John Wiley and Sons, pp. 103-152.

Corte, E. de, L. Verschaffel and C. Masui (2004), "The CLIA-Model: a Framework for Designing Powerful Learning Environments for Thinking and Problem Solving", *European Journal of Psychology of Education*, Vol. 19, No 4, pp. 365-384.

Corte, E. de, L. Verschaffel and F. Depaepe (in press), "Enhancing Mathematical Problem Solving in Upper Primary School Children: Lessons from Design Experiments", in O.A. Barbarin and B. Wasik (eds.), *The Handbook of Developmental Science and Early Education, Volume III: Teaching Math and Scientific Inquiry in Early Childhood*, New York: Guilford Publications, Inc.

Depaepe, F., E. de Corte and L. Verschaffel (2007), "Unravelling the Culture of the Mathematics Classroom: A Video-Based Study in Sixth Grade", *International Journal of Educational Research*, Vol. 46, No. 5, pp. 266-279.

De Ribaupierre, A. and L. Rieben (1996), "Piaget's Theory of Human Development", in E. de Corte and F.E. Weinert (eds.), *International Encyclopaedia of Developmental and Instructional Psychology*, Oxford, UK: Elsevier Science, pp. 97-101.

Dewey, J. (1916), *Democracy and Education*, New York: Macmillan.

Dignath, C and G. Büttner (2008), "Components of Fostering Self-Regulated Learning among Students. A Meta-Analysis on Intervention Studies at Primary and Secondary School Level", *Metacognition and Learning*, Vol. 3, No. 3, pp. 231-264.

Dignath, C., G. Buettner and H.P. Langfeldt (2008), "How Can Primary School Students Learn Self-Regulated Learning Strategies Most Effectively? A Meta-Analysis on Self-Regulation Training Programs", *Educational Research Review*, Vol. 3, pp. 101-129.

Dochy, F.J.R.C. (1996), "Prior Knowledge and Learning", in E. De Corte and F.E. Weinert (eds.), *International Encyclopaedia of Developmental and Instructional Psychology*, Oxford, UK: Elsevier Science, pp. 459-464.

Eisner, E.W. (1994), *The Educational Imagination: On the Design and Evaluation of School Programs, Third edition,* New York: Macmillan.

Ernest, P. (1996), "Varieties of Constructivism: A Framework for Comparison", in L.P. Steffe, P. Nesher, P. Cobb, G.A. Goldin and B. Greer (eds.), *Theories of Mathematical Learning,* Mahwah, NJ: Lawrence Erlbaum Associates, pp. 335-350.

Frijda, N.H. and A.D. De Groot (eds.) (1981), *Otto Selz: His Contribution to Psychology,* The Hague, The Netherlands: Mouton Publishers.

Gardner, H. (1985), *The Mind's New Science,* New York: Basic Books.

Glaser, R. (1977), *Adaptive Education: Individual Diversity and Learning,* New York: Holt, Rinehart and Winston.

Glaser, R. and M. Bassok (1989), "Learning Theory and the Study of Instruction", *Annual Review of Psychology,* Vol. 40, pp. 631-666.

Greeno, J.G. (1989), "A Perspective on Thinking", *American Psychologist,* Vol. 44, No. 2, pp. 134-141.

Greeno, J.G., A.M. Collins and L.B. Resnick (1996), "Cognition and Learning", in D.C. Berliner and R.C. Calfee (eds.), *Handbook of Educational Psychology,* New York: Macmillan, pp. 15-46.

Gruber, H., L.C. Law, H. Mandl and A. Renkl (1995), "Situated Learning and Transfer", in P. Reimann and H. Spada (eds.), *Learning in Humans and Machines, Towards an Interdisciplinary Learning Science,* Oxford, UK: Elsevier Science Ltd, pp. 168-188.

Hatano, G. (1996), "A Conception of Knowledge Acquisition and Its Implications for Mathematics Education", in L.P. Steffe *et al.* (eds.), *Theories of Mathematical Learning,* Mahwah, NJ: Lawrence Erlbaum Associates, pp. 197-217.

Hatano, G. and K. Inagaki (1986), "Two Courses of Expertise", in H.A.H. Stevenson and K. Hakuta (eds.), *Child Development and Education in Japan,* New York: Freeman, pp. 262-272.

Hatano, G. and Y. Oura (2003), "Commentary Reconceptualising School Learning Using Insight from Expertise Research", *Educational Researcher,* Vol. 32, No. 8, pp. 26-29.

James, W. (1899/1983), *Talks to Teachers on Psychology and to Students on Some of Life's Ideal,* Cambridge, MA: Harvard University Press.

Kirschner, D. and J.A. Whitson (eds.) (1997), *Situated Cognition: Social, Semiotic, and Psychological Perspectives,* Mahwah, NJ: Lawrence Erlbaum Associates.

Kirschner, P.A., J. Sweller and R.E. Clark (2006), "Why Minimal Guidance during Instruction does not Work: An Analysis of the Failure of Constructivist, Discovery, Problem-Based, Experiential, and Inquiry-Based Teaching", *Educational Psychologist*, Vol. 41, No. 2, pp. 75-86.

Knoers, A. (1996), "Paradigms in Instructional Psychology", in E. De Corte and F.E. Weinert (eds.), *International Encyclopaedia of Developmental and Instructional Psychology*, Oxford, UK: Elsevier Science, pp. 317-321.

Lave, J., M. Murthaugh and O. de la Rocha (1984), "The Dialectic of Arithmetic in Grocery Shopping", in B. Rogoff and J. Lave (eds.), *Everyday Cognition: Its Development in Social Context*, Cambridge, MA: Harvard University Press, pp. 67-94.

Lehtinen, E. (2003), "Computer-Supported Collaborative Learning: An Approach to Powerful Learning Environments", in E. De Corte *et al.* (eds.), *Powerful Learning Environments: Unravelling Basic Components and Dimensions* (Advances in Learning and Instruction Series.), Oxford, UK: Elsevier Science Ltd, pp. 35-53.

Luria, A.R. (1976), *Cognitive Development: Its Cultural and Social Foundations,* Cambridge, MA: Harvard University Press.

Mayer, R.E. (1996), "History of Instructional Psychology", in E. De Corte and F.E. Weinert (eds.), *International Encyclopaedia of Developmental and Instructional Psychology,* Oxford, UK, Elsevier Science Ltd, pp. 26-33.

Mayer, R.E. (2001), "Changing Conceptions of Learning: A Century of Progress in the Scientific Study of Education", in L. Corno (ed.), *Education across a Century: The Centennial Volume. Hundredth Yearbook of the National Society for the Study of Education*, Chicago, IL: National Society for the Study of Education, pp. 34-75.

Mayer, R.E. (2004), "Should There Be a Three-Strikes Rule against Pure Discovery Learning", *American Psychologist,* Vol. 59, No. 1, pp. 14-19.

National Research Council (2000), *How People Learn: Brain, Mind, Experience, and School,* J.D. Bransford, A.L. Brown and R.R. Cocking (eds.), Committee on Developments in the Science of Learning and Committee on Learning Research and Educational Practice, Washington, DC: National Academy Press.

National Research Council (2005), *How Students Learn: History, Mathematics, and Science in the Classroom.* Committee on How People Learn, a Targeted Report for Teachers, M.S. Donovan and J.D. Bransford (eds.), Division of Behavioural and Social Sciences and Education, Washington, DC: National Academy Press.

Nunes, T., A.D. Schliemann and D.W. Carraher (1993), *Street Mathematics and School Mathematics,* Cambridge, UK: Cambridge University Press.

Phillips, D.C. (1995), "The Good, the Bad, and the Ugly: The Many Faces of Constructivism", *Educational Researcher*, Vol. 24, No. 7, pp. 5-12.

Phillips, D.C. (ed.) (2000), *"Constructivism in Education: Opinions and Second Opinions on Controversial Issues", Ninety-Ninth Yearbook of the National Society for the Study of Education, Part I,* Chicago, IL: National Society for the Study of Education.

Piaget, J. (1955), *The Child's Construction of Reality,* London: Routledge and Kegan Paul.

Remillard, J.T. (2005), "Examining Key Concepts in Research on Teachers' Use of Mathematics Curricula", *Review of Educational Research*, Vol. 75, No. 2, pp. 211-246.

Resnick, L.B. (1983), "Toward a Cognitive Theory of Instruction", in S.G. Paris, G.M. Olson and H.W. Stevenson (eds.), *Learning and Motivation in the Classroom*, Hillsdale, NJ: Erlbaum.

Resnick, L.B. (1989), "Introduction", in L.B. Resnick (ed.), *Knowing, Learning, and Instruction: Essays in Honour of Robert Glaser*, Hillsdale, NJ, Lawrence Erlbaum Associates, pp. 1-24.

Rogoff, B. and J. Lave (eds.) (1984), *Everyday Cognition: Its Development in Social Context,* Cambridge, MA: Harvard University Press.

Salomon, G. (ed.) (1993), *Distributed Cognition, Psychological and Educational Considerations,* Cambridge, UK: Cambridge University Press.

Salomon, G. and D.N. Perkins (1998), "Individual and Social Aspects of Learning", in P.D. Pearson and A. Iran-Nejad (eds.), *Review of Research in Education,* Vol. 23, No. 1, pp. 1-24.

Sawyer, R.K. (ed.) (2006), *Cambridge Handbook of the Learning Science,* Cambridge, UK: Cambridge University Press.

Schmidt, H.G., S.M.M. Loyens, T. van Gog and F. Paas (2007), "Problem-Based Learning is Compatible with Human Cognitive Architecture: Commentary on Kirschner, Sweller and Clark (2006)", *Educational Psychologist*, Vol. 42, No. 2, pp. 91-97.

Selz, O. (1913), *Uber die Gesetze des geordneten Denkverlaufs,* Stuttgart: Spemann.

Sfard, A. (1998), "On Two Metaphors for Learning and the Dangers of Choosing Just One", *Educational Researcher*, Vol. 27, No. 2, pp. 4-13.

Shuell, T.J. (1988), "The Role of the Student in Learning from Instruction", *Contemporary Educational Psychology,* Vol. 13, No. 3, pp. 276-295.

Simon, H.A. (1979), "Information Processing Models of Cognition", *Annual Review of Psychology,* Vol. 30, No. 1, pp. 363-396.

Simons, P.R.J., J. van der Linden and T. Duffy (eds.) (2000a), *New Learning,* Dordrecht, The Netherlands: Kluwer Academic Publishers.

Simons, P.R.J., J. van der Linden and T. Duffy (2000b), "New Learning: Three Ways to Learn in a New Balance", in P.R.J. Simons, J. van der Linden and T. Duffy (eds.), *New Learning,* Dordrecht, The Netherlands: Kluwer Academic Publishers, pp. 1-20.

Skinner, B.F. (1953), *Science and Human Behaviour,* New York: Macmillan.

Steffe, L.P. and J. Gale (eds.) (1995), *Constructivism in Education,* Hillsdale, NJ: Lawrence Erlbaum Associates.

Stokes, L.M., N.E. Sato, M.W. McLaughlin and J.E. Talbert (1997), *Theory-Based Reform and Problems of Change: Contexts that Matter for Teachers' Learning and Community,* Stanford, CA: Centre for Research on the Context of Secondary Teaching, School of Education, Stanford University.

The Design-Based Research Collective (2003), "Design-based Research: An Emerging Paradigm for Educational Inquiry", *Educational Researcher,* Vol. 32, No. 1, pp. 5-8.

Thorndike, E.L. (1922), *The Psychology of Arithmetic,* New York: Macmillan.

Timperley, H. (2008), *Teacher Professional Learning and Development.* (Educational Practices Series, 18), Geneva: International Bureau of Education.

Van der Linden, J., G. Erkens, H. Schmidt and P. Renshaw (2000), "Collaborative Learning", in R.J. Simons, J. van der Linden and T. Duffy (eds.), *New learning,* Dordrecht, The Netherlands: Kluwer Academic Publishers, pp. 37-54.

Verschaffel, L., E. De Corte, S. Lasure, G. Van Vaerenbergh, H. Bogaerts and E. Ratinckx (1999), *Learning to Solve Mathematical Application Problems: A Design Experiment with Fifth Graders,* Mathematical Thinking and Learning, Vol. 1, No. 3, pp. 195-229.

Vosniadou, S. (1996), "Towards a Revised Cognitive Psychology for Advances in Learning and Instruction", *Learning and Instruction,* Vol. 6, No. 2, pp. 95-109.

Vosniadou, S. (2001), *How Children Learn. (Educational Practices Series, 7),* Geneva: International Bureau of Education.

Vosniadou, S. (2005), "The Problem of Knowledge in the Design of Learning Environments", in L. Verschaffel, *et al.* (eds.), *Powerful Environments for Promoting Deep Conceptual and Strategic Learning,* Leuven: Leuven University Press, pp. 19-29.

Vosniadou, S. and X. Vamvakoussi (2006), "Examining Mathematics Learning from a Conceptual Change Point of View: Implications for the Design of Learning Environments", in L. Verschaffel, *et al.* (eds.), *Instructional Psychology: Past, Present and Future Trends. Sixteen Essays in Honour of Erik De Corte (Advances in Learning and Instruction Series)*, Oxford, UK: Elsevier Science Ltd, pp. 55-70.

Vygotsky, L.S. (1978), *Mind in Society: The Development of Higher Psychological Processes,* Cambridge, MA: Harvard University Press.

Webb, N.M. and A.S. Palincsar (1996), "Group Processes in the Classroom", in D.C. Berliner and R.C. Calfee (eds.), *Handbook of Educational Psychology*, New York, NY: Macmillan, pp. 841-873.

Weinert, F.E. and E. De Corte (1996), "Translating Research into Practice", in E. De Corte and F.E.Weinert (eds.), *International Encyclopedia of Developmental and Instructional Psychology*, Oxford, UK: Elsevier Science, pp. 43-50.

Wertheimer, M. (1945), *Productive Thinking*, Harper, New York.

Wood, T., P. Cobb and E. Yackel (1991), "Change in Teaching Math3ematics: A Case Study", *American Educational Research Journal,* Vol. 28, No. 3, pp. 587-616.

Zimmerman, B.J. (1994), "Dimensions of Academic Self-Regulation: A Conceptual Framework for Education", in D.H. Schunk and B.J. Zimmerman (eds.), *Self-Regulation of Learning and Performance: Issues and Educational Applications*, Hillsdale, NJ: Lawrence Erlbaum Associates, pp. 3-21.

Zimmerman, B.J. and R. Risemberg (1997), "Self-Regulatory Dimensions of Academic Learning and Motivation", in G.D. Phye (ed.), *Handbook of Academic Learning: Construction of Knowledge*, San Diego, CA: Academic Press, pp. 105-125.

Chapter 3

The cognitive perspective on learning: ten cornerstone findings

Michael Schneider and Elsbeth Stern
ETH Zurich, Institute for Behavioural Research

Michael Schneider and Elsbeth Stern place knowledge acquisition at the very heart of the learning process, albeit that the quality of the knowledge is as necessary as the quantity and that "knowledge" should be understood much more broadly than (but including) knowing facts. They summarise the cognitive perspective through ten "cornerstones". Learning: i) is essentially carried out by the learner; ii) should take prior knowledge importantly into account; iii) requires the integration of knowledge structures; iv) balances the acquisition of concepts, skills and meta-cognitive competence; v) builds complex knowledge structures by hierarchically organising more basic pieces of knowledge; vi) can valuably use structures in the external world for organising knowledge structures in the mind; vii) is constrained by the capacity limitations of human information-processing; viii) results from a dynamic interplay of emotion, motivation and cognition; ix) should develop transferable knowledge structures; x) requires time and effort.

The cognitive perspective on learning – an introduction

Imagine the following scenario:

An experienced teacher explains to a class of ten motivated and intelligent elementary school children that the earth is a sphere moving through space. The teacher uses simple, precise and convincing wording. (S)he explains the similarities and differences between the earth, its moon and the sun. A week later the students are asked to draw a picture of the earth and they produce a number of wrong depictions, including a spherical but hollow earth with people living on the bottom of the inside. Why did the teaching not work as expected?

This situation, loosely based on a study conducted by Vosniadou and Brewer (1992), illustrates that many factors that must interact optimally for learning to occur and even then successful learning is not guaranteed. Even with many positive educational factors being present – experienced teachers, small class sizes, motivated students – learning did not improve as these factors did not lead ultimately to the successful acquisition of new knowledge. In this chapter, we will use this example and others to illustrate how teaching and learning can be better understood and improved by implementing the findings of cognitive science. After elaborating the key assumptions of the cognitive perspective, the chapter presents ten cornerstone findings and conclusions.

Rationale and assumptions underpinning the cognitive perspective

The cognitive perspective on learning is based on the assumption that knowledge acquisition lies at the very heart of learning. Once children acquire new information in learning environments, they are supposed to use that information in completely different situations later in life. This is only possible if they have understood it correctly and stored it in a well-organised manner in their long-term memory.

Cognitive research on learning has the goal of uncovering the mechanisms underlying knowledge acquisition and storage. Many of these mechanisms can be understood as transformation of information, similar to how a computer transforms data by means of algorithms. Therefore, information-processing theories have always been and are still central to cognitive research on learning. Researchers use laboratory experiments and computer simulations of dynamic information-processing models to advance this line of research.

Over the years, however, researchers have broadened their scope and gained insights into how interactions with the social and physical environment shape our knowledge structures. Socially-shared symbol systems such as languages, pictograms and diagrams are important prerequisites for learning. Computers and the Internet, for instance, are providing new settings for the exchange of information. Researchers also started to recognise the active role students play in learning: how students acquire knowledge depends on their goals in life, their more specific learning goals, their learning strategies, their confidence in themselves as problem-solvers and other similar factors.

Due to the broad scope of modern-day cognitive science it is ubiquitous in research on learning. When browsing through leading journals that publish advances in research on learning, such as the *Journal of Educational Psychology* or the *Journal of the Learning Sciences*, it is hard to find any study free of ideas or methods originating in cognitive science. Consequently, the cognitive perspective on learning does not compete with other perspectives (for example, the biological perspective or motivational psychology), but instead overlaps with them – usually with huge gains for both sides.

A paradigm shift: from the amount of knowledge to the structure of knowledge

Researchers, teachers, policy makers, parents and students for long judged the success of learning in terms of how much knowledge a student had acquired. In contrast, modern-day cognitive science assumes that the **quality** of knowledge is at least as important as its quantity (Linn, 2006; de Corte, this volume), because knowledge is multi-faceted. There is knowledge about abstract concepts, about how efficiently to solve routine problems, knowledge about how to master complex and dynamic problem situations, knowledge about learning strategies, knowledge about how to regulate one's own emotions and so forth. All these facets interact in contributing to a person's competence. These facets (also called "pieces of knowledge"; diSessa, 1988) can differ in their functional characteristics. They can be isolated or inter-related, context-bound or context-general, abstract or concrete, implicit or conscious, inert or accessible to different degrees. When knowledge is structured in detrimental ways, the person can have a high amount of knowledge in a domain but may still not be able to apply it to solve relevant real-life problems.

It is commonplace when someone refers to "knowledge" that they mean only knowledge of facts. In that view, knowledge is something that has to be acquired in addition to other favourable learning outcomes such as conceptual understanding, skills, adaptive competence, or literacy in a domain. In contrast, modern-day cognitive science shows that even these complex competences arise from well-organised underlying knowledge structures (*e.g.* Baroody and Dowker, 2003; Taatgen, 2005). In this chapter as well as in cognitive science in general, therefore, the term "knowledge" is used as a generic term referring to the cognitive bases of many kinds of competence. While some of these competences are brittle and limited (*e.g.* some memorised facts), others are broad, flexible and adaptive – depending on the cognitive organisation of the underlying knowledge.

Ten cornerstone findings from cognitive research on learning

Because cognitive research on learning spans different disciplines and is methodologically diverse, it is impossible to give a comprehensive review of its outcomes here. Instead, we will present ten cornerstone results from cognitive research, which are relevant to all who try to understand and improve learning. The ten points illustrate well the questions typically asked in cognitive research on learning. Each point also highlights a different aspect of how learners can build up well-organised knowledge structures.

1. Learning is an activity carried out by the learner

Teachers cannot put their hands into the heads of their students and insert new pieces of knowledge. The knowledge a person has can only be directly accessed by this person. As a consequence, learners have to create new knowledge structures by themselves.

Although this seems obvious, the implications are profound. It means that the student is the most important person in the classroom. The teacher typically knows more than the student, has more resources to hand, is more experienced, prepares the classes, provides materials, implements teaching methods, etc. This can give the impression that it is the activity of the teacher that fully determines what students learn and, indeed, teachers' actions influence the quality of instruction to a high degree. However, learning – the main goal of learning environments – takes place in the heads of the students and requires the students to be mentally active. Our introductory example illustrated this: the teacher provided the students with scientifically correct and comprehensive information but what the students stored in their memories was quite different from what the teacher said in class.

As a consequence, teachers need not only good **pedagogical knowledge** about teaching methods and good **content knowledge** about the topics they teach but they also need **pedagogical content knowledge**, that is, an awareness of how students construct knowledge in a content domain (Schulman, 1987). Pedagogical content knowledge comprises insights into the difficulties students often have in a domain and how these difficulties can be overcome. Teachers with good pedagogical content knowledge employ teaching methods not as ends to themselves, but as the means to stimulate their students' idiosyncratic knowledge construction processes. Consequently, future teachers should be trained to use teaching methods flexibly and to adapt them to the needs of their students as well as to the requirements of the content area.

2. Optimal learning takes prior knowledge into account

Teachers can only help their students when they know the students' knowledge during the teaching. People generally try to make sense of new information by linking it to their prior knowledge. Thus, what students already know substantially influences their subsequent learning processes.

In the example given in the chapter introduction, the teacher did not account for the students' prior knowledge. Elementary school children have experienced many times that the ground they stand on is flat and that things put on the underside of a sphere fall down. When a teacher tells children that the earth they live on is a sphere, this conflicts with their prior knowledge. When the children try to combine the new information with their prior knowledge, they come up with completely new conceptions of the shape of the earth. Teaching that explicitly addresses children's prior knowledge and shows how it relates to the new knowledge can avoid these problems.

Making sense of new information by interpreting it in the light of prior knowledge is not limited to elementary school children. It is a fundamental characteristic of all human thinking. Even newborns have some rudimentary and implicit knowledge. This so-called "core knowledge" gives babies intuitions about the basic properties of our world and helps them to structure the flood of perceptions they encounter every day. Other studies with adolescents and adults have found domain-specific prior knowledge to be one of the most important determinants of subsequent learning (Schneider, Grabner and Paetsch, in press). Prior knowledge in a domain is usually an even better predictor of future competence in that domain than intelligence (Stern, 2001). The importance of prior knowledge is not limited to specific content domains. Even learning in formal domains, for instance, mathematics or chess, depends heavily on prior knowledge (Grabner, Stern and Neubauer, 2007; Vosniadou and Verschaffel, 2004). Studies have found interactions between students' prior knowledge and learning processes in various academic disciplines, including physics, astronomy, biology, evolution, medicine and history (Vosniadou, 2008).

Students' prior knowledge stems from various formal and informal contexts including everyday-life observations, hobbies, media, friends, parents and school instruction. Students have different parents, use different media and have different interests. Therefore, even students in the same class can possess vastly different prior knowledge. This requires teachers to adapt their instruction not only to the competence level of their classes but also to the individual prior knowledge of their students. Since this knowledge changes during instruction, teachers must continuously assess and diagnose children's knowledge during class. This approach differs substantially from the traditional practice of first teaching a topic and only then assessing children's knowledge in a final test (Pellegrino, Chudowsky and Glaser, 2001).

Recently, educational researchers have developed a number of tools and techniques for assessing students' knowledge during on-going instruction (so-called "formative assessment"; *e.g.* Angelo and Cross, 1993; Wiliam, this volume). All teachers should have a working knowledge of the diagnostic methods appropriate for their subject and age group. It is also important to view the mistakes students make as signs of on-going knowledge construction and use them to diagnose these processes (Stigler and Hiebert, 1999).

3. Learning requires the integration of knowledge structures

The fact that students' knowledge stems from a wide variety of sources gives rise to another issue: learners often fail to see the abstract relations between pieces of knowledge acquired in superficially different situations (diSessa, 1988). For example, when children hear that the earth is a sphere but do not understand how this relates to their prior knowledge, they might simply assume that two earths exist – the flat ground they stand on and a spherical earth flying through the sky above them (Vosniadou and Brewer, 1992). This phenomenon has been observed in other age groups and content areas, too. When children already hold incorrect conceptions in a domain and the correct concept is taught to them without linking it to their prior knowledge, the children can simultaneously hold incorrect and correct concepts without even noticing the contradiction. The child will activate one of the two concepts depending on the nature of a situation (*e.g.* conversations with friends in everyday life vs. tests in school) (Taber, 2001).

A weaker form of this phenomenon can be observed when a person holds several correct pieces of knowledge without seeing how they relate at an abstract level. For example, making clothes dirty and then washing them puts them back to their original state. The task $5 + 3 - 3$ can be solved without computation by simply stating 5 as the answer. Taking three cookies out of a jar and putting three other cookies into it later, brings back the original number of cookies. From $b - b = 0$ follows $a + b - b = a$. Most adults can see easily how these different statements relate to each other – they all describe an inverse relation between two operations. However, empirical research shows that children often do not see this (Schneider and Stern, 2009). Dirty cloths, numerical computations, cookies and algebraic equations – they each belong to different domains of learners' lives and thus, commonly, to different domains of their thinking.

Teachers should remember that the same content domain can look highly relational and well-organised from their point of view but, at the same time, fragmented and chaotic from their students' point of view. Helping students gradually to adopt the perspective of experts by successively linking more and more pieces of knowledge in the students' minds is a major aim of teaching (Linn, 2006). All instructional practices focusing on abstract relations are helpful for achieving this goal. For example, diagrams can help to visualise connections between concepts; students often discover abstract relations by comparing similarities and differences between superficially different examples of the same abstract idea.

Integration of knowledge across subjects can be fostered by projects in which students discuss the same phenomenon (*e.g.* the shape of the earth) from the perspectives of different subjects (mathematics, physics, geography, history). Equally, perhaps even more, important is for teachers to point their students toward the multitude of small links that exist between subjects during class. Proportional reasoning (*i.e.* one variable as the quotient of two other variables), the use of symbol systems (*e.g.* diagrams or formulas), the usefulness and limits of computers, the interpretation of empirical data, differences between scientific reasoning and everyday thinking, how to contribute productively to a discussion – these are just some examples of the many topics that are relevant to many subjects and that can be used to integrate knowledge structures across subject boundaries. Finally, good communication about lesson content between the different teachers who participate in the students' educational programme is a precondition for knowledge integration across subjects.

4. Optimally, learning balances the acquisition of concepts, skills and meta-cognitive competence

An important aspect of integrating students' knowledge structures is helping them to link their concepts and their procedures. Concepts are abstract and general statements about principles in a domain. For example, students with good conceptual knowledge in algebra understand that a + b equals b + a (*i.e.* the "principle of commutativity"). Students with good conceptual knowledge in physics understand that density is mass per unit volume and what implications this has, for example, for whether objects float or sink in liquids. Procedures differ from concepts in that they are rules specifying how to solve problems. They are like recipes in that they specify the concrete steps that have to be executed in order to reach a goal. Good procedures can, for example, enable students efficiently to solve a quadratic equation or to construct a toy ship which will actually float on water.

In the past, philosophers and educators debated the relative importance of concepts and procedures (Star, 2005). Some argued that only procedures help to solve the problems we encounter in everyday life; that practising efficient use of procedures is thus the most important learning activity while abstract concepts are of little help. Others responded that such routine expertise is too limited and brittle for solving the complex and dynamic problems of real life, claiming that education should focus primarily on teaching concepts; the assumption being that a person who fully understands the concepts behind a problem can easily construct a solution when necessary. Today, there is widespread agreement that concepts and procedures are both important parts of competence (Siegler, 2003). Well-practiced procedures help students to solve routine problems efficiently and with minimal cognitive resources. The resources becoming available can then be used instead to solve newer and more complex problems on the basis of a deeper conceptual understanding.

It is not enough, however, for students to have just concepts and procedures. Students also need to see how concepts and procedures relate to each other (Baroody, 2003; Rittle-Johnson, Siegler and Alibali, 2001). For example, building a toy ship from household materials can improve one's concepts about buoyancy force and how buoyancy relates to object density, because the practical problem offers many opportunities for testing the implications of the concepts and to connect abstract ideas to concrete experiences. On the other hand, the acquisition of abstract concepts helps learners to understand why their procedures work, under what conditions they function, and how they can be adapted to new problem types. The teacher in our introductory example had a difficult task because the shape of the earth is a content area with many concepts but only a few procedures that could help students explore and experience the concrete meanings of these concepts. One possible solution in such cases is the use of physical models, for example, a globe.

The mutual reinforcement of concepts and procedures can be strengthened further by helping learners to reflect on their knowledge acquisition processes. This is usually labelled *meta-cognition*, that is, cognition about one's own cognition (Hartman, 2001). Meta-cognition helps students actively to monitor, evaluate, and optimise their acquisition and use of knowledge. Without meta-cognition, students do not notice inconsistencies in their knowledge base. On the other hand, meta-cognition is not an end in itself but serves as a means to knowledge acquisition. Thus, meta-cognition and knowledge acquisition in concrete content domains are inseparably intertwined and cannot be taught or learned independently of each other.

5. Learning optimally builds up complex knowledge structures by organising more basic pieces of knowledge in a hierarchical way

Different people all with high competence in a domain can have very different knowledge structures, depending on their individual preferences and their learning histories. One characteristic is nevertheless common to the knowledge of all competent persons: it is structured in hierarchical ways. This is true for perception, language processing, abstract concepts and problem-solving procedures.

Tihs sencente mkeas snese to you, eevn thgoh the lretets are sclrabmed up, because people do not encode letters independently of each other. Instead, people use hierarchic memory representations with letters at the basic level and words at a higher level. Thus, knowledge about letters helps to identify words and knowledge about words helps to identify letters. By means of this mutual support, intact knowledge on one level can help to correct wrong or incomplete information on the other level.

The same applies to taxonomic knowledge (Murphy and Lassaline, 1997) and more complex concepts (Chi, Slotta and Leeuw, 1994). Imagine a person without any background knowledge about the American Goldfinch. When this person is told that the Goldfinch is a bird, (s)he immediately knows many things about it. Birds lay eggs, so the Goldfinch lays eggs. Birds belong to the super-ordinate category "animal", and animals breathe, so the Goldfinch breathes. Birds are animals that are distinct from mammals, so the Goldfinch does not feed milk to its young.

The hierarchical organisation of knowledge is also important for procedures. For example, planning a house is a complex problem consisting of many sub-problems. Novices with little prior knowledge can quickly get lost in this complexity. In contrast, experts will break the big problem down into a series of smaller and more manageable sub-problems (*e.g.* first planning the position and shape of the outer walls, and then planning the inner walls on each floor). In a next step, experts will break these problems down into even smaller and manageable sub-problems (*e.g.* first planning the staircase and the bathrooms and then fitting in the other planned rooms) and so forth. The result is a large number of small and easy-to-solve problems. In the literature, this process is also referred to as "task (or goal) decomposition". A large number of empirical studies and computer simulations demonstrate the ubiquity and power of this problem-solving approach (*e.g.* Ritter, Anderson, Koedinger and Corbett, 2007).

6. Optimally, learning can utilise structures in the external world for organising knowledge structures in the mind

Teachers are supposed to make sure that students acquire rich, well-balanced, well-organised knowledge structures and yet they cannot put these knowledge structures directly into their students' heads. So, what can teachers do? The answer is that they can provide optimal learning opportunities by preparing well-structured learning environments (Vosniadou, Ioannides, Dimitrakopoulou and Papademetriou, 2001). This strategy works because structured information in the learners' social and physical environment will help them to structure information in their minds. There are many ways to provide structures on many different levels in learning environments. Some examples are the temporal organisation of a curriculum, the order of ideas or tasks introduced to the students in a lesson, the outline of a book, the informal social structures of groups of students working together, the design of work sheets, technical terms, formulas, diagrams, and specific formulations in the teacher's language. We will take a closer look at some of the most important examples in this section.

Teachers can only prepare structured learning environments to the degree they are aware of the structure of the content area they are teaching in, the structure of students' prior knowledge, and the knowledge structures the learners are supposed to build up during the teaching. This is often hampered by the fact that curricula are formulated as a list or table specifying what content is to be taught at what grade level. This could result in teachers thinking linearly and simply in terms of sequences of contents or teaching methods. While this may be correct so far as it goes, it has to be completed with a second perspective: teachers must be aware of the hierarchical structure of the knowledge they are trying to communicate (see Point 5).

Language is one of the most powerful tools for providing structure in a learning environment. Grammatical constructions can emphasise the relations between concepts and procedures (Gentner and Loewenstein, 2002; Loewenstein and Gentner, 2005). By carefully choosing their words, teachers can emphasise that two pieces of knowledge conflict with each other (*e.g.* "… whereas…"), that one idea explains or justifies another idea (*e.g.* "… therefore…"), that two variables form a proportion (*e.g.* "… per…") and so on. The use of labels for groups of objects can emphasise commonalities of the objects within each group and differences between objects not in the same group (Lupyan, Rakison and McClelland, 2007). For example, in everyday life, people often speak of the "sun and the stars in the sky". This might cause children to think that the sun is basically different from stars. By labelling the sun a "star", a teacher can help children integrate their knowledge about stars and about the sun.

A second function of language is the structuring of classroom discourse. Discussion between students is important because it helps them to exchange ideas and learn about the existence of different perspectives and opinions. This helps teachers to assess their students' knowledge. It is important to keep in mind, however, that the discourse serves a clear purpose within a lesson. By asking good questions, and opposing, re-phrasing, or summarising students' statements, teachers can structure a discussion; they can make sure that it is not an aimless collection of different statements but a goal-directed social construction of new insights (Hardy, Jonen, Möller and Stern, 2006).

Structuring time well also provides structure. A semester, a topic within a semester, a lesson within a topic – all need to be structured effectively with an orienting and motivating introduction, a main part and a consolidating summary. This sounds easy, but it means that teachers have to use a considerable amount of their time planning ahead, because it is not enough for them just to prepare one script and stick to it. Teachers can only react to the unfolding social interactions in their classrooms when they improvise to some degree while simultaneously providing structure and guidance. This requires teachers to anticipate the potential reactions of their students and prepare appropriate responses.

Technical equipment can be a great help for structuring learning environments (Winn, 2002). PowerPoint presentations, movies, audio recordings, experiments, computer programmes, and interactive internet pages provide structure by stimulating some thinking processes while preventing others. An important rationale is that even the best technical equipment can never replace but only complement teachers and face-to-face interactions in class (Koedinger and Corbett, 2006).

Technical equipment is a tool used by a teacher to stimulate specific learning activities. Thus, technology is not generally good or bad for teaching. It is unproductive when it is used as a means in itself. It is productive when it is used skilfully as a tool for fostering students' construction of specific knowledge structures (cf. Mayer, this volume). For example, replacing a teacher monologue about the earth as a sphere by Internet pages with the same content is of little help. Using an interactive computer animation showing the earth from different perspectives, on the other hand, can help students to understand that the same earth looks very different when you are standing on it from when you see it from a point in space thousands of kilometres away.

Finally, providing structure in learning environments implies that teacher and learners must be aware of the learning goals (Borich, 2006). Whether students are practising routine tasks, working on a cross-subject project, or seeing a movie, they will learn little unless the teacher uses learning goals to focus the students' attention on the relevant aspects of these complex situations. Students need to understand the reasons behind their learning activities.

It took mankind several thousand years until it discovered some of the contents taught in middle schools today, for example, the laws of classical mechanics, the Cartesian coordinate system, or the mechanisms of photosynthesis. These ideas were not developed by average people but usually by a genius, often after years of intense research. Normal learners cannot be expected to acquire many of these concepts through incidental or informal learning, for example, during visits to a museum or to a factory, participation in a community project, or during their various hobbies. Instead, they need structured and professionally-designed learning opportunities that carefully guide their knowledge construction. Informal learning settings can still be helpful for acquiring self-regulatory competence, optimising motivation, practising the application of knowledge etc. From a cognitive point of view, however, informal learning experiences can only complement but never replace more formal – more structured – settings for learning.

7. Learning is constrained by capacity limitations of the human information-processing architecture

The architecture of human cognition has some basic properties relevant for the design of optimally structured learning materials (Sweller, Merrienboer and Paas, 1998). These properties include **working memory**, where information is actively processed, and **long-term memory**, where information is stored. Working memory has a limited capacity, and information stored in working memory is quickly lost when it is not updated within seconds. In contrast, long-term memory has an almost unlimited capacity and can retain information for days or even years. New information can only enter long-term memory through working memory. However, not all information is transferred from working memory to long-term memory because new information is filtered. The more meaningful, more important, or more frequently-recurring the information, the more likely it is to be transferred from working memory to long-term memory. Teachers can make information more meaningful and more important to students by linking it to their prior knowledge and by using appealing examples that demonstrate the usefulness for solving real-life problems.

Due to its limited capacity, working memory is a bottleneck for the transfer of knowledge to long-term memory. Even though learners build up a complex web of knowledge in their long-term memory, their working memory can only hold up to about seven pieces of information at a time (Miller, 1956). Therefore, taking up information from the environment and integrating it with prior knowledge already in long-term memory requires a series of many small steps carried out in working memory (Anderson and Schunn, 2000).

Teachers can aid this process by reducing unnecessary working memory load (see Mayer, this volume). Structuring information hierarchically helps, because it enables learners to hold a super-ordinate piece of knowledge in working memory instead of its many subordinate components. For example, someone who tries to remember the number 01202009 has to hold 8 digits in working memory. Others might be able to subsume the number under the super-ordinate label "date of Obama's inauguration as president of the United States". They can remember all the digits by storing this one label in working memory. Thus, structuring knowledge hierarchically, or "chunking" as it is often called, can help overcome working memory limitations.

Unnecessary working memory load can further be reduced (*cf.* Mayer and Moreno, 2003) if pieces of information that can only be understood together are presented together. For example, a coordinate system with several line graphs is easier to understand if each graph is labelled directly rather than if this same information is given in a key under the coordinate system. In the latter case, learners have to jump back and forth between the coordinate system and the key. This creates an unnecessary working memory load. For the same reason, when a formula with many new symbols is presented in a book, the symbols should be explained directly next to the formula and not somewhere else. When a text explains a complex figure, it can help to present the text in auditory form, so the learners can look at the figure while listening to the text instead of jumping back and forth between a printed figure and a written text.

Another way to reduce unnecessary working memory load is to keep learning materials as simple as possible. For example, when a quantitative function can be visualised in a two-dimensional graph, it should not be presented in a three-dimensional figure just because the latter looks more impressive. Likewise, computer-presented slides should not contain any more cartoons, cross-fading effects, or animation than necessary to grab the attention of the audience. The same applies to language: the simpler the language used to explain complex relations, the better and faster students will understand such concepts.

When students are learning to solve new problems with multiple steps (*e.g.* equation systems), their working memory quickly reaches its maximum capacity. This is because the students must not only execute the concrete steps necessary to solve the problem but they must also find the abstract principle that underlies the problem solution. In this case, working memory load can be reduced by worked-out examples. By studying solutions instead of generating them, students can focus solely on the big idea behind the solution and not worry about carrying out the concrete solution steps at the same time (Renkl, 2005).

8. Learning results from a dynamic interplay of emotion, motivation and cognition

At the beginning of cognitive science research, many researchers imagined human cognition to be similar to information processing by a computer. As a consequence, little attention was paid to the emotional and motivational aspects of human cognition. Since the 1960s, however, things have changed considerably. Motivation and emotion are now recognised as important determinants of thinking and learning.

Many laypersons and teachers, and maybe even some researchers, tend to see motivation as the motor that drives learning. When the motor is running, learning takes place; when the motor stands still, no learning occurs. Empirical research shows that there are at least three things wrong with this picture. First, motivation gradually and dynamically changes: it is not either "on" or "off". Second, while motivation drives cognitive learning processes, it also results from cognitive processes such as learning and reasoning about one's own competence. Third, the picture creates a false dichotomy between cognition and motivation. The two concepts have to be broken up into their constituents to understand how they influence each other. Students' learning goals and goals in life, their thoughts about their own competence, and their attributions of academic success or failure on various potential causes, and their interests and hobbies all contribute to the complex interplay of cognition and motivation.

For this reason, good learning environments do not treat motivation as a motor that simply has to be started up in order for knowledge acquisition to take place. Instead, they treat knowledge acquisition and motivation as multi-faceted and dynamically interacting systems that can strengthen or weaken each other in a multitude of ways.

9. Optimal learning builds up transferrable knowledge structures

Even when students are motivated and build up sophisticated knowledge structures, this does not necessarily mean they acquire competence that is useful for their lives. There are many more concepts and procedures that are relevant for life than can be taught in school. Teachers do not know for sure which pieces of knowledge will be relevant for their students later in life because life is so diverse and unpredictable. Two potential approaches for solving this problem are discussed in the scientific literature – the training of domain-general competences and fostering knowledge transfer.

The training of domain-general competences (*e.g.* intelligence, working memory capacity, or brain efficiency) is based on the idea that these competences help to solve a very wide range of problems independently of their domain. It follows that if time is set aside from other subjects in school and used for the training of domain-general competences, students might gain competence that is not restricted to specific content areas. This idea appeals to many because it seems to be an efficient way of acquiring competence – practising a single competence and then being able to solve a limitless number of problems. Decades of intense research have shown, however, that this hope is not realistic. Domain-general competences, such as intelligence, are extremely difficult and costly to train. They can be increased only within narrow limits, and the increases are usually not stable over time. Even more importantly, domain-general competences do not help to solve a problem when a person lacks knowledge about the problem at hand and its solution. The highest intelligence, largest working memory capacity, or the most efficient brain cannot help to solve a problem if the person has no meaningful knowledge to process.

A related misconception is that formal training, for example, learning Latin or mental exercises with more or less randomly chosen content (commonly called "brain jogging"), makes subsequent learning in all content domains more efficient. According to the empirical research so far, this is not the case. Even though the brain is plastic, it cannot be trained with just any exercise as if it was a muscle (Stanford Center on Longevity and Max Planck Institute for Human Development, 2009; Chi, Glaser and Farr, 1988). For all of these reasons, teaching domain-general competences at the expense of concrete content knowledge is an ineffective instructional approach (Stern, 2001).

A more effective alternative for broadening competences is to teach concrete content knowledge in ways that aid subsequent transfer to new situations, problem-types and content domains. This flexible kind of expertise, however, does not develop on its own. Practitioners and researchers alike are often surprised at how frequently learners who have competently mastered one problem are then unable to solve basically the same problem when only small aspects of its presentation change (*e.g.* the wording or the illustrative context) (Greeno and The Middle School Mathematics Through Applications Project Group, 1998). Yet, the ability to apply knowledge flexibly and adaptively to new situations is one of the most important characteristics of the human mind (Barnett and Ceci, 2002).

Teachers should do all they can to help learners use this potential to its fullest extent (Bereiter, 1997). One important precondition for transfer is that students must focus on the common deep-structure underlying two problem situations rather than on their superficial differences. Only then will they apply the knowledge acquired in one situation to solve a problem in another. This can be accomplished by pointing out to students that two problem solutions require similar actions (Chen, 1999); by using diagrams to visualise the deep-structures of different problems (Novick and Hmelo, 1994; Stern, Aprea and Ebner, 2003); by fostering comparisons between examples that highlight their structural similarities or differences (Rittle-Johnson and Star, 2007); and by the careful use of analogies between phenomena arising in different domains (Gentner, Loewenstein and Thomson, 2003). People are less likely to transfer isolated pieces of knowledge than they are to transfer parts of well-integrated hierarchical knowledge structures (Wagner, 2006). The more connections a learner sees between the educational world of learning environments and the outside world, the easier the transfer will be.

Teachers should thus make use of meaningful real-life problems whenever possible (Roth, van Eijck and Hsu, 2008; The Cognition and Technology Group at Vanderbilt, 1992). In addition, parents, museums, media, computer learning programmes etc. can foster knowledge transfer by illustrating to learners the relevance of scientific concepts and approaches in the context of everyday life (Renkl, 2001; Barron and Darling-Hammond, this volume).

10. Learning requires time and effort

Building up complex knowledge structures requires hard work over long periods of time for both students and teachers. Consequently, time and effort invested in practising problem-solving and extending one's knowledge base are among the most important factors influencing the success of learning (Ericsson, Krampe and Tesch-Römer, 1993).

Some self-proclaimed experts claim that students could become competent without investing serious time and effort if only the teaching was more fun, more brain-adequate, more computer-based, or if it occurred earlier in life. None of these claims is justified by the results of empirical research. These features can assist learning to some degree if they are used in the right amount and at the right times. However, none of them can substitute for the acquisition of complex knowledge structures nor even guarantee that knowledge acquisition would actually occur. To the extent that they do stimulate learning, it is still as time-consuming and difficult to achieve as learning processes generally are (*cf.* Anderson and Schunn, 2000). Learning can and should be fun, but the type of fun that it is to climb a mountain – not the fun of sitting at the top and enjoying the view.

Conclusions

Only certain areas of cognitive science investigate learning processes. Since it is impossible to summarise all the findings from cognitive science or even just from cognitive research on learning in a single book chapter, we present ten cornerstone findings from cognitive research on learning to illustrate typical questions, approaches and outcomes in this field. The ten points focus on knowledge acquisition, because cognitive research shows that well-structured knowledge underlies more complex competences including conceptual understanding, efficient skills and adaptive expertise. Learners lacking such knowledge are unable to take advantage of the multitude of social, ecological, technological, cultural, economical, medical and political resources that surround them.

The ten points described in this chapter have direct implications for the design of effective learning environments. Since they are derived from general principles of how the human mind works, they can be applied to all age groups, school forms and subjects. Good learning environments: stimulate learners to be mentally active; address prior knowledge; integrate fragmented pieces of knowledge into hierarchical knowledge structures; balance concepts, skills and meta-cognitive competence; provide expedient structures in the environment that help learners to develop well-organised knowledge structures; and present information adequately for efficient processing in the human mind given its inherent limitations for processing (such as limited working memory capacity). Good learning environments foster transfer between content domains as well as between the learning situation and everyday life. They do not try to circumvent the hard work that learning entails. Instead, they maximise motivation by making sure that the content to be learned is meaningful for the students, by clarifying the goals of their lessons, by emphasising the relevance for life outside of the learning environment, and by sensitivity to their students' interests, goals and self-perceptions.

References

Anderson, J.R. and C.D. Schunn (2000), "Implications of the ACT-R Learning Theory: No Magic Bullets", in R. Glaser (ed.), *Advances in Instructional Psychology: Educational Design and Cognitive Science*, Erlbaum, Mahwah, NJ, Vol. 5, pp. 1-34.

Angelo, T.A. and K.P. Cross (1993), *Classroom Assessment Techniques: A Handbook for College Teachers*, Jossey-Bass, San Francisco.

Barnett, S.M. and S.J. Ceci (2002), "When and Where Do We Apply What We Learn? A Taxonomy for Far Transfer", *Psychological Bulletin*, Vol. 128, No. 4, pp. 612-637.

Baroody, A.J. (2003), "The Development of Adaptive Expertise and Flexibility: The Integration of Conceptual and Procedural Knowledge", in A.J. Baroody and A. Dowker (eds.), *The Development of Arithmetic Concepts and Skills: Constructing Adaptive Expertise*, Erlbaum, Mahwah, NJ, pp. 1-33.

Bereiter, C. (1997), "Situated Cognition and How to Overcome It", in D. Kirshner and J.A. Whitson (eds.), *Situated Cognition: Social, Semiotic, and Psychological Perspectives,* Erlbaum, Hillsdale, NJ, pp. 281-300.

Borich, G.D. (2006), *Effective Teaching Methods: Research-Based Practice*, Prentice Hall, Upper Saddle River, NJ.

Chen, Z. (1999), "Schema Induction in Children's Analogical Problem Solving", *Journal of Educational Psychology*, Vol. 91, No. 4, pp. 703-715.

Chi, M.T.H., R. Glaser and M.J. Farr (1988), *The Nature of Expertise*, Erlbaum, Hillsdale, NJ.

Chi, M.T.H., J.D. Slotta and N. de Leeuw (1994), "From Things to Processes: A Theory of Conceptual Change for Learning Science Concepts", *Learning and Instruction*, Vol. 4, No.1, pp. 27-43.

diSessa, A.A. (1988), "Knowledge in Pieces", in G. Forman and P.B. Pufall (eds.), *Constructivism in the Computer Age*, Erlbaum, Hillsdale, NJ, pp. 49-70.

Ericsson, K.A., R.T. Krampe and C. Tesch-Römer (1993), "The Role of Deliberate Practice in the Acquisition of Expert Performance", *Psychological Review*, Vol. 100, No. 3, pp. 363-406.

Gentner, D. and J. Loewenstein (2002), "Relational Language and Relational Thought", in E. Amsel and J. P. Byrnes (eds.), *Language, Literacy, and Cognitive Development: The Development and Consequences of Symbolic Communication,* Erlbaum, Mahwah, NJ, pp. 87-120.

Gentner, D., J. Loewenstein and L. Thomson (2003), "Learning and Transfer: A General Role for Analogical Encoding", *Journal of Educational Psychology*, Vol. 95, No. 2, pp. 393-408.

Grabner, R., E. Stern and A. Neubauer (2007), "Individual Differences in Chess Expertise: A Psychometric Investigation", *Acta Psychologica*, Vol. 124, No. 3, pp. 398-420.

Greeno, J.G. and The Middle School Mathematics through Applications Project Group (1998), "The Situativity of Knowing, Learning, and Research", *American Psychologist*, Vol. 53, No. 1, pp. 5-26.

Hardy, I., A. Jonen, K. Möller and E. Stern (2006), "Effects of Instructional Support within Constructivist Learning Environments for Elementary School Students' Understanding of 'Floating and Sinking'", *Journal of Educational Psychology*, Vol. 98, No. 2, pp. 307-326.

Hartman, H. J. (2001), *Metacognition in Learning and Instruction*, Kluver, Dordrecht.

Koedinger, K. R. and A.T. Corbett (2006), "Cognitive Tutors: Technology Bridging Learning Science to the Classroom", in K. Sawyer (ed.), *Cambridge Handbook of the Learning Sciences*, Cambridge University Press, New York, pp. 61-78.

Linn, M. C. (2006), "The Knowledge Integration Perspective on Learning and Instruction", in R. K. Sawyer (ed.), *The Cambridge Handbook of the Learning Sciences*, Cambridge University Press, New York, pp. 243-264.

Loewenstein, J. and D. Gentner (2005), "Relational Language and the Development of Relational Mapping", *Cognitive Psychology*, Vol. 50, No. 4, pp. 315-353.

Lupyan, G., D.H. Rakison and J.L. McClelland (2007), "Language Is not Just for Talking: Redundant Labels Facilitate Learning of Novel Categories", *Psychological Science*, Vol. 18, No. 12, pp. 1077-1083.

Mayer, R.E. and R. Moreno (2003), "Nine Ways to Reduce Cognitive Load in Multimedia Learning", *Educational Psychologist*, Vol. 38, No. 1, pp. 43-52.

Miller, G.A. (1956), "The Magical Number Seven, Plus or Minus Two: Some Limits on Our Capacity for Processing Information", *Psychological Review*, Vol. 63, No. 2, pp. 81-97.

Murphy, G.L. and M.E. Lassaline (1997), "Hierarchical Structure in Concepts and the Basic Level of Categorization", in K. Lamberts and D. Shanks (eds.), *Knowledge, Concepts, and Categories*, Psychology Press, Hove, pp. 93-132.

Novick, L.R. and C.E. Hmelo (1994), "Transferring Symbolic Representations across Nonisomorphic Problems", *Journal of Experimental Psychology: Learning, Memory, and Cognition*, Vol. 20, No. 6, pp. 1296-1321.

Pellegrino, J. P., N. Chudowsky and R. Glaser (eds.) (2001), *Knowing What Students Know: The Science and Design of Educational Assessment*, National Academy Press, Washington, DC.

Renkl, A. (2001), "Situated Learning, Out of School and in the Classroom", in P.B. Baltes and N.J. Smelser (eds.), *International Encyclopedia of the Social and Behavioral Sciences*, Pergamon, Amsterdam, Vol. 21, pp. 14133-14137.

Renkl, A. (2005), "The Worked-Out Examples Principle in Multimedia", in R.E. Mayer (ed.), *The Cambridge Handbook of Multimedia Learning*, Cambridge University Press, New York, pp. 229-246.

Ritter, S., J.R. Anderson, K.R. Koedinger and A. Corbett (2007), "Cognitive Tutor: Applied Research in Mathematics Education", *Psychonomic Bulletin and Review*, Vol. 14, No. 2, pp. 249-255.

Rittle-Johnson, B. and J.R. Star (2007), "Does Comparing Solution Methods Facilitate Conceptual and Procedural Knowledge? An Experimental Study on Learning to Solve Equations", *Journal of Educational Psychology*, Vol. 99, No. 3, pp. 561-574.

Rittle-Johnson, B., R.S. Siegler and M.W. Alibali (2001), "Developing Conceptual Understanding and Procedural Skill in Mathematics: An Iterative Process", *Journal of Educational Psychology*, Vol. 93, No. 2, pp. 346-362.

Roth, W.M., M. van Eijck, G. Reis and P.L. Hsu (2008), *Authentic Science Revisited*, Sense, Rotterdam.

Schneider, M. and E. Stern (2009), "The Inverse Relation of Addition and Subtraction: A Knowledge Integration Perspective", *Mathematical Thinking and Learning*, Vol. 11, No. 1, pp. 92-101.

Schneider, M., R.H. Grabner and J. Paetsch (2009), "Mental Number Line, Number Line Estimation, and Mathematical Achievement: Their

Interrelations in Grades 5 and 6", *Journal of Educational Psychology*, Vol. 101, No. 2, pp. 359-372.

Shulman, L. (1987), "Knowledge and Teaching: Foundations of a New Reform", *Harvard Educational Review*, Vol. 57, No. 1, p. 1-22.

Siegler, R.S. (2003), "Implications of Cognitive Science Research for Mathematics Education", in J. Kilpatrick, W.B. Martin and D.E. Schifter (eds.), *A Research Companion to Principles and Standards for School Mathematics*, National Council of Teachers of Mathematics, Reston, VA, pp. 219-233.

Stanford Center on Longevity and Max Planck Institute for Human Development (2009), *Expert Consensus on Brain Health*, *http://longevity. stanford.edu/about/pressreleases/CognitiveAgingConsensus*.

Star, J.R. (2005), "Re-Conceptualizing Procedural Knowledge: Innovation and Flexibility in Equation Solving", *Journal for Research in Mathematics Education*, Vol. 36, No. 5, pp. 404-411.

Stern, E. (2001), "Intelligence, Prior Knowledge, and Learning", in N.J. Smelser and P.B. Baltes (eds.), *International Encyclopedia of the Social and Behavioral Sciences*, Elsevier Science, Oxford, Vol. 11, pp. 7670-7674.

Stern, E., C. Aprea and H.G. Ebner (2003), "Improving Cross-Content Transfer in Text Processing by Means of Active Graphical Representation", *Learning and Instruction*, Vol. 13, No. 2, pp. 191-203.

Stigler, J.W. and J. Hiebert (1999), *The Teaching Gap: Best Ideas from the World's Teachers for Improving Education in the Classroom*, Free Press, New York.

Sweller, J., J.J.G. van Merrienboer and F.G.W.C. Pass (1998), "Cognitive Architecture and Instructional Design", *Educational Psychology Review*, Vol. 10, No. 3, pp. 251-296.

Taatgen, N.A. (2005), "Modeling Parallelization and Flexibility Improvements in Skill Acquisition: From Dual Tasks to Complex Dynamic Skills", *Cognitive Science*, Vol. 29, No. 33, pp. 421-455.

Taber, K.S. (2001), "Shifting Sands: A Case Study of Conceptual Development as Competition between Alternative Conceptions", *International Journal of Science Education*, Vol. 23, No. 7, pp. 731-753.

The Cognition and Technology Group at Vanderbilt (1992), "The Jasper Series as an Example of Anchored Instruction: Theory, Program Description and Assessment Data", *Educational Psychologist*, Vol. 27, No. 3, pp. 291-315.

Vosniadou, S. (ed.) (2008), *International Handbook of Research on Conceptual Change*, Routledge, London.

Vosniadou, S. and W.F. Brewer (1992), "Mental Models of the Earth: A Study of Conceptual Change in Childhood", *Cognitive Psychology*, Vol. 24, No. 4, pp. 535-585.

Vosniadou, S., C. Ioannides, A. Dimitrakopoulou and E. Papademetriou (2001), "Designing Learning Environments to Promote Conceptual Change in Science", *Learning and Instruction*, Vol. 11, No. 4-5, pp. 381-419.

Vosniadou, S. and L. Verschaffel (2004), "Extending the Conceptual Change Approach to Mathematics Learning and Teaching", *Learning and Instruction*, Vol. 14, No. 5, pp. 445-451.

Wagner, J.F. (2006), "Transfer in Pieces", *Cognition and Instruction*, Vol. 24, No. 1, pp. 1-71.

Winn, W. (2002), "Current Trends in Educational Technology Research: The Study of Learning Environments", *Educational Psychology Review*, Vol. 14, No. 3, pp. 331-351.

Chapter 4

The crucial role of motivation and emotion in classroom learning

Monique Boekaerts
Leiden University, Netherlands
and
Katholieke Universiteit, Leuven, Belgium

Monique Boekaerts posits that the role of emotions and motivations has been seriously neglected in the design of learning arrangements and teacher professional development. She summarises knowledge about the key role of emotions and motivations around a small number of principles. Students are more motivated to engage in learning when: they feel competent to do what is expected of them and perceive stable links between actions and achievement; they value the subject and have a clear sense of purpose; they experience positive emotions towards learning activities and, contrariwise, turn away from learning when they experience negative emotions; and when they perceive the environment as favourable for learning. Students free up cognitive resources when they are able to influence the intensity, duration and expression of their emotions, and are more persistent in learning when they can manage their resources and deal with obstacles efficiently.

Introduction

Motivation and emotion are essential to education because – together – they ensure that students acquire new knowledge and skills in a meaningful way. If all classroom activities were interesting and fun, students would engage in them naturally. But students face many tasks that they do not like or in which they are not interested or do not feel competent. Teachers thus need to be aware of how to adapt the curriculum and their teaching so that students find the classroom activities more interesting, purposeful and enjoyable, and feel more competent to do them. Students become more effective learners when they understand how their learning and motivation systems work and how they can boost their own motivation, whatever the teacher might do.

Most theories of learning and instruction may acknowledge but do not integrate motivational constructs, treating them as largely given to the learning situation. Competence models mainly focus on the domain-specific knowledge that students need to acquire, and the cognitive and meta-cognitive processes that they need to access in order to become strategic learners. However, not all students acquire knowledge in the same way and they differ in the value they attach to new knowledge and newly-acquired strategies. This means that the models commonly used to design teaching and learning do not capture all of the complexity that students bring to their learning. Unless the students' cognitions and emotions about learning are adequately factored in, these models do not represent well the dynamics of the learning process.

In this chapter, I review the research that has investigated the wide spectrum of motivational and affective processes involved, and discuss theoretical insights and empirical studies shedding light on how the motivation system works. There is, however, no all-encompassing motivation theory that explains why students are or are not motivated for school learning. Instead, we have a limited set of mini-theories that together provide insight into how students' perceptions, cognitions, emotions and commitments energise the learning process, which I summarise as a set of "principles". Recent in-class studies have helped to clarify how students' engagement is associated with specific classroom features, teaching and evaluation practices.

The effect of motivational beliefs and emotions on learning

The following example illustrates well how emotions and motivations form an integral part of learning:

> Julie failed her math exam and has to re-sit it. She is motivated to work hard during the week running up to it. Her idea is to review all the exercises they did in class. She has divided the year's work into 7 units and plans to do one unit a day. After two days of hard work,

Julie has already covered three units. She feels proud and relaxed, and decides to take the day off to go swimming. But, the fourth and fifth units are much more difficult and at the end of Day 4 she feels tired and disappointed because she has only partially covered the fourth unit. She decides to have an early start the next day, in which to finish the fourth unit by lunch time and cover most of the fifth unit before bed. If she can accomplish that there is still hope that she can cover all the material before the exam. Julie works mindfully all morning and does not allow herself any breaks. She is relieved that she understands the material well and can solve most of the problems, yet she realises that her progress is slow. At the end of Day 5, Julie starts feeling anxious because she realises that hard work may not be enough. On Day 6, Julie has problems concentrating; she keeps imagining her mother's face if she would fail the exam. She is not sure that she understands all the problems well enough to solve similar ones in the exam. By the end of Day 6, Julie has barely finished the fifth unit. She has been plagued by ruminating thoughts and anticipatory shame. After lunch, she is aware of how hot it is in her room and how tired and unhappy she feels. Julie feels out of control: she cannot cover all the material in time due to bad planning. She is certain that she will fail the exam.

In this example, Julie has a clear and concrete goal – to prepare well for the exam. During preparation, she experiences positive and negative emotions. She appraises the situation based on prior knowledge and her beliefs about what she can or cannot do in a week – her "meta-cognitive and motivational beliefs". For example, she thought that she could cover one unit per day, anticipating a steady rate of progress. Her progress was initially faster than that and she experienced positive emotions (pride, joy, feeling relaxed) and adjusted her plan: she began coasting. Likewise, when she first experienced negative emotions (disappointment), she interpreted it as slow progress and adjusted her action plan by speeding up and taking no breaks. Julie's cognitions and emotions thus work in concert to determine her actions. She observed that her strategy change had resulted in progress but relief turned to worry when she realised that she could not attain her goal. Ruminating thoughts competed for limited processing capacity in her working memory which slowed her down and introduced errors into her work (Pekrun, Frenzel, Goetz and Perry, 2007).

Emotions signal that a deviation in either direction from a predetermined standard has been detected, and this signal needs to be interpreted for change to occur (Carver, 2003). Students use these moment-to-moment variations in goal-related emotions, as well as the distance still to be covered to reach the goal, to select and modify the strategies needed to reach it. Students' motivational beliefs act as a favourable or unfavourable internal context for learning. Researchers have examined how new knowledge and skills are acquired based on how students observe and interact with their teachers and peers; social-cognitive theories provide constructs to describe students' motivational beliefs based on their previous experiences and how they are affected by the social and educational context.

Motivational beliefs are cognitions about the self in a domain (for example learning mathematics): they refer to the knowledge and opinions that students have about how their motivation system functions in different subjects and about the effect of different teaching practices on their motivation. All this is also called "meta-motivation". Students use their motivational beliefs to give meaning to learning tasks and situations and to their social and educational context. Many different types of motivational beliefs have been identified. There are the beliefs students hold about their own capability to do something (self-efficacy), that certain actions will lead to success and others to failure (outcome expectations), about the purpose of a learning activity (goal orientation), about how interesting or boring activities are (value judgments), and perceived causes of success and failure (attributions).

Motivational beliefs can be positive or negative. They are based on direct experiences in the domain (say, mathematics), but also on observations of how others perform and on what teachers, parents and peers have had to say. Motivational beliefs are important because they determine the choices students make as well as how much effort they will invest and how long they will persist in the face of difficulties.

Emotions signal to the learner that action is needed

"Emotion" refers to a wide range of affective processes, including feelings, moods, affects and well-being. Traditionally, the term has been reserved for the six primary emotions: joy, sadness, anger, fear, surprise and disgust. Many educational psychologists would also include "secondary emotions", such as envy, hope, sympathy, gratitude, regret, pride, disappointment, relief, hopelessness, shame, guilt, embarrassment and jealousy. Frijda (1986) argues that emotions have two major functions. First, they give high priority warning signals that interrupt ongoing activities and inform us that we are facing a highly valuable or threatening situation. This produces an increased level of arousal, alerting us that something needs our immediate attention. The second important function is to prepare us to react swiftly in response. The increased level of arousal coincides with a secretion of hormones into the bloodstream, producing physical changes and providing the physiological and motivational energy to allow us to take action. We can observe in ourselves many of these changes, such as the heart beating faster, breathing becoming shallower, or our hands feeling clammy.

As we saw with Julie, students detect changes in the levels of arousal and act accordingly. Some cues have the same effect in all students, for example, speaking in public increases the level of arousal while a long wait in silence decreases it. It is not the increased or decreased level of arousal itself that influences the learning outcomes, but the way that students interpret it. Those who interpret increased levels of arousal before an exam with negative emotions (anxiety, worry) will be more impeded in their exam performance than students who positively label it as a challenge. Some of these emotions, such as anger, relief and joy, are short-lived and have little significance for further learning. Other emotions, such as shame and hopelessness, have enduring relevance to classroom learning because they are tagged to a learning situation and will be activated when a student is confronted with similar tasks in the future.

Emotions have diagnostic value for the teacher because they reveal underlying cognitions, commitments and concerns. Teachers need to be aware of their students' motivational beliefs and be sensitive to their emotions as this information can inform the design of the learning process. Their own behaviour and their teaching and evaluation practices trigger specific emotions and motivational beliefs in the students, which in turn affect the quality of the learning which takes place.

Motivational beliefs and regulation strategies are integral to self-regulation

Faced by a new learning task, students first observe specific features of the task and its educational context. Second, they activate domain-specific knowledge and relevant meta-cognitive strategies. Third, they activate – the key point here – motivational beliefs and regulation strategies. Integrated models of motivation and learning, such as "dual processing self-regulation", consider motivation as a key aspect of self-regulated learning (Boekaerts, 2006; Boekaerts and Niemivirta, 2000): students orient themselves to new learning situations using all three sources of information, not just the first two. All this information is brought into working memory to determine: i) how students perceive and appraise a specific learning assignment; ii) their commitment to tackling it; and iii) how they regulate their motivation during learning.

Appraisals – task-specific motivational beliefs – play a central role in self-regulation. One of their key functions is to assign meaning and purpose to the learning activity: how relevant, boring or interesting it is; what outcome is expected; why one needs to do it; whether one feels effective or not; what causes success and failure. An equally important function is to direct activities in the self-regulation system, either towards expanding personal resources (extending knowledge, or improving learning strategy or competence) or to set bounds on well-being (*e.g.* feeling safe, secure, satisfied). Motivational beliefs thus influence willingness to engage in learning activities, even without students being aware of them.

Students' appraisals of the learning task and hence their commitment to it may change midstream, as we saw with Julie. Obstacles or distractions may come along while working on it. Changing internal and external conditions may thus alter the appraisals and trigger negative emotions with the result that the learner is no longer committed to the task in question (Boekaerts and Niemivirta, 2000). Although students may continue on the task "on automatic pilot", they have re-directed attention to their emotions (*e.g.* Julie's ruminating thoughts) or to unfavourable features of the learning environment (she noticed how uncomfortable was the room). At such a point, students need to use emotion regulation strategies to reduce their level of arousal (Key Principle 6, see below) and to volitional strategies to sustain their motivation (Key Principle 7). Students without these strategies need help from the teacher (external regulation) or their peers (co-regulation) to re-direct them in the learning.

Key motivation principles

This section presents eight "key principles" which underpin motivational beliefs (Principles 1-5), motivation regulation strategies (Principles 6-7), and the learning environment (Principle 8), together with some discussion of their implications for teaching.

Key Principle 1: Students are more motivated when they feel competent to do what is expected of them

Numerous studies have reported that students who think that they have what it takes to do specific tasks in a domain (high self-efficacy) will choose more challenging problems, invest more effort, persist longer, and will enrol in courses that are not obligatory (Pintrich and Schunk, 1996; Schunk and Pajares, 2004; Wigfield and Eccles, 2002). High self-belief and efficacy and expectations of success are positively and consistently linked to positive outcomes, such as higher recall of learned material, better strategy use, and higher grades in native language learning and mathematics. These beliefs can predict grades even better than prior grades do.

Wigfield and Eccles (2002) found that students' sense of competence becomes more differentiated and generally declines as they advance through primary school: older children more often compare themselves with peers and become more accustomed to grading and evaluation procedures. Successful students use this information to enhance their sense of self-efficacy and expectations and may simultaneously increase the value attached to learning tasks, while the motivational beliefs of unsuccessful students decline without them realising why.

Students with judgments which are well calibrated, *i.e.* in line with actual performance, are much more effective at self-regulated learning (Winne and Jamieson-Noel, 2002). They possess more accurate information about how to monitor their performance and they know how to (re)direct their learning to improve achievement. Poorly calibrated students either over-estimate or under-estimate their performance (Schunk and Pajares, 2004). The latter feel uncertain and tend uncritically to adopt other people's viewpoints and solutions (Efklides, 2006). These students may also be reluctant to try, thus delaying skill acquisition. By contrast, students who are overconfident may be highly motivated and show resolve to find a solution but they are also inclined to coast. When these students fail unexpectedly they are disappointed and may turn against the learning activity.

Bandura (1997) suggests that self-efficacy judgments which slightly exceed actual performance are beneficial for learning: these motivational beliefs raise effort and persistence without too many disappointments, while repeated failure despite high self-efficacy judgments leads to decreased effort and abandonment. Schunk and Pajares (2009) advise teachers against hasty encouragements of "give it a try" or telling students that success will come if they just invest effort. Unwarranted encouragement makes students overconfident without the necessary skills to back up their high self-efficacy. Several studies have shown that the way that teachers organise classroom practices influences their students' sense of efficacy and their outcome expectations, either in a supportive or in an inhibitory way (*e.g.* Nolen, 2007). Brophy (2001) argues that teachers should keep constantly current their expectations of what their students – alone or with the help of others – are capable of achieving by monitoring their progress closely. Teacher expectations tend to shape what students come to expect from themselves, and should be communicated to the students up front, positively yet realistically. Students' self-efficacy beliefs and expectations can be enhanced through live or symbolic modelling, catchphrases, and by encouragement to self-instruction.

Key Principle 2: Students are more motivated to engage in learning when they perceive stable links between specific actions and achievement

Some students think that the teacher is in control of learning outcomes, others believe they are in control and can specify what to do to achieve well. Evidence shows that students expect to do well on tasks that they have done well on in the past. Weiner (1986) suggests, however, that it is not actual success or failure that has an effect on future performance. Rather, the causes as understood by students about what lies behind their success or failure shape their motivational beliefs and, in this way, student expectations about future performance. Weiner argues that a poor performance on, say, a science test is seen by students and teachers alike as due to specific causes such as limited capacity in science, low invested effort, a difficult test, or simply bad luck. He found that attributing failure to low ability may have a devastating effect on students' self-concept, with them not feeling in control and discouraged from further effort.

Seligman (1975) coined the term for this stable attribution pattern "learned helplessness", reflecting students' beliefs that they have low ability and that whatever they do will not make a difference. By contrast, when students attribute a poor performance to low effort or to having used the wrong strategy (variable, internal attribution) they do not feel out of control. Such an attribution protects them from negative emotions (Key Principle 5) and negative reactions from the teacher and classmates – because low effort or using the wrong strategies are considered controllable.

Zimmerman and Kitsantas (1997) show that attributing failure to having used the wrong strategies is beneficial for motivation: students who had deliberately planned and used a specific strategy for problem solving were more likely to attribute their poor results to the strategy than to low ability. This helps them to sustain a sense of efficacy despite poor results. Students who attribute their results to the strategy chosen tend to persist until all the strategies they have available have been tried. By contrast, several studies have shown that students do not invest effort in preparing for exams when they do not perceive stable links between their strategies and the expected outcome (Boekaerts, 2006). In our example, Julie had high self-efficacy and expectations at the start of the week but while her efficacy remained high her outcome expectation changed when she observed that what she was doing was not bearing fruit. She attributed her problems to bad planning (strategy failure), leaving her self-efficacy in place but prompting her to modify her planning next time.

Teachers need to ensure that students attribute results in a healthy way that fosters motivation, including after poor performance. Students need to know beforehand what the desired outcomes are and which strategies they will use. On completion, they need to reflect on the adequacy of the strategies they have used. Students need to perceive the learning outcomes as **contingent** on the use of specific cognitive and meta-cognitive strategies. They need to perceive stable links between their own actions (such as re-reading a text, highlighting the main ideas and paraphrasing the message) and their achievement so as to attribute the results to the strategy used.

Key Principle 3: Students are more motivated to engage in learning when they value the subject and have a clear sense of purpose

Students are not likely to initiate activities and maintain effort if the perceived value of the task is minimal. The anticipated pleasure and pride in accomplishing a task energises them. Wigfield and Eccles (2002) conclude that the importance, interest and relevance students attach to a domain are the best predictors of whether they will persist, whether they select challenging or easy tasks and whether they will enrol in courses in that subject. Competency beliefs are the best predictors of a student's actual achievement. Dweck (1986) has argued that students develop short cuts for assigning meaning to learning tasks: they tend to adopt either "mastery" or "performance" goal orientations. Students with a performance orientation want to demonstrate their ability for the task, to obtain a high grade and out-perform others. By contrast, students with a mastery orientation engage in learning in order to understand the new material and increase their competence. The perceived purpose is fundamentally different in the two cases.

Numerous studies have shown that mastery orientation is associated with interest and is beneficial for learning (deep learning strategies). Initially, studies argued against the performance goal orientation because it depends on two unfavourable motivational beliefs: first, that one needs high ability to be successful and second that success should be demonstrated with little effort. Ames (1992) argues that such beliefs create anxiety when someone is faced with complex or ambiguous tasks – students hide errors as they view them as a sign of low ability and they do not ask for feedback. They believe that others will think they are less competent than they pretend they are. It leads to behaviour such as making less effort, refusing help, procrastination and task avoidance. Mastery orientation is instead based on favourable motivational beliefs, such as faith that effort leads to success and confidence in the benefits of feedback, scaffolding and help. Such constructive beliefs trigger positive emotions and prompt students to solicit feedback and help in order to improve.

More recent studies have revisited these conclusions by distinguishing between "performance approach" (wanting to demonstrate ability) and "performance avoidance" (wanting to hide incompetence). Harackiewicz, Barron, Pintrich, Elliot and Thrash (2002) show that only performance avoidance goals are detrimental for learning. Performance approach goals – together with mastery goals – actually lead to better cognitive engagement and achievement than either goal orientation by itself.

Teachers can promote either a mastery or performance orientation (Ames, 1984). When they give competitive instructions, emphasise grades and draw students' attention to the difficulty of the task, most students tend to adopt a performance orientation and view the purpose as having to demonstrate their ability. Ryan and Sapp (2005) warn against a strong emphasis on evaluation procedures, competition, and high-stakes testing because these tend to reward only those students who have high ability and want to demonstrate it. Even these achievement-oriented students may be at risk of negative side-effects, because they are being encouraged to display superficial learning, to depend on extrinsic motivation, and are rewarded for avoidance. By contrast, teachers, who give non-competitive instructions, linking learning tasks to students' interests and personal goals, develop mastery-oriented students (Nolen (2007). These students understand the role of effort and monitor their performance for lack of comprehension. They ask the teacher to scaffold their performance, when appropriate.

Key Principle 4: Students are more motivated to engage in learning when they experience positive emotions towards learning activities

Different learning histories shape students' emotions towards academic work. Positive and negative emotions become integrated into specific mental representations. Positive emotions prime encoded information in long-term memory to signal that one is doing well, leading to a positive mood state and favourable judgments of one's own performance (Bower, 1991). Positive emotions serve to signal fulfilment of one's psychological needs – need for competence, autonomy and social relatedness – encouraging active, constructive engagement (Ryan and Deci, 2000). Positive feelings also signal that one has sufficient personal resources to deal with a particular situation and this coincides with openness for change and playful activities (Aspinwall and Taylor, 1997). Positive emotions energise students because they direct attention towards relevant cues in the task and the learning environment to create an optimal internal environment for learning, self-regulation and achievement.

The positive emotions of pleasure and pride that things go well experienced during a challenging math or writing task create "task attraction" and "task satisfaction" (sometimes called "situational interest") which encourage students to seek similar learning tasks. Similarly, the feelings of pride and self-respect which comes with effortful accomplishment – "intrinsic motivation" – are valued more highly than getting tangible reward. Unfortunately, pride and satisfaction are not experienced on every occasion of successful accomplishment. According to Weiner (2007), the success must be self-attributed and this involves recall of prior successes or comparisons with a social norm. He maintains that students will experience positive emotions when they attribute success to stable, internal causes (*e.g.* capacity and persistence) and failure to variable, external causes (*e.g.* bad luck, being tired, not getting enough time or help). Such patterns of attribution diminish the negative emotions when the student performs poorly. Instead, (s)he will show social emotions (disappointment, anger) directed at what is seen to have caused the failure, *e.g.* "the teacher did not allow us enough time to finish the task". This is a healthy attribution style because it allows students to encode the learning task into a positive set of associations: a positive self-concept is established and favourable reactions will be triggered on comparable future occasions.

Unjustified positive emotions may be considered misplaced by others. For example, students resent it when someone shows pride for getting good grades after copying somebody else's work; they think that relief or being thankful would be more appropriate. Positive emotions which are triggered by the task or its context may evaporate quickly, but they may also develop into personal interest under the right circumstances. Personal interest develops from stimulated situational interest being sustained over time, with the educational context allowing an elaborate understanding of the course content to develop. Personal interest is thus like intrinsic motivation for a school subject. Intrinsically motivated students report that positive feelings are triggered automatically when they engage in tasks in that school subject, provided that they can work with some autonomy (see Key Principle 8). A meta-analysis by Cameron and Pierce (1994) showed that giving extrinsic rewards for something which students would have done anyway decreased intrinsic motivation, with a detrimental effect on creativity, invested effort and performance.

Key Principle 5: Students direct their attention away from learning when they experience negative emotions

Performance anxiety is the best known negative emotion in relation to learning, but shame, boredom, anger, disappointment and hopelessness are others. Negative emotions produce ruminating thoughts (recall Julie's example) that inhibit performance. Negative emotions prime encoded information in long-term memory and signal to the student that something is wrong (Bower, 1991). This triggers a negative mood and unfavourable judgments of the task and one's performance of it. Negative emotions may also indicate that the learner's psychological needs for competence, autonomy and social relatedness are frustrated.

As children move up the school system, they become increasingly aware of their own needs. At the same time, they realise the limits of their ability to do school tasks relative to their peers, so affecting their self-worth. Weiner (1986, 2007) and Covington (1992) have described the devastating effect that students' reactions to failure may have on their self-worth, especially those who ascribe failure to stable, internal causes ("I am not capable of doing that"). This will activate negative emotions and unfavourable motivational beliefs next time – low expectations and self-efficacy and performance avoidance – and reinforce negative learning experiences.

Common advice to teachers seeking to break the vicious circle is to programme a series of success experiences. But, when these students enjoy unexpected success they do not experience the usual positive emotions but instead feel relieved that it did not go wrong and are grateful to the teacher, peers, or even to favourable circumstances that they thought caused the success. Their way of attributing cause does not allow them to establish a positive view, even when they enjoy success. As such, these students will continue to encode learning activities in a negative way.

These students also consider effort as a threat to their self-esteem. Most students lose face when they fail despite having tried, because they think that others will perceive it as a sign of low ability (Covington and Omelich, 1979). To avoid the demoralising feeling, they use ego-protective, inhibiting behaviours. Shame and personal dissatisfaction are greatest when students have studied hard for a test and failed anyhow, and least when they fail but have made little effort. This research suggests that shame and dissatisfaction are reduced considerably by acceptable excuses for why they had not tried hard (*e.g.* having been taught by a temporary teacher).

Teachers need to break the vicious circle by providing learning tasks that are slightly above the students' current level of competence and giving non-threatening feedback. Dweck (1986) advised teachers to avoid reference to their students' intelligence, social comparisons, and personal criticism but to invite them to assess their own performance and to push them to listen carefully to the teacher's feedback. Teachers should emphasise that mistakes are inherent to learning and that one can learn a lot from them (Brown, 1994). They should encourage students to reflect on their own and other students' strengths and take pleasure in accomplishments that needed effort. When failure occurs, teachers should use responses such as: "You gave it a good try but it did not work. Do you have any idea why?" or "Could you think of another way to do this next time?" Less successful students should be given the chance to answer these questions. Wiebe Berry (2006) advised teachers not to over-help their students and to make sure that they are part of the discussion. Such students also need to be placed in the role of help providers, because peers interpret getting help without also providing it as a sign that they have nothing of value to contribute.

Key Principle 6: Students free up cognitive resources for learning when they are able to influence the intensity, duration and expression of their emotions

Students experience many stressful situations in the classroom that can harm their self-concept and elicit negative emotions and produce ruminating thoughts that interfere with information processing (Key Principle 5). Students need to remove these internal road blocks and re-direct their attention to the learning task. They should either express their emotions or turn down the level and duration of arousal caused by these emotional triggers. At times, it is beneficial to express one's emotions so that others can take account of one's feelings (such as showing disappointment or irritation if someone takes credit for something they did not do). At other times, it is essential to temper one's emotions because they hinder the learning process. Not all students are able to control their emotions swiftly to continue with the task in hand, yet they may realise that how they regulate their emotions influences learning and social interaction in the classroom.

"Emotion regulation strategies" (also called "coping" or "affect regulation strategies") refer to the capacity to use one's emotions as a source of energy and to modify them when they interfere with the pursuit of goals. Such strategies may take the form of reappraising the relevance of the task that caused the negative feeling, emotion suppression, anxiety or danger control, relaxation and distraction. Gross and John (2002) argue that emotion regulation can be preventive or remedial. Students may reflect on emotion regulation strategies **before** the negative emotions are triggered, *e.g.* anticipated shame due to feeling incompetent may be prevented by pre-arranging support from a more advanced peer in case one's own strategies would fail. Students may also try to reduce the impact of the emotion by forcing themselves to stay calm, holding a conversation with oneself, deliberate distraction (*e.g.* go and sit somewhere else), or avoidance. An effective way may be re-appraisal of the situation ("Is it really so bad that I cannot solve this problem? Yesterday, I did seven of them."). Re-appraisal is beneficial by being positively associated with self-efficacy, positive mood and sharing emotions, and negatively associated with neuroticism (Gross and John, 2002). Since re-appraisal occurs early in the episode, it does not require continuous monitoring and hence does not overload the student's processing capacity. Suppression of emotion comes at a cost, however, as it is associated with feelings of loss of control and depression. It reduces cognitive resources for ongoing and upcoming activities because it requires continuous monitoring during the emotion episode.

The types of emotion regulation strategies that students bring to the classroom are affected by parental modelling and coaching, as well as by the social support parents provide. Students who experience many negative emotions and find it difficult to regulate them need support from the teacher and their peers. These students will benefit if their teachers model effective emotion regulation strategies and scaffold their development. This is a new area of research and only a few studies have demonstrated the benefits for achievement of training in emotion regulation strategies (*e.g.* Punmongkol, 2009).

Key Principle 7: Students are more persistent in learning when they can manage their resources and deal with obstacles efficiently

Normally, the curriculum and the teacher specify what needs to be learned and in what time frame. Students are expected to make sense of the learning tasks and complete them in the time allotted, soliciting feedback and help when needed. As seen, motivational beliefs influence the way students assign meaning and purpose to their learning and they provide information on how students can enhance and sustain motivation. Ideally, students should orient themselves to a learning task before they start with it, so that they can determine its purpose and the outcomes to be reached. Establishing a clear and concrete learning goal helps students to select appropriate strategies and to assess how much time and effort will be needed. However, things may turn out differently than expected. Students may re-appraise the activity as more difficult, boring, or time-consuming than anticipated (recall Julie). They may meet with unexpected obstacles and distractions. Hence, they need "motivation regulation strategies" (also called "volitional strategies"). These remind students why it is important to complete the task and help to protect their willingness to learn, particularly when the work is difficult.

Students may be aware that different volitional strategies exist and they may use them occasionally. Examples are anticipating rewards for completion and the negative consequences of giving up, self-talk (thoughts about the purpose of finishing the task), interest enhancement, removing distractions that reduce the likelihood of completion (environmental control) and good work habits.

Students often detect too late that their learning is problematic and this because they lack the necessary volitional strategies. People often confuse good intention or commitment with their ability to translate it into action (Gollwitzer, 1999). Gollwitzer proposes that people should combine implementation intentions with specific volitional strategies ("**when** I come home from school, I will go to **my room** and start my homework **immediately**"). Such implementation intentions (when-where plans) encourage students to initiate good work habits via specific environmental cues. Gollwitzer found that when students formulated specific implementation intentions, it facilitated both the detection of obstacles and the ability to address them. The initiation of the plan is immediate and efficient, and protects the student from unwanted negative emotions once obstacles arise.

Less successful students need the help of teachers to accomplish long-term goals. These students benefit from training in good work habits and from sharing effective volitional strategies with their peers. Students of all ages benefit when their teachers model good work habits and scaffold the development of motivation regulation (Corno, 2004). Students like to share and build up information about the best use of personal resources and how to deal with obstacles and distractions. Observational learning is beneficial: students have been found to be more motivated to acquire new skills after observing a model succeed after struggling with road blocks than after watching a flawless performance (Zimmerman and Kitsantas, 2002). They appreciated realistic models who recognised the obstacles they had encountered, described what they had done to tackle the problem, and where they still needed scaffolding from an expert performer.

Key Principle 8: Students are more motivated to engage in learning and use motivation regulation strategies when they perceive the environment as favourable for learning

Students learn in social and classroom contexts which interact with their personal characteristics, motivational beliefs and personal strategies. Students observe teachers demonstrating a new skill, and they listen to teacher questions and feedback as well as to reprimands and appreciative statements. They participate in learning activities with others and observe their successes and failures. In sum, students come to understand and integrate learning strategies through observing and participating in social learning activities. Their appraisal of the task and its context are **co-constructed** in the specific educational and social context (Perry, Turner and Meyer, 2006).

Different educational situations provide different levels of structural, motivational, social and emotional support. The tasks that teachers select and the learning environment in which they are located motivate students differently. Aspects of the learning task – novelty, diversity, authenticity, relevance, fantasy – may or may not capture student interest. The way that teachers structure learning and design the social environment may or may not be favourable to maintaining interest. I have already referred to aspects of the learning environment that enhance a performance goal orientation (Key Principle 3), instructional practices detrimental to learning (Key Principles 2 and 5), and environments that meet psychological needs (Key Principle 4).

Students learn best when teachers cater to individual preferences but it is difficult to take account of all these preferences. Some students like collaborative work more than individual seatwork, but only if the conditions are right. Some feel frustrated when the teacher tells them exactly what to do while others feel threatened when they have to direct their own learning. There are marked individual differences in student preferences for the type and intensity of structural, motivational, social and emotional support, making it impossible to specify the most engaging tasks and environments for each and every student.

Recent in-class studies (*e.g.* Nolen, 2007; Perry, Turner and Meyer, 2006) suggest that tasks are engaging when teachers and students can manipulate them to suit their current teaching and learning needs. This dynamic approach is based on how students learn effectively. What it implies is that, at any moment, both students and teachers know who regulates the learning process, whether the teacher (external regulation), the learners (self-regulation), or jointly (co-regulation).

Teachers should check whether their students are responsive to instructions and can detect from them who should assume the primary responsibility for different aspects of the learning. Lack of understanding of the interdependence that the teacher had in mind for a particular activity causes frustration. Students may feel that the learning activities do not increase their competence, that they are not given sufficient latitude or are obliged to work on tasks that have low authenticity, variety, novelty and relevance (Ryan and Deci, 2000). They may find that the tasks are too difficult to do alone but resent the help needed to succeed. Over-helped students who are shut out of discussion display resistance, using strategies such as withdrawal, being silly, or refusing to cooperate (Nolen, 2007). These strategies come at a cost: they confirm that the student has a problem, which may bring peer rejection and teacher sanctions, while reducing the student's opportunities for skill development.

In-class observations have shown that primary school children are able to co-regulate and self-regulate their learning when given complex, meaningful writing tasks that address multiple goals and lead to varied writing products over extended periods (Nolen, 2007; Perry, 1998). Complex writing assignments allow students more ways to satisfy their needs and preferences compared with tasks that steered them to predetermined written outcomes. Teachers who encourage their students to plan their own writing and who scaffold the monitoring and evaluation process, have students who report feeling more in control of their writing and more motivated to express their ideas. Even low-achieving students display fewer negative emotions and react more favourably to corrective and constructive feedback; they use fewer self-handicapping strategies than low-achieving students in classrooms where all students worked on the same tasks.

It is important that teachers select a range of learning activities from which students can chose the ones that they think will work for them. Teachers should encourage students to self-regulate their learning, providing as much constructive feedback as needed. They should emphasise students' strengths rather than their weaknesses and encourage them to learn from and with each other. Asking students to share meaningful products and discuss efficient and less efficient strategies in a non-threatening way creates interest, opportunities to improve strategy use, and builds a community of learners (Brown, 1994).

Implications for policy

Motivation research has direct implications for the design of effective learning environments. Teachers need to understand how cognitive and motivation systems work and how they interact. The eight key principles presented exemplify how favourable cognitions and positive emotions act together to energise students. The principles also demonstrate how negative emotions and unhealthy attributions can inhibit learning and demoralise.

Students will not take the risk of losing face and accept responsibility for learning if their teachers have not created a foundation of trust. Teachers need to be aware that motivational messages are embedded in their own discourse, their selection of learning tasks, and in their teaching practices. Students pick up these unintended messages, and appraise the climate as either favourable or unfavourable for learning.

I began this chapter by stating that theories of learning and instruction have mostly failed to represent the dynamics of the learning process, by treating motivation as largely an unrelated matter. Unfortunately, such theories are still being studied in teacher education programmes. There is an urgent need for a wind of change. Teachers need to factor in the motivational beliefs and concomitant emotions that students bring to bear on their learning and – even more importantly – to use this information to determine the zones of cognitive **and motivational** competence that are just above the students' current levels. The cognitive and motivational needs of students change as their expertise in different fields develops, and optimal learning conditions therefore also change.

It is essential that experts in cognition, motivation, teaching and learning work together to design programmes that inform teachers on how the cognitive and motivation systems work together during the learning process which then lead to hands-on training units to implement these insights. Such courses and training programmes should: (1) make teachers aware of the motivational beliefs that students bring to bear on learning, and (2) of the positive and negative emotions that affect learning. The programmes should also guide teachers (3) on how to recognise and take account of these beliefs and emotions, and (4) on how they can help students to deal with counter-productive beliefs and emotions. Teachers need to be trained in how they can (5) model and scaffold good work habits and other volitional and emotion regulation strategies, so that their students can deal with internal and external road blocks themselves.

References

Ames, C. (1984), "Competitive, Co-operative, and Individualistic Goal Structures: A Cognitive Motivational Analysis", in R.E. Ames and C. Ames (eds.), *Research on Motivation in Education* (Vol. 1, pp. 177-208), Academic Press, New York.

Ames, C. (1992), "Classrooms: Goals, Structures, and Student Motivation", *Journal of Educational Psychology,* Vol. 84, No. 3, pp. 261-271.

Aspinwall, L.G. and S.E. Taylor (1997), "A Stich in Time: Self-Regulation and Proactive Coping", *Psychological Bulletin*, Vol. 121, No. 3, pp. 417-436.

Bandura, A. (1997), *Self-efficacy: The exercise of control,* Freeman, New York.

Boekaerts, M. (2006), "Self-Regulation and Effort Investment", in E. Sigel and K.A. Renninger (eds.), *Handbook of Child Psychology*, Vol. 4, Child Psychology in Practice, John Wiley and Sons, Hoboken, NJ, pp. 345-377.

Boekaerts, M. and M. Niemivirta (2000), "Self-Regulated Learning: Finding a Balance between Learning Goals and Ego Protective Goals", in M. Boekaerts, P.R. Pintrich and M. Zeidner (eds.), *Handbook of Self-Regulation*, Academic Press , New York, pp. 417-450.

Bower, G.H. (1991), "Mood Congruity of Social Judgment", in J. Forgas (ed.), *Emotion and Social Judgment*, Pergamon , Oxford, UK, pp. 31-54.

Brophy, J. (2001), *Teaching*, in the Educational Practice Series of the International Academy of Education, International Bureau of Education, UNESCO, Geneva.

Brown, A.L. (1994), "The Advancement of Learning", *Educational Researcher*, Vol. 23, No. 8, pp. 4-12.

Cameron, J. and W.D. Pierce (1994), "Reinforcement, Reward, and Intrinsic Motivation: A Meta-Analysis", *Review of Educational Research*, Vol. 64, No. 3, pp. 363-423.

Carver, C.S. (2003), "Pleasure as a Sign You Can Attend to Something Else: Placing Positive Feelings within a General Model of Affect", *Cognition and Emotion,* Vol. 17, No. 2, pp. 241-261.

Corno, L. (2004), "Work Habits and Work Styles: The Psychology of Volition in Education", *Teachers College Record*, Vol. 106, No. 9, pp. 1669-1694.

Covington, M.V. (1992), *Making the Grade: A Self-Worth Perspective on Motivation and School Reform*, New York: Cambridge University Press.

Covington, M.V. and C.L. Omelich (1979), "Effort: the Double-Edged Sword in School Achievement", *Journal of Educational Psychology*, Vol. 71, No. 2, pp. 169-182.

Dweck, C.S. (1986), "Motivational Process Affecting Learning", *American Psychologist*, Vol. 41, No. 10, pp. 1040-1048.

Efklides, A. (2006), "Metacognition and Affect: What Can Metacognitive Experiences Tell Us about the Learning Process?", *Educational Research Review*, Vol. 1, No. 1, pp. 3-14.

Frijda, N.H. (1986), *The Emotions*, Cambridge University Press, Cambridge, UK.

Gollwitzer, P.M. (1999), "Implementation Intentions: Strong Effects of Simple Plans", *American Psychologist,* Vol. 54, No. 7, pp. 493-503.

Gross, J.J. and O.P. John (2002), "Wise Emotion Regulation", in F.F. Barrett and P. Salovey (eds.), *The Wisdom in Feeling: Psychological Processes in Emotion Intelligence*, Guilford Press, New York, pp. 297-318.

Harackiewicz, J.M., K.E. Barron, P.R. Pintrich, A.J. Elliot and T.M. Thrash (2002), "Revision of Achievement Goal Theory: Necessary and Illuminating", *Journal of Educational Psychology,* Vol. 94, No. 3, pp. 638-645.

Nolen, S.B. (2007), "Young Children's Motivation to Read and Write: Development in Social Contexts", *Cognition and Instruction*, Vol. *25*, No. 2-3, pp. 219-270.

Pekrun, R., A.C. Frenzel, T. Goetz and R.P. Perry (2007), "Theoretical Perspectives on Emotion in Education", in P. Schutz, R. Pekrun and G. Phye (eds.), *Emotion in Education*, Academic Press, San Diego, CA, pp. 13-36.

Perry, N.E. (1998), "Young Children's Self-Regulated Learning and the Contexts that Support It", *Journal of Educational Psychology,* Vol. 90, No. 4, pp. 715-729.

Perry, N.E., J.C. Turner and D.K. Meyer (2006), "Classrooms as Contexts for Motivated Learning", in P.A. Alexander and P.H. Winne (eds.), *Handbook of Educational Psychology*, Lawrence Erlbaum, Mahwah, NJ, pp. 327-348.

Pintrich, R.R.and D.H. Schunk (1996), *Motivation in Education: Theory, Research, and Applications,* Englewood Cliffs, Prentice-Hall, Inc., New Jersey.

Punmongkol, P. (2009), "The Regulation of Academic Emotions", PhD Thesis, University of Sydney, NSW, Australia.

Ryan, R.M. and E. Deci (2000), "Intrinsic and Extrinsic Motivations: Classic Definitions and New Directions", *Contemporary Educational Psychology*, Vol. 25, No. 1, pp. 54-67.

Ryan, R.M. and A. Sapp (2005), "Zum Einfluss Testbasierter Reformen: High Stake Testing (HST)", *Unterrichtswissenschaft,* Vol. 33, No. 2, pp. 143-159.

Schunk, D.H. and F. Pajares (2004), "Self-Efficacy in Education Revisited: Empirical and Applied Evidence", in D.M. McInerney and S. Van Etten (eds.), *Big Theories Revisited*, Information Age Publishing, Greenwich, CT, pp. 115-138.

Schunk, D.H. and F. Pajares (2009), "Self-Efficacy Theory", in K. Wentzel and A. Wigfield (eds.), *Handbook of Motivation at School*, Routledge, New York and London.

Seligman, M.E.P. (1975), *Helplessness: on Depression Development and Death*, Freeman, San Francisco.

Weiner, B. (1986), *An Attributional Theory of Motivation and Emotion,* Springer-Verlag, New York.

Weiner, B. (2007), "Examining Emotional Diversity in the Classroom: An Attribution Theorist Considers the Moral Emotions", in P. Schutz, R. Pekrun and G. Phye (eds.), *Emotion in Education*, Academic Press, San Diego, CA, pp. 75-88.

Wiebe Berry, R.A. (2006), "Inclusion, Power, and Community: Teachers and Students Interpret the Language of Community in an Inclusion Classroom", *American Educational Research Journal,* Vol. 43, No. 3, pp. 489-529.

Wigfield, A. and J.S. Eccles (2002), "The Development of Competence Beliefs, Expectancies for Success, and Achievement Values from Childhood through Adolescence", in A. Wigfield and J.S. Eccles (eds.), *Development of Achievement Motivation*, Academic Press, San Diego, CA, pp. 91-120.

Winne, P.H. and E. Jamieson-Noel (2002), "Exploring Students' Calibration of Self-Reports about Study Tactics and Achievement", *Contemporary Educational Psychology,* Vol. 27, No. 4, pp. 551-572.

Zimmerman, B. and A. Kitsantas (1997), "Developmental Phases in Self-Regulation: Shifting from Process to Outcome Goals", *Journal of Educational Psychology,* Vol. 89, No. 1, pp. 29-36.

Zimmerman, B and A. Kitsantas (2002), "Acquiring Writing Revision and Self Regulatory Skill through Observation and Emulation", *Journal of Educational Psychology,* Vol. 94, No. 4, pp. 660-668.

Chapter 5

Learning from the developmental and biological perspective

Christina Hinton and Kurt W. Fischer
Harvard Graduate School of Education

Christina Hinton and Kurt Fischer consider first how genetics and experience interact to guide development, and how learning experiences literally shape the physical structure of the brain. They stress how cognition and emotion work in tandem. The chapter reviews research on how the brain acquires core academic abilities, including language, literacy and mathematics, and discuss atypical development of these abilities. The brain is biologically primed to acquire language, while the capacity for literacy, on the other hand, is built over time with cumulative neural modifications and varies depending on the language in question. Similarly, different instruction shapes the neural circuitry underlying mathematical abilities. Neuro-scientific research has underpinned key findings regarding learning, such as the extent of individual differences and the essential social nature of human learning, which means that learning environments should incorporate multiple means of representation, assessment and engagement.

Introduction

How do nature and nurture interact to guide brain development? How does the brain translate learning experiences into neurological signals? Why do children and adolescents often struggle with emotional regulation? Why do children seem to master the accent of a foreign language virtually effortlessly? How does the brain support reading? Are children's brains ready to begin mathematics instruction in primary school? What is the neurological basis of empathy, and what is its role in learning? The emerging field of mind, brain and education is beginning to answer these kinds of questions. With recent technological and methodological breakthroughs, such as brain imaging technologies and innovative cognitive methods for mapping learning pathways, this new field is poised to make a major contribution to our understanding of learning (Hinton, Miyamoto and della Chiesa, 2008; Fischer *et al.*, 2007; OECD, 2007).

This chapter provides an overview of principles emerging from this field and considers their educational implications. It first explains how genetics and experience interact to guide development, how learning experiences literally shape the physical structure of the brain, and how cognition and emotion work in tandem. It then reviews recent mind, brain and education research on how the brain acquires core academic abilities, including language, literacy and mathematics. Finally, it considers the central role of social interaction and cultural context in how people use their brains to learn, and concludes by considering implications for learning environments.

Research in mind, brain and education

The field of mind, brain and education, also referred to as "educational neuroscience", is comprised of many disciplines, including neuroscience, cognitive science and education (Fischer *et al.*, 2007; OECD, 2007). Educational research has accumulated an extensive knowledge base, and research from the field of mind, brain and education can complement this work. Education research often links policies and practices with learning outcomes. Research in mind, brain and education allows us to uncover key causal mechanisms underlying these relationships. For example, education research established that policies and practices that delay exposure to a second language until after adolescence often result in significant deficits in the processing of grammar and the sounds of words (Fledge and Fletcher, 1992). Neuroscience provides a causal explanation for this finding, revealing that children learn differently depending on the maturity of their brains. When they are young, they learn best through talking with others in the language being learned. When they become adolescent or adult, they learn better when instruction includes a focus on the rules of the language (grammar, sound, discussion)* (Neville and Bruer, 2001). By connecting work across disciplines, the field of mind, brain and education can shed light on how and why certain policies and practices may lead to more or less favourable outcomes.

Working across disciplines nevertheless brings new challenges as well as new opportunities (della Chiesa, Christoph and Hinton, 2009). Biology, cognitive science and education each have deeply-rooted disciplinary cultures with field-specific language and methods, which make it difficult for experts in the different fields to collaborate. There is a lack of consensus about the meaning of even fundamental terms, such as "learning" and methodological tools of measurement are not yet aligned across fields. Scientists working in laboratories are unplugged from the world of educational policies, school cultures and student differences. As a result, they often carry out research with limited practical relevance (OECD, 2007).

On the other side, educators – a term used throughout this chapter very broadly to refer to all adults who are involved in helping children and adolescents learn – are often unable accurately to determine the educational implications of scientific results (Goswami, 2006; Pickering and Howard-Jones, 2007). Moreover, statements of ideas in neuro-scientific language and the deployment of brain images make educators more likely to believe such statements and can lead some commercial and political organisations to promote their ideas about learning as "brain-based" even when there is no robust neuroscience to support their claims (McCabe and Castel, 2008). Without a background understanding of biology and cognitive science, educational policy makers and practitioners are sometimes unable to distinguish these "neuro-myths" from sound neuroscience (OECD, 2007).

We should therefore be cautious when considering educational implications of brain research (Bruer, 1997). Researchers, policy makers and practitioners should collaborate to steer researchers toward relevant areas and help policy makers and practitioners to identify the educational implications of scientific findings. Continued progress therefore requires the creation of an infrastructure that supports this type of collaboration (Hinton and Fischer, 2008; Fischer, 2009; Shonkoff and Phillips, 2000). As the field develops, research in mind, brain and education can play a key role in designing effective education policies and practices.

---

*Though it is easier for people to use their brain to master the grammar of a language early in life, it is still possible to learn the grammar of a language in adulthood. In addition, some other aspects of language are learned more easily by adults (Snow and Hoefnagel-Hohle, 1978).

Nature meets nurture

Why do some students whiz through algebra, while others struggle? How does a young student become a talented musician? Why do some students work hard and persist in the face of adversity? Why do some shy children grow up to be outgoing adults? The answer to these types of questions is not a simple one. Development involves a complex interplay of nature and nurture, with genetics and experience working hand-in-hand (Hinton, Miyamoto and della Chiesa, 2008). For example, a genetic predisposition for shyness may be counterbalanced by socialisation in gregarious culture. Similarly, a genetic predisposition for perfect pitch may become a singing talent because of a mother's encouragement, a teacher's guidance and the child's passion for performance. Throughout life, genetics and experience interact to shape development.

Genetics provide a plan for the brain's basic organisation. Just as an architect supplies a blueprint that lays out a plan for building a house, genetics provide a plan for the basic connectivity patterns within and among brain networks. These connectivity patterns define genetic predispositions for later development, which are realised to a greater or lesser extent in response to the environment. In the same way that a carpenter adjusts a house as it is being built, the environment shapes the architecture of the brain. The first few years of life bring rapid proliferation, with 700 new connections forming every second (Shonkoff and Phillips, 2000). Connections are then reduced through a process called "pruning" as the brain is sculpted to fit the needs of its environment. Lower-level circuits, such as those for sensory capacities like vision and hearing, are shaped earliest. Higher-level networks, such as those supporting cognitive functions, then follow.

How people use their brains to learn

The brain networks involved in learning can be broadly classified into the "recognition", "strategic" and "affective" networks (Figure 5.1) (Rose and Meyer, 2000). The recognition network, which includes sensory areas such as the visual cortex, receives information from the environment and transforms it into knowledge. It identifies and categorises what children see, hear, or read. The strategic network, which includes the prefrontal cortex, is used for planning and coordinating goal-oriented actions. Finally, the affective network encompasses areas of the limbic system, such as the amygdala. It is involved in emotional dimensions of learning such as interest, motivation and stress. When faced with a learning task, such as reading a Shakespearean sonnet, all of these networks work together to guide the learning process – the recognition network identifies letters, words and Shakespeare's tone; the strategic network focuses attention on the goal of understanding the text and monitors progress toward that goal; and the affective network manages the motivation to continue reading.

Figure 5.1. **Broad classification of brain networks involved in learning**

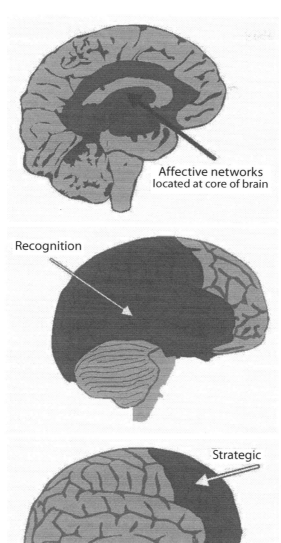

These networks are made up of specialised nerve cells called neurons and supporting glial cells. Learning experiences are translated into electrical and chemical signals that gradually modify connections between neurons (Kaczmarek, 1997). Each neuron has three distinguishable parts: dendrites, a cell body and an axon (Figure 5.2). Dendrites receive chemical signals from other cells in response to experience. They then relay signals to the cell body, which contains the nucleus with DNA and is the main site of protein synthesis (which is crucial for converting short-term memory into long-term memory). If the signal is above a certain threshold, it triggers an electrical signal called an action potential. The action potential then travels along the axon, a long process covered by a fatty myelin sheath which surrounds and insulates axons, and increases the speed at which messages can be sent. When it reaches the end of the axon, it prompts the release of chemical signals to the dendrites of other cells. A neuron that is sending information is termed a "presynaptic neuron" and a neuron that is receiving information is termed a "postsynaptic neuron". There is a small space called the "synaptic cleft" between the axon of a presynaptic neuron and the dendrites of a postsynaptic neuron.

Figure 5.2. **The connection between two neurons**

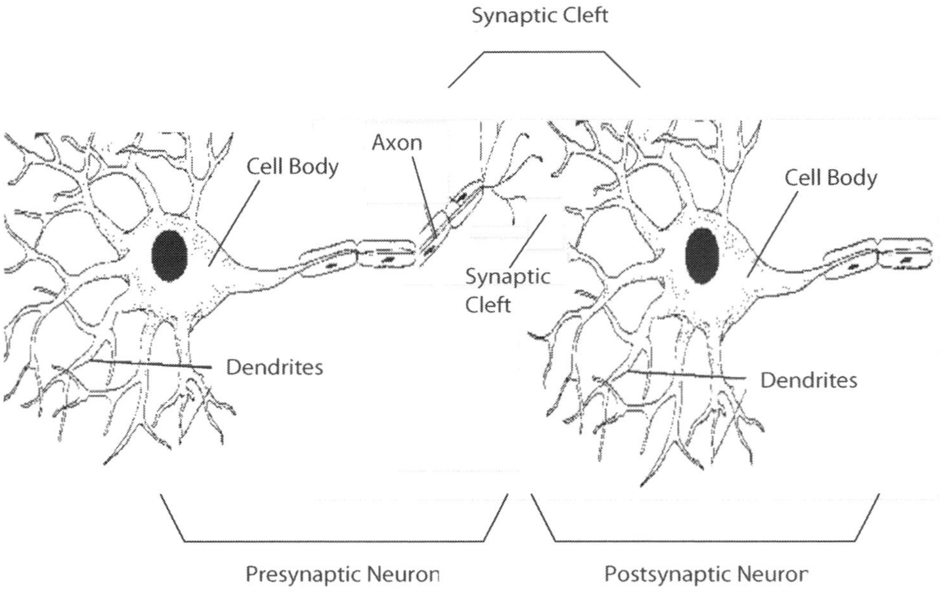

Changes in synaptic connections are modified by learning experiences following the "use it or lose it" rule. Figure 5.2 is simplified in that, in reality, the axon terminals of many presynaptic neurons converge on the dendrites of each postsynaptic neuron. Presynaptic inputs may be strengthening or inhibiting; those that are the most active relative to other inputs on that post-synaptic neuron are strengthened, while those that are relatively less active are weakened (and can eventually be eliminated). This strengthening and weakening raises or lowers the threshold at which an action potential will fire in the presynaptic cell. The initial facilitation or inhibition of the connection is temporary, and thought to underlie short-term memory. However, repeated activity, or lack of it, eventually leads to long-term changes in synaptic con-nections that are mediated by protein synthesis; these robust changes appear to underlie long-term memory (Squire and Kandel, 1999).

Over time, these alterations in cellular connectivity aggregate to produce significant changes in the configuration of the recognition, strategic and affec-tive networks (Buonomano, Merzenich, 1998). For example, as a child learns to play the violin, neuronal connections are gradually tuned which, over time, manifests itself in changes in cortical organisation. As he or she practises, the neuronal connections underlying finger dexterity in the hand are active which further strengthens these connections. In fact, the cortical area representing the fingers of the left hand is larger in violinists than in non-musicians (Ebert *et al.*, 1995). Similarly, the neuronal connections needed for processing musi-cal notes are reinforced through practising the violin and the cortical area representing musical tones is larger in violinists than non-musicians (Pantev *et al.*, 1998). Over time, brain networks gradually reorganise to reflect learning experiences, and this reorganisation influences future learning.

The main message of all of this research for educators is that the brain is powerfully shaped by experience. This fact is good news because it means that a good educational experience can dramatically improve children and adolescents' brain development. However, it also underscores a great respon-sibility for society since it means that a bad educational experience can threaten the physical integrity of children and adolescents' brains.

Emotion and cognition are inextricably linked in the brain

Emotional experiences are also built into the architecture of the devel-oping brain. In fact, emotion and cognition operate seamlessly in the brain (Barrett, 2006; Barrett *et al.*, 2005; Damasio, 1994, 2003). The brain is organ-ised into assemblies of neurons with specialised properties and functions. A stimulus elicits a network response of various assemblies to produce a learning experience. Particular components of this experience can usefully be labelled cognitive or emotional, but the distinction between the two is theoretical since they are integrated and inseparable in the brain.

Emotion and cognition work together to guide learning processes (Hinton, Miyamoto and della Chiesa, 2008; Fischer and Bidell, 2006). Children and adolescents have emotionally charged goals, and cognitively appraise the degree to which a situation is hindering or promoting attainment of those goals, which leads to emotional reactions. For example, consider the following scenario. A teacher returns an exam face-down onto the desk of Francisco, a high school student. He flips the paper over to reveal an F staring back at him. Francisco recruits cortical structures to appraise the situation cognitively: this grade will thwart his goals to do well in the class, please his mother and convince her that he deserves an *iPhone* for his upcoming birthday. As he realises this, his limbic system structures, including the amygdala,** launch an emotional response, and he begins to experience negative emotions (MacLean, 1952). These negative emotions can disrupt learning processes in the brain (OECD, 2007).

We can learn to cognitively regulate emotional reactions, however, which can serve as an effective coping mechanism. Neuro-scientific research shows that emotional regulation can reduce negative emotion, which is reflected in both decreased amydala activation and a more positive subjective emotional experience (Ochsner *et al.*, 2004). Effective emotional regulation strategies include reinterpretation and depersonalisation. Reinterpretation involves reframing a situation in a more positive way while depersonalisation involves considering a situation objectively rather than taking it personally. Consider how this kind of emotional regulation could be helpful for Francisco in the example above. He could cognitively regulate his emotional reaction: reinterpreting his test grade as only a small contribution to his final grade, and depersonalising his failure by characterising the exam as difficult for everyone. These regulatory strategies are reflected in both an increase in activity in the cortical areas implicated in cognitive control and in an attenuated amygdala response. This regulation cools the emotional reaction, allowing him to concentrate in class despite the emotional setback. Emotional regulation skills can help children and adolescents to learn more effectively.

Children are not very skilled at emotional regulation, and these skills need to be developed throughout childhood and adolescence: children up to age 12 years have been found to be virtually unable to reduce negative affect, and adolescents (aged 13-17 years) demonstrated only half the regulatory control of adults (Gabrieli, 2004). These differences likely have a neurobiological basis. One study examined the neurobiological response in children and adolescents (ages 9 to 17) to perception of fearful facial expressions, a common emotion-evoking laboratory stimulus (Killgore *et al.*, 2001). Neuro-imaging

---

**The limbic system is made up of many deep brain structures – including the amygdala, hippocampus, septum and basal ganglia – that are involved in emotion, memory and certain aspects of movement. The amygdala is a deep brain structure that is involved in emotions and memory.

revealed a relative decrease in amygdala-to-cortical activation with the development of the young person. This can be interpreted as a progressive increase in the cognitive regulation of emotion. Another study investigated differences in attention-mediated processing of emotional stimuli between children and young people aged 9 to 17 years and adults (Monk *et al.*, 2003). Participants were asked to perform a task requiring attention while viewing emotional stimuli. This manipulation resulted in greater cortical activation in adults than children, representing a stronger goal-directed response in adults as compared with the raw stimulus-driven response in children. Emotional regulation skills need to be developed gradually as the person matures.

Since neuroscience confirms that the emotional and cognitive dimensions of learning are inextricably entwined, the long-standing ideological debate as to whether learning institutions should be involved in learners' emotional development becomes irrelevant – if learning institutions are responsible for cognitive development, they are automatically involved in emotional development as well (Hinton, Miyamoto and della Chiesa, 2008). Therefore, educators should guide the development of emotional regulation skills just as they guide the development of meta-cognitive skills.

Language and literacy

The brain is biologically primed to acquire language, but the capacity for literacy is built over time through cumulative neural modifications. As expressed by Pinker (1995), "Children are wired for sound, but print is an optional accessory that must be painstakingly bolted on." There are brain structures that are designed and shaped by evolution for language, including Broca's area and Wernike's area (OECD, 2007). Literacy is built "on top of" these language areas as children grain experience with print.

The brain structures dedicated to language acquisition are differentially receptive to experience across the lifespan. There are periods when certain structures most readily acquire experience-dependent changes. There is a developmental sensitivity for learning the grammar and accent of a language: in general, the earlier a language is learned, the more efficiently the brain can master its grammar and accent (Neville and Bruer, 2001). Exposing the brain to a foreign language in early childhood leads grammar to be processed by the left hemisphere as in a native speaker, while delaying exposure until adolescence leads to less efficient processing (OECD, 2007). Similarly, there is a sensitive period for learning the accent of a language such that the brain can acquire an accent most effectively before adolescence (OECD, 2007). These sensitivities mean that early language learning is most efficient and effective. However, it is certainly possible to learn a foreign language at any age.

Recent neuroscience research has made important strides in identifying brain networks involved in reading. Though neuroscientists are just beginning to study reading at the level of whole sentences, they have made significant progress in understanding of reading at the level of the word. The "dual route theory" provides a comprehensive framework for describing how the brain processes reading at the level of a word (Jobard, Crivello and Tzourio-Maxoyer, 2003); this is true for English at least since the research supporting this theory has been conducted primarily with English speakers and cannot be automatically extended to learning to read in other languages. As you look at the words on this page, this stimulus is first processed by the primary visual cortex, which is part of the recognition network in the brain (it is in the region of the occipital cortex where most visual information first arrives). The dual route theory posits that after that initial recognition processing then follows one of two complementary pathways. One pathway involves an intermediate step of converting letters/words into sounds, bringing in Broca's area, located in the frontal lobe of the left hemisphere involved in the production of speech. The other pathway consists of a direct transfer of letters/word to meaning and involves the "visual word form area" (VWFA).

This research suggests that in reading both phonological processing and direct processing of meaning play key roles in the brain. This informs the classic debate between phonetics and "whole language" text immersion techniques for reading instruction. The dual importance of both of these processes in the brain suggests that a balanced approach to literacy instruction that incorporates both the development of phonetic skills and "whole language" learning may be most effective, for English native speakers at least.

However, the neural circuitry underlying reading is not entirely the same across different languages. Language brain structures, such as Broca's area and Wernicke's area, play an important role in reading across languages. However, reading in different languages brings in distinct brain areas that support the particular skills for that language. Reading in languages with relatively simple orthography – in which the letter-to-sound correspondence is close – involves partially distinct neural circuitry. An example is Italian, which relies less on the direct route for accessing meaning than reading in languages with complex orthographies, such as English such that the visual word form area (VWFA) is less critical for Italian speakers than English native-speakers (Paulesu *et al.*, 2001). This difference likely arises because Italian speakers can rely more heavily on phonological processing when reading since the letter-to-sound correspondence is more consistent in Italian than English. Learning to read in Italian actually builds different neural circuitry than in English, such that Italian speakers recruit different neural circuitry even when reading in English. Since the circuitry underpinning reading differs across languages with different orthographic structures, the most effective balance of phonetics and "whole language" instruction varies across different languages.

The way literacy develops in the brain seems to be influenced by the forms of words in a language as well. Brain imaging studies reveal that Chinese native speakers engage areas of the brain associated with spatial information processing, which come into play because of the spatial representation of Chinese ideograms (Tan *et al.*, 2003). Again, these areas are involved even when Chinese native speakers read in English, indicating that the brain circuitry involved reading develops in a different way in Chinese than in English native speakers. Together, this research shows that there are many ways for literacy to develop in the brain, and the most appropriate reading instruction will vary depending on particular properties of a certain language.

Some children and adolescents struggle to learn to read with traditional instructional techniques because of a biologically based language impairment called dyslexia. Dyslexia is variable and multifaceted, but commonly involves difficulties in phonological processing (Lyon, Shaywitz and Shaywitz, 2003). Neuroscientists are making great strides in identifying atypical cortical features underpinning dyslexia, enabling researchers to design targeted interventions so that children with dyslexia are able to learn to read. Neuroscience research on language and literacy is rapidly accumulating, and a biological perspective on these skills should be taken into account in the design of education policies and practices.

Mathematics

Mathematics in the brain is analogous to language and literacy in that the brain is biologically primed to have a basic number sense, but formal mathematic abilities are built over time through experience. Babies are born with a number sense that is used as a perceptual tool to interpret the world numerically. Children and adolescents build on this understanding as they learn about mathematics.

Babies are born with several quantitative abilities (Wynn, 1998). They have a concept of "one", "two" and "three", and can precisely discriminate these quantities from one another and from larger quantities. Babies can also approximately discriminate among larger numbers. There is evidence that they can even perform simple mathematical operations (Wynn, 1992). When one object is placed behind a screen followed by a second object, they expect to see two objects when the screen is removed, suggesting that they know that one plus one should equal two. This basic quantitative sense most likely resides in the parietal lobe (OECD, 2007).

The parietal circuit is also involved in the representation of space, and number and space seem to be intertwined (Dehaene, 1997). Young children often conceptualise number as spatially oriented before being formally introduced to numbers and there appears to be a biological predisposition to associate number with space. Therefore, teaching tools such as the number line and concrete spatial manipulatives (*i.e.* blocks, rods, board games, measuring tools, etc.) can reinforce and solidify children's intuitive mathematical understandings. Indeed, mathematics instruction that connects number with space can be very successful: in experiments in one programme using the number line and variety of concrete manipulatives that link number and space propelled children who were lagging behind their peers to the top of their class after forty 20-minute sessions (Griffin, Case and Siegler,1994).

Since the brain areas that support formal mathematics are built through experience, different instruction actually shapes the neural circuitry underlying mathematical abilities. For example, when children learn by drill, by memorising an association between a specific result and two operands, it is encoded in a different neural location than when they learn by strategy, which consists of applying a sequence of arithmetic operations (Delazer *et al*, 2005). Therefore, though two children may both answer that 10 plus 10 equals 20, if one child has memorised this fact while the other is applying the strategy of double-digit addition, the children are engaging distinct neural circuitry in each case.

Some children have serious difficulties with mathematics. Two of the most common difficulties are dyscalculia and math anxiety. Dyscalculia is the mathematical analogue of dyslexia. It is caused by a biologically based impairment of the early basic number sense, but scientists are only beginning to investigate its neural underpinnings (Landerl, Bevan and Butterworth, 2004). Maths anxiety is characterised by an acute fear of mathematics which disrupts cognitive strategies and working memory (Ashcraft, 2002). Further research is needed on the underlying causes of dyscalculia and maths anxiety to develop targeted interventions.

People use their brains differently, following different learning pathways

Educators have long known that new knowledge is built in different ways based on previous learning, and neuroscientists recognise this as a fundamental principle of how the brain learns (OECD, 2007; Schwartz and Fischer, 2003; Tobin and Tippins, 1993). Teachers understand that when they read Cinderella to their class, each child actively constructs a different understanding of it as they relate it to past experience. For one child, Cinderella's fairy godmother may elicit warm feelings based on her relationship with her own godmother, while for another child the fairy godmother may stir up memories of a magic show he once saw. As each child listens to the story, his or her brain processes it in a different way based on previous experience.

As children learn, this new information shapes the brain which then biases it to process future information in certain ways. Reading provides an illustration of this principle. As a child learns to read in a certain language, the neural circuitry supporting literacy is tuned to experience with that language, and this biases the brain to use that neural circuitry for future reading. For example, as a child learns to read in English, he or she develops the neural circuitry described in the "dual route theory", with both the indirect pathway involving Broca's area (which converts letters/words into sounds and then into meaning), and the direct pathway converting letters/words directly into meaning involving the VWFA. By contrast, as a child learns to read in Italian, he or she develops neural circuitry for reading that relies primarily on the indirect pathway. If both of these individuals are later given a text to read in English (assuming the Italian native speaker learns English later in life), their brains process the text differently: the English native speaker will process the words using both pathways and engaging Broca's area and the VWFA area, while the Italian native speaker will processes the words relying primarily on the indirect pathway including Broca's area.

As the example of reading illustrates, children and adolescents develop different underlying brain structures for a given academic ability. In other words, they follow different learning pathways. Educators can therefore facilitate learning by using multiple means of representation, assessment and engagement to accommodate a wide range of individual differences (Rose and Meyer, 2002). Information can be presented in many ways to give children and adolescents various "ways in" to understanding a core concept (Gardner, 1983). For example, when children are learning about fractions, they could bake a cake with measuring cups, create a store and practise making change with money or build a birdhouse taking measurements of its component pieces. Such varied activities encourage children to construct personal meaning of partial numbers, which will help many of them better to understand fractions.

Children and adolescents' learning can also be guided by multiple means of assessment. Traditional summative assessments, such as grades, diplomas and certificates, can be aligned with formative assessment (OECD, 2005). Formative assessment involves frequent assessment of progress with a variety of assessment techniques, including portfolios, logbooks and rubrics, which are used to shape both learning and teaching. Formative assessment allows educators to guide learning throughout the process and tailor their instruction to meet individual needs (see Wiliam, this volume).

As a component of formative assessment, educators can empower children and adolescents to guide their own learning by developing the meta-cognitive skills of "learning how to learn" (Schoenfeld, 1987). Since formative assessment emphasises the process of learning, it encourages children and adolescents to develop meta-cognitive skills about various components of the learning process. Meta-cognitive skills include defining goals, assessing progress and appropriately adjusting learning strategies. Teaching learners meta-cognitive skills is a powerful tool for meeting a wide range of individual differences because it allows them to be self-directed learners who can guide their own progress.

Using multiples means of engagement can also help to accommodate individual differences. What motivates children and adolescents can be as varied as their learning needs, and learning environments should provide experiences that tap into many different interests. For example, when teaching about measurement, this could be related to science ("how do scientists measure light waves?"), fashion ("how do dressmakers take measurements when making a dress?"), mathematics ("how many feet of yarn do we need to cut four strings 7-inches each?"), cooking ("what is the conversion between teaspoons and cups?") and so forth. Relating a core concept to multiple topics can help motivate children and adolescents with a wide range of interests.

People use their brains to learn through social interaction in a cultural context

Children and adolescents learn in a social context, and the human brain is primed for social interaction. The brain is tuned to experience empathy, which intimately connects us to others' experiences. Neurons in the brain – called "mirror neurons" – fire to simulate others' experiences (Dobbs, 2006). When a child sees his or her mother build a tower of blocks, some of the same neurons in the child's brain fire as when the child builds a tower of blocks himself or herself. Similarly, when a teacher sees an adolescent cry, some of the same neurons in the teacher's brain fire as when the teacher cries himself or herself. These mirror neurons are thought to be the neurological basis for empathy, and serve both bonding and learning.

Mirror neurons biologically prime children and adolescents to attune to others and bond with them, which sustains interactions with adults and peers that support learning. Adults and more-expert peers provide scaffolding that enables children and adolescents to grapple with advanced knowledge, which leads to richer and more rapid learning than would be possible through individual exploration (Vygotsky, 1978). For example, as a child struggles to understand why a wooden block floats in water despite its large size, the parent can guide the child towards understanding by strategically suggesting other objects to test. The bond between the parent and child facilitates this interaction, with the child attuning to the parent and trusting the suggestions. These types of social interactions are fundamental to learning – environments that promote positive relationships and a sense of community promote learning.

As children and adolescents interact with members of their family, school and community, they are socialised into society, and internalise many of its beliefs and values. These cultural beliefs and values are developed over many generations. Generation after generation, societies build meaning – a process called "cumulative cultural evolution" (Tomasello, 1999). This sea of meaning makes up the cultural context in which children and adolescents learn (Smagorinsky, 2001). The brain's plasticity allows these bits of cultural meaning to be integrated into the biology of children and adolescents; as they grow and learn in a society, their brains are shaped by these culturally-situated experiences.

The brain therefore develops "on the shoulders of" the meanings created by previous generations. Children and adolescents carve up bits of meaning with tools created by society and piece them together to construct under-standings. Languages, for example, have culturally constrained properties that reflect the values of a society and influence how its youth construct meaning. It is important for children and adolescents to learn about this proc-ess and become aware of their cultural biases. Cross-cultural studies can help children and adolescents understand various perspectives in their own society and develop an appreciation for other cultures and ways of life. This cultural sensitivity is crucial in an increasingly globalised world.

Implications for the design of learning environments

Mind, brain and education research should be integrated with knowledge from other fields to create effective learning environments. Principles emerg-ing from this new field have important implications for the design of learning environments (Hinton, Miyamoto and della Chiesa, 2008). Hence, the main conclusions from the chapter are recast in terms of these implications.

Focus on the learning environment

Nature and nurture continuously interact to shape brain development. Though certain genetic predispositions exist, the environment powerfully influences how the brain develops. It is therefore often possible and desir-able to shift policy from a focus on treating the individual toward a focus on restructuring the environment.

Recognise the importance of emotions

Since neuroscience confirms that the emotional and cognitive dimensions of learning are inextricably entwined, the long-standing debate as to whether learning institutions should be involved in learners' emotional development is no longer relevant – if institutions are responsible for cognitive development, they are inherently involved in emotional development as well and should promote emotional regulation skills.

Consider sensitive periods for language learning

The earlier that foreign language instruction begins, the more efficiently and effectively the brain is able to learn its accent and grammar. Beginning foreign language instruction in early learning environments therefore gives children a biological advantage for learning certain aspects of that language.

Inform reading instruction with neuroscience findings

The dual importance of phonological and direct semantic processing in the brain during reading suggests that a balanced approach to literacy instruction may be most effective for "non-shallow" (with weaker letter-to-sound correspondence) alphabetic languages such as English. However, the optimal approach will vary according to the language in question. Learning environments should be informed by information about literacy in the brain. Teachers should be trained to recognise indicators of dyslexia because early dyslexia interventions prevent children from suffering in school for years before they are diagnosed and helped.

Inform mathematics instruction with neuroscience findings

It would be useful to inform the design of learning environments with information about mathematics and the brain. Learning environments can be structured to build on young children's biological inclination to understand the world numerically and their informal knowledge base to facilitate their understanding of formal mathematics. For example, learning environments can incorporate instructional methods that connect number and space since these capacities are closely linked in the brain.

Incorporate multiple means of representation, assessment and engagement

Learning environments should be flexible and capable of meeting a wide range of individual differences. The brain is dynamic and academic abilities can be built through many different learning pathways. This suggests that learning environments should incorporate multiple means of representation, assessment, and engagement to meet the various learning needs and interests of children and adolescents. Learning environments should incorporate formative assessment, which can powerfully guide the development of abilities, and they should support the development of meta-cognitive skills.

Build strong learning communities

Learning is a social endeavour, positive relationships facilitate learning, and so learning environments should be community-oriented. The brain is primed to relate to others and learn from them. Adults and knowledgeable peers can provide scaffolding that enables children and adolescents to grapple with advanced knowledge, leading to richer and more rapid learning than would be possible through individual exploration.

Create culturally-sensitive learning environments

Learning environments should be culturally sensitive. Societies build meaning generation after generation, and each new generation learns in this cultural context. Learning environments should ensure that children and adolescents are aware that their beliefs and practices are powerfully shaped by culture. Cultural awareness promotes cross-cultural understanding and appreciation for other ways of life, which is ever more important in an increasingly globalised world.

Continually adapt learning environments to incorporate new knowledge

As the field of mind, brain and education continues to develop, learning environments should be informed by this new research, to be considered along with findings from other fields and in light of cultural context.

References

Ashcraft, M.H. (2002), "Math Anxiety: Personal, Educational, and Cognitive Consequences", *Current Directions in Psychological Science*, Vol. 11, No. 5, pp. 181-185.

Barrett, L.F. (2006), "Are Emotions Natural Kinds?", *Perspectives on Psychological Science*, Vol. 1, No. 1, pp. 28-58.

Barrett, L.F., P.M. Niedenthal and P. Winkielman (eds.) (2005), *Emotion and Consciousness*, Guilford, New York.

Bruer, J. (1997), "Education and the Brain: A Bridge Too Far", *Educational Researcher*, Vol. 26, No. 8, pp. 4-16.

Buonomano, D.V. and M.M. Merzenich (1998), "Cortical Plasticity: From Synapses to Maps", *Annual Review of Neuroscience*, Vol. 21, No. 1, pp. 149-186.

Damasio, A.R. (1994), *Descartes' Error: Emotion, Reason, and the Human Brain*, Grosset/Putnam, New York.

Damasio, A.R. (2003), *Looking for Spinoza: Joy, Sorrow, and the Feeling Brain*, Harcourt/Harvest, New York.

Dehaene, S. (1997), *The Number Sense: How the Mind creates Mathematics*, Oxford University Press.

Delazer, M., A Ischebeck, F Domahs, L Zamarian, F Koppelstaetter, C.M Siedentopf, L Kaufmann, T Benke and S Felber (2005), "Learning by Strategies and Learning by Drill – Evidence from an fMRI Study", *Neuroimage*, Vol. 25, No. 3, pp. 838-849.

della Chiesa, B., V. Christoph and C. Hinton (2009), "How Many Brains Does It Take to Build a New Light? Knowledge Management Challenges of a Trans-Disciplinary Project", *Mind, Brain, and Education*, Vol. 3, No. 1, pp. 17-26.

Dobbs, D. (2006), "A Revealing Reflection: Mirror neurons seem to effect everything from how we learn to speak to how we build culture", *Scientific American Mind*, May/June.

Elbert, T, C. Pantev, C. Wienbruch, B. Rockstroh and E. Taub (1995), "Increased Cortical Representation of the Fingers of the Left hand in String Players", *Science,* Vol. 270, No. 5234, pp. 305-307.

Fischer, K.W. (2009), "Mind, Brain, and Education: Building a Scientific Groundwork for Learning and Teaching", *Mind, Brain, and Education,* Vol. 3, No. 1, pp. 2-15.

Fischer, K.W. and T.R. Bidell (2006), "Dynamic Development of Action, Thought and Emotion" in W. Damon and R. M. Lerner (eds.), *Theoretical Models of Human Development, Handbook of Child Psychology,* Wiley, New York, Vol. 1, pp. 331-339.

Fischer, K.W., D.B. Daniel, M.H. Immordino-Yang, E. Stern, A. Battro and H. Koizumi (2007), "Why Mind, Brain and Education? Why Now?", *Mind, Brain and Education,* Vol. 1, No. 1, pp. 1-2.

Fledge, J. and K. Fletcher (1992), "Talker and Listener Effects on Degree", *Journal of the Acoustical Society of America,* Vol. 91, No. 1, pp. 370-389.

Gabrieli, J. (2004), *Development of Emotions and Learning: A Cognitive Neuroscience Perspective,* Building Usable Knowledge in Mind, Brain, and Education, Cambridge, MA.

Gardner, H. (1983), *Frames of Mind: The Theory of Multiple Intelligences,* Basic, New York.

Goswami, U. (2006), "Neuroscience and Education: From Research to Practice", *Nature Reviews Neuroscience,* Vol. 7, No. 5, pp. 406-413.

Griffin, S., R. Case and R. Siegler (1994), "Rightstart: Providing the Central Conceptual Prerequisites for First Formal Learning of Arithmetic to Students At-risk for School Failure" in K. McGilly (Ed.), *Classroom Lessons: Integrating Cognitive Theory and Classroom Practice,* Cambridge, MA: Bradford Books MIT Press, pp. 24-49.

Hinton, C. and K.W. Fischer (2008), "Research Schools: Grounding Research in Education Practice", *Mind, Brain and Education,* Vol. 2, No. 4, pp. 157-160.

Hinton, C., K. Miyamoto and B. della Chiesa (2008), "Brain Research, Learning and Emotions: Implications for Education Research, Policy, and Practice", *European Journal of Education,* Vol. 43, No. 1, pp. 87-103.

Jobard, G., F. Crivello and N. Tzourio-Mazoyer (2003), "Evaluation of the Dual Route Theory of Reading: A Metanalysis of 35 Neuroimaging Studies", *NeuroImage,* Vol. 20, No. 2, pp. 693-712.

Kaczmarek, L. (1997), *The Neuron,* Oxford University Press, New York.

Killgore, W.D.S., M. Oki and D.A. Yurgelun-Todd (2001), "Sex-Specific Developmental Changes in Amygdala Responses to Affective Faces", *Neuroreport*, Vol. 12, No. 2, pp. 427-433.

Landerl, K., A. Bevan and B. Butterworth (2004), "Developmental Dyscalculia and Basic Numerical Capacities: A Study of 8-9-year-old Students", *Cognition*, Vol. 93, No. 2, pp. 99-125.

Lyon, G.R., S.E. Shaywitz and B.A. Shaywitz (2003), "A Definition of Dyslexia", *Annals of Dyslexia*, Vol. 53, pp. 1-14.

MacCabe, D.P. and A.D. Castel (2008), "Seeing is Believing: The Effect of Brain Images on Judgments of Scientific Reasoning, *Cognition*, Vol. 107, No. 1, pp. 343-352.

MacLean, P.D. (1952), "Some Psychiatric Implications of Physiological Studies on Frontotemporal Portion of Limbic System (visceral brain)", *Electroencephalography and Clinical Neurophysiology*, Vol. 4, pp. 407-418.

Monk, C.S., E.B. McClure, E.E. Nelson, E. Zarahn, R.M. Bilder, E. Leibenluft, D.S. Charney, M. Ernst and D.S. Pine (2003), "Adolescent Immaturity in Attention-Related Brain Engagement to Emotional Facial Expression", *NeuroImage,* Vol. 20, No. 1, pp. 420-428.

Neville, H.J. and J.T. Bruer (2001), "Language Processing: How Experience Affects Brain Organisation", in D.B. Bailey, J.T. Bruer, F.J. Symons and J.W. Lichtman (eds.), *Critical Thinking about Critical Periods*, Paul H. Brookes Publishing Co., Maryland, pp.151-172.

Ochsner, K.N., R.D. Ray, J.C. Cooper, E.R. Robertson, S. Chopra, J.D. Gabrieli, J.J. Gross (2004), "For Better or for Worse: Neural Systems Supporting the Cognitive Down-and Up-regulation of Negative Emotion", *NeuroImage*, Vol. 23, No. 2, pp. 483-499.

OECD (2005), *Formative Assessment: Improving Learning in Secondary Classrooms*, OECD Publishing, Paris.

OECD (2007), *Understanding the Brain: The Birth of a Learning Science*, OECD Publishing, Paris.

Pantev, C., R. Oostenveld, A. Engelien, B. Ross, L.E. Roberts, M. Hoke (1998), "Increased Auditory Cortical Representation in Musicians", *Nature,* Vol. 23, No. 392, pp. 811-814.

Paulesu, E., J.F. Démonet, F. Fazio, E.MC Crory, V. Chamoine, N. Brunswick, F. Cappa, G. Cossu, M. Habib, C.D. Frith and U. Frith (2001), "Dyslexia: Cultural Diversity and Biological Unity", Science, Vol. 291, No.5511, pp.2165-2167.

Pickering, S.J. and P. Howard-Jones (2007), "Educators' Views on the Role of Neuroscience in Education: Findings from a Study of UK and International Perspectives", *Mind, Brain and Education*, Vol. 1, No. 3, pp. 109-113.

Pinker, S. (1995), *The Language Instinct. How the Mind Creates Language*, Harper Collins, New York.

Rose, D. and A. Meyer (2000), "Universal Design for Individual Differences", *Educational Leadership*, Vol. 58, No. 3, pp. 39-43.

Rose, D. and A. Meyer (2002), *Teaching Every Student in the Digital Age: Universal Design for Learning*, CAST, Massachusetts.

Schoenfeld, A. (1987), "What's All the Fuss about Metacognition?" in A. Schoenfeld (ed.), *Cognitive Science and Mathematics Education*, Lawrence Erlbaum Associates, New Jersey, pp. 189-215.

Schwartz, M.S. and K.W. Fischer (2003), "Building vs. Borrowing: The Challenge of Actively Constructing Ideas", *Liberal Education*, Vol. 89, No. 3, pp. 22-29.

Shonkoff, J.P. and D.A. Phillips (eds.) (2000), *From Neurons to Neighborhoods: The Science of Early Childhood Development*, National Academy Press, Washington, DC

Smagorinsky, P. (2001), "If Meaning is Constructed, What is it Made of? Toward a Cultural Theory of Reading", *Review of Educational Research*, Vol. 71, No. 1, pp. 133-169.

Squire L.R. and E.R. Kandel (1999), *Memory: From Mind to Molecules*, New York: Scientific American Library.

Tan, L.H., J.A. Spinks, C.M. Feng, W.T. Siok, C.A. Perfetti, J. Xiong, P.T. Fox and J.H. Gao (2003), "Neural Systems of Second Language Reading Are Shaped by Native Language," *Human Brain Mapping*, Vol. 18, No. 3, pp. 158-166.

Tobin, K. and D. Tippins (1993), "Constructivism as a Referent for Teaching and Learning" in K. Tobin (ed.), *The Practice of Constructivism in Science Education*, Lawrence Erlbaum Associates, New Jersey, pp. 3-21.

Tomasello, M. (1999), *The Cultural Origins of Human Cognition*, Harvard University Press, Massachusetts.

Vygotsky, L.V. (1978), *Mind in Society*, Harvard University Press, Massachusetts.

Wynn, K. (1992), "Addition and Subtraction by Human Infants", *Nature*, Vol. 358, No. 6389, pp. 749-750.

Wynn, K. (1998), "Numerical Competence in Infants", in C. Donlan (ed.), *The Development of Mathematical Skills*, Psychology Press, East Sussex, UK.

Chapter 6

The role of formative assessment in effective learning environments

Dylan Wiliam
Institute of Education, University of London

Dylan Wiliam describes assessment as the bridge between teaching and learning. The concept of "formative assessment" emerged with recognition of the importance of feedback and application of navigational metaphors about staying on course through corrective steering. There is substantial evidence, reviewed here, on how feedback improves learning but most studies suffer from weak conceptualisation and neglect of longer-term impacts. The definition here emphasises the role of assessment in improving the quality of instructional decisions. It can be seen as entailing five "key strategies":

1. Clarifying, sharing and understanding learning intentions and criteria for success.

2. Engineering classroom activities that elicit evidence of learning.

3. Providing feedback that moves learners forward.

4. Activating students as instructional resources for one another.

5. Activating students as owners of their own learning.

Formative assessment is proposed as a process of capitalising on, "moments of contingency" for the purpose of regulating learning processes.

Introduction

Assessment plays a number of roles in modern societies, including the certification of student achievement and holding educational institutions to account. Over the past approximately 40 years, however, there has also been increasing interest in the role it can play in supporting learning, often called "formative assessment" or "assessment for learning". This chapter presents a brief overview of how the concept of formative assessment has developed in recent years; in particular, how the central idea has expanded from an original focus on feedback to a wider perspective on classroom practice. It presents evidence on the impact of formative assessment on learning and discusses definitional issues. It concludes with discussion on how formative assessment relates to instructional design through the "regulation" of learning processes.

Why assessment is central to learning

If what students will learn as the result of a particular sequence of activities were predictable, designing learning would be simple. Provided that we ascertain that students possess the correct prerequisites for a particular learning sequence, we could be sure that they all would have learned what was intended after engaging in the specified activities. However, as Denvir and Brown found (1986a; 1986b), even when teachers design high quality learning activities aimed at particular skills, and even when they take into account the student's prior knowledge, what is learned can often be quite different from the intended goal.

Yet, in most classrooms across the world, evidence about the success of learning activities is typically collected only at the end of the learning sequence. It is as if the crew of an aircraft on a long journey concentrated only on following the optimal course from their starting point to their destination, and paid no attention to whether they were, in fact, on course. As all pilots know, this is an unreliable strategy. This is why, in addition to plotting a careful course, aircrew also take readings of their position as they are heading towards their destination and make adjustments as conditions dictate.

In a similar vein over 40 years ago, Benjamin Bloom suggested that in addition to assessment used at the end of a learning process to establish what had been learned, assessment could also be used "to provide feedback and correctives at each stage in the teaching-learning process" (Bloom, 1969 p. 48). He also noted that, while such assessments "may be graded and used as part of the judging and classificatory function", it is much more effective "if it is separated from the grading process and used primarily as an aid to teaching" (p. 48).

David Ausubel stated many years ago: "If I could reduce all of educational psychology to one principle, I would say this: the most important single factor influencing learning is what the learner already knows. Ascertain this and teach him accordingly" (Ausubel, 1968 p. iv). Assessment is central to effective learning, therefore, because even if learners start in roughly the same place with respect to a particular piece of learning, they will very quickly be at different places due to the differences in what they have learned.

This is the fundamental idea explored in this chapter: the design of learning environments needs to take account of the fact that learning is unpredictable so that assessment has a key role to play by relating the instructional activities that teachers plan to the consequent increase in learner capabilities. In other words, assessment functions as the bridge between teaching and learning. The aim of this chapter is to provide a clear theoretical basis for the ways in which assessment can support learning, to show how the different formulations of the notion of formative assessment proposed over the last 40 years can be encompassed within a broader over-arching framework, and to use that framework to understand research in related areas.

Formative assessment as feedback

Course correction in navigation as discussed above is an example of a "feedback" system, developed originally in the field of systems engineering (see Wiener, 1948). Wiener noted that sometimes the effect of the "feedback loop" is to drive the system further in the direction it is already going, such as population growth with plentiful food and no predators or inflationary price/wage spirals in economics. Such feedback is called "positive feedback" because the effect of the feedback and the tendency of the system operate in the same direction. In other situations, the effect of the feedback is to oppose the tendency, restoring stability by returning the system to a steady state, as with population growth when food supply is limited or the familiar room thermostat. This is called "negative feedback" by engineers since its effect is in the opposite direction to the tendency of the system. In engineering, positive feedback is unhelpful because it means instability leading either to explosive growth or collapse. In contrast, negative feedback helps to restore the system to a stable state.

The metaphor of "feedback" is widespread in education but it is important to note that there are significant differences between the usage of the term in engineering and in education. First, to qualify as feedback for an engineer, the system must be able to use the information to affect its performance: "Feedback is information about the gap between the actual level and the reference level of a system parameter which is used to alter the gap in some way." (Ramaprasad, 1983, p. 4) In contrast, in education the term "feedback" is often used to describe any information given back to a learner about their performance, irrespective of whether that information has the capacity to alter the gap (Sadler, 1989). In other words, if we use the term as an engineer would, feedback is not just information given to students about their performance. It must direct their future actions in productive ways.

Second, not only the term "feedback" but the qualifiers "positive" and "negative" are also applied in somewhat different ways. In engineering, they refer to the effect of the feedback in relation to the tendency of the system. In education, the terms tend to be used instead as value judgments on the effects of the feedback. Feedback that suggests that the learner is on the right track, so reinforcing the learning, would be described as "positive" both by educators and engineers. However, consider the situation in which a student received critical evaluations, made less effort, got even worse evaluations and made even less effort, ultimately disengaging from learning altogether. To an educator, this is an example of negative feedback but to an engineer this is positive feedback, since it drives the system (student) in the direction it is already heading.

Third, and perhaps most importantly, we want in education to encourage the development of autonomy in learning – for students to be able to develop their own skills of self-regulation of learning so that their need for feedback diminishes. In contrast, no-one would criticise a room thermostat because the furnace had not yet learned when to decide for itself when to turn itself on and off.

While these may appear to be semantic distinctions, in fact they go to the heart of the problems encountered in the design of effective feedback systems in education. Crooks (1988) reviewed over two hundred studies of the impact of classroom evaluation practices on students and concluded that the power of assessments to guide learning was not being realised because the summative function of assessment – providing grades and other measures of how much had been learned – is dominant.

Evidence on the impact of feedback

Studies have found that feedback can substantially improve educational outcomes but we should be aware of certain caveats by way of introduction. The results of many studies are given in terms of a "standardised effect size" ["effect size" for short: this following Cohen (1988) is the difference in performance between two groups (*e.g.* those given and those not given feedback) divided by a measure of the spread of scores in the population (the standard deviation)]. While the standardised effect size has undoubted advantages over reporting the level of statistical significance attained in experimental comparisons (Harlow, Mulaik and Steiger, 1997), it nevertheless suffers from limitations as a metric with which to compare findings from different experimental studies. In particular, where the range of outcomes is restricted (*e.g.* studies on specific sub-populations such as students with special educational needs), the effect size is inflated because the divisor in the calculation is smaller (Black and Wiliam, 1998a). Second, measures of educational outcomes differ greatly in their sensitivity to the effects of education and whether the measure relates directly to what students have been learning or is more remote, as with many national tests and examinations (Wiliam, 2008). This means that it is difficult to give hard-and-fast rules about how to interpret effect sizes. Nevertheless, as a general guide, at least on standardised measures of educational achievement, effect sizes of around 0.4, which are typical in studies of feedback, indicate an increase of at least 50% in the rate of learning. In other words, students were learning in 8 months what other students were taking a year to learn. These are therefore rather substantial increases in educational productivity, especially if they can be scaled across an entire national system.

A more general caveat is that evaluations are used in schools for a multiplicity of purposes and comparisons are misleading when evaluations are compared in terms of functions for which they were not designed (*e.g.* Natriello, 1987). For example, finding that differentiated feedback has more impact on directing future student learning than on grades may show nothing more than that systems generally do more effectively those things they are designed to do than those things they are not designed to do.

Such limitations notwithstanding, the first substantial finding is that just being assessed regularly can have a significant impact on learning. For instance, students who took at least one test over a 15-week period scored 0.5 standard deviations higher than those who did not, and more frequent testing was associated with higher levels of achievement, although testing more frequently than once every two weeks conferred no additional benefit (Bangert Drowns, Kulik, Kulik and Morgan, 1991). The quality of feedback and how it is used, however, are much more important than its frequency. A review of 40 research reports on the effects of feedback in "test-like" events (such as questions embedded in programmed learning materials or review tests at the end of a block of teaching) found that the way feedback was provided and the kind of feedback given were both critical (Bangert-Drowns *et al.*, 1991). Where students could look ahead and "peek" at the answers before they had attempted the questions, they learned less than when studies controlled for this "pre-search availability" (effect size: 0.26). More importantly, when feedback is given through the details of the correct answer, students learn more than when they are just told whether their answer is correct or not (effect size: 0.58).

Feedback can also be useful to teachers. Fuchs and Fuchs (1986) conducted a meta-analysis of 21 different reports on the use of the feedback to and by teachers, with frequencies of between 2 and 5 times per week. The mean effect size on achievement between experimental and control groups was 0.70 standard deviations. In about half the studies reviewed, teachers set rules about reviews of the data and actions to follow and in these cases the mean effect size was significantly higher at 0.92; when actions were left to teachers' judgments the effect size was only 0.42. In those studies in which teachers produced graphs of the progress of individual children as a guide and stimulus to action, the effect was larger (mean effect size: 0.70) than in those where this was not done (mean effect size: 0.26).

These findings appear to be affected by the kind of learning being considered. Dempster (1991) found that many of the available research studies measured achievement in terms of content knowledge and low-level skills so that it is not clear that such findings would necessarily generalize to higher-order thinking. In a subsequent paper, Dempster (1992) argued that while the benefits of integrating assessment with instruction are clear, and there is an emerging consensus in the research for the conditions for effective assessment – frequent testing soon after instruction, cumulating demand, with feedback soon after testing – assessment is neglected in teacher education and current practices in schools are far from these ideals.

A review by Elshout-Mohr (1994), published originally in Dutch and reviewing many studies not available in English, suggested that for more complex tasks, knowledge of correct answers is less useful than it is for simple tasks. Learning is not just a matter of correcting what is wrong but of developing new capabilities and this requires feedback more as dialogue rather than simply giving correct answers. This requires the learner to become active in managing the process.

Much of this work had focused on the effects of feedback in schools. In 1996, Kluger and DeNisi published a review of the effects of feedback in schools, colleges and workplaces.[1] Across all the studies, the average effect size for the feedback is 0.41 standard deviations, but the effects vary considerably across the different studies. Most notably in 50 out of the 131 studies (38%) feedback actually **lowered** average performance.

As part of a broader research programme on the development of intelligent tutoring environments, Shute (2008) examined research on feedback to students.[2] This review identified major gaps in the literature and, as might be expected, concluded that there was no simple answer to the question, "What feedback works?". But, it also endorsed the findings of earlier reviews on the size of the effects that could be expected from feedback (standardized effect sizes in the range 0.4 to 0.8 standard deviations).

Some pointers regarding effective feedback

In seeking to understand why feedback may sometimes lower performance, Kluger and DeNisi (1996) looked for "moderators" of feedback effects. They found that feedback was least effective when it focused attention on the self, more effective when it focused on the task in hand, and most effective when it focused on the details of the task and involved goal-setting.

However, even the limited benefits of feedback identified by Kluger and DeNisi might sometimes be counter-productive. They pointed out that feedback might make the learner work harder, which is presumably beneficial, but it might also lead the learner to channel her or his efforts in a particular direction, to modify or reject the goal, or to ignore the feedback entirely. Even when feedback produced a positive impact on learning, this might be by emphasising instrumental goals and inhibiting deep learning. In their conclusion, they suggested that it is more important to examine the processes induced by the feedback rather than whether feedback in general improves performance.

Shute (2008) offers a number of "preliminary guidelines" for the design of effective feedback, both in relation to enhancing learning and in terms of timing.

Feedback should focus on the specific features of the task, and provide suggestions on how to improve, rather than focus on the learner; it should focus on the "what, how and why" of a problem rather than simply indicating to students whether they were correct or not; elaborated feedback should be presented in manageable units and, echoing Einstein's famous dictum, should be "as simple as possible but no simpler." However, feedback should not be so detailed and specific that it "scaffolds" the learning to such an extent that the students do not need to think for themselves. Feedback is also more effective when from a trusted source (whether human or computer).

The optimum timing of feedback appears to depend strongly on the kind of learning being undertaken: immediate feedback appears to be most helpful for procedural learning or when the task is well beyond the learner's capability at the beginning of the learning, while delayed feedback appears to be more appropriate for tasks well within the learner's capability or when transfer to other contexts is sought.

The recent review by Hattie and Timperley (2007) defines the purpose of feedback as reducing discrepancies between current understandings or performance and a desired goal (as proposed by Ramaprasad, 1983). Building on the work of Deci and Ryan (1994) and Kluger and DeNisi (1996), their model posits that students can reduce the discrepancy either by employing more effective strategies or increasing effort, on the one hand, or by abandoning, blurring or lowering the goals they have set for themselves, on the other. Teachers can reduce the discrepancy by changing the difficulty or specificity of the goals or by providing more support to the students. Their model specifies three kinds of questions that feedback is designed to answer (Where am I going? How am I going? Where next?), and each feedback question operates at four levels: feedback about the task (FT), feedback about the processing of the task (FP), feedback about self-regulation (FR), and feedback about the self as a person (FS). They demonstrate that FS is the least effective form of feedback; FR and FP "are powerful in terms of deep processing and mastery of tasks"; FT is powerful when the feedback is used either to improve strategy processing, or for enhancing self-regulation (although these conditions are rarely met in practice).

Formative assessment as part of teaching

The studies summarised above show that some form of feedback to learners in the course of their learning has positive effects on learning, but that such effects cannot be taken for granted. The effects depend not just on the quality of the feedback but on the learning milieu in which it is provided, the orientations and motivations of the learner, and a range of other contextual factors (Boekaerts, this volume). For this reason, when Paul Black and I sought to update the reviews of Natriello and Crooks, we deliberately took a broad view of the field. (We noted that the reviews by Natriello and Crooks had cited 91 and 241 references respectively, and yet only 9 references were common to both papers, and neither cited the review by Fuchs and Fuchs.) Rather than relying on electronic search methods, we consulted each issue of 76 of the journals considered most likely to contain relevant research between 1987 and 1997. Our review (Black and Wiliam, 1998a), based on 250 studies, found that effective use of classroom assessment yielded improvements in student achievement between 0.4 and 0.7 standard deviations, albeit noting the already-mentioned problems with the interpretation of effect sizes.

Black and Wiliam presented a number of "examples in evidence" – the meta-analysis by Fuchs and Fuchs and seven classroom-based studies – that illustrate features of effective formative assessment. Perhaps the most important one is that, to be effective, formative assessment has to be integrated into classroom practice, requiring a fundamental re-organisation of classroom operations:

> It is hard to see how any innovation in formative assessment can be treated as a marginal change in classroom work. All such work involves some degree of feedback between those taught and the teacher, and this is entailed in the quality of their interactions which is at the heart of pedagogy. (Black and Wiliam, 1998a, p. 16)

We also noted that for assessment to function formatively, the feedback information has to be used, and thus the differential treatments that are incorporated in response to the feedback are at the heart of effective learning. Moreover, for these differentiated treatments to be selected appropriately, teachers need adequate models of how students might react to, and make use of, the feedback. As Perrenoud (1998) observes in his commentary on the Black and Wiliam paper, "…the feedback given to pupils in class is like so many bottles thrown into the sea. No one can be sure that the message they contain will one day find a receiver."

In order to address this, we examined the **student** perspective, the role of **teachers**, and some of the **systems** for the organisation of teaching in which formative assessment is a major component. In drawing out implications for the policy and practice of formative assessment, we concluded:

There does not emerge, from this present review, any one optimum model on which … policy might be based. What does emerge is a set of guiding principles, with the general caveat that the changes in classroom practice that are needed are central rather than marginal, and have to be incorporated by each teacher into his or her practice in his or her own way …. That is to say, reform in this dimension will inevitably take a long time and need continuing support from both practitioners and researchers. (p. 62)

Most of the work reviewed by Natriello, Crooks, Kulik and his colleagues, and Black and Wiliam focused on school-age students (*i.e.* up to the age of 18). Nyquist (2003) examined studies of feedback with college-age learners. He reviewed approximately 3000 studies of the effects of feedback, of which 86 met the criteria that they:

- Involved experimental manipulation of a characteristic relevant to feedback.

- Used a sample of college-age learners.

- Measured academic performance.

- Provided sufficient quantitative information for an effect size to be calculated.

From the 86 studies it was possible to derive 185 effect sizes. After a number of technical adjustments (limiting extreme values to 2 standard deviations from the mean effect, and correcting for small sample bias across the studies), the analysis yielded a mean effect size of 0.40 standard deviations – almost identical to that found by Kluger and DeNisi. This mean effect reduced slightly to 0.35 (SE = 0.17) once adjustments were made (weighting the effects so that the contribution to the mean effect was proportional to their reliability), although the effects themselves were highly variable (ranging from -0.6 to 1.6 SDs).

To investigate "moderators" of effect, Nyquist developed the following typology of different kinds of formative assessment:

- **Weaker feedback only**: students are given only the knowledge of their own score or grade; often described as "knowledge of results".

- **Feedback only**: students are given their own score or grade, together with either clear goals to work towards or feedback on the correct answers to the questions they attempted; often described as "knowledge of correct results".

- **Weak formative assessment**: students are given information about the correct results, together with some explanation.

- **Moderate formative assessment**: students are given information about the correct results, some explanation, and some specific suggestions for improvement.

- **Strong formative assessment**: students are given information about the correct results, some explanation, and specific activities to undertake in order to improve.

The average standardized effect size for each type of intervention is given in Table 6.1.

Table 6.1. **Effect sizes for different kinds of feedback intervention**

	N	Effect
Weaker feedback only	31	0.14
Feedback only	48	0.36
Weaker formative assessment	49	0.26
Moderate formative assessment	41	0.39
Strong formative assessment	16	0.56
Total	185	

Source: Nyquist, 2003. The figures are corrected values provided in a personal communication and not the same as given in the original thesis.

Nyquist's results echo the findings of Bangert-Drowns *et al.* discussed above. Just giving students feedback about current achievement produces relatively little benefit, but where feedback engages students in mindful activity, the effects on learning can be profound.

The research reviews conducted by Natriello (1987), Crooks (1988), Bangert-Drowns *et al.* (1991), and Black and Wiliam (1998a) underline that not all kinds of feedback to students about their work are equally effective. As a further example, Meisels, Atkins-Burnett, Xue, Bickel and Son (2003) explored the impact of the Work Sample System (WSS) – a system of curriculum-embedded performance assessments – and the achievement of WSS students was significantly and substantially higher in reading, but in mathematics there was no significant difference. The details of the system in use, how it is implemented, and the nature of the feedback provided to students appear to be crucial variables, with small changes often producing large impacts on effectiveness.

Though many of the studies included in the reviews focus on older students, attitudes to learning are shaped by the feedback they receive from a very early age. In a year-long study of eight kindergarten and first grade classrooms in six schools in England, Tunstall and Gipps (1996a; 1996b) identified a range of roles played by feedback. Like Torrance and Pryor (1998), they found that much of the feedback given by teachers to students focused on socialisation: "I'm only helping people who are sitting down with their hands up" (p. 395). Beyond this socialisation role, they identified four types of feedback on academic work.

The first two types are essentially **evaluative** in form. The first covers feedback that rewards or punishes the students for their work (*e.g.* students being allowed to leave for lunch early when they had done good work, or threatened with not being allowed to leave for lunch if they hadn't completed assigned tasks). The second type of feedback is also evaluative, but indicates the teacher's level of approval (*e.g.* "I'm very pleased with you" vs. "I'm very disappointed in you today"). The two other types of feedback identified by Tunstall and Gipps are termed "descriptive". The third focuses on the adequacy of the work in terms of the teacher's criteria for success, ranging from the extent to which the work already satisfies the criteria at one end (*e.g.* "This is extremely well explained") to the steps the student needs to take to improve (*e.g.* "I want you to go over all of them and write your equals sign in each one"). The fourth kind of feedback emphasises process, with the teacher playing the role of facilitator rather than evaluator. As Tunstall and Gipps (1996a) explain, teachers engaging in this kind of feedback "conveyed a sense of work in progress, heightening awareness of what was being undertaken and reflecting on it" (p. 399).

Most of the research reviewed above was published in English. In order to provide a more comprehensive overview of research in this area, the OECD study of formative assessment (Looney, 2005) commissioned reviews of relevant research published in French (Allal and Lopez, 2005) and German (Köller, 2005).

Allal and Lopez report that research in France and French-speaking parts of Belgium, Canada and Switzerland, has focused much more on theoretical than empirical work, with very few controlled empirical studies. They suggest that the most important finding of their review of over 100 studies of the previous thirty years is that the studies of assessment practices in French-speaking classrooms have utilized an "enlarged conception of formative assessment" along the lines adopted by Black and Wiliam. Allal and Lopez argue that central to feedback within the Anglophone tradition (as exemplified by Bloom), is "remediation," which they summarise as "feedback + correction". In contrast, within much of the research undertaken in francophone countries, the central concept is "regulation", summarised as "feedback + adaptation" (p. 245).[3]

Allal and Lopez identify four major developments in this French-language research literature. In the first, which they term "focus on instrumentation", the emphasis was on the development of assessment tools such as banks of diagnostic items and adaptive testing systems. In the second ("search for theoretical frameworks"), the emphasis shifted to a "search for theories that can offer conceptual orientation for conducting assessment". The third development – "studies of existing assessment practices in their contexts" – provides a grounding for the search for theoretical frameworks by articulating it with the study of how formative assessment is practised in real classrooms. The fourth, and most recent, development has been "development of active student involvement in assessment" which has examined student self-assessment, peer-assessment, and the joint construction of assessment by students and teachers together.

The notion of formative assessment as being central to the regulation of learning processes has been adopted by some Anglophone researchers (see, for example, Wiliam, 2007), and the broadening of the understanding of formative assessment was noted by Brookhart (2007). Her review of the literature on "formative classroom assessment" charted the development of the concept of formative assessment as a series of nested formulations (p. 44):

- Information about the learning process.

- Information about the learning process that teachers can use for instructional decisions.

- Information about the learning process that teachers can use for instructional decisions and students can use in improving their performance.

- Information about the learning process that teachers can use for instructional decisions and students can use in improving their performance in ways that motivate them.

In general, however, there appear to be few links between the strong theoretical work in the francophone tradition and the empirical work undertaken particularly in the United States. Allal and Lopez conclude that the French-language work on formative assessment is in need of considerably more empirical grounding. (p.256)

The review of German-language literature by Köller (2005) began with an approach similar to that adopted by Black and Wiliam, with searches of on-line databases supplemented by scrutiny of all issues of the six most relevant German-language journals from 1980 to 2003. Köller noted that while there were many developments related to formative assessment reported in academic journals, there was little evaluation of the outcomes of formative assessment practices for students, although there were confirmations of some findings in the Anglophone literature. He reports the work of Meyer who, like Kluger and DeNisi, found that praise can sometimes have a negative impact on learning, while criticism, even blame, can sometimes be helpful. Another important strand of work mentioned by Köller concerns differences between teachers' uses of "reference norms." A number of studies, notably those by Rheinberg, have shown that students learn more when taught by teachers who judge a student's performance against his or her previous performance (individual reference norm) rather than teachers who compare students with others in the class (social reference norm).

Theoretical syntheses: formative assessment and assessment for learning

Over the last dozen or so years, a number of definitions of the term "formative assessment" have been proposed. Black and Wiliam (1998a) defined formative assessment "as encompassing all those activities undertaken by teachers, and/or by their students, which provide information to be used as feedback to modify the teaching and learning activities in which they are engaged" (p. 7). Cowie and Bell (1999) adopted a slightly more restrictive definition by limiting the term to assessment conducted **and acted upon** while learning was taking place by defining formative assessment as "the process used by teachers and students to recognise and respond to student learning in order to enhance that learning, **during the learning**" (p. 32, my emphasis). The requirement that the assessment be conducted during learning was also embraced by Shepard, Hammerness, Darling-Hammond, Rust, Snowden, Gordon, Gutierez and Pacheco (2005) in defining formative assessment as "assessment carried out during the instructional process for the purpose of improving teaching or learning" (p. 275).

The OECD review of formative assessment practices across eight national and provincial systems also emphasised the principle that the assessment should take place during instruction: "Formative assessment refers to frequent, interactive assessments of students' progress and understanding to identify learning needs and adjust teaching appropriately" (Looney, 2005, p. 21). In similar vein, Kahl (2005) wrote: "A formative assessment is a tool that teachers use to measure student grasp of specific topics and skills they are teaching. It's a 'midstream' tool to identify specific student misconceptions and mistakes while the material is being taught" (p. 11).

Broadfoot, Daugherty, Gardner, Gipps, Harlen, James and Stobart (1999) argue that using assessment to improve learning depends on five key factors: 1) the provision of effective feedback to pupils; 2) the active involvement of pupils in their own learning; 3) adjusting teaching to take account of the results of assessment; 4) a recognition of the profound influence assessment has on the motivation and self-esteem of pupils, both of which are crucial influences on learning; and 5) the need for pupils to be able to assess themselves and understand how to improve. They suggest that the term "formative assessment" is unhelpful to describe such uses of assessment because "the term 'formative' itself is open to a variety of interpretations and often means no more than that assessment is carried out frequently and is planned at the same time as teaching" (p. 7). Instead, they suggest the term "assessment for learning", as proposed originally by James (1992).

Black, Harrison, Lee, Marshall and Wiliam (2004) suggest keeping both terms in that "assessment for learning" refers to any assessment for which the first priority in its design and practice is to serve the purpose of promoting students' learning, and that this "becomes 'formative assessment' when the evidence is actually used to adapt the teaching work to meet learning needs" (p. 10).

Taking this into account, I propose the following definition based on Black and Wiliam (2009), which subsumes and extends previous definitions: "An assessment functions formatively to the extent that evidence about student achievement is elicited, interpreted, and used by teachers, learners, or their peers, to make decisions about the next steps in instruction that are likely to be better, or better founded, than the decisions they would have taken in the absence of that evidence."

Several features of this definition are worth noting:

- It is based on the function served by the information yielded by the assessment, rather than a property of the assessment itself.

- The assessment can be carried out by the teacher, the learner, or her peers.

- The focus of the definition is on decisions regarding next steps in instruction, rather than intentions or outcomes.

- The definition is probabilistic.

- The assessment need not change the direction of instruction (it might merely confirm that the planned subsequent actions were appropriate).

Any assessment that provides evidence that has the potential to improve instructional decision-making by teachers, learners, or their peers can therefore be formative. Suppose a class has taken a test that assesses the ability to find the largest or smallest fraction in a given set. The raw scores achieved by students would provide a "monitoring assessment", indicating which students might benefit from additional instruction or explanation. If, in addition, the teacher noticed that many students gaining low scores were more successful in examples that involved unitary fractions (those with 1 as the numerator) than with more complex fractions, this would provide a "diagnostic assessment", providing specific information about sources of difficulty. The teacher would then be able to focus additional instruction on non-unitary fractions. If the teacher can see from the responses that many students are operating with a strategy that the smallest fraction is the one with the largest denominator, and the largest fraction is the one with the smallest denominator – a strategy that works with unitary fractions (Vinner, 1997) – then this provides information for the teacher that is "instructionally tractable". Such assessments and interpretations of them not only signal the problem (monitoring) and locate it (diagnosing), but they also situate the problem within a theory of action that suggests measures to be taken to improve learning. The best formative assessments are prospective rather than retrospective, therefore, in that they identify recipes for future action.

Any assessment is potentially formative, therefore, since any assessment can support decisions that would not have been possible, or would not be made so well, without the assessment information. However, this does not mean that all formative uses of assessment information are equally effective. By definition, assessments giving diagnostic insights are likely to lead to better decisions about teaching than those that simply monitor student achievement, and those that yield insights that are instructionally tractable are, in all likelihood, better still.

One of the differences between assessments that monitor, those that diagnose, and those that provide insights that are instructionally tractable is the specificity of the information yielded: to be instructionally tractable, the assessment needs to provide more information than simply whether learning is taking place or, if it is not, what specifically is not being learned: it must also incorporate theories of curriculum and of learning. This is because the focus is on "what next?" and this implies a clear notion of a learning progression – a description of the "knowledge, skills, understandings, attitudes or values that students develop in an area of learning, in the order in which they typically develop them" (Forster and Masters, 2004, p.65). Instructional tractability also entails a theory of learning because, before a decision can be made about what evidence to elicit, it is necessary to know not just what comes next in learning, but also what kinds of difficulties learners have in making those next steps. The links between formative assessment and theories of learning are examined in greater detail in Black and Wiliam (2005), Brookhart (2007), Wiliam (2007), and Black and Wiliam (2009).

Cycle lengths for formative assessment

In the example of the fractions test discussed above, the action taken by the teacher follows quickly from generating the evidence about student achievement. In general, however, the definition of formative assessment proposed above allows for cycles of elicitation, interpretation and action of any length, provided the information is used to inform decisions about teaching, which decisions are likely to be better than those made in the absence of that evidence. The length of the formative assessment cycle should also be attuned to the capacity of the system to respond to the evidence generated – there is little point in generating information on a daily basis if the decisions that the evidence is to inform are taken only monthly (Wiliam and Thompson, 2007).

Not all examples consistent with this definition would be considered as formative assessment under some of the other definitions discussed above. For example, Cowie and Bell (1999), Looney (2005), Shepard (2007) and Kahl (2005) would all probably resist using the term "formative" for assessment that seems remote from its collection. The research literature reviewed above indeed confirms that formative assessment that is less remote is more likely to increase learning and by a greater amount. However, as I have elsewhere noted (Wiliam, 2009), it seems odd to reserve the term "formative" only for assessments that make a significant difference to student outcomes. Rather, it makes more sense to this author to describe assessment as "formative" when it **forms** the direction of future learning but to acknowledge that there are different cycle-lengths involved, as shown in Table 6.2.

Table 6.2. **Cycle lengths for formative assessment**

Type	Focus	Length
Long-cycle	Across marking periods, quarters, semesters, years	4 weeks to 1 year
Medium-cycle	Within and between instructional units	1 to 4 weeks
Short-cycle	Within and between lessons	Day by day: 24 to 48 hours Minute by minute: 5 seconds to 2 hours

Source: Wiliam and Thompson (2007).

Formative assessment: key instructional processes

In order to understand what kinds of formative assessments are likely to be most effective, it is necessary to go beyond the functional definition of formative assessment and look in more detail at the underlying processes. The "systems" metaphor adopted by Ramaprasad (1983), which provides the basis for the definition of assessment for learning adopted by the Assessment Reform Group (Broadfoot *et al.*, 2002), draws attention to three key instructional processes in terms of establishing:

1. Where the learners are in their learning.

2. Where they are going.

3. What needs to be done to get them there.

While many approaches to formative assessment emphasise the role of the teacher, the definition adopted here acknowledges the roles that the learners themselves and their peers have to play. Crossing the process dimension (where learners are in their learning, where they are going, how to get there) with that of the agent in the instructional process (teacher, peer, learner) produces a matrix of nine cells. However, while some of the nine cells generated in this way make sense on their own, it also makes sense to look at other cells in combination. For example, if we consider the role of students in establishing where they are in their learning, and how to reach their desired goal, this can be presented as a process of "activating students as owners of their own learning", which subsumes a range of important aspects of learning, such as meta-cognition (see Schneider and Stern, this volume). In the same way, the role of peers in establishing where students are in their learning and how they can reach their desired goal, can be presented as "activating students as instructional resources for one another" (see Barron and Darling-Hammond, this volume). Finally, the three cells involving "where the learner is going" can be presented as "clarifying, sharing, and understanding learning intentions and criteria for success". The result is that the nine cells can be collapsed into the five "classroom strategies" of formative assessment marked 1-5 in Table 6.3. Details of the research base for each of these five strategies can be found in Wiliam (2007), and details of how teachers have implemented these strategies in their own classrooms can be found in Leahy, Lyon, Thompson and Wiliam (2005).

Table 6.3. **Classroom strategies for formative assessment**

	Where the learner is going	Where the learner is right now	How to get there
Teacher	Clarifying learning intentions and sharing and criteria for success (1)	Engineering effective classroom discussions, activities and tasks that elicit evidence of learning (2)	Providing feedback that moves learners forward (3)
Peer	Understanding and sharing learning intentions and criteria for success (1)	Activating students as instructional resources for one another (4)	
Learner	Understanding learning intentions and criteria for success (1)	Activating students as the owners of their own learning (5)	

Source: Leahy, Lyon, Thompson and Wiliam, 2005.

Formative assessment and the regulation of learning processes

In the remainder of this chapter, I discuss how the approach to formative assessment outlined here can be integrated into a larger perspective on instructional design through a focus on the regulation of learning processes (Perrenoud, 1991; 1998).

Within such a framework, the actions of the teacher, the learners, and the context of the classroom can be evaluated with respect to how well the intended learning proceeds towards the intended goal. As Schneider and Stern (this volume) point out, teachers do not create learning; only learners can do this and so many have called for a shift in the role of the teacher from the "sage on the stage" to the "guide on the side." The danger with such a characterisation is that it is often interpreted as relieving the teacher of responsibility for ensuring that learning takes place. What I propose here is that the teacher be regarded as responsible for "engineering" a learning environment, both in its design and its operation.

An effective learning environment creates student engagement and is well-regulated. As a growing body of research on cognitive development shows, the level of engagement in cognitively challenging environments influences not only achievement, but also IQ itself (Dickens and Flynn, 2001; Mercer, Dawes, Wegerif and Sams, 2004). As well as creating engagement, effective learning environments need to be designed so that, as far as possible, they afford or scaffold the learning that is intended ("proactive regulation"). If the intended learning is not occurring, then this should become apparent so that appropriate adjustments may be made ("interactive regulation"). Finally, it is also possible for teachers to engage in "retroactive regulation"; for example, when a teacher realises that a particular instructional sequence might be improved for one group of students as a result of experiences with other groups of students.

Proactive regulation is achieved "upstream" of the lesson itself (*i.e.* before the lesson begins). The regulation can be unmediated as when, for example, a teacher "does not intervene in person, but puts in place a 'meta-cognitive culture', mutual forms of teaching and the organisation of regulation of learning processes run by technologies or incorporated into classroom organisation and management" (Perrenoud, 1998, p. 100). For example, a teacher's decision to use realistic contexts in mathematics can provide a source of regulation since students will be able to evaluate how reasonable are their answers. When a teacher develops in the students the skills of consulting and productively supporting each other, this too is an example of proactive regulation.

At other times, particularly when it is hard to predict how students will respond to instructional activities, it may be more appropriate to regulate learning interactively – for example, by creating questions, prompts or activities that evoke responses from the students that the teacher can use to determine the progress of the learning and, if necessary, to make adjustments. Often, these questions or prompts will be open-ended, requiring higher-order thinking – indeed such questions are essential to creating learning environments that foster student engagement. But closed questions have a role here, too. "Is calculus exact or approximate?", "What is the pH of 10 molar NaOH?", or, "Would your mass be the same on the moon?" are all closed questions with a single correct answer, but are valuable because they frequently reveal student conceptions that are different from those intended by the teacher (many students believe that calculus is approximate, that a pH cannot be greater than 14, and that one's mass depends on gravity like one's weight does).

"Upstream" planning of good questions like those above therefore creates the possibility that the learning activities "downstream" may change course in light of the students' responses. These "moments of contingency" – points in the instructional sequence when the instruction can proceed in different directions according to the responses of the students – are at the heart of the regulation of learning. Indeed, Black and Wiliam (2009) propose that formative assessment is, in essence, concerned with "the creation of, and capitalisation upon, 'moments of contingency' in instruction for the purpose of the regulation of learning processes" (p. 6). A theory of formative assessment is therefore much narrower than an overall theory of teaching and learning, although it links in significant ways to other aspects of teaching and learning, since how teachers, learners, and their peers create and capitalise on these moments of contingency entails considerations of instructional design, curriculum, pedagogy, psychology and epistemology.

Summary

This chapter has traced a number of significant strands in the development of the concept of formative assessment, although the account is of necessity highly selective. The earliest uses of the term drew heavily on the idea of feedback and on navigational metaphors, focusing on feedback as a corrective measure to restore learning to its intended trajectory. Over the last hundred years, literally thousands of studies have sought to determine what kinds of feedback interventions improve learning, and by how much, but these studies are of limited value due to weak conceptualisation of the feedback intervention itself, of the kinds of learning under study, and a failure to consider long-term impacts. Over the last twenty years, there has been considerable interest in the use of formative assessment not in isolation but as an integral feature of high-quality educational practice in classroom settings, and a number of definitions have been proposed.

In this chapter, a definition of formative assessment has been presented emphasising the role of assessment in improving the quality of instructional decisions, which subsumes previous definitions of "formative assessment". Consequences of this definition have been drawn out; specifically, it is suggested that formative assessment can usefully be thought of as entailing five key strategies:

1. Clarifying, sharing and understanding learning intentions and criteria for success.

2. Engineering effective classroom discussions, activities and tasks that elicit evidence of learning.

3. Providing feedback that moves learners forward.

4. Activating students as instructional resources for one another.

5. Activating students as the owners of their own learning.

Finally, it is suggested that formative assessment is concerned with the creation of, and capitalisation upon, "moments of contingency" in instruction with a view to regulating learning processes, which allows a clear demarcation between formative assessment and other aspects of instructional design and pedagogy.

Notes

1. They began by identifying approximately 3 000 potentially relevant research studies, and excluded all those with fewer than 10 participants, where there was not a comparison group of some kind, and those with too few details for effect sizes to be computed. They were left with just 131 publications, reporting 607 effect sizes and involving 23 663 observations of 12 652 participants.

2. From an initial screening involving on-line databases which generated 180 relevant studies, a total of 141 publications met the inclusion criteria (103 journal articles, 24 books and book chapters, 10 conference proceedings and 4 research reports).

3. The French word *régulation* has a much more specific meaning than the English word "regulation". There are two ways to translate the word "regulation" into French – *règlement* and *régulation*. The former of these is used in the sense of "rules and regulations," while the latter is used in the sense of adjustment in the way that a thermostat "regulates" the temperature of a room.

References

Allal, L. and L.M. Lopez (2005), "Formative Assessment of Learning: A Review of Publications in French" in J. Looney (ed.), *Formative Assessment: Improving Learning in Secondary Classrooms*, Paris, France: Organisation for Economic Cooperation and Development, pp. 241-264.

Ausubel, D.P. (1968), *Educational Psychology: A Cognitive View*, Holt, Rinehart and Winston, New York.

Bangert-Drowns, R., C. Kulik, J. Kulik and M. Morgan (1991), "The Instructional Effect of Feedback in Test-Like Events", *Review of Educational Research,* Vol. 61, No. 2, pp. 213-238.

Black, P., C. Harrison, C. Lee, B. Marshall and D. Wiliam (2004), "Working Inside the Black Box: Assessment for Learning in the Classroom", *Phi Delta Kappan,* Vol. 86, No. 1, pp. 9-21.

Black, P. and D. Wiliam (1998a), "Assessment and Classroom Learning", *Assessment in Education: Principles Policy and Practice,* Vol. 5, No. 1, pp. 7-73.

Black, P. and D. Wiliam (2005), "Developing a Theory of Formative Assessment", in J. Gardner (ed.), *Assessment and learning*, Sage, London, UK, pp. 81-100.

Black, P. and D. Wiliam (2009), "Developing the Theory of Formative Assessment", *Educational Assessment, Evaluation and Accountability,* Vol. 21, No. 1, pp. 5-31.

Bloom, B.S. (1969), "Some Theoretical Issues Relating to Educational Evaluation", in R.W. Tyler (ed.), *Educational Evaluation: New Roles, New Means: The 68th Yearbook of the National Society for the Study of Education (part II)* (Vol. 68, No. 2, pp. 26-50), University of Chicago Press, Chicago, IL.

Broadfoot, P., R. Daugherty, J. Gardner, W. Harlen, M. James and G. Stobart (1999), *Assessment for Learning: Beyond the Black Box*, University of Cambridge School of Education, Cambridge, UK.

Broadfoot, P., R. Daugherty, J. Gardner, W. Harlen, M. James and G. Stobart (2002), *Assessment for Learning: 10 principles*, University of Cambridge School of Education, Cambridge, UK.

Brookhart, S.M. (2004), "Classroom Assessment: Tensions and Intersections in Theory and Practice", *Teachers College Record,* Vol. 106, No. 3, pp. 429-458.

Brookhart, S.M. (2007), "Expanding Views about Formative Classroom Assessment: A Review of the Literature", in J.H. McMillan (ed.), *Formative Classroom Assessment: Theory into Practice*, Teachers College Press, New York, NY, pp. 43-62.

Cowie, B. and B. Bell (1999), "A Model of Formative Assessment in Science Education", *Assessment in Education: Principles Policy and Practice,* Vol. 6, No. 1, pp. 32-42.

Crooks, T.J. (1988), "The Impact of Classroom Evaluation Practices on Students", *Review of Educational Research,* Vol. 58, No. 4, pp. 438-481.

Deci, E.L. and R.M. Ryan (1994), "Promoting Self-Determined Education", *Scandinavian Journal of Educational Research,* Vol. 38, No. 1, pp. 3-14.

Dempster, F.N. (1991), "Synthesis of Research on Reviews and Tests", *Educational Leadership,* Vol. 48, No. 7, pp. 71-76.

Dempster, F.N. (1992), "Using Tests to Promote Learning: A Neglected Classroom Resource", *Journal of Research and Development in Education,* Vol. 25, No. 4, pp. 213-217.

Denvir, B. and M.L. Brown (1986a), "Understanding of Number Concepts in Low-Attaining 7-9 year olds: Part 1. Development of Descriptive Framework and Diagnostic Instrument", *Educational Studies in Mathematics,* Vol. 17, No. 1, pp. 15-36.

Denvir, B. and M.L. Brown (1986b), "Understanding of Number Concepts in Low-Attaining 7-9 year olds: Part II, The Teaching Studies", *Educational Studies in Mathematics,* Vol. 17, No. 2, pp. 143-164.

Dickens, W. and J.R. Flynn (2001), "Heritability Estimates vs. Large Environmental Effects: The IQ Paradox Resolved", *Psychological Review*, Vol. 108, No. 2, pp. 346-369.

Elshout-Mohr, M. (1994), "Feedback in Self-Instruction", *European Education,* Vol. 26, No. 2, pp. 58-73.

Forster, M. and G. Masters (2004), "Bridging the Conceptual Gap between Classroom Assessment and System Accountability", in M. Wilson (ed.), *Towards Coherence between Classroom Assessment and Accountability*, University of Chicago Press, Chicago.

Fuchs, L.S. and D. Fuchs (1986), "Effects of Systematic Formative Evaluation – A Meta-Analysis", *Exceptional children,* Vol. 53, No. 3, pp. 199-208.

Harlow, L.L., S.A. Mulaik and J.H. Steiger (eds.) (1997), *What If There Were No Significance Tests?,* Lawrence Erlbaum Associates, Mahwah, NJ.

Hattie, J. and H. Timperley (2007), "The Power of feedback", *Review of Educational Research,* Vol. 77, No. 1, pp. 81-112.

James, M. (1992), "Assessment for Learning", annual conference of the Association for Supervision and Curriculum Development (Assembly session on 'Critique of Reforms in Assessment and Testing in Britain') held in New Orleans, LA, University of Cambridge Institute of Education, Cambridge, UK.

Kahl, S. (2005), "Where in the World are Formative Tests? Right under Your Nose!", *Education Week,* Vol. 25, No. 4, pp. 11.

Kluger, A.N. and A. DeNisi (1996), "The Effects of Feedback Interventions on Performance: A Historical Review, A Meta-Analysis, and A Preliminary Feedback Intervention Theory", *Psychological Bulletin,* Vol. 119, No. 2, pp. 254-284.

Köller, O. (2005), "Formative Assessment in Classrooms: A Review of the Empirical German Literature", in J. Looney (ed.), *Formative Assessment: Improving Learning in Secondary Classrooms,* OECD Publishing, Paris, pp. 265-279.

Leahy, S., C. Lyon, M. Thompson and D. Wiliam (2005), "Classroom Assessment: Minute-by-Minute and Day-by-Day", *Educational Leadership,* Vol. 63, No. 3, pp. 18-24.

Looney, J. (ed.) (2005), *Formative Assessment: Improving Learning in Secondary Classrooms,* OECD Publishing, Paris.

Meisels, S.J., S. Atkins-Burnett, Y. Xue, J. Nicholson, D.D. Bickel and S.-H. Son (2003), "Creating a System of Accountability: The impact of Instructional Assessment on Elementary Children's Achievement Test Scores", *Education Policy Analysis Archives,* Vol. 11, No. 9.

Mercer, N., L. Dawes, R. Wegerif and C. Sams (2004), "Reasoning as a Scientist: Ways of Helping Children to Use Language to Learn Science", *British Educational Research Journal,* Vol. 30, No. 3, pp. 359-377.

Natriello, G. (1987), "The Impact of Evaluation Processes on Students", *Educational Psychologist,* Vol. 22, No. 2, pp. 155-175.

Nyquist, J.B. (2003), *The Benefits of Reconstruing Feedback as a Larger System of Formative Assessment: A Meta-Analysis,* Unpublished Master of Science, Vanderbilt University.

Perrenoud, P. (1991), "Towards a Pragmatic Approach to Formative Evaluation", in P. Weston (ed.), *Assessment of Pupils' Achievement: Motivation and School Success*, Amsterdam: Swets & Zeitlinger, pp. 77-101.

Perrenoud, P. (1998), "From Formative Evaluation to a Controlled Regulation of Learning Towards a Wider Conceptual Field", *Assessment in Education: Principles Policy and Practice*, Vol. 5, No. 1, pp. 85-102.

Ramaprasad, A. (1983), "On the Definition of Feedback", *Behavioural Science*, Vol. 28, No. 1, pp. 4-13.

Sadler, D.R. (1989), "Formative Assessment and the Design of Instructional Systems", *Instructional Science*, Vol. 18, No. 2, pp. 119-144.

Shepard, L.A. (2007), "Formative Assessment: Caveat Emptor", in C.A. Dwyer (ed.), *The Future of Assessment: Shaping Teaching and Learning*, Lawrence Erlbaum Associates, Mahwah, NJ, pp. 279-303.

Shepard, L., K. Hammerness, L. Darling-Hammond and F. Rust (2005), "Assessment", in L. Darling-Hammond and J. Bransford (eds.), *Preparing Teachers for a Changing World: What Teachers Should Learn and Be Able to Do*, Jossey-Bass, San Francisco, CA, pp. 275-326.

Shute, V.J. (2008), "Focus on Formative Feedback", *Review of Educational Research*, Vol. 78, No. 1, pp. 153-189.

Torrance, H. and J. Pryor (1998), *Investigating Formative Assessment*, Open University Press, Buckingham, UK.

Tunstall, P. and C.V. Gipps (1996a), "Teacher Feedback to Young Children in Formative Assessment: A Typology", *British Educational Research Journal*, Vol. 22, No. 4, pp. 389-404.

Tunstall, P. and C.V. Gipps (1996b), "'How Does Your Teacher Help You to Make Your Work Better?' Children's Understanding of Formative Assessment", *The Curriculum Journal*, Vol. 7, No. 2, pp. 185-203.

Vinner, S. (1997), From Intuition to Inhibition – Mathematics, Education and Other Endangered Species, in E. Pehkonen (ed.), *Proceedings of the 21st Conference of the International Group for the Psychology of Mathematics Education* (Vol. 1), University of Helsinki Lahti Research and Training Centre, Lahti, Finland, pp. 63-78.

Wiener, N. (1948), *Cybernetics, or the Control and Communication in the Animal and the Machine*, John Wiley, New York, NY.

Wiliam, D. (2007), "Keeping Learning on Track: Classroom Assessment and the Regulation of Learning", in F.K. Lester Jr (ed.), *Second Handbook of Mathematics Teaching and Learning*, Information Age Publishing, Greenwich, CT, pp. 1053-1098.

Wiliam, D. (2009), "An Integrative Summary of the Research Literature and Implications for a New Theory of Formative Assessment", in H.L. Andrade and G.J. Cizek (eds.), *Handbook of Formative Assessment*, Routledge, Taylor and Francis, New York.

Wiliam, D. and P.J. Black (1996), "Meanings and Consequences: A Basis for Distinguishing Formative and Summative Functions of Assessment?", *British Educational Research Journal,* Vol. 22, No. 5, pp. 537-548.

Wiliam, D. and M. Thompson (2007), "Integrating Assessment with Instruction: What Will it Take to Make it Work?", in C.A. Dwyer (ed.), *The Future of Assessment: Shaping Teaching and Learning*, Lawrence Erlbaum Associates, Mahwah, NJ, pp. 53-82.

Chapter 7

Co-operative learning: what makes group-work work?

Robert E. Slavin
University of York and Johns Hopkins University

Robert Slavin reviews the substantial body of studies of co-operative learning in schools, in particular those using control groups being taught with more traditional methods. There are two main categories – "Structured Team Learning" and "Informal Group Learning Methods" – each reviewed and illustrated. As regards affective outcomes, co-operative learning overwhelmingly shows beneficial results. For achievement outcomes, positive results depend heavily on two key factors. One is the presence of group goals (the learner groups are working towards a goal or to gain reward or recognition), the other is individual accountability (the success of the group depends on the individual learning of every member). The chapter presents alternative perspectives to explain the benefits of co-operative learning – whether it acts via motivations, social cohesion, cognitive development, or "cognitive elaboration". Despite the very robust evidence base of positive outcomes, co-operative learning "remains at the edge of school policy" and is often poorly implemented.

Introduction

There was once a time when it was taken for granted that a quiet class was a learning class, when principals walked down the hall expecting to be able to hear a pin drop. In more recent times, however, teachers are more likely to encourage students to interact with each other in co-operative learning groups. Yet having students work in groups can be enormously beneficial or it can be of little value. How can teachers make best use of this powerful tool?

Co-operative learning has been suggested as the solution for wide array of educational problems. It is often cited as a means of emphasising thinking skills and increasing higher-order learning; as an alternative to ability grouping, remediation, or special education; as a means of improving race relations; and as a way to prepare students for an increasingly collaborative work force. How many of these claims are justified? What effects do the various collaborative learning methods have on student achievement and other outcomes? Which forms of co-operative learning are most effective, and what components must be in place for co-operative learning to work?

To answer these questions, this chapter reviews the findings of studies of co-operative learning in elementary and secondary schools that have compared co-operative learning with control groups studying the same objectives but taught using traditional methods.

Co-operative learning methods

There are many quite different forms of co-operative learning, but all of them involve having students work in small groups or teams to help one another learn academic material. Co-operative learning usually supplements the teacher's instruction by giving students an opportunity to discuss information or practise skills originally presented by the teacher. Sometimes co-operative methods require students to find or discover information on their own. Co-operative learning has been used and investigated in every subject at all grade levels.

Co-operative learning methods fall into two main categories. One set – "Structured Team Learning" – involves rewards to teams based on the learning progress of their members, and they are also characterised by individual accountability, which means that team success depends on individual learning, not group products. A second set – "Informal Group Learning Methods" – covers methods more focused on social dynamics, projects, and discussion than on mastery of well-specified content.

Structured team learning methods

Student Team Learning

Student Team Learning (STL) techniques were developed and researched at Johns Hopkins University in the United States. More than half of all experimental studies of practical co-operative learning methods involve STL methods. All co-operative learning methods share the idea that students work together and are responsible for one another's learning as well as their own. STL also emphasises the use of team goals and collective definitions of success, which can only be achieved if all members of the team learn the objectives being taught. That is, in *Student Team Learning* the important thing is not to **do** something together but to **learn** something as a team.

Three concepts are central to all *Student Team Learning* methods: **team rewards**, **individual accountability** and **equal opportunities for success**. In classes using STL, teams earn certificates or other team rewards if they achieve above a designated criterion. "Individual accountability" means that the team's success depends on the individual learning of all team members. This focuses team activity on explaining concepts to one another and making sure that everyone on the team is ready for a quiz or other assessment that they will be taking without teammate help. With equal opportunities for success, students contribute to their teams by improving over their past performances, so that high, average and low achievers are equally challenged to do their best and the contributions of all team members are valued.

The findings of these experimental studies indicate that team rewards and individual accountability are essential elements for enhancing basic skills achievement (Slavin, 1995, 2009). It is not enough simply to tell students to work together. They must have a reason to take one another's achievement seriously. Further, if students are rewarded for doing better than they have in the past, they will be more motivated to achieve than if they are rewarded based on their performance in comparison to others – rewards for improvement make success neither too difficult nor too easy for students to achieve.

Four principal Student Learning methods have been extensively developed and researched. Two are general co-operative learning methods adaptable to most subjects and grade levels: *Student Team-Achievement Divisions* (STAD) and *Teams-Games-Tournament* (TGT). The remaining two are comprehensive curriculums designed for use in particular subjects at particular grade levels: *Team Assisted Individualisation* (TAI) for mathematics in years 3-6 and *Co-operative Integrated Reading and Composition* (CIRC) for reading and writing instruction in years 3-5.

Student Teams-Achievement Divisions (STAD)

In STAD (Slavin, 1994), students are assigned to four-member learning teams which are mixed in performance level, sex and ethnicity. The teacher presents a lesson, and the students work within their teams to make sure that all team members have mastered the lesson. Finally, all students take individual quizzes on the material, at which time they are not allowed to help one another.

Students' quiz scores are compared to their own past averages, and points are awarded based on the degree to which students can meet or exceed their own earlier performances. These points are then summed to form team scores, and teams that meet certain criteria earn certificates or other rewards. The whole cycle of activities, from teacher presentation to team practice to quiz, usually takes three to five class periods.

STAD had been used in a wide variety of subjects, from mathematics to language arts and social studies. It has been used from grade 2 through college. STAD is most appropriate for teaching well-defined objectives, such as mathematical computations and applications, language usage and mechanics, geography and map skills, and science facts and concepts. Typically, it is a co-operative learning programme in which students work in 4-member heterogeneous teams to help each other master academic content and teachers follow a schedule of teaching, team work and individual assessment. The teams receive certificates and other recognition based on the average scores of all team members on weekly quizzes. This team recognition and individual accountability are held by Slavin (1995) and others to be essential for positive effects of co-operative learning.

Numerous studies of STAD have found positive effects of the programme on traditional learning outcomes in mathematics, language arts, science and other subjects (Slavin, 1995; Mevarech, 1985, 1991; Slavin and Karweit, 1984; Barbato, 2000; Reid, 1992). For example, Slavin and Karweit (1984) carried out a large, year-long randomised evaluation of *STAD* in Math 9 classes in Philadelphia. These were classes for students not felt to be ready for Algebra I, and were therefore the lowest-achieving students. Overall, 76% of students were African American, 19% were White, and 6% were Hispanic. Forty-four classes in 26 junior and senior high schools were randomly assigned within schools to one of four conditions: *STAD, STAD* plus *Mastery Learning, Mastery Learning*, or control. All classes, including the control group, used the same books, materials and schedule of instruction, but the control group did not use teams or mastery learning. In the Mastery Learning conditions, students took formative tests each week, students who did not achieve at least an 80% score received corrective instruction, and then students took summative tests.

The four groups were very similar at the start. Shortened versions of the standardised Comprehensive Test of Basic Skills (CTBS) in mathematics served as a pre- and post-test, and the purpose was to identify the effect size[*] of those being taught using the co-operative methods (using 2 x 2 nested analyses of covariance). There was a significant advantage noted for the STAD groups (Effect Size = +0.21, p<.03), in other words, their post-test levels were about a fifth of a standard deviation ahead of the control group, and these gains were similar for high, average and low-achieving students as measured by their pre-test scores. The gain was slightly larger for those who had had the teams methods combined with Mastery Learning (the effect size compared to the control group was +0.24), while that for *STAD* without Mastery Learning was +0.18. There was no significant main effect for Mastery Learning by itself.

Teams-Games-Tournament (TGT)

Teams-Games-Tournament uses the same teacher presentations and team-work as in STAD, but replaces the quizzes with weekly tournaments (Slavin, 1994). In these, students compete with members of other teams to contribute points to their team score. Students compete at three-person "tournament tables" against others with a similar past record in mathematics. A procedure changes table assignments to keep the competition fair. The winner at each tournament table brings the same number of points to his or her team, regardless of which table it is; this means that low achievers (competing with other low achievers) and high achievers (competing with other high achievers) have equal opportunity for success. As in STAD, high performing teams earn certificates or other forms of team rewards. TGT is appropriate for the same types of objectives as STAD. Studies of TGT have found positive effects on achievement in math, science and language arts (Slavin, 1995).

Team Assisted Individualisation (TAI)

Team Assisted Individualisation (TAI; Slavin *et al.* 1986) shares with STAD and TGT the use of the four-member mixed-ability learning teams and certificates for high-performing teams. But where STAD and TGT use a single pace of instruction for the class, TAI combines co-operative learning with individualised instruction. Also, where STAD and TGT apply to most subjects at grade levels, TAI is specifically designed to teach mathematics to students in grades 3-6 or older students not ready for a full algebra course.

---

[*]An effect size (ES) is the proportion of a standard deviation by which experimental groups exceed control groups, after adjusting for any pre-test differences.

In TAI, students enter an individualised sequence according to a placement test and then proceed at their own rates. In general, team members work on different units. Teammates check each others' work against answer sheets and help one another with any problems. Final unit tests are taken without teammate help and are scored by student monitors. Each week, teachers total the number of units completed by all team members and give certificates or other team rewards to teams that exceed a criterion score based on the number of final tests passed, with extra points for perfect papers and completed homework.

Because students take responsibility for checking each others' work and managing the flow of materials, the teacher can spend most of the class time presenting lessons to small groups of students drawn from the various teams who are working at the same point in the mathematics sequence. For example, the teacher might call up a decimals group, present a lesson, and then send the students back to their teams to work on problems. The teacher might then call up the fractions group, and so on. Several large evaluations of TAI have shown positive effects on mathematics achievement in the upper-elementary grades (*e.g.* Slavin and Karweit, 1985; Stevens and Slavin, 1995).

Co-operative Integrated Reading and Composition (CIRC)

A comprehensive programme for teaching reading and writing in the upper elementary grades is called *Co-operative Integrated Reading and Composition* (CIRC) (Stevens *et al.* 1987). In CIRC, teachers use reading texts and reading groups, much as in traditional reading programmes. However, all students are assigned to teams composed of two pairs from two different reading groups. While the teacher is working with one reading group, the paired students in the other groups are working on a series of engaging activities, including reading to one another, making predictions about how narrative stories will come out, summarising stories to one another, writing responses to stories, and practising spelling, decoding and vocabulary. Students work as a team to master "main idea" and other comprehension skills. During language arts periods, students engage in writing drafts, revising and editing one another's work and finalising the team books.

In most CIRC activities, students follow a sequence of teacher instruction, team practice, team pre-assessments and quizzes so that they do not take the quiz until their teammates have determined that they are ready. Certificates are given to teams based on the average performance of all team members on all the reading and writing activities.

Research on CIRC and similar approaches has found positive effects on measures of reading performance in upper-elementary and middle schools (Stevens and Slavin, 1995a, 1995b; Stevens, Madden, Slavin and Farnish,

1987; Stevens and Durkin, 1992). CIRC has been adopted as the upper-elementary and middle school component of the *Success for All* comprehensive reform models and is currently disseminated under the name *Reading Wings* by the *Success for All Foundation* (see Slavin and Madden, 2009).

An example of the positive evaluations can be found in Stevens *et al.* (1987, Study 2). They evaluated CIRC over a 6-month period in a middle class suburb of Baltimore, with 450 3rd and 4th graders, of whom about a fifth (22%) were minority and 18% disadvantaged as indicated by entitlement to free or reduced-price lunches. CIRC was used in 9 classes in 4 schools, and there were 13 control classes in 5 schools matched on California Achievement Test (CAT) reading scores and demographics. Using the CAT measures to identify the impact of the different types of teaching showed the clear positive gains for the CIRC students (effect sizes were +0.35 (p<.002) for Reading Comprehension, +0.11 (p<.04) for Reading Vocabulary, and +0.23 (p<.01) for CAT Total). On standards of oral reading (using individually-administered Durrell Oral Reading Tests for six randomly-selected students in each class), the CIRC students scored substantially higher than the control groups, averaging ES = +0.54 across five measures (p<.02). Combining the effects found using the California Achievement Test with those for oral reading using Durrell gave a mean effect size of +0.45.

Even larger impacts were measured for special needs students. Separate analyses for students in special education found CAT effect sizes of +0.99 for Reading Comprehension and +0.90 for Reading Vocabulary; analyses for remedial reading students found effect sizes of +0.40 for Reading Comprehension and +0.26 for Reading Vocabulary.

Peer-Assisted Learning Strategies (PALS)

Peer Assisted Learning Strategies (PALS) is a learning approach in which pairs of children take turns as teacher and learner. The children are taught simple strategies for helping each other, and are rewarded based on the learning of both members of the pair. Research on PALS in elementary and middle school mathematics and reading has found positive effects of this approach on student achievement outcomes (*e.g.* Mathes and Babyak, 2001; Fuchs, Fuchs and Karns, 2001; Calhoon *et al.*, 2006; Fuchs, Fuchs, Kazden and Allen, 1999, Calhoon, 2005).

For example, Fuchs, Fuchs, Kazdan and Allen (1999) evaluated PALS in a 21-week study in Grades 2-3. Two forms of PALS were evaluated. In PALS, students worked 35 minutes 3 times a week in pairs, alternating roles as teacher and learner. They engaged in partner reading, summarisation, identification of main ideas, and predictions. Teachers of 16 classes were randomly assigned to PALS or control classes. They designated one low, one average, and one high-achieving student, and only these students were assessed (even though all children in each class participated in the treatments). Students were pre- and post-tested on the Reading Comprehension subtest of the Standard Diagnostic Reading Test (SDRT). The results were very positive for the students using PALS compared with the others, at nearly three-quarters of a standard deviation in front (ES = +0.72). Positive learning effects of a similar programme called *Classwide Peer Tutoring* (Greenwood, Delquardi and Hall, 1989) have also been found. Two Belgian studies (Van Keer and Verhenge, 2005, 2008) also found positive effects for same-age tutoring.

IMPROVE

IMPROVE (Mevarech, 1985) is an Israeli mathematics programme that uses co-operative learning strategies similar to those used in *STAD* but also emphasises teaching of meta-cognitive skills and regular assessments of mastery of key concepts and re-teaching of skills missed by many students. Studies of *IMPROVE* have found positive effects on the mathematics achievement of elementary and middle school students in Israel (Mevarech and Kramarski, 1997; Kramarski, Mevarech and Lieberman, 2001). For example, Mevarech and Kramarski (1997, Study 1) evaluated this approach in four Israeli junior high schools at seventh grade over one semester with matched controls using the same books and objectives. The experimental classes were selected from among those taught by teachers with experience teaching *IMPROVE*, and matched control classes were selected as well. Students were given pre- and post-tests certified by the Israeli superintendent of mathematics as fair to all groups. Pre-test scores were similar across groups. The results significantly favoured the *IMPROVE* classes on scales assessing introduction to algebra (ES = +0.54) as well as mathematical reasoning (ES = +0.68), for an average effect size of +0.61. That is, the achievements of those students following the co-operative methods exceeded the others by over three-fifths of a standard deviation, and these positive impacts were similar whether the students were low, average, or high achievers.

Informal group learning methods

Jigsaw

Jigsaw was originally designed by Elliot Aronson and his colleagues (1978). In Aronson's *Jigsaw* method, students are assigned to six-member teams to work on academic material that has been broken down into sections (for example, a biography might be divided into early life, first accomplishments, major setbacks, later life and impact on history). Each team member reads his or her section. Members of different teams who have studied the same sections then meet in "expert groups" to discuss their sections, after which the students return to their teams and take turns teaching their teammates about what they have learnt with the others sharing the same section material.

Since the only way students can learn material other than their own is to listen carefully to their teammates, they are motivated to support and show interest in one another's work. Slavin (1994) developed a modification of *Jigsaw* at Johns Hopkins University and then incorporated it in the Student Team Learning programme. In this method, called *Jigsaw II*, students work in four-or five-member teams as in TGT and STAD. Instead of each student being assigned a particular section of text, all students read a common narrative, such as a book chapter, a short story, or a biography but each student also receives a topic – such as "climate" in a unit on France – on which to become an expert. Students with the same topics meet in expert groups to discuss them, after which they return to their teams to teach what they have learned to their teammates. Then students take individual quizzes, which result in team scores based on the STAD improvement assessment system. Teams that meet preset standards earn certificates. *Jigsaw* is primarily used in social studies and other subjects where learning from text is important (Mattingly and Van Sickle, 1991).

Learning Together

David Johnson and Roger Johnson at the University of Minnesota developed the *Learning Together* models of co-operative learning (Johnson and Johnson, 1999). These involve students working on assignment sheets in four- or five-member heterogeneous groups. The groups hand in a single sheet and receive praise and rewards based on the group product. Their methods emphasise team-building activities before students begin working together and regular discussions within groups about how well they are collaborating.

Group Investigation

Group Investigation, developed by Shlomo Sharan and Yael Sharan (1992) at the University of Tel-Aviv, is a general classroom organisation plan in which students work co-operatively in small groups with inquiry, group discussion, and shared planning and project realisation. In this method, students form their own two- to six-member groups. After choosing sub-topics from a unit being studied by the entire class, the groups further break their sub-topics into individual tasks and carry out the activities necessary to prepare group reports. Each group then makes a presentation or display to communicate its findings to the entire class. A study in Israel by Sharan and Shachar (1988) found positive effects of *Group Investigation* on achievement in language and literature.

What makes co-operative learning work?

Co-operative learning methods are among the most extensively evaluated alternatives to traditional instruction in use today. Use of co-operative learning almost always improves affective outcomes. Students love to work in groups and they feel more successful and like subjects taught co-operatively. They have more friends of different ethnic groups and are more accepting of others different from themselves (see Slavin, 1995). Regarding achievement, however, outcomes depend a great deal on how co-operative learning is used. In general, two elements must be present if co-operative learning is to be effective: **group goals** and **individual accountability** (Slavin 1995, 2009; Rohrbeck *et al.*, 2003; Webb, 2008). That is, groups must be working to achieve some goal or to earn rewards or recognition, and the success of the group must depend on the individual learning of every group member.

Why are group goals and individual accountability so important? To understand this, consider the alternatives. In some forms of co-operative learning, students work together to complete a single worksheet or to solve a problem together. In such methods, there is little reason for more able students to take time to explain what is going on to their less able group-mates or to ask their opinions. When the group task is to **do** something, rather than to learn something, the participation of less able students may be seen as interference rather than help. It may be easier in this circumstance for students to give each other answers than to explain concepts or skills to one another.

In contrast, when the group's task is to ensure that every group member **learns** something, it is in the interests of every group member to spend time explaining concepts to his or her group-mates. Studies of student behaviour within co-operative groups have consistently found that the students who gain most from co-operative work are those who give and receive elaborated explanations (Webb, 1985, 2008); in fact, giving and receiving answers without explanations were negatively related to achievement gain in these studies. Group goals and individual accountability motivate students to give explanations and to take one another's learning seriously, instead of simply giving answers.

A review of 99 studies of co-operative learning of durations of at least four weeks in elementary and secondary schools compared the achievement gains of the co-operative approaches with control group learning. Of sixty-four studies of co-operative learning methods that provided group rewards based on the sum of members' individual learning (categorised here as *Structured Team Learning Methods*), fifty (78%) found significantly positive effects on achievement, and none found negative effects (Slavin, 1995). The median effect size for the studies from which effect sizes could be computed was +.32 (*i.e.* nearly one-third of a standard deviation separated co-operative learning and control treatments). In contrast, studies of informal group learning methods which used group goals based on a single product from the work or provided no rewards, found few positive effects, with a median effect size of only +.07. Comparisons of alternative treatments within the same studies found similar patterns: group goals based on the sum of individual learning performances were a necessary ingredient to the instructional effectiveness of the co-operative models (*e.g.* Chapman, 2001; Fantuzzo, Polite and Grayson, 1990; Fantuzzo, Riggio, Connelly and Dimeff, 1989; Huber, Bogatzki and Winter, 1982).

Co-operative learning methods generally work equally well for all types of students. While occasional studies find particular advantages for high or low achievers, boys or girls, the great majority find equal benefits for all types of students. Teachers or parents sometimes worry that co-operative learning will hold back the high-achievers. The research provides no support for this claim: high achievers gain from co-operative learning (relative to high achievers in traditional classes) as much as do low and average achievers (Slavin, 1995).

Theoretical perspectives on co-operative learning

While there is a general consensus among researchers about the positive effects of co-operative learning on student achievement, there remains a controversy about why and how they affect achievement and, most importantly, under what conditions they have these effects. Different groups of researchers investigating co-operative learning effects on achievement begin with different assumptions and conclude by explaining the effects of in terms that are substantially unrelated or conflicting. In earlier work, Slavin (1995, 2009; Slavin, Hurley and Chamberlain, 2001) identified *motivationalist, social cohesion, cognitive-developmental* and *cognitive-elaboration* as the four major theoretical perspectives held by different researchers on the achievement effects of co-operative learning.

The motivationalist perspective presumes that task motivation has the greatest impact on the learning process, and that the other processes (such as planning and helping) are driven by individuals' motivated self interest. Motivationalist scholars focus especially on the reward or goal structure under which students operate. By contrast, the social cohesion perspective (also called "social interdependence theory") suggests that the effects of co-operative learning are largely dependent on the cohesiveness of the group. In this perspective, students help each other to learn because they care about the group and its members and come to derive the benefits of self-identity from group membership (Johnson and Johnson, 1989; 1999; Hogg, 1987).

The two cognitive perspectives focus on the interactions among groups of students, holding that these interactions themselves lead to better learning and thus better achievement. The cognitive developmentalists attribute these effects to processes outlined by scholars such as Piaget and Vygotsky. The cognitive elaboration perspective instead asserts that learners must engage in some manner of cognitive restructuring (elaboration) of new materials in order to learn them; co-operative learning is seen to facilitate that process.

Slavin *et al.* (2003) have proposed a theoretical model intended to acknowledge the contributions of each of the major theoretical perspectives and the likely role that each plays in co-operative learning processes. They explore conditions under which each may operate, and suggest research and development needed to advance co-operative learning scholarship so that educational practice may truly benefit the lessons of thirty years of research.

The different perspectives on co-operative learning may be seen as complementary, not as exclusive alternatives. For example, motivational theorists would not argue that the cognitive theories are unnecessary but instead assert that motivation drives cognitive process, which in turn produces learning. They would argue that it is unlikely that over the long haul students would engage in the kind of elaborated explanations found by Webb (1989, 2008) to be essential to profiting from co-operative activity, without a goal structure designed to enhance motivation. Similarly, social cohesion theorists might identify the utility of extrinsic incentives to lie in their contribution to group cohesiveness, caring and pro-social norms among group members, which in turn affects cognitive processes.

A model of how co-operative learning might improve learning, adapted from Slavin (1995), is shown in Figure 7.1, depicting the main components of group learning interaction and representing the functional relationships among the different theoretical approaches.

Figure 7.1. **Different factors that influence the effectiveness of co-operative learning**

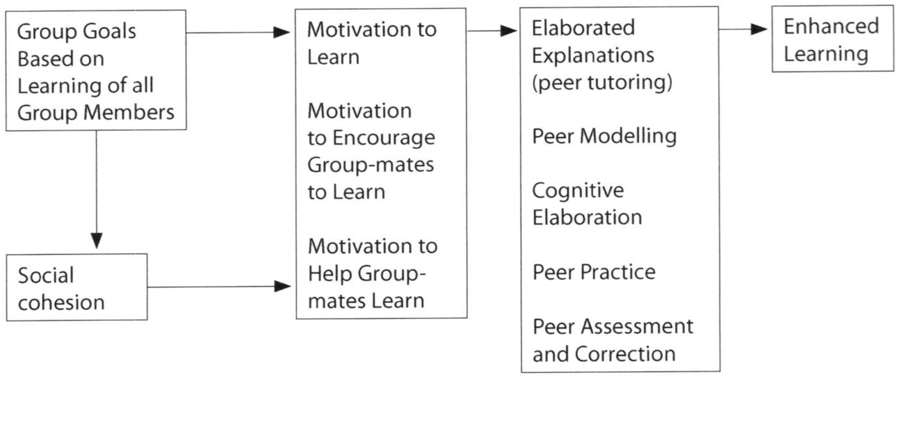

This diagram of the interdependent relationships among the components begins with a focus on group goals or incentives based on the individual learning of all group members. It assumes that motivation to learn and to encourage and help others to do so activates co-operative behaviours that will result in learning. This includes both task motivation and motivation to interact in the group. In this model, motivation to succeed leads directly to learning, and it also drives the behaviour and attitudes that foster group cohesion, which in turn facilitates the types of group interactions – peer modelling, equilibration and cognitive elaboration – that yield enhanced learning and academic achievement.

Co-operative learning in learning environments for the 21st century

Learning environments for the 21st century must be ones in which students are actively engaged with learning tasks and with each other. Today, teachers are in competition with television, computer games, and all sorts of engaging technology, and the expectation that children will learn passively is becoming increasingly unrealistic. Co-operative learning offers a proven, practical means of creating exciting social and engaging classroom environments to help students to master traditional skills and knowledge as well as develop the creative and interactive skills needed in today's economy and society. Co-operative learning itself is being reshaped for the 21st century, particularly in partnership with developments in technology.

Co-operative learning has established itself as a practical alternative to traditional teaching, and has proven its effectiveness in hundreds of studies throughout the world. Surveys find that a substantial proportion of teachers claim to use it regularly (*e.g.* Puma, Jones, Rock and Fernandez, 1993). Yet observational studies (*e.g.* Antil, Jenkins, Wayne and Vadasy, 1998) find that most use of co-operative learning is informal, and does not incorporate the group goals and individual accountability that research has identified to be essential. Clearly, co-operative learning can be a powerful strategy for increasing student achievement, but fulfilling this potential depends on the provision of professional development for teachers that is focused on the approaches most likely to make a difference.

Training in effective forms of co-operative learning is readily available, such as from the *Success for All Foundation* in the United States and the United Kingdom (*www.successforall.org*), as well as the US-based *Peer-Assisted Learning Strategies* (*www.peerassistedlearningstrategies.net*) and *Kagan Publishing and Professional Development* (*www.kaganonline.com*). Training should include not only workshops, but also follow-up into teachers' classes by knowledgeable coaches, who can give feedback, do demonstrations and provide support.

In comparison with schooling practices that are often supported by governments – such as tutoring, technology use and school restructuring – co-operative learning is relatively inexpensive and easily adopted. Yet, thirty years after much of the foundational research was completed, it remains at the edge of school policy. This does not have to remain the case: as governments come to support the larger concept of evidence-based reform, the strong evidence base for co-operative learning may lead to a greater focus on this set of approaches at the core of instructional practice. In the learning environments of the 21st century, co-operative learning should play a central role.

References

Antil, L.R., J.R. Jenkins, S.K. Wayne and P.F. Vadasy (1998), "Co-operative Learning: Prevalence, Conceptualizations, and the Relation between Research and Practice", *American Educational Research Journal*, Vol. 35, No. 3, pp. 419-454.

Barbato, R. (2000), *Policy Implications of Co-operative Learning on the Achievement and Attitudes of Secondary School Mathematics Students*, Unpublished Doctoral Dissertation, Fordham University.

Calhoon, M. (2005), "Effects of a Peer-Mediated Phonological Skill and Reading Comprehension Program on Reading Skill Acquisition for Middle School Students with Reading Disabilities", *Journal of Learning Disabilities,* Vol. 38, No. 5, pp. 424-433.

Chapman, E. (2001), *More on Moderators in Co-operative Learning Outcomes,* Paper presented at the annual meeting of the American Educational Research Association, Seattle, WA.

Fantuzzo, J.W., K. Polite and N. Grayson (1990), "An Evaluation of Reciprocal Peer Tutoring across Elementary School Settings", *Journal of School Psychology*, Vol. 28, No. 4, pp. 309-323.

Fantuzzo, J.W., R.E. Riggio, S. Connelly and L.A. Dimeff (1989), "Effects of Reciprocal Peer Tutoring on Academic Achievement and Psychological Adjustment: A Component Analysis", *Journal of Educational Psychology*, Vol. 81, No. 2, pp. 173-177.

Fuchs, L.S., D. Fuchs, S. Kazdan and S. Allen (1999), "Effects of Peer-Assisted Learning Strategies in Reading with and without Training in Elaborated Help Giving", *The Elementary School Journal,* Vol. 99, No. 3, pp. 201-221.

Hogg, M.A. (1987), "Social Identity and Group Cohesiveness" (pp. 89-116), in J.C. Turner (ed.), *Rediscovering the Social Group: A Self-Categorization Theory*, Basil Blackwell, Inc., New York

Huber, G.L., W. Bogatzki and M. Winter (1982*), Kooperation als Ziel Schulischen Lehrens und Lehrens*, Arbeitsbereich Pädagogische Psychologie der Universität Tübingen, Tübingen, Germany.

Johnson, D.W and R.T. Johnson (1999), *Learning Together and Alone* (5th ed), Prentice-Hall, Englewood Cliffs, N.J..

Kramarski, B., Z.R. Mevarech and A. Liberman (2001), "The Effects of Multilevel-versus Unilevel-metacognitive training on mathematical reasoning", *The Journal of Educational Research*, Vol. 94, No. 5, pp. 292-300.

Mathes, P.G. and A.E. Babyak (2001), "The Effects of Peer-Assisted Literacy Strategies for First-Grade Readers with and without Additional Mini-Skills Lessons", *Learning Disabilities Research and Practice*, Vol. 16, No. 1, pp. 28-44.

Mattingly, R.M. and R.L. Van Sickle (1991), "Co-operative Learning and Achievement in Social Studies: Jigsaw II", *Social Education*, Vol. 55, No. 6, pp. 392-395.

Mevarech, Z.R. (1985), "The Effects of Co-operative Mastery Learning Strategies on Mathematics Achievement", *Journal of Educational Research*, Vol. 78, No. 3, pp. 372-377.

Mevarech, Z.R. (1991), "Learning Mathematics in Different Mastery Environments", *Journal of Educational Research*, Vol. 84, No. 4, pp. 225-231.

Mevarech, Z.R. and B. Kramarski (1997), "Improve: A Multidimensional Method for Teaching Mathematics in Heterogeneous Classrooms", *American Educational Research Journal*, Vol. 34, No. 2, pp. 365-394.

Puma, M.J., C.C. Jones, D. Rock and R. Fernandez (1993), *Prospects: The Congressionally Mandated Study of Educational Growth and Opportunity. Interim Report*, Abt Associates, Bethesda, MD.

Reid, J. (1992), "Effects of Cooperative Learning on Achievement and Attitude among Students of Color", *The Journal of Educational Research*, Vol. 95, No. 6, pp. 359-366.

Rohrbeck, C.A., M. Ginsburg-Block, J.W. Fantuzzo and T.R. Miller (2003), "Peer-Assisted Learning Interventions with Elementary School Students: A Meta-Analytic Review", *Journal of Educational Psychology*, Vol. 95, No. 2, pp. 240-257.

Sharan, S. and C. Shachar (1988), *Language and Learning in the Co-operative Classroom*, Springer-Verlag, New York.

Sharan, Y. and S. Sharan (1992), *Expanding Co-operative Learning through Group Investigation*, Teachers College Press, New York.

Slavin, R.E. (1994), *Using Student Team Learning, 3rd Ed*, Success for All Foundation. Elementary and Middle Schools, Johns Hopkins University, Baltimore, MD:

Slavin, R.E. (1995), *Co-operative Learning: Theory, Research, and Practice* (2nd edition), Allyn and Bacon, Boston.

Slavin, R.E. (2009), "Cooperative Learning", in G. McCulloch and D. Crook (eds.), *International Encyclopedia of Education*, Routledge, Abington, UK.

Slavin, R.E., E.A. Hurley and A.M. Chamberlain (2001), "Co-operative Learning in Schools", in N.J. Smelser and B.B. Paul (eds.), *International Encyclopedia of the Social and Behavioral Sciences*, Pergamon, Oxford, England, pp. 2756-2761.

Slavin, R.E. and N. Karweit (1984), "Mastery Learning and Student Teams: A Factorial Experiment in Urban General Mathematics Classes", *American Educational Research Journal,* Vol. 21, No. 4, pp. 725-736.

Slavin, R.E., M.B. Leavey and N.A. Madden (1986), *Team Accelerated Instruction Mathematics*, Mastery Education Corporation Watertown, Mass.

Slavin, R.E and N.A. Madden (eds.) (2009), *Two Million Children: Success for All*, Corwin, Thousand Oaks, CA.

Stevens, R.J. and S. Durkin (1992), *Using Student Team Reading and Student Team Writing in Middle Schools: Two Evaluations*, Report No. 36, Johns Hopkins University, Centre for Research on Effective Schooling for Disadvantaged Students, Baltimore, MD.

Stevens, R.J. and R.E. Slavin (1995), "Effects of a Co-operative Learning Approach in Reading and Writing on Handicapped and Nonhandicapped Students' Achievement, Attitudes, and Metacognition in Reading and Writing", *Elementary School Journal,* Vol. 95, No. 3, pp. 241-262.

Stevens, R.J. and R.E. Slavin (1995), "The Co-operative Elementary School: Effects on Students' Achievement, Attitudes, and Social Relations", *American Educational Research Journal,* Vol. 32, No. 2, pp. 321-351.

Stevens, R.J., N.A. Madden, R.E. Slavin and A.M. Farnish (1987), "Co-operative Integrated Reading and Composition: Two field experiments", *Reading Research Quarterly,* Vol. 22, No. 4, pp. 433-454.

Van Keer, H. and J. Verhaeghe (2005), "Comparing Two Teacher Development Programs for Innovating Reading Comprehension Instruction with regard to Teachers' Experiences and Student Outcomes", *Teaching and Teacher Education,* Vol. 21, No. 5, pp. 543-562.

Van Keer, H. and J. Verhaeghe (2008), *Strategic Reading in Peer Tutoring Dyads in Second and Fifth-grade Classrooms,* unpublished report, Ghent University, Belgium.

Webb, N. (1985), "Student Interaction and Learning in Small Groups: A Research Summary", in R. Slavin, *et al.* (eds.), *Learning to Cooperate, Cooperating to Learn,* New York: Plenum.

Webb, N. (2008), "Co-operative Learning", in T.L. Good (ed.), *21st Century Education: A Reference Handbook,* Sage, Thousand Oaks, CA.

Chapter 8

Learning with technology

Richard E. Mayer
University of California, Santa Barbara

Richard Mayer argues that few of the many strong claims made for the transformative potential of new technologies have been convincingly tested against research evidence. A major reason is that too often a "technology-centred", as opposed to a "learning-centred", approach is followed. A convincing theory of how people learn with technology can be based on three important principles: "dual channels" (people process sound and visual images separately), "limited capacity" (people can only process a small amount of sound or image at a time), and "active processing" (meaningful learning depends on engagement in appropriate cognitive processing). These are explained and applied to argue that effective instruction with technology helps cognitive processing in learners without overloading their cognitive system; this can be achieved by reducing extraneous processing, managing essential processing, and fostering generative processing. How this can be done applying different techniques and principles, together with supportive evidence, are presented in detail.

Introduction: learning with technology

Consider the following examples of learning situations: a student is interested in how the digestive system works so she goes to her laptop, clicks on an entry entitled "The Digestive System" in a multimedia encyclopaedia, and receives a 90-second narrated animation on how the human digestive system works. A second student goes to a government health agency site and clicks on an article about digestion, which contains five frames of text and illustrations. Finally, a third student finds a digestion game that involves moving around within a virtual world of the digestive system. These are all examples of learning with technology – situations in which learners use technology (such as a computer-based multimedia lesson or simulation game) in order to learn.

Many strong claims are made for the potential of new technologies to transform education and training around the world, but few of the claims have been substantiated by research evidence or even tested in rigorous scientific research (Lowe and Schnotz, 2008; Mayer, 2009; O'Neil and Perez, 2003, 2006; PyllikZillig, Bodvarsson and Bruning, 2005; Reiser and Dempsy, 2007; Rouet, Levonen and Biardeau, 2001; Spector *et al.*, 2008). For example, predictions include that education will be improved by providing students with access to hand-held devices (such as PDAs) or virtual reality game environments, by converting face-to-face instruction to online venues, or even by providing access to inexpensive laptops for all children in developing countries. The goal of this chapter is to explore what research tells us about how people learn with technology (the science of learning) and how to use technology to help people learn (the science of instruction).

Topics in learning with technology

Learning with technology refers to situations in which someone uses technology with the goal of promoting learning. Current interest in learning with technology reflects what Lowyck (2008, p. xiii) calls "a common impulse to (try to) use available technology for schooling purposes." The most common learning technologies of today involve computers and information technology:

> Karl Benz's invention of an automobile with a built-in internal combustion engine in 1885 caused a world-wide revolution, not only in the technology field but also in all segments of human life … The rise of personal computers and network facilities in the second half of the 20th century eventually … revolutionised information development and exchange. In contrast to the gas-fuelled engine, information and communication technologies suggest a sensitivity toward lifelong learning issues. (Lowyck, 2008, p. xiii)

In particular, the Internet has become an important venue for online courses from schools, training for jobs and informal learning – all of which are forms of eLearning (Clark and Kwinn, 2007; Clark and Mayer, 2008; O'Neil, 2005). eLearning refers to instruction delivered on a computer.

What are some currently promising forms of learning with technology? Graesser and colleagues (Graesser, Chipman, and King, 2008; Graesser and King, 2008) suggest ten genres of technology-based learning environments:

1. *Computer-based training:* lessons, tests and feedback that are presented on a computer screen, usually in a mastery format in which the learner goes on to the next section after passing a test on the current section.

2. *Multimedia:* instruction that consists of pictures (such as illustrations, photos, animation, or video) and words (such as printed or spoken text).

3. *Interactive simulation:* simulations over which the learner has some control, such as being able to slow down an animation or set input parameters and observe what happens.

4. *Hypertext and hypermedia*: instructional material consisting of click-able links, such as used in web pages.

5. *Intelligent tutoring systems:* instructional systems that track the knowledge of the learner and adjust what is presented accordingly.

6. *Inquiry-based information retrieval:* such as using Google for web searches.

7. *Animated pedagogical agents:* on-screen characters who help guide the learner through a computer-based lesson.

8. *Virtual environments with agents:* visually realistic environments that simulate interactions with real people, often using natural language.

9. *Serious games:* games that are intended to serve an instructional function.

10. *Computer-supported collaborative learning:* in which groups of learn-ers work together on a common task by communicating via computers.

Similarly, *The Cambridge Handbook of Multimedia Learning* (Mayer, 2005) examines conventional computer-based presentations as well as five advanced computer-based learning settings that have received research attention: animated pedagogical agents (corresponding to 7 above); virtual reality (corresponding to 8 above); games, simulations and microworlds (including 3 and 9 above); hyper-media (corresponding to 4 above); and e-Courses (including 1, 2 and 5 above). In this chapter, I focus on basic concepts and exemplary research that are relevant to a broad range of technology-based learning environments.

Two approaches to learning with technology

Table 8.1 summarises the important distinction between **technology-centred** and **learner-centred** approaches to learning with technology. In the technology-centred approach, the focus is on using technology in education through providing access to cutting-edge technology. The main problem with the technology-centred approach is that during the 20th century it has produced several major cycles of big promises, some implementation in schools... and failure.

In the 1920s, for example, the cutting-edge educational technology of the day was motion pictures. At that time, Thomas Edison predicted that "the motion picture is destined to revolutionise our educational system" and "books will soon to obsolete in our schools" (Cuban, 1986, p. 9-11). Yet classroom use of film remains rare. In the 1930s and 1940s, the cutting-edge educational technology was radio, which promoters touted as a means to "bring the world to the classroom" yielding the prediction that "a portable radio receiver will be as common in the classroom as the blackboard" (Cuban, 1986, p. 19). In spite of valiant efforts to develop "schools of the air", radio was never widely accepted in education. Next, in the 1950s educational television was promoted as an educational technology that would revolutionise education, but it was never widely used in schools (Cuban, 1986). In the 1960s, computer-based pro-grammed instruction was offered as the technology that would revolutionise education, but again, despite large-scale development efforts such as PLATO and TICCIT, programmed instruction did not have much impact (Cuban, 1986; 2001). During the late 20th century, information technology was spotlighted as a cutting-edge educational technology that would cause major changes in education, but Cuban (2001, p. 195) concludes: "The introduction of informa-tion technologies into schools over the past two decades has achieved neither the transformation of teaching and learning nor the productivity gains that a coalition of corporate executives, public officials, parents, academics, and educators have sought."

Table 8.1. **The distinction between technology-centred and learner-centred approaches to learning with technology**

Approach	Focus	Role of technology	Goal
Technology-centred	What technology can do	Provide access to instruction	Use technology for teaching
Learner-centred	How the human mind works	Aid human learning	Adapt technology to promote learning

Writing in 1990, Saettler's (1990/2004) vision of the cutting-edge educational technologies of the future included instructional television, computer-assisted instruction, interactive multimedia systems and intelligent tutoring systems, but he noted that none had yet produced a major breakthrough in improving education. What is wrong with the technology-centred approach? The answer is that it fails to take the learner into account, and assumes that learners and teachers will adapt to the requirements of the new technology rather than the new technology adapt to the needs of learners and teachers (Norman, 1993).

In contrast, in taking a learner-centred approach, we begin with a focus on how people learn and view technology as an aid to human learning. It follows that technology should be adapted to fit the needs of learners and teachers – an approach that often is lacking when we solely seek to provide access to new technologies for learners. As we explore ways to incorporate computer and information technology in 21st century education, it is worthwhile to consider Saettler's (1990/2004, p. 538) observation: "The most frequent failing of technological futurists is to predict the future with little or no reference to the past." In short, most of yesterday's optimistic predictions about the impact of educational technology have failed to materialise. Given this disappointing history, I take a learner-centred approach to learning with technology.

Science of learning: how people learn with technology

In order to use technology effectively in education, it is worthwhile to ground educational practice with an understanding of how people learn. In this section, I explore what the science of learning contributes to understanding how learning with technology works.

What is the science of learning?

The science of learning is the scientific study of how people learn. Much educational practice involving learning with technology is based on the opinions of experts or on what is considered to be best practice. Rather than basing a theory of learning on opinions or fads, the science of learning is based on research evidence.

What is learning?

Learning is a long-lasting change in the learner's knowledge attributable to the learner's experience. This definition has three parts: (a) learning is a long-lasting change in a learner, (b) what is changed is the learner's knowledge, and (c) the cause of the change is something that the learner experiences.

Knowledge is at the centre of learning. Cognitive and educational scientists (Anderson *et al.*, 2001; Mayer, 2008) have identified five kinds of knowledge required for proficiency in most educational domains:

- *Facts:* statements about the characteristics or states of things, such as "the earth is the third planet from the sun".

- *Concepts:* categories, models, schemas, or principles, such as "in the number 23, the 2 represents the number of tens".

- *Procedures:* step-by-step processes that generate output, such as knowing the procedure for 22 x 115 = ___.

- *Strategies:* general methods, such as "break a problem into smaller parts".

- *Beliefs:* cognitions about one's learning, such as "I am not good in statistics".

Perhaps the single most important individual differences dimension concerns the prior knowledge of the learner: Kalyuga (2005) has shown that effective instructional methods for low-knowledge learners may be ineffective or even detrimental for high-knowledge learners.

What is learning with technology?

Learning with technology involves learning situations in which the instructional experience is created with the aid of a physical device, such as a computer or the Internet. At some level almost all learning involves technology. For example, in a traditional lecture, an instructor may use chalk and a chalkboard, thereby employing an old but reliable technology. Similarly, a textbook constitutes a form of technology albeit one with a 500-year old history. In this chapter, I focus mainly on learning with computer-based technology. An important feature of computer-based technology, and possible advantage if used appropriately, is that it allows for the presentation of multimedia instructional messages (Mayer, 2001, 2009) – that is, instructional messages consisting of words (such as spoken or printed words) and pictures (such as animation, video, illustrations, or photos). Computer-based technology also allows for levels of interactivity, computational power, graphic rendering and information retrieval that may not otherwise be feasible.

How does learning work?

During the past 100 years, psychologists and educators have developed three visions of how learning works, which I refer to as three "metaphors of learning" (Mayer, 2001, 2009; see also de Corte, this volume). As shown in the top portion of Table 8.2, the *response-strengthening* view, which developed in the first half of the 20th century, is based on the idea that learning involves the strengthening and weakening of associations. When a response is rewarded, its association with the situation is strengthened and when a response is punished that association is weakened. Technology can be used to solicit responses from a learner and to administer subsequent reward or punishment, such as in drill-and-practice teaching machines. For example, "2 + 5 = ___" appears on the screen, the learner enters "7" as a response, and clapping hands appear on the screen as a reward.

Table 8.2. **Three metaphors of how learning works**

Metaphor	Learner	Teacher	Role of technology
Response-strengthening	Passive recipient of rewards and punishments	Dispenser of rewards and punishments	Solicit response, provide feedback
Information acquisition	Passive recipient of information	Dispenser of information	Provide access to information
Knowledge construction	Active sense maker and knowledge builder	Cognitive guide	Guide learner's cognitive processing during learning

As shown in the middle portion of Table 8.2, the *information acquisition* view, which developed in the mid-20th century, is based on the idea that learning involves adding information to the learner's memory. When a teacher presents information, the learner stores the information in memory. The corresponding role of technology is to deliver information to the learner, such as with a multimedia encyclopaedia or a Power Point presentation.

As shown in the bottom row of Table 8.2, the *knowledge construction* view, which became popular in the later decades of the 20th century, is based on the idea that learning occurs when the learner builds a cognitive representation of the presented material based on his or her learning experience. The learner is a sense-maker who tries to make sense of the presented material while the teacher is a cognitive guide who helps guide the learner's cognitive processing during learning. The role of technology in this case is not only to present information but also to help guide the learner's cognitive processing during learning.

Although all three views of learning have had strong impacts on the development of educational technology, I focus on the knowledge construction view in this chapter because I am most interested in promoting meaningful learning. In the cognitive revolution, as Saettler notes in his comprehensive history of educational technology: "the learner becomes an active participant in the process of acquiring and using knowledge" (1990/2004,

p. 15). The concept of active learning has important implications for learning with technology, as described in the following sections.

How does learning with technology work?

In developing a theory of how people learn with technology, I focus on three important principles from research in cognitive science:

- **Dual channels**: people have separate channels for processing verbal and visual material (Paivio, 1986, 2007).

- **Limited capacity**: people can process only small amounts of material in each channel at any one time (Baddeley, 1999; Sweller, 1999).

- **Active processing**: meaningful learning occurs when learners engage in appropriate cognitive processing during learning, such as attending to relevant material, organising it into a coherent representation, and integrating it with relevant prior knowledge (Mayer, 2008; Wittrock, 1989).

These three principles are consistent with the cognitive theory of multimedia learning shown in Figure 8.1 (Mayer, 2001, 2009). This is an information-processing model relevant to learning with technology. The information-processing system in Figure 8.1 consists of three kinds of memory stores:

- **Sensory memory**: holds all incoming visual information in visual form for a short time (in "visual sensory memory") and all incoming sounds in auditory form for a short time ("auditory sensory memory").

- **Working memory**: holds a limited number of selected words and images for further processing.

- **Long-term memory**: unlimited storehouse of knowledge.

As shown on the left side of Figure 8.1, pictorial material and printed words enter the learner's cognitive system through the eyes and are held briefly in visual sensory memory whereas spoken words enter the learner's cognitive system through his or her ears and are held briefly in auditory sensory memory. If the learner attends to the incoming visual material some can be transferred to working memory for further processing as indicated by the *selecting images* arrow, and if the learner attends to the incoming auditory material some can be transferred to working memory for further processing as represented by the *selecting words* arrow. Visually-presented words can be converted and moved to the verbal channel in working memory, hence the arrow "from image to sound" in working memory in Figure 8.1. The *organising images* arrow represents how learners can construct a pictorial model by mentally organising the images into a coherent representation and similarly, as indicated by the *organising words* arrow, learners can construct a verbal model by mentally organising the words into a coherent representation. Finally, learners can make connections between the verbal and

Figure 8.1. **Cognitive theory of multimedia learning**

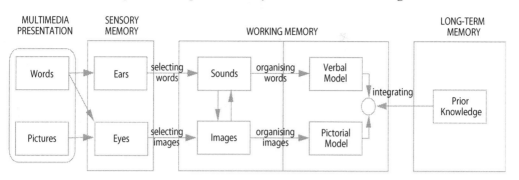

Table 8.3. **Cognitive processes required for active learning with technology**

Process	Description	Location
Selecting	Paying attention to relevant words and pictures	Transfer information from sensory memory to working memory
Organizing	Organizing selected words and pictures into coherent mental representations	Manipulate information in working memory
Integrating	Connecting verbal and pictorial representations with each other and with prior knowledge	Transfer knowledge from long term memory to working memory

pictorial models and with relevant knowledge from long-term memory, as shown by the *integrating* arrows. Table 8.3 summarises the three kinds of active cognitive processing required for meaningful learning using multimedia technology – **selecting, organising** and **integrating**.

Science of instruction: how to help people learn with technology

In this section, I explore what the science of instruction contributes to understanding how to help people learn with technology.

What is the science of instruction?

The science of instruction is the scientific study of how to cause cognitive changes in learners. A central goal of instructional science is the development of evidence-based principles for how to design instruction that is effective for particular kinds of learners and particular kinds of instructional objectives. Consistent with the science of instruction, evidence-based practice refers to instructional practices that are grounded in empirical research.

What is instruction?

"Instruction" is the manipulation of the learner's environment by the instructor(s) in order to foster learning. It thus involves: (1) manipulating what the learner experiences, and (2) intention to cause learning. An "instructional method" refers to a technique that is intended to foster learning – such as modelling how to solve example problems ("worked example method") or asking students to solve problems on their own ("discovery method"). An instructional objective is a statement that specifies the cognitive change intended for the learner, such as being able to add and subtract single-digit signed numbers. In short, an instructional objective describes what we want the learner to know.

The effectiveness of instruction is generally measured by retention tests – in which the learner should recall or recognise what was presented – and by transfer tests – in which the learner is asked to solve problems that involve using the information in new ways. Table 8.4 lists three kinds of learning outcomes: no learning, which is reflected in poor retention and poor transfer performance; rote learning, characterised by good retention but poor transfer performance; and meaningful learning, in which both retention and transfer performance are good. My interest in this chapter is on promoting meaningful learning so I focus on transfer tests.

Table 8.4. **Three kinds of learning outcomes**

Learning outcome	Cognitive description	Retention test score	Transfer test score
No learning	No knowledge	Poor	Poor
Rote learning	Fragmented knowledge	Good	Poor
Meaningful learning	Integrated knowledge	Good	Good

What is instruction with technology?

Instruction with technology involves using technology – such as computer and information technology – to support instruction. It covers both instructional media – the physical devices used to deliver the instruction – and instructional methods – the way that the material is presented to the learner. As shown in Table 8.5, media research focuses on which instructional medium is best for accomplishing a particular objective for a particular kind of learner, such as, "Are computers more effective than textbooks for teaching arithmetic to beginners?" In contrast, research on instructional methods focuses on how best to present material to learners (Mayer, 2008).

Although there is a long history of media research (Saettler, 1990/2004), media scholars have come to the conclusion that further media research is not productive (Clark, 2001). The main problem for media research is that learning is caused by the instructional method rather than the instructional medium. It is possible to design ineffective or effective approaches using either books or computers. For example, Moreno and Mayer (2002) have shown that the same instructional methods are effective across different instructional media, such as a desktop simulation or an immersive virtual reality simulation. To focus on instructional media becomes important when a certain medium affords an instructional method that might not be feasible using a different medium. In short, although instructional media may be the most salient aspect of learning with technology, **it is the instructional method that causes learning**.

Table 8.5. **The distinction between media and method in learning with technology**

Type of research	Research focus	Research question	Example
Media research	Focus on physical devices	Which instructional medium is most effective?	Are computers more effective than books?
Method research	Focus on instructional methods	Which instructional method is most effective?	Is discovery more effective than direct instruction?

How does instruction with technology work?

Table 8.6 summarises three demands on the learner's cognitive capacity during learning: *extraneous processing*, *essential processing* and *generative processing*. Extraneous processing – which Sweller (1999) refers to as "extraneous cognitive load" – is cognitive processing during learning which does not support the instructional objective and is caused by poor layout or extraneous material in the lesson. For example, when text is on one page but the corresponding graphic is on another page, the need to scan back and forth creates extraneous processing. Thus, the first goal of instructional design with technology is to **reduce extraneous processing by keeping the learning setting as simple as possible**.

Essential processing (which Sweller, 1999, refers to as "intrinsic cognitive load") is cognitive processing during learning aimed at mentally representing the essential material and is caused by the inherent complexity of the material. Thus, the second goal of instructional design with technology is **to manage essential processing**.

Generative processing (which Sweller, 1999, calls "germane cognitive load") is cognitive processing aimed at mentally organising the material and integrating it with other relevant knowledge. For example, a fast-paced narrated animation on how lightning storms develop consists of many inter-related events that may overload the learner's cognitive system. Even when the learner has sufficient cognitive capacity, she or he may not exert effort to make sense of this material, perhaps being simply not interested. Thus, the third goal of instructional design with technology is **to foster generative processing**.

The central challenge of instruction with technology is to support the learner's active cognitive processing during learning (essential and generative processing) without overloading the learner's cognitive capacity.

To sum up, with this model of cognitive load, we can derive three main goals of instruction with technology: a) reduce extraneous processing, b) manage essential processing, and c) foster generative processing.

Table 8.6. **How does instruction with technology work?**

Three demands on the learner's cognitive capacity during instruction

Type of processing	Description	Learning processes
Extraneous	Cognitive processing that does not support the objective of the lesson; caused by poor instructional design	None
Essential	Basic cognitive processing is required to represent mentally the presented material; caused by the inherent complexity of the material	Selecting
Generative	Deep cognitive processing required to make sense of the presented material; caused by learner's motivation to make an effort to learn	Organising and integrating

Principles of instructional design for learning with technology

Consider what happens when someone learns from an on online narrated animation, a multimedia presentation, or an instructional computer game. This section summarises twelve research-based principles for designing instruction in learning environments such as these. Each principle is based on a set of experimental comparisons (Mayer, 2009) in which one group of learners received a lesson that was based on the design principle (treatment group) and another group received an identical lesson except that it was not based on the design principle (control group). We computed an effect size (d) by subtracting the mean transfer test score of the control group from the mean transfer score of the treatment group, and dividing the difference by the pooled standard deviation. Following Cohen (1988), an effect size of +0.8 is large, +0.5 is medium, and +0.2 or less is small, so I am particularly interested in design principles that generate large effect sizes (*i.e.* effect sizes equal to or greater than 0.8).

Techniques to reduce extraneous processing

A major obstacle to learning with technology occurs when the amount of cognitive processing required for learning exceeds the learner's cognitive capacity. In particular, when the instructional message is poorly designed or contains extraneous material, the learner has to engage in extraneous processing, which may leave insufficient cognitive capacity for the essential and generative processing really needed for learning. For example, a lesson on how digestion works may include some anecdotes about sword swallowing or medical devices that must be swallowed – which constitute interesting but extraneous material. Table 8.7 lists five techniques for reducing extraneous processing: the "coherence principle", the "signalling principle", the "redundancy principle", the "spatial contiguity principle", and the "temporal contiguity principle".

The "coherence principle" is illustrated by comparing learning from a lesson that contains extraneous material – such as interesting anecdotes, attention-grabbing photos, background music, or computational details – versus from a lesson that contains only the essential words and pictures. As can be seen in the first line of Table 8.7, in 13 out of 14 experimental comparisons involving lessons on lightning, brakes and ocean waves, students

Table 8.7. **Five evidence-based and theoretically-grounded principles for reducing extraneous processing**

Principle	Definition	Effect size	Number of tests
Coherence	Reduce extraneous material.	0.97	13 of 14
Signalling	Highlight essential material.	0.52	6 of 6
Redundancy	Do not add on-screen text to narrated animation.	0.72	5 of 5
Spatial contiguity	Place printed words next to corresponding graphics.	1.12	5 of 5
Temporal contiguity	Present corresponding narration and animation at the same time.	1.31	8 of 8

performed better on transfer tests when extraneous material was removed from the lesson, yielding a large median effect size. When extraneous material cannot be deleted from a lesson, an alternative – using the "signalling principle" – is to highlight the essential material such as by using outlines, headings and bold font. As can be seen in the second line of Table 8.7, in six out of six experimental comparisons involving airplane lift, lightning and biology, students performed better on transfer tests when essential material was highlighted (signalled) rather than not signalled, yielding a medium effect size.

The remaining lines in Table 8.7 show that students performed better on transfer tests when they received animation and narration rather than animation, narration, but also on-screen text that duplicates the existing information ("redundancy principle"); when explanatory text was printed next to the corresponding part of the graphic rather than as a caption or on another page ("spatial contiguity principle"); and when corresponding narration and animation were presented simultaneously rather than separated in time ("temporal contiguity principle").

In short, an important instructional goal is to reduce the need to engage in extraneous processing during learning, thereby allowing the learner to use his or her cognitive capacity for essential and generative processing needed for meaningful learning.

Techniques that manage essential processing

Even if we could eliminate extraneous processing, another potential obstacle to learning with technology occurs when the amount of cognitive processing required for essential processing exceeds the learner's cognitive capacity. This situation ("essential overload") can occur when the to-be-learned material is complex and the learner lacks sufficient prior knowledge to organise it. In this case, as the material is essential it cannot be eliminated as with the extraneous examples, but rather the learner needs guidance in how to manage the essential processing that is required for mentally representing this complex material. Table 8.8 lists three techniques for managing essential processing: the "segmenting principle", the "pre-training principle" and the "modality principle".

The "segmenting principle" can be understood by comparing learning from a lesson that contains a narrated animation as a single continuous presentation (the control group) with one where it is broken down into segments that are presented under learned control (segmented group), as shown in the top row of Table 8.8. In 3 out of 3 experimental comparisons involving lessons on lightning and electric motors, students performed better on transfer tests when narrated animations were segmented, with a large effect size.

Table 8.8. **Three evidence-based and theoretically-grounded principles for managing essential processing**

Principle	Definition	Effect size	Number of tests
Segmenting	Present animation in learner-paced segments	0.98	3 of 3
Pre-training	Provide pre-training in the name, location and characteristics of key components	0.85	5 of 5
Modality	Present words as spoken text rather than printed text	1.02	17 of 17

When essential material cannot be segmented in a lesson, an alternative is to provide the learner with pre-training in the names and characteristics of the main concepts or components in the lesson – which I call the "pre-training principle". As reported in the second line of the table, in five out of five experimental comparisons involving brakes, pumps and geology, pre-trained students performed better on transfer tests than did non-pre-trained students, also yielding a large effect size.

Finally, the visual channel can become overloaded with essential processing when a fast-paced animation is presented along with concurrent on-screen captions. The "modality principle" calls for presenting words as narration so some essential processing is off-loaded from the visual channel onto the verbal channel (the third line of Table 8.8). In 17 out of 17 experimental comparisons involving lightning, brakes, pumps, electrical motors, biology, ecology and aircraft, students performed better on transfer tests when they learned from animation with narration rather than having to read on-screen text at the same time as following the animation and on-screen text. This also yielded a large effect size. In short, an important instructional goal is to guide the learner's processing of essential processing in ways that minimise demands on cognitive capacity.

Techniques for fostering generative processing

The foregoing techniques are intended to ensure that the cognitive processing required for meaningful learning does not overload the learner's cognitive capacity. However, even when cognitive capacity is available, learners may not be motivated to exert the effort to engage in the "generative processing" necessary for deep learning. Thus, a third challenge of instructional designers is to encourage learners to engage in generative processing. Table 8.9 lists two techniques intended to foster generative processing: the "multimedia principle" and the "personalisation principle". The "multimedia principle" is based on the idea that people learn more deeply when they are encouraged to build connections between words and pictures (such as corresponding animation and narration).

As shown in the first line of Table 8.9, in 11 out of 11 experimental comparisons, students performed better on transfer tests when they received both words and pictures than when they received words alone, yielding a large effect size.

Table 8.9. **Two evidence-based and theoretically-grounded principles for fostering generative processing**

Principle	Definition	Effect size	Number of tests
Multimedia	Present words and pictures rather than words alone.	1.39	11 of 11
Personalisation	Present words in conversational style rather than formal style.	1.11	11 of 11

The "personalisation principle" is based on the idea that people try harder to make sense out of instructional messages when they feel a social companionship with the speaker, such as when the speaker adopts a conversational style including use of "I" and "you." As reported in the second line of Table 8.9, in 11 out of 11 experimental comparisons involving lightning, botany, lungs and engineering, students performed better on transfer tests when the speaker used a conversational style rather than a more formal style; this also yielded a large effect size. Other techniques offer potential for motivating learners to process the presented material more deeply – for example, instructional games (O'Neil and Perez, 2008) and animated pedagogical agents (Moreno, 2005) – but more research is needed on how to promote deep processing in learners.

Other issues which have received some research attention concern the role of animation (Lowe and Schnotz, 2008), interactivity (Betracourt, 2005), collaboration (Jonassen, Lee, Yang and Laffey, 2005), worked-out examples (Renkl, 2005), discovery (de Jong, 2005) and motivation (Moreno and Mayer, 2007).

Summary

Learning with technology includes learning from an online encyclopaedia, a multimedia presentation, or a computer game. Common topics include computer-based instruction, multimedia, interactive simulation, hypermedia, intelligent tutoring systems, inquiry-based information retrieval, games, computer-supported collaborative learning, animated pedagogical agents, virtual reality, and e-courses. Technology-centred approaches focus on providing access to technology in education, whereas learner-centred approaches adapt technology to serve as a cognitive tool for learners.

How do students learn? Meaningful learning occurs when learners engage in appropriate cognitive processing during learning – including selecting relevant information from the presented material, organising the incoming information into a coherent mental representation, and integrating the incoming information with existing knowledge. This processing takes place in the learner's working memory, which is limited in capacity and has separate channels for processing verbal and pictorial information. Learning is a long-lasting change in a person's knowledge attributable to experience.

How can we help students learn with technology? Effective instruction with technology seeks to help the learner engage in appropriate cognitive processing during learning without overloading her or his cognitive system. This overarching goal can be achieved by reducing extraneous processing, managing essential processing and fostering generative processing. Instruction is the manipulation of the learner's environment in order to promote learning. Learning with technology is caused by instructional methods not by instructional media.

Effective instructional techniques for reducing extraneous processing accord with one or another of a set of alternative principles: these include principles relating to coherence, signalling, redundancy, spatial contiguity and temporal contiguity. Effective instructional techniques for managing essential processing include the "segmenting", "pre-training" and "modality" principles. Effective instructional techniques for fostering generative processing include the "multimedia" and "personalisation" principles.

References

Anderson, L. and D. Krathwohl (2001), *A Taxonomy of Learning for Teaching: A Revision of Bloom's Taxonomy of Educational Objectives*, Longman, New York.

Baddeley, A. (1999), *Human Memory*, Allyn and Bacon, Boston.

Betracourt, M. (2005), "The Animation and Interactivity Principles in Multimedia Learning", in R.E. Mayer (ed.), *The Cambridge Handbook of Multimedia Learning*, Cambridge University Press, New York, pp. 287-296.

Clark, R.C. and A. Kwinn (2007), *The New Virtual Classroom*, Pfeiffer, San Francisco.

Clark, R.C. and R.E. Mayer (2008), *E-Learning and the Science of Instruction: Second Edition*, Pfeiffer, San Francisco.

Clark, R.E. (2001), *Learning from Media*, Information Age Publishing, Greenwich, CT.

Cohen, J. (1988), *Statistical Power Analysis for the Behavioral Sciences*, Erlbaum, Hillsdale, NJ.

Cuban, L. (1986), *Teachers and Machines: The Classroom Use of Technology Since 1920*, Teachers College Press, New York.

Cuban, L. (2001), *Oversold and Underused: Computers in the Classroom*, Harvard University Press, Cambridge, MA.

De Jong, T. (2005), "The Guided Discovery Principle in Multimedia Learning", in R.E. Mayer (ed.), The Cambridge Handbook of Multimedia Learning, Cambridge University Press, New York, pp. 215-228.

Graesser, A.C., P. Chipman and B.G. King (2008), "Computer-Mediated Technologies", in J.M. Spector, *et al.* (eds.), Handbook of Research on Educational Communications and Technology (3rd Edition), Erlbaum, New York, pp. 211-224.

Graesser, A.C. and B. King (2008), "Technology-Based Training", in J.J. Blascovich and C.R. Hartel (eds.), Human Behavior in Military Contexts (pp. 127-149), National Academies Press, Washington, DC.

Jonassen, D.H., C.B. Lee, C.C. Yang and J. Laffey (2005), "The Collaboration Principle in Multimedia Learning", in R.E. Mayer (ed.), The Cambridge Handbook of Multimedia Learning, Cambridge University Press, New York, pp. 247-270.

Kalyuga, S. (2005), "The Prior Knowledge Principle in Multimedia Learning", in R.E. Mayer (ed.), The Cambridge Handbook of Multimedia Learning, Cambridge University Press, New York, pp. 325-228.

Lowe, R. and W. Schnotz (eds.) (2008), *Learning with Animation: Research Implications for Design*, Cambridge University Press, New York.

Lowyck, J. (2008), "Foreword", in J.M. Spector, *et al.* (eds.), Handbook of Research on Educational Communications and Technology (3rd Edition), Erlbaum, New York, pp. xiii-xv.

Mayer, R.E. (2001), *Multimedia Learning*, Cambridge University Press, New York.

Mayer, R.E. (ed.) (2005), *The Cambridge Handbook of Multimedia Learning*, Cambridge University Press, New York.

Mayer, R.E. (2008), *Learning and Instruction: Second Edition*, Merrill Pearson Prentice Hall, Upper Saddle River, NJ.

Mayer, R.E. (2009), *Multimedia Learning: Second Edition*, Cambridge University Press, New York.

Moreno, R. (2005), "Multimedia Learning with Animated Pedagogical Agents", in R.E. Mayer (ed.), *The Cambridge Handbook of Multimedia Learning*, Cambridge University Press, New York, pp. 507-524.

Moreno, R.E. and R.E. Mayer (2002), "Learning Science in Virtual Reality Environments: Role of Methods and Media", *Journal of Educational Psychology*, Vol. 94, No. 3, pp. 598-610.

Moreno, R. and R.E. Mayer (2007), "Interactive Multimodal Learning Environments", *Educational Psychology Review*, Vol. 19, No. 3, pp. 309-326.

Norman, D.A. (1993), *Things that Make us Smart*, Addison-Wesley, Reading, MA.

O'Neil, H.F. (ed.) (2005), *What Works in Distance Education: Guidelines*, Information Age Publishing, Greenwich, CT.

O'Neil, H.F and R.S. Perez (eds.) (2003), *Technology Applications in Education: A Learning View*, Erlbaum, Mahwah, NJ.

O'Neil, H.F. and R.S. Perez (eds.) (2006), Web-Based Learning: Theory, Research, and Practice, Erlbaum, Mahwah, NJ.

O'Neil, H.F.and R.S. Perez (eds.) (2008), *Computer Games and Team and Individual Learning*, Elsevier, Amsterdam.

Paivio, A. (1986), *Mental Representations: A Dual Coding Approach*, Oxford University Press, Oxford, UK.

Paivio, A. (2007), *Mind and Its Evolution*, Erlbaum, Mahwah, NJ.

Pytllik Zillig, L.M., M. Bodvarsson and R. Bruning (eds.) (2005), *Technology-Based Education*, Information Age Publishing, Greenwich, CT.

Reiser, R.A. and J.V. Dempsey (eds.) (2007), *Trends and Issues in Instructional Design and Technology*, Pearson Merrill Prentice Hall, Upper Saddle River, NJ.

Renkl, A. (2005), "The Worked-Out Example Principle in Multimedia Learning", in R.E. Mayer (ed.), The Cambridge Handbook of Multimedia Learning, Cambridge University Press, New York, pp. 229-246.

Rouet, J-F., J.J. Levonen and A. Biardeau (eds.) (2001), *Multimedia Learning: Cognitive and Instructional Issues*, Pergamon, Oxford, UK.

Saettler, P. (2004), *The Evolution of American Educational Technology*, Information Age Publishing, Greenwich, CT. [Originally published in 1990.]

Spector J.M., M.D. Merrill, J. Van Merrienboer and M.P. Driscoll (eds.) (2008), *Handbook of Research on Educational Communications and Technology (3rd Edition)*, Erlbaum, New York.

Sweller, J. (1999), *Instructional Design in Technical Areas*, ACER Press Camberwell, Australia.

Wittrock, M.C. (1989), "Generative Processes of Comprehension", *Educational Psychologist*, Vol. 24, No. 4, pp. 345-376.

Chapter 9

Prospects and challenges for inquiry-based approaches to learning

Brigid Barron and Linda Darling-Hammond
Stanford University School of Education

Brigid Barron and Linda Darling-Hammond summarise three, often overlapping, families of inquiry-based learning: "project-based", "problem-based" and "learning through design". A first key conclusion of their review of research evidence is that students learn more deeply when they can apply classroom-gathered knowledge to real-world problems; inquiry-based approaches are important ways to nurture communication, collaboration, creativity and deep thinking. Second, inquiry-based learning depends on the application of well-designed assessments, both to define the learning tasks and to evaluate what has been learned. Third, however, the success of inquiry approaches tends to be highly dependent on the knowledge and skills of those implementing them. If these approaches are poorly understood and mistaken for being unstructured, their benefits are substantially reduced compared with when they are implemented by those appreciating the need for extensive scaffolding and constant assessment to inform their direction.

The need for inquiry-based learning to support 21st century skills

Enthusiasm for educational approaches that connect knowledge to its applications has been on the upswing since the 1980s. Recommendations from a wide array of organisations have emphasised the need to support 21st century skills through learning that supports inquiry, application, production and problem-solving. Nearly two decades ago, the SCANS Report (Secretary's Commission on Achieving Necessary Skills, 1991) suggested that for today's students to be prepared for tomorrow's workplace they need learning environments that allow them to explore real-life situations and consequential problems. These arguments have been echoed in scholarly research (*e.g.* Levy and Murnane, 2004), national commission reports (*e.g.* NCTM, 1989; NRC, 1996) and policy proposals (*e.g.* NCREL, 2003; Partnership for 21st Century Skills, 2004), urging instructional reforms to help students gain vital media literacies, critical thinking skills, systems thinking, and interpersonal and self-directional skills that allow them to manage projects and competently find resources and use tools.

In order for these capacities to be nurtured, the reports argue, students must be given opportunities to develop them in the context of complex, meaningful projects that require sustained engagement, collaboration, research, management of resources, and development of an ambitious performance or product. The rationale for these recommendations has come in part from research demonstrating that students do not routinely develop the ability to analyse, think critically, write and speak effectively, or solve complex problems from working on more constrained tasks that emphasise memorisation and call only for responses that demonstrate recall or the application of simple algorithms. In addition, there is a growing body of research indicating that students learn more deeply and perform better on complex tasks when they have had the opportunity to engage in more "authentic" learning.

A set of studies has found positive effects on student learning of instruction, curriculum and assessment practices that requires students to construct and organise knowledge, consider alternatives, apply disciplinary processes to content central to the discipline (*e.g.* use of scientific inquiry, historical research, literary analysis, or the writing process) and communicate effectively to audiences beyond the classroom and school (Newmann, 1996). For example, a study of more than 2 100 students in 23 restructured schools found significantly higher achievement on intellectually challenging performance tasks for students who experienced this kind of "authentic pedagogy" (Newmann, Marks and Gamoran, 1996). The use of these practices predicted student performance more strongly than any other variable, including student background factors and prior achievement.

While this kind of research is promising, the chequered history of efforts to implement "learning by doing" makes clear the need for greater knowledge about how successfully to manage problem- and project-based approaches in the classroom (Barron, *et al.*, 1998). The teaching suggested by these descriptions is not straightforward and requires knowledge of the characteristics of successful strategies and highly skilled teachers to implement them. In this chapter, we focus on both the design and implementation of inquiry-based curriculum that engages children in extended constructive work, often in collaborative groups, and subsequently demands a good deal of self-regulated inquiry. The research we review spans the K-12 years, college and graduate education and can be found across core disciplines and in interdisciplinary programmes of study. Research on the implementation and efficacy of these approaches for learning is yielding two major conclusions:

1. Small group inquiry approaches can be extremely powerful for learning. To be effective, they need to be guided by thoughtful curriculum with clearly defined learning goals, well designed scaffolds, ongoing assessment and rich informational resources. Opportunities for professional development that include a focus on assessing student work increase the likelihood that teachers will develop expertise in implementing these approaches.

2. Assessment design is a critical issue for **revealing the benefits** of inquiry approaches for group efforts and individual learning as well as for promoting the success of learning. Specifically, if one only looks at traditional learning outcomes, inquiry-based and traditional methods of instruction appear to yield similar results. Benefits for inquiry learning are found when the assessments require application of knowledge and measure quality of reasoning. Consequently, we also take up a discussion of "performance assessment" and its role in both supporting and evaluating meaningful learning.

An historical perspective on inquiry-based learning

The family of approaches that can be described as "inquiry-based" includes project-based learning, design-based learning and problem-based learning. Projects, proposed as a means for making schooling more useful and readily applied to the world, first became popular in the early part of the century in the United States. The term "project" represented a broad class of learning experiences. For example, in early works one sees the label applied to activities as diverse as making a dress, watching a spider spin a web, or writing a letter. The key idea behind such projects was that learning was strengthened when "whole heartedness of purpose was present" (Kilpatrick, 1918).

Enthusiasm and belief in the efficacy of such approaches for school-aged children has waxed and waned, as project-based learning has been rejected as too unstructured during several eras of "back to the basics" backlash, or as policymakers have assumed that applied projects are only needed for vocational training. Critics of the progressive movement argued that discovery learning approaches led to "doing for the sake of doing" rather than doing for the sake of learning. There is a growing consensus that authentic problems and projects afford unique opportunities for learning but that authenticity in and of itself does not guarantee learning (Barron, *et al.*, 1998; Thomas, 2000).

It is critical how these complex approaches are implemented. For example, in the curricular reforms of the post-Sputnik years, initiatives using inquiry-based approaches (typically called "discovery learning" or project learning) were found in a number of studies to produce comparable achievement on basic skills tests while contributing more to students' problem-solving abilities, curiosity, creativity, independence and positive feelings about school (Horwitz, 1979; Peterson, 1979; McKeachie and Kulik, 1975; Soar, 1977; Dunkin and Biddle, 1974; Glass *et al.*, 1977; Good and Brophy, 1986; Resnick, 1987). This kind of meaning-oriented teaching – once thought to be appropriate only for selected high-achieving students – proved to be more effective than rote teaching for students across a wide spectrum of initial achievement levels, family income, and cultural and linguistic backgrounds (Garcia, 1993; Knapp, 1995; Braddock and McPartland, 1993).

However, new curriculum initiatives focused on inquiry using complex instructional strategies were found more often to promote significant increases in learning gains among students taught by the early adopters – teachers who were extensively involved in design and piloting of the curriculum and who were given strong professional development. These effects were not always sustained as curriculum reforms were "scaled up" and used by teachers who did not have the same degree of understanding or skill in implementation.

At the present time, there is still controversy over whether open-ended approaches are effective and efficient for developing students' basic knowledge of a domain. And implementation issues continue to be a concern of both practitioners and researchers. Classroom research indicates that well-designed, carefully thought-out materials and connected classroom practices are needed to capitalise on inquiry-based approaches. Without careful planning, students may miss opportunities to connect their project work with key concepts underlying a discipline (Petrosino, 1998).

In recent years, the research base on inquiry approaches has grown to include both comparative studies and more descriptive classroom investigations of teaching and learning processes. There is a growing consensus on the importance of a number of design principles that characterise successful inquiry-based learning environments and that can be used by teachers as they embark on developing or enacting new curricula.

Research evaluations of inquiry-based learning

We summarise below the relevant research base on the different approaches to inquiry-based learning.

Project-based learning

Project-based learning (PBL) involves the completion of complex tasks that typically result in a realistic product, event, or presentation to an audience. Thomas (2000) defines productive project-based learning as 1) central to the curriculum, 2) organised around driving questions that lead students to encounters central concepts or principles of a discipline, 3) focused on a constructive investigation that involves inquiry and knowledge building, 4) student-driven, in that students are responsible for making choices and for designing and managing their work, and 5) authentic, by posing problems that occur in the real world and that people care about.

Generally, research on the benefits of project-based learning concludes that students who engage in this approach experience gains in factual learning that are equivalent or superior to those who engage in traditional forms of instruction (Thomas, 2000). The goals of PBL are broader, however. The approach aims to enable students to transfer their learning more powerfully to new kinds of situations and problems and to use knowledge more proficiently in performance situations.

There is a number of studies demonstrating these kinds of outcomes in both short- and long-term learning situations. As noted, however, the goals of PBL are broader than simply the development of content knowledge. This approach aims to take learning one step further by enabling students to **transfer** their learning to new kinds of situations and problems and to use knowledge more proficiently in performance situations. Some examples help to illustrate this point.

Shepherd (1998) studied the results of a unit in which a group of fourth and fifth graders completed a nine-week project to define and find solutions related to housing shortages in several countries. In comparison to the control group, the students engaged in project-based learning demonstrated a significant increase in scores on a critical-thinking test, as well as increased confidence in their learning.

A more ambitious, longitudinal comparative study by Boaler (1997, 1998) followed students over three years in two British schools that were comparable with respect to students' prior achievement and socio-economic status, but that used either a traditional curriculum or a project-based curriculum. The traditional school featured teacher-directed whole class instruction organised around texts, workbooks and frequent tests in tracked classrooms. Instruction in the other school used open-ended projects in heterogeneous classrooms. Using a pre- and post-test design, the study found that although students had comparable learning gains when tested on basic mathematics procedures, those who had participated in the project-based curriculum did better on conceptual problems presented in the national examination. Significantly more students in the project-based school passed the exam in year three of the study than those in the traditional school. Boaler noted that, although students in the traditional school "thought that mathematical success rested on being able to remember and use rules," the PBL students had developed a more flexible, useful kind of mathematical knowledge that engaged them in "exploration and thought" (Boaler, 1997, p. 63).

A third study, designed to assess the impact of the development of multimedia projects on student learning, showed similar gains. In this example, researchers created a performance task in which students participating in the Challenge 2000 Multimedia Project and a comparison group developed a brochure informing school officials about problems faced by homeless students (Penuel, Means and Simkins, 2000). The students in the multimedia programme earned higher scores than the comparison group on content mastery, sensitivity to audience and coherent design. They performed equally well on standardised test scores of basic skills.

Many other studies have recorded student and teacher reports of positive changes in motivation, attitudes toward learning and skills as a result of participating in PBL, including work habits, critical thinking skills and problem-solving abilities (*e.g.* Bartscher, Gould and Nutter, 1995; Peck, Peck, Sentz and Zasa, 1998). Some have found that some students who do less well in traditional instructional settings excel when they have the opportunity to work in a PBL context which better matches their learning style or preference for collaboration and activity type (*e.g.* Boaler, 1997; Rosenfeld and Rosenfeld, 1998). One interesting study observed four PBL classrooms in the fall and spring of a school year, finding much larger increases in five critical thinking behaviours (synthesising, forecasting, producing, evaluating and reflecting) and five social participation behaviours (working together, initiating, managing, inter-group awareness and inter-group initiating) for initially low-achieving students over the course of the year than for initially high-achieving students (Horan, Lavaroni and Beldon, 1996).

Problem-based learning

Problem-based learning approaches represent a close cousin of project-based learning, and are often configured as a specific type of project that aims to teach problem definition and solution strategies. In problem-based learning, students work in small groups to investigate meaningful problems, identify what they need to learn in order to solve a problem, and generate strategies for solution (Barrows, 1996; Hmelo-Silver, 2004). The problems are realistic and ill-structured, meaning that they are not perfectly formulated textbook problems but rather are like those in the real world with multiple solutions and methods for reaching them. In addition, research that has sought to establish the characteristics of "good" problems suggests that they should resonate with students' experiences, promote argumentation, provide opportunities for feedback, and allow repeated exposure to concepts.

Much work on this approach has been associated with medical education. For example, student physicians are presented with a patient profile, including a set of symptoms and a history, and the small group's task is to generate possible diagnosis and a plan to differentiate possible causes by conducting research and pursuing diagnostic tests. The instructor typically plays a coaching role, helping to facilitate the group's progress though a set of activities that involve understanding the problem scenario, identifying relevant facts, generating hypotheses, collecting information (*e.g.* interviewing the patient, ordering tests), identifying knowledge deficiencies, learning from external resources, applying knowledge and evaluating progress. The steps in the cycle may be revisited as work progresses (*e.g.* new knowledge deficiencies may be noticed at any point and more research might be carried out). Meta-analyses of studies of medical students have found that across studies, students who are enrolled in problem-based curricula score higher on items that measure clinical problem-solving and actual ratings of clinical performance (Vernon and Blake, 1992; Albanese and Mitchell, 1993).

Similar problem- or case-based approaches have been used in business, law and teacher education to help students learn to analyse complex, multi-faceted situations and develop knowledge to guide decision-making (*e.g.* Lundeberg, Levin and Harrington, 1999; Savery and Duffy, 1995; Williams, 1992). In all problem-based approaches, students take an active role in knowledge construction. The teacher plays an active role in making thinking visible, guides group process and participation, and asks questions to solicit reflections. The goal is to model good reasoning strategies and support the students to take on these roles themselves. At the same time teachers also provide instruction in more traditional ways such as providing lectures and explanation which are crafted and timed to support inquiry.

Studies of the efficacy of problem-based learning suggest that, like other project-based approaches, it is comparable, though not always superior, to more traditional instruction in facilitating factual learning, but it is better in supporting flexible problem-solving, application of knowledge and hypothesis generation (for a meta-analysis, see Dochy *et al.*, 2003). Additional quasi-experimental studies have demonstrated more accurate hypothesis generation and more coherent explanations for students who participated in problem-based experiences (Hmelo, 1998a, 1998b; Schmidt *et al.*, 1996), greater ability to support claims with well-reasoned arguments (Stepien *et al.*, 1993), and larger gains in conceptual understanding in science (Williams, Hemstreet, Liu and Smith, 1998).

Learning through design

A third genre of instructional approaches has grown out of the idea that children learn deeply when they are asked to design and create an artefact that requires the understanding and application of knowledge. It is believed that design-based projects have several features that make them ideal for the development of technical and subject matter knowledge (Newstetter, 2000). For example, design activity supports revisions and iterative activity as projects require cycles of *defining* → *creating* → *assessing* → *redesigning*. The complexity of the work often dictates the need for collaboration and distributed expertise. Finally, a variety of valued cognitive tasks are employed such as setting constraints, generating ideas, prototyping, and planning through "storyboarding" or other representational practices. These are all critical 21st century skills.

Design-based approaches can be found in science, technology, art, engineering and architecture. Non-school based projects organised around contests such as the FIRST robotics competitions (www.usfirst.org) or the *Thinkquest* competition (www.thinkquest.org) also stress design using technological tools and collaborative project work. For example, *Thinkquest* is an international competition in which teams of students from 9- to 19-years-old come together to build websites designed for youth about an educational topic. Teams of three to six are mentored by a teacher who provides general guidance throughout the several months of the design process but leaves the specific creative and technical work to the students. Teams receive and offer feedback during a peer review of the initial submissions and then they use this information to revise their work. To date, more than 30 000 students have participated and there are currently more than 5 500 sites available in the on-line library (*www.thinkquest.org/library/*). Topics range from art, astronomy, and programming to issues like foster care or the use of humour for mental health – almost anything is fair game.

Despite the wide range of applications of learning through design, much of the research-based curriculum development and assessment has taken place in the domain of science (Harel, 1991; Kafai, 1995; Kafai and Ching, 2001; Lehrer and Romberg, 1996; Penner, Giles, Leher and Schauble, 1997). For example, a group from University of Michigan has been developing an approach called *Design-based Science* (Fortus *et al.*, 2004), and a group from TERC (2000) developed a *Science by Design* series including four high school units focused on constructing gloves, boats, greenhouses and catapults. A separate group from the Georgia Institute of Technology has been developing an approach they call *Learning by Design,*™ also used in science (Kolodner, 1997; Puntambeckar and Kolodner, 2005).

Within the relatively small body of research that uses control group designs, the research on learning reported by Kolodner and colleagues (2003) shows large consistent differences between the *Learning by Design*™

classes and their comparisons. Their measures assess groups' abilities to complete performance tasks before and after instruction. Each task has three parts: first, students design an experiment that would provide a fair test; second, they run an experiment and collect data (the design is specified by the researchers); third, they analyse the data and use it to make recommendations. The researchers also score group interaction from videotaped records on seven dimensions: negotiation during collaboration; distribution of the work; attempted use of prior knowledge; adequacy of prior knowledge; science talk; science practice; and self-monitoring. They report that the Learning by Design students consistently outperform non-LBD students on collaborative interaction and aspects of meta-cognition (*e.g.* self monitoring).

The importance of assessment in inquiry-based approaches

As the discussion above suggests, collaborative and inquiry-approaches to learning require that we consider classroom activities, curriculum, and assessment as a system in which each interdependent aspect is important for providing an environment that will promote robust learning. Indeed, our ability to assess – both formatively and summatively – has enormous implications for what we teach, and how effectively. At least three elements of assessment are especially important for meaningful learning of the kind we have been describing:

- The design of **intellectually ambitious performance assessments** that define the tasks students will undertake in ways that allow them to learn and apply the desired concepts and skills in authentic and disciplined ways.

- The creation of guidance for students' efforts in the form of **evaluation tools** such as assignment guidelines and rubrics that define what constitutes good work (and effective collaboration).

- The frequent use of **formative assessments** to guide feedback to students and teachers' instructional decisions throughout the process.

The nature of assessments defines the cognitive demands of the work students are asked to undertake. Research suggests that thoughtfully structured performance assessments can support improvements in the quality of teaching, and that inquiry-based learning demands such assessments both to define the task and to properly evaluate what has been learned. Some studies have also found that teachers who are involved in scoring performance assessments with other colleagues and discussing their students' work find the experience has helped them change their practice to become more problem-oriented and more diagnostic (*e.g.* Darling-Hammond and Ancess, 1994; Goldberg and Rosewell, 2000; Murnane and Levy, 1996).

There are many ways in which authentic assessments contribute to learning. For example, exhibitions, projects and portfolios provide occasions for review and revision toward a polished performance. These opportunities help students examine how they learn and how they can perform better. Students are often expected to present their work to an audience – groups of faculty, visitors, parents, other students – to ensure that their apparent mastery is genuine. Presentations of work also signal to students that their work is important enough to be a source of public learning and celebration, and provide opportunities for others in the learning community to see, appreciate and learn from student work. Performances create living representations of school goals and standards so that they remain vital and energising, and develop important life skills. As Ann Brown (1994) observed:

> Audiences demand coherence, push for high levels of understanding, require satisfactory explanations, request clarification of obscure points... There are deadlines, discipline, and most important, reflection on performance. We have cycles of planning, preparing, practicing, and teaching others. Deadlines and performance demand the setting of priorities – what is important to know?

Planning, setting priorities, organising individual and group efforts, exerting discipline, thinking through how to communicate effectively with an audience, understanding ideas well enough to answer the questions of others – all of these are tasks people engage in outside of school in their life and work. Good performance tasks are complex intellectual, physical and social challenges. They stretch students' thinking and planning abilities while also allowing student aptitudes and interests to serve as a springboard for developing competence.

In addition to designing tasks that are intellectually powerful, teachers need to provide guidance to students about the quality of work and interactions they are aiming for. The benefits of clear criteria given in advance have been documented by many studies (*e.g.* Barron *et al.*, 1998). For example, Cohen and her colleagues tested the idea that clear evaluation criteria could improve student learning by improving the nature of the conversation (Cohen *et al.*, 2002). They found that the introduction of evaluation criteria led groups to spend more time discussing content, discussing the assignment and evaluating their products than groups who were not given criteria. They also found that individual learning scores were significantly correlated with the amount of evaluative and task-focused talk.

The criteria used to assess performances should be multidimensional, representing the various aspects of a task rather than a single grade, and openly expressed to students and others in the learning community, rather than kept secret in the tradition of content-based examinations (Wiggins, 1989). For example, a research report might be evaluated for its use of evidence, accuracy of information, evaluation of competing viewpoints, development of a clear argument, and attention to conventions of writing. When work is repeatedly assessed, the criteria guide teaching and learning and students become producers and self-evaluators while teachers become coaches. A major goal is to help students develop the capacity to assess their own work against standards, to revise, modify, and redirect their energies, taking initiative to promote their own progress. This is an aspect of self-directed work and self-motivated improvement required of competent people in many settings, including a growing number of workplaces.

Use of performance tasks is also important so that we can adequately assess the benefits of problem and project-based approaches for learning and application of knowledge. For example, Bransford and Schwartz (1999) and Schwartz and Martin (2004) have carried out research demonstrating that the outcomes of different instructional conditions might look similar on "sequestered problem-solving tasks" but look very different on assessments that gauge students' "preparation for future learning". The preparation for future learning tasks asked students to read new material that was composed to include opportunities to learn. On this kind of task they found that students who had been in a learning condition where they were first asked to invent a solution to a problem, were more likely to learn from the new material than students who had been given traditional instruction consisting of explanations, examples, and practice.

Finally, formative assessment is a critical element in learning generally, and is especially important in the context of long-term collaborative work. Formative assessment is designed to provide feedback to students that they can then use to revise their understanding and their work. It is also used to inform teaching so it can be adapted to meet students' needs. The benefits of formative assessment for learning have been documented in a classic review article (Black and Wiliam, 1998a, 1998b) which documented that substantial learning gains result from providing students with frequent feedback about their learning, especially when that feedback takes the form of specific comments that can guide students' ongoing efforts.

A theme in the literature on formative assessment is that feedback seems to be more productive to the extent that it is focused on student process rather than product, and keyed on the quality of the work (task-involving) rather than quality of the worker (ego-involving), for example providing comments rather than grades for students to consider (Butler, 1988; Deci and Ryan, 1985; Schunk, 1996a, 1996b). Shepard (2000) suggests that the focus on process and task allows students to see cognitive prowess not as a fixed individual trait, but as a dynamic state that is primarily a function of the level of effort in the task at hand (see also, Black and Wiliam, 1998a, 1998b). This can support their motivation as they sustain confidence in their own ability to learn.

There is a set of related practices of importance in the activities we have described, including the integration of assessment and instruction, the systematic use of iterative cycles of reflection and action, and ongoing opportunity for students to improve their work – which is grounded in a conception of learning as developmental and the belief that all students will learn from experience and feedback, rather than being constrained by innate ability.

While formative assessment may be introduced as part of a change in classroom pedagogy, it may also create fundamental changes in teachers' abilities to teach effectively. As Darling-Hammond, Ancess and Falk (1995) observed in a study of the use of performance assessments in five schools to drive high-quality learning: "as [teachers] use assessment and learning dynamically, they increase their capacity to derive deeper understanding of their students' responses; this then serves to structure increased learning opportunities".

Supporting collaboration within inquiry approaches

Much of the work involving inquiry-based learning involves students working in pairs or groups to solve a problem, complete a project, or design and build an artefact. Co-operative small-group learning, which Cohen (1994b) defines as "students working together in a group small enough that everyone can participate on a collective task that has been clearly assigned," has been the subject of hundreds of studies and several meta-analyses (Cohen, Kulik and Kulik, 1982; Cook, Scruggs, Mastropieri and Castro, 1985; Hartley, 1977; Johnson, Maruyama, Johnson, Nelson and Skon, 1981; Rohrbeck, Ginsburg-Block, Fantuzzo and Miller, 2003). Overall, these analyses come to the same conclusion: there are significant learning benefits for students who work together on learning activities (Johnson and Johnson, 1981, 1989).

Co-operative group work benefits students in social and behavioural areas as well, including improvement in student self-concept, social interaction, time on task and positive feelings toward peers (Cohen *et al.*, 1982; Cook *et al.*, 1985; Hartley, 1977; Ginsburg-Block, Rohrbeck and Fantuzzo, 2006; Johnson and Johnson, 1999). Ginsburg-Block and colleagues (2006) focused on the relationship between academic and non-academic measures. They found that both social and self-concept measures were related to academic outcomes. Larger effects were found for classroom interventions that used same-gender grouping, interdependent group rewards, structured student roles, and individualised evaluation procedures. They also found that low-income students benefited more than those from high-income backgrounds and that urban students benefited more than those from suburban areas. Racial and ethnic minority students benefited even more from co-operative group work than non-minority students, a finding repeated over several decades (see Slavin and Oickle, 1981).

Nevertheless, effective co-operative learning can also be complex to implement. The classroom teacher plays a critical role in establishing and modelling practices of productive learning conversations. Aspects of the larger classroom learning environment shape small group interactions. Observing a group's interactions can provide a substantial amount of information about the degree to which the work is productive, as well as an opportunity for formative feedback and the provision of support for aligning understandings and goals among group members. Computer-based tools can also be useful in establishing ways of working and supporting productive collaborative exchanges. One of the best and most documented examples is the Computer-Supported Intentional Learning project (CSILE; Scardamalia, Bereiter and Lamon, 1994) that includes a knowledge-gathering and improvement tool to support inquiry and knowledge-building discourse. Beyond any specific tool or technique, a particularly important role for the teacher is to establish, model and encourage norms of interaction that reflect good inquiry practices (Engle and Conant, 2002).

A great deal of work has been done to specify the kinds of tasks, accountability structures and roles that help students to collaborate well (Aronson *et al.*, 1978). In Johnson and Johnson's summary (1999b) of 40 years of research on co-operative learning, they identify five "basic elements" of co-operation that have emerged as important across different models and approaches: positive interdependence, individual accountability, structures that promote face-to-face interaction, social skills and group processing.

A range of activity structures has been developed to support group work, from co-operative-learning approaches where students are simply asked to help each other complete individually-assigned traditional problem sets to approaches where students are expected to define projects collectively and generate a single product that reflects the continued work of the entire group. Many approaches fall between these two extremes. Some approaches assign children in the group to management roles (*e.g.* Cohen, 1994a, 1994b), conversational roles (O'Donnell, 2006; King, 1990), or intellectual roles (Palincsar and Herrenkohl, 1999, 2002; Cornelius and Herrenkohl, 2004; White and Frederiksen, 2005).

When designing co-operative group work, teachers should pay careful attention to various aspects of the work process and to the interaction among students (Barron, 2000; 2003). For example, Slavin (1991) argues: "it is not enough to simply tell students to work together. They must have a reason to take one another's achievement seriously." He developed a model that focuses on external motivators that reside outside the group, such as rewards and individual accountability established by the teacher. His meta-analysis found that group tasks with structures promoting individual accountability produce stronger learning outcomes (Slavin, 1996).

Cohen's review of research (1994b) on productive small groups focuses on internal group interaction around the task. She and her colleagues developed Complex Instruction, one of the best-known and well-researched approaches to co-operative small-group learning. Complex Instruction uses carefully designed activities that require diverse talents and interdependence among group members. Teachers are encouraged to pay attention to unequal participation among group members, which often results from status differences among peers, and are given strategies that allow them to bolster the status of infrequent contributors (Cohen and Lotan, 1997). In addition, roles are assigned to support equal participation, such as recorder, reporter, materials manager, resource manager, communication facilitator and harmoniser. A major component of the approach is development of "group-worthy tasks" that are both sufficiently open-ended and multi-faceted that they require and benefit from the participation of every member of the group. Tasks that require a variety of skills – such as research, analysis, visual representation and writing – are well suited to this approach.

There is strong evidence supporting the success of Complex Instruction strategies in promoting student academic achievement (Cohen *et al.*, 1994; Cohen, 1994a, 1994b; Cohen and Lotan, 1995; Cohen *et al.*, 1999, 2002). In recent studies, evidence of this success has been extended to the learning gains of new English language learners (Lotan, 2008; Bunch, Abram, Lotan and Valdés, 2001).

Challenges of inquiry approaches to learning

Many challenges have been identified with the management of the approaches just reviewed, as the pedagogies required to implement them are much more complex than the direct transmission of knowledge to students via textbooks or lectures. In fact, inquiry approaches to learning have frequently been found to be highly dependent on the knowledge and skills of teachers involved (Good and Brophy, 1986). When these approaches are poorly understood, teachers often think of inquiry or other student-centred approaches as "unstructured," rather than appreciating that they require extensive scaffolding and constant assessment and redirection as they unfold.

Research on these approaches signals a number of specific challenges that emerge when students lack prior experiences or modelling regarding particular aspects of the learning process. Regarding disciplinary understanding, students can have difficulty generating meaningful questions or evaluating their questions to understand if they are warranted by the content of the investigation (Krajcik *et al.*, 1998), and they may lack background knowledge needed to make sense of the inquiry (Edelson, Gordon and Pea, 1999). Regarding general academic skills, students may have difficulty developing logical arguments and evidence to support their claims (Krajcik *et al.*, 1998). Regarding management of tasks, students often have difficulty figuring out how to work together, managing their time and the complexity of the work, and sustaining motivation in the face of difficulties or confusion (Achilles and Hoover, 1996; Edelson, Gordon and Pea, 1999).

Teachers may also encounter challenges as they try to juggle the time needed for extended inquiry. They need to learn new approaches to classroom management, design and support inquiries that illuminate key subject matter concepts, balance students' needs for direct information with their opportunities to inquire, scaffold the learning of many individual students (providing enough, but not too much, modelling and feedback for each one), facilitate the learning of multiple groups, and develop and use assessments to guide the learning process (Blumenfeld *et al.*, 1991; Marx *et al.*, 1994, 1997; Rosenfeld *et al.*, 1998). Without supports to learn these complex skills, teachers may be unable to use inquiry approaches to best advantage, engaging students in "doing" but not necessarily in disciplined learning that has a high degree of transfer.

How can teachers support productive inquiry?

Successful inquiry-based approaches require planning and well thought out approaches to collaboration, classroom interaction and assessment. Classroom research (Barron *et al*, 1998; Gertzman and Kolodner, 1996; Puntambeckar and Kolodner, 2005) has shown that simply providing students with rich resources and an interesting problem (*e.g.* design a household robot with arthropod features) are not enough. Students need help understanding the problem, applying science knowledge, evaluating their designs, explaining failures and engaging in revision. Students often neglect to use informational resources unless explicitly prompted. Several research groups have offered design principles that can help guide curriculum efforts (Barron *et al.*, 1998; Engle and Conant, 2002; Puntambekar and Kolodner, 2005). Below we summarise the primary design principles from these groups.

Projects must be well designed with well-defined learning goals guiding the nature of activities.

Subject matter can be problematised by encouraging students to define problems and treat claims and explanatory accounts, even those offered by "experts," as needing evidence. The teacher should encourage students to question all sources. Rather than ignoring differences across sources, the teacher can draw attention to them and encourage them to look for converging sources.

Resources can scaffold both teachers and student learning

Resources such as models, public forums, tools, books, films or fieldtrips can support inquiry and discussion. Access to experts and a variety of informational resources are key in allowing students to find a broad range of topics, contradictions and perspectives. Discrepancies across sources can be important for driving debates but also for developing students' reasoning and sophistication in using different types of evidence. Another important resource is time. Students must be given plenty of time to investigate questions, carry out designs and share the group's current thinking and disagreements with one another and with the teacher.

Teachers must develop participation structures and classroom norms that encourage accountability, use of evidence and a collaborative stance

Students can be given authority to address disciplinary problems by personally identifying them with claims, explanations, or designs in ways that encourage them to be authors and producers of knowledge. The teacher can communicate an enthusiasm for debate and productive conflict. Public performances like presentations can encourage the ability to adopt a particular perspective as well as attention to quality. Students should be encouraged to address others' viewpoints even if they disagree. Disciplinary norms, such as paying attention to evidence and citing sources, should be modelled and nurtured. The teacher can encourage the students to incorporate a wide range of sources into their research. Students can also constantly be made aware of the requirement that they help their group members learn.

Well-designed formative assessment and opportunities for revision support learning and well designed summative assessments can be useful learning experiences

Formative opportunities for reflection on collaborative processes and work progress should be built in to help students self-assess and revise their course of action if needed. It is important to find a balance between having students work on design activities and reflecting on what they are learning, so that they can guide their progress. Incorporating reflective activities is important to encourage understanding. The criteria used for summative assessment should be multidimensional, representing the various aspects of a task rather than a single grade, and openly expressed to students and others in the learning community, rather than kept secret in the tradition of content-based examinations.

Summary and conclusions

The current conversation about 21st century skills calls for classroom and other learning environments that, in addition to including the core subjects of schooling, encourage students to develop new media literacies, critical and systems thinking, interpersonal and self directional skills. This chapter has presented classroom approaches that support sustained inquiry and collaborative work. Such approaches are critical for preparing students for future learning. Three main conclusions may be drawn from our review.

1. Students learn more deeply when they can apply classroom knowledge to real-world problems. Inquiry and design-based approaches are an important way to nurture communication, collaboration, creativity and deep thinking. Attention to the processes, as well as the content, of learning is beneficial.

2. Inquiry approaches to learning are challenging to implement. They are highly dependent on the knowledge and skills of the teachers engaged in trying to implement them. When these approaches are poorly understood, teachers often think of them as "unstructured," rather than appreciating that they require extensive scaffolding and constant assessment and redirection as they unfold. Teachers need time and a community to support their capacity to organise sustained project work. It takes significant pedagogical sophistication to manage extended projects in classrooms so as to maintain a focus on "doing with understanding" rather than "doing for the sake of doing". Fortunately there is a wealth of examples and articulated design principles that can help teachers to do these things.

3. Assessment strategies must be designed to support both formative and summative evaluation. The nature of assessments defines the cognitive demands of the work students are asked to undertake. Research suggests that thoughtfully-structured performance assessments can support improvements in the quality of teaching, and that inquiry-based learning demands such assessments, both to define the task and to evaluate properly what has been learned.

As the international community explores strategies to prepare students for an increasingly complex and interconnected world, inquiry and design approaches to learning provide a well researched approach that has the potential to transform important aspects of teaching and learning. Students develop critical collaborative and academic skills, and teachers are given opportunities to deepen their repertoire for nurturing 21st century learners. International collaboration among researchers and educators can only strengthen the possibilities for imagining and enacting transformative pedagogies that support deep engagement and learning for all.

References

Achilles, C.M. and S.P. Hoover (1996), *Transforming Administrative Praxis: The Potential of Problem-Based Learning (PBL) as a School-Improvement Vehicle for Middle and High Schools,* Annual Meeting of the American Educational Research Association, New York.

Albanese, M.A. and S.A. Mitchell (1993), "Problem-Based Learning: A Review of Literature on Its Outcomes and Implementation Issues." *Academic Medicine,* Vol. 68, No. 1, pp. 52-81.

Aronson, E., C. Stephen, J. Sikes, N. Blaney and M. Snapp (1978), *The Jigsaw Classroom*, Sage, Thousand Oaks, CA.

Barron, B. (2000a), "Achieving Coordination in Collaborative Problem-Solving Groups", *Journal of the Learning Sciences,* Vol. 9, No. 4, pp. 403-436.

Barron, B. (2000b), "Problem Solving in Video-Based Microworlds: Collaborative and Individual Outcomes of High-Achieving Sixth-Grade Students", *Journal of Educational Psychology,* Vol. 92, No. 2, pp. 391-398.

Barron, B. (2003), "When Smart Groups Fail", *Journal of the Learning Sciences,* Vol. 12, No. 3, pp. 307-359.

Barron, B.J.S., D.L. Schwartz, N.J. Vye, A. Moore, A. Petrosino, L. Zech, J.D. Bransford and CTGV (1998), "Doing with Understanding: Lessons from Research on Problem- and Project-Based Learning", *Journal of the Learning Sciences,* Vol. 7, No. 3-4, pp. 271-311.

Barrows, H.S. (1996), "Problem-Based Learning in Medicine and Beyond: A Brief Overview", in *New Directions for Teaching and Learning,* No. 68, Jossey-Bass, San Francisco, pp. 3-11.

Bartscher, K., B. Gould and S. Nutter (1995), *Increasing Student Motivation through Project-based Learning,* Master's Research Project, Saint Xavier and IRI Skylight.

Black, P.J. and D. Wiliam (1998a), "Assessment and Classroom Learning", *Assessment in Education: Principles, Policy and Practice,* Vol. 5, No. 1, pp. 7-73.

Black, P. and D. Wiliam (1998b), "Inside the Black Box: Raising Standards through Classroom Assessment", *Phi Delta Kappan,* Vol. 80, No. 2, pp. 139-148.

Blumenfeld, P.C., E. Soloway, R.W. Marx, J.S. Krajcik, M. Guzdial and A. Palincsar (1991), "Motivating Project-based Learning: Sustaining the Doing, Supporting the Learning", *Educational Psychologist,* Vol. 26, Nos. 3-4, pp. 369-398.

Boaler, J. (1997), *Experiencing School Mathematics: Teaching Styles, Sex, and Settings,* Open University Press, Buckingham UK.

Boaler, J. (1998), "Open and Closed Mathematics: Student Experiences and Understandings", *Journal for Research in Mathematics Education,* Vol. 29, No. 1, pp. 41-62.

Braddock, J.H. and J.M. McPartland (1993), "The Education of Early Adolescents", in L. Darling-Hammond (ed.), *Review of Research in Education* 19, American Educational Research Association, Washington, DC

Bransford, J. D. and D. L. Schwartz (1999), "Rethinking Transfer: A Simple Proposal with Multiple Implications", *Review of Research in Education,* A. Iran-Nejad and P. D. Pearson (eds.), Chapter 3, Vol. 24, American Educational Research Association, Washington, D.C, pp. 61-100.

Brown, A. L. (1994), "The Advancement of Learning", *Educational Researcher,* Vol. 23, No. 8, pp. 4-12.

Bunch, G. C., P.L. Abram, R.A. Lotan and G. Valdés (2001), "Beyond Sheltered Instruction: Rethinking Conditions for Academic Language Development", *TESOL Journal,* Vol. 10, No. 2-3, pp. 28-33.

Butler, R. (1988), "Enhancing and Undermining Intrinsic Motivation: The Effects of Task-Involving and Ego-Involving Evaluation of Interest and Performance", *British Journal of Educational Psychology,* Vol. 58, No. 1, pp. 1-14.

Cohen, E.G. (1994a), *Designing Groupwork: Strategies for Heterogeneous Classrooms,* Revised edition, Teachers College Press, New York.

Cohen, E.G. (1994b), "Restructuring the Classroom: Conditions for Productive Small Groups", *Review of Educational Research,* Vol. 64, No. 1, pp. 1-35.

Cohen, E.G. and R.A. Lotan (1995), "Producing Equal-Status Interaction in the Heterogeneous Classroom, *American Educational Research Journal*", Vol. 32, No. 1, pp. 99-120.

Cohen, E.G. and R.A. Lotan (eds.) (1997), *Working for Equity in Heterogeneous Classrooms: Sociological Theory in Practice,* Teachers College Press, New York.

Cohen, E.G., Lotan, R. A., Abram, P.L., Scarloss, B.A., Schultz, S.E. (2002), "Can Groups Learn?", *Teachers College Record,* Vol. 104, No. 6, pp. 1045-1068.

Cohen, E.G., Lotan, R.A., Scarloss, B.A. and Arellano, A. R. (1999), "Complex Instruction: Equity in Co-operative Learning Classrooms", *Theory into Practice,* Vol. 38, No. 2, pp. 80-86.

Cohen, E.G., R.A. Lotan, J.A. Whitcomb, M. Balderrama, R. Cossey and P. Swanson (1994), "Complex Instruction: Higher-order Thinking in Heterogeneous Classrooms" in S. Sharan (ed.), *Handbook of Cooperative Learning Methods,* Greenwood, Westport CT.

Cohen, P.A., J.A. Kulik and C.C. Kulik (1982), "Education Outcomes of Tutoring: A Meta-Analysis of Findings", *American Educational Research Journal,* Vol. 19, No. 2, pp. 237-248.

Cook, S. B., T.E Scruggs, M.A. Mastropieri and G. Casto (1985), "Handicapped Students as Tutors", *Journal of Special Education,* Vol. 19, No. 4, pp. 483-492.

Cornelius, L.L. and L.R. Herrenkohl (2004), "Power in the Classroom: How the Classroom Environment Shapes Students' Relationships with Each Other and with Concepts", *Cognition and Instruction,* Vol. 22, No. 4, pp. 467-498.

Darling-Hammond, L. and J. Ancess (1994), *Graduation by Portfolio at Central Park East Secondary School,* National Center for Restructuring Education, Schools, and Teaching, Teachers College, Columbia University, New York.

Darling-Hammond, L., J. Ancess and B. Falk (1995), *Authentic Assessment in Action: Studies of Schools and Students at Work*, Teachers College Press, New York.

Deci, E.L. and R.M. Ryan (1985), *Intrinsic Motivation and Self-Determination in Human Behavior,* Plenum, New York.

Dochy, F., M. Segers, P. van den Bossche and D. Gijbels (2003), "Effects of Problem-Based Learning: A Meta-Analysis", *Learning and Instruction,* Vol. 13, No. 5, pp. 533-568.

Dunkin, M. and B. Biddle (1974), *The Study of Teaching,* Holt, Rinehart and Winston, New York.

Edelson, D., D. Gordon and R. Pea (1999), "Addressing the Challenges of Inquiry-Based Learning through Technology and Curriculum Design", *Journal of the Learning Sciences,* Vol. 8, Nos. 3 and 4, pp. 391-450.

Engle, R.A. and F.R. Conant (2002), "Guiding Principles for Fostering Productive Disciplinary Engagement: Explaining an Emergent Argument in a Community of Learners Classroom", *Cognition and Instruction,* Vol. 20, No. 4, pp. 399-483.

Fortus, D., R.C. Dershimer, R.W. Marx, J. Krajcik, R. Mamlok-Naaman (2004), "Design-Based Science (DBS) and Student Learning", *Journal of Research in Science Teaching,* Vol. 41, No. 10, pp. 1081-1110.

Garcia, E. (1993), "Language, Culture, and Education", in L. Darling-Hammond (ed.), *Review of Research in Education 19,* American Educational Research Association, Washington, DC.

Gertzman, A. and J.L. Kolodner (1996), "A Case Study of Problem-Based Learning in Middle-School Science Class: Lessons Learned" in *Proceedings of the Second Annual Conference on the Learning Sciences,* Evanston, Chicago, pp. 91-98.

Ginsburg-Block, M.D., C.A. Rohrbeckand and J.W. Fantuzzo (2006), "A Meta-Analytic Review of Social, Self-concept, and Behavioral Outcomes of Peer-Assisted Learning", *Journal of Educational Psychology,* Vol. 98, No. 4, pp. 732-749.

Glass, G.V., D. Coulter, S. Hartley, S. Hearold, S. Kahl, J. Kalk and Sherretz (1977), *Teacher "Indirectness" and Pupil Achievement: An Integration of Findings,* Laboratory of Educational Research, University of Colorado, Boulder.

Goldberg, G.L. and B.S. Rosewell (2000), "From Perception to Practice: The Impact of Teachers' Scoring Experience on the Performance Based Instruction and Classroom Practice", *Educational Assessment,* Vol. 6, No. 4, pp. 257-290.

Good, T.L. and J.E. Brophy (1986), *Educational Psychology* (3rd edition), Longman, New York.

Harel, I. (1991), *Children Designers,* Ablex, Norwood CT.

Hartley, S.S. (1977), *A Meta-Analysis of Effects of Individually Paced Instruction in Mathematics,* unpublished doctoral dissertation, University of Colorado at Boulder.

Hmelo, C.E. (1998a), "Cognitive Consequences of Problem-Based Learning for the Early Development of Medical Expertise", *Teaching and Learning in Medicine,* Vol. 10, No. 2, pp. 92-100.

Hmelo, C.E. (1998b), "Problem-Based Learning: Effects on the Early Acquisition of Cognitive Skill in Medicine", *Journal of the Learning Sciences,* Vol. 7, No. 2, pp. 173-208.

Hmelo-Silver, C.E. (2004), "Problem-Based Learning: What and How Do Students Learn?", *Educational Psychology Review,* Vol. 16, No. 3, pp. 235-266.

Horan, C., C. Lavaroni and P. Beldon (1996), *Observation of the Tinker Tech Program Students for Critical Thinking and Social Participation Behaviors,* Buck Institute for Education, Novato, CA.

Horwitz, R.A. (1979), "Effects of the 'Open' Classroom", in H.J. Walberg (ed.), *Educational Environments and Effects: Evaluation, Policy and Productivity,* McCutchan, Berkeley, CA.

Johnson, D.W. and R.T. Johnson (1981), "Effects of Co-operative and Individualistic Learning Experiences on Interethnic Interaction", *Journal of Educational Psychology,* Vol. 73, No. 3, pp. 444-449.

Johnson, D.W. and R.T. Johnson (1989), *Cooperation and Competition: Theory and Research,* Interaction Book Company, Edina, MN.

Johnson, D.W. and R.T. Johnson (1999), "Making Co-operative Learning Work", *Theory into Practice,* Vol. 38, No. 2, pp. 67-73.

Johnson, D.W., G. Maruyama, R. Johnson, D. Nelson and L. Skon (1981), "Effects of Co-operative, Competitive, and Individualistic Goal Structures on Achievement: A Meta-Analysis", *Psychological Bulletin,* Vol. 89, No. 1, pp. 47-62.

Kafai. Y (1995), *Minds in Play: Computer Game Design as a Context for Children's Learning,* Lawrence Erlbaum Publishers, Hillsdale NJ.

Kafai, Y.B. and C.C. Ching (2001), "Talking Science within Design: Learning through Design as a Context", *Journal of the Learning Sciences,* Vol. 10, No. 3, pp. 323-363.

Kilpatrick, W.H. (1918), "The Project Method", *Teachers College Record,* Vol. 19, No 4, pp. 319-335.

King, A. (1990), "Enhancing Peer Interaction and Learning in the Classroom through Reciprocal Peer Questioning", *American Educational Research Journal,* Vol. 27, No. 4, pp. 664-687.

Knapp, M.S. (ed.) (1995), *Teaching for Meaning in High-Poverty Classrooms,* Teachers College Press, New York.

Kolodner, J.L. (1997), "Educational Implications of Analogy: A View from Case-Based Reasoning", *American Psychologist,* Vol. 52, No. 1, pp. 57-66.

Kolodner, J.L., P. J. Camp, D. Crismond, B. Fasse, J. Gray, J. Holbrook, S. Puntambekar and M. Ryan (2003), "Problem-Based Learning Meets Case-Based Reasoning in the Middle-School Science Classroom: Putting *Learning by Design*™ into Practice", *Journal of the Learning Sciences,* Vol. 12, No. 4, pp. 495-547.

Krajcik, J.S., P.C. Blumenfeld, R.W. Marx, K.M. Bass, J. Fredricks and E.Soloway (1998), "Inquiry in Project-Based Science Classrooms: Initial Attempts by Middle School Students, *Journal of the Learning Sciences,* Vol. 7, Nos. 3-4, pp. 313-350.

Lehrer, R. and T. Romberg (1996), "Exploring Children's Data Modeling", *Cognition and Instruction,* Vol. 14, No. 1, pp. 69-108.

Levy, F. and R. Murnane (2004), *The New Division of Labor: How Computers Are Creating the Next Job Market,* Princeton University Press, Princeton NJ.

Lotan, R.A. (2008), "Developing Language and Content Knowledge in Heterogeneous Classrooms", in R. Gillies, A. Ashman and J.Terwel (eds.), *The Teacher's Role in Implementing Cooperative Learning in the Classroom,* Springer, New York.

Lundeberg, M., B.B. Levin and H.L. Harrington (1999), *Who Learns What from Cases and How? The Research Base for Teaching and Learning with Cases,* Lawrence Erlbaum Associates, Mahwah, NJ.

Marx, R.W., P. C. Blumenfeld, J.S. Krajcik, M. Blunk, B. Crawford, B. Kelley and K.M. Meyer (1994). "Enacting Project-based Science: Experiences of Four Middle Grade Teachers", *Elementary School Journal,* Vol. 94, No. 5, p. 518

Marx, R.W., P.C. Blumenfeld, J.S. Krajcik and E. Soloway (1997), "Enacting Project-based Science: Challenges for practice and policy", *Elementary School Journal,* 97, 341-358.

McKeachie, W.J. and J.A. Kulik (1975), "Effective College Teaching", in F. N. Kerlinger (ed.), *Review of Research in Education* Vol. 3, Peacock, Itasca, IL.

Murnane, R. and F. Levy (1996), *Teaching the New Basic Skills,* Free Press, New York.

National Council of Teachers of Mathematics (NCTM) (1989), *Curriculum and Evaluation Standards for School Mathematics,* NCTM, Reston VA.

National Research Council (1996), *National Science Education Standards,* National Academy Press, Washington, DC.

NCREL (2003), *21st century Skills: Literacy in the Digital Age,* North Central Regional Educational Laboratory (NCREL), retrieved 2 October, 2005 from *www.ncrel.org/engauge/skills/skills.htm.*

Newmann, F.M. (1996), *Authentic Achievement: Restructuring Schools for Intellectual Quality,* Jossey-Bass, San Francisco.

Newmann, F.M., H.M. Marks and A. Gamoran (1996), "Authentic Pedagogy and Student Performance", *American Journal of Education,* Vol. 104, No. 4, pp. 280-312.

Newstetter, W. (2000), "Bringing Design Knowledge and Learning Together", in C. Eastman, W. Newstetter and M. McCracken (eds.), *Design Knowing and Learning: Cognition in Design Education,* Elsevier Science Press, New York.

O'Donnell, A.M. (2006), "The Role of Peers and Group Learning", in P. Alexander and P. Winne (eds.), *Handbook of Educational Psychology* (2nd edition.), Erlbaum, Mahwah, NJ.

Palincsar, A.S. and L. Herrenkohl (1999), "Designing Collaborative Contexts: Lessons from Three Research Programs", in A.M. O'Donnell and A. King (eds.), *Cognitive Perspectives on Peer Learning,* Erlbaum, Mahwah, NJ.

Palincsar, A.S. and L. Herrenkohl (2002), "Designing Collaborative Learning Contexts", *Reading Teacher,* Vol. 41, No. 1, pp. 26-32.

Partnership for 21st Century Skills (2004), *Learning for the 21st Century,* Washington, DC, available at *www.21stcenturyskills.org.*

Peck, J.K., W. Peck, J. Sentz and R. Zasa (1998), "Students' Perceptions of Literacy Learning in a Project-Based Curriculum", in E. G. Sturtevant, J. A. Dugan, P. Linder and W. M. Linek (eds.) *Literacy and Community,* College Reading Association, Texas A&M University.

Penner, D.E., N.D. Giles, R. Lehrer and L. Schauble (1997), "Building Functional Models: Designing an Elbow", *Journal of Research in Science Teaching,* Vol. 34, No. 2, pp. 1-20.

Penuel, W.R., B. Means and M.B. Simkins (2000), "The Multimedia Challenge", *Educational Leadership,* Vol. 58, No. 2, pp. 34-38.

Peterson, P. (1979), "Direct Instruction Reconsidered", in P. Peterson and H. Walberg (eds.), *Research on Teaching: Concepts, Findings, and Implications,* McCutchan, Berkeley, CA.

Petrosino, A.J. (1998), *The Use of Reflection and Revision in Hands-On Experimental Activities by At-Risk Children,* Unpublished Doctoral Dissertation, Vanderbilt University, Nashville, TN.

Puntambekar, S. and J.L. Kolodner (2005), "Toward Implementing Distributed Scaffolding: Helping Students Learn Science from Design", *Journal of Research in Science Teaching,* Vol. 42, No. 2, pp. 185-217.

Resnick, L. (1987), *Education and Learning to Think,* National Academy Press, Washington, DC.

Rohrbeck, C.A., M.D. Ginsburg-Block, J. W., Fantuzzo and T. R. Miller (2003), "Peer-Assisted Learning Interventions with Elementary School Students: A Meta-Analytic Review", *Journal of Educational Psychology,* Vol. 95, No. 2, pp. 240-257.

Rosenfeld, M. and S. Rosenfeld (1998), "Understanding the 'Surprises' in PBL: An Exploration into the Learning Styles of Teachers and Their Students", paper presented at the 8th European Association for Research in Learning and Instruction (EARLI), Gothenburg, Sweden.

Savery, J.R. and T.M. Duffy (1995), "Problem based learning: an instructional model and its constructivist framework", *Educational Technology,* Vol. 35, No. 5, pp. 31-38.

Scardamalia, M., C. Bereiter and M. Lamon (1994), "The CSILE Project: Trying to Bring the Classroom into World 3", in K. McGilly (ed.), *Classroom Lessons: Integrating Cognitive Theory and Classroom Practice,* MIT Press, Cambridge, MA.

Schmidt, H.G., M. Machiels-Bongaerts, H. Hermans, T. ten Cate, R. Venekamp and H. Boshuizen(1996), "The Development of Diagnostic Competence: A Comparison between a Problem-Based, an Integrated, and a Conventional Medical Curriculum", *Academic Medicine,* Vol. 71, No. 6, pp. 658-664.

Schunk, D.H. (1996a), "Motivation in Education: Current Emphases and Future Trends", *Mid-Western Educational Researcher,* Vol. 9, No. 2, pp. 5-11, 36, Spr.

Schunk, D.H. (1996b), "Goal and Self-evaluative Influences during Children's Cognitive Skill Learning", *American Educational Research Journal,* Vol.33, No. 2, pp. 359-382.

Schwartz, D.L. and T. Martin (2004), "Inventing to Prepare for Future Learning: The Hidden Efficiency of Encouraging Original Student Production in Statistics Instruction", *Cognition and Instruction*, Vol. 22, No. 2, pp. 129-184.

Secretary's Commission on Achieving Necessary Skills (SCANS) (1991), *What Work Requires of Schools*, report published by the National Technical Information Service (NTIS), U.S. Department of Commerce.

Shepard, L.A. (2000), "The Role of Assessment in the Learning Culture", *Educational Researcher*, Vol. 29, No. 7, pp. 4-14.

Shepherd, H.G. (1998), "The Probe Method: A Problem-based Learning Model's Effect on Critical Thinking Skills of Fourth- and Fifth-grade Social Studies Students", *Dissertation Abstracts International*, Section A: Humanities and Social Sciences, September 1988, Vol. 59 (3-A), p. 0779.

Slavin, R. (1991), "Synthesis of Research on Co-operative Learning", *Educational Leadership*, Vol. 48, No. 5, pp. 71-82.

Slavin, R. (1996), "Research on Co-operative Learning and Achievement: What We Know, What We Need to Know", *Contemporary Educational Psychology*, Vol. 21, No. 1, pp. 43-69.

Slavin, R. and E. Oickle (1981), "Effects of Co-operative Learning Teams on Student Achievement and Race Relations: Treatment by Race Interactions", *Sociology of Education*, Vol. 54, No. 3, pp. 174-180.

Soar, R.S. (1977), "An Integration of Findings from Four Studies of Teacher Effectiveness", in G.D. Borich (ed.), *The Appraisal of Teaching: Concepts and Process*, Addison-Wesley, Reading, MA.

Stepien, W.J., S.A. Gallagher and D. Workman (1993), "Problem-Based Learning for Traditional and Interdisciplinary Classrooms", *Journal for the Education of the Gifted Child*, Vol. 16, No. 4, pp. 338-357.

TERC (2000), *Construct-A-Glove*, NSTA Press, Cambridge, MA.

Thomas, J.W. (2000), *A Review of Project Based Learning*, report prepared for Autodesk Foundation, San Rafael, CA.

Vernon D.T. and R.L. Blake (1993), "Does problem-based learning work? A meta-analysis of evaluation research", *Academic Medicine*; Vol. 68, No. 7, pp. 550-563.

White, B. and J. Frederiksen (2005), "A Theoretical Framework and Approach for Fostering Metacognitive Development", *Educational Psychologist*, Vol. 40, No. 4, pp. 211-223.

Wiggins, G. (1989), "Teaching to the (authentic) Test", *Educational Leadership,* Vol. 46, No. 7, pp. 41-47.

Williams, D.C., S. Hemstreet, M. Liu and V.D. Smith (1998), *Examining How Middle Schools Students Use Problem-Based Learning Software,* Proceedings of the ED-MEDIA/ED-Telecom 10th World Conference on Educational Multimedia and Hypermedia, Freiburg, Germany.

Williams, S.M. (1992), "Putting Case-Based Instruction into Context: Examples from Legal and Medical Education", *Journal of the Learning Sciences,* Vol. 2, No. 4, pp. 367-427.

Chapter 10

The community as a resource for learning: an analysis of academic service-learning in primary and secondary education

Andrew Furco
University of Minnesota

Andrew Furco's chapter reviews "academic service learning": i.e. experiential learning that takes place in the community as an integral part of the curriculum. These approaches are arousing substantial international interest and embrace pedagogies of engagement; pedagogies of empowerment; national service programmes; values education initiatives; citizenship education programmes; and community resource programmes. They lie between community service and volunteer work, at the service end of the spectrum, and field education and internships, at the learning end. Different forms of service learning are of value in themselves as good education. They also positively influence cognitive achievements in ways discussed in other chapters of this volume, such as by giving opportunities for authentic learning, engaging students actively, fostering co-operation and collaboration, meeting individual interests, empowering learners and extending horizons beyond comfort zones. However, the evidence base on associated outcomes and on what works best and why reveals some emerging, positive findings but remains seriously under-developed.

The rising tide of service-learning

In western Argentina, a group of students, age 12, is exploring the history of their land as part of the history curriculum. The area in which they live is dry and barren. The local residents, mostly part of the Huarpe Indian people, live in poverty and suffer from a lack of abundant food and water. In studying the history of their land, the students come to learn that their Indian ancestors were farmers who lived on fertile land that grew corn and other crops. The students decide to explore why today their land is so dry and barren. In their investigation, they come to learn that 25 years earlier, the local water was diverted to a nearby region to irrigate the vineyards of some newly established wineries. Seeking to make their land fertile again, the students develop a plan to reclaim their water. They ultimately make a successful case to the provincial government to re-divert some of the water back to their province. The students design and construct an aqueduct which carries the water back to their community. They also bring direct water access to local residents who have had to rely on collecting water from the town's common watering well. The students plant various vegetables and establish an education program designed to advance residents' capacity to cultivate nutritious and saleable grains and vegetables.

The students in this example participated in an educational experience known as **academic service-learning**. At its most basic level, academic service-learning is an experiential learning pedagogy in which education is delivered by engaging students in community service that is integrated with the learning objectives of core academic curricula. Academic service-learning is premised on providing students with contextualised learning experiences that are based on authentic, real-time situations in their communities. Using the community as a resource for learning, the primary goal of academic service-learning is to enhance students' understanding of the broader value and utility of academic lessons within the traditional disciplines (*e.g.* science, mathematics, social studies, language arts and fine arts), all while engaging young people in social activities through which they derive and implement solutions to important community issues (Scheckley and Keeton, 1997). Ideally, the community service the students perform helps them learn better how the academic concepts taught in the classroom can be applied to situations in their everyday lives. In this regard, academic service-learning seeks simultaneously to enhance students' academic achievement and their civic development (Eyler and Giles, 1999; Tapia, 2007).

Today, service-learning is one of the fastest growing educational initiatives in contemporary primary, secondary and post-secondary education. Substantial national service-learning initiatives are now part of the education systems of

Argentina, Singapore and the United States, and are emerging in many OECD and non-OECD countries, including Australia, Canada, Chile, Columbia, Germany, Ireland, Italy, Japan, Mexico, South Africa, Spain and the United Kingdom. While a world-wide, comprehensive assessment of school-sponsored service-learning initiatives is not available, evidence of its rising tide in educational settings is suggested by the growing body of publications, conferences and international networks devoted to advancing the practice and study of service-learning in primary, secondary and tertiary education.

The extant literature and other materials suggest that academic service-learning experiences can be generated from curriculum in any discipline and involve students at all educational levels (Cairn and Kielsmeier, 1991; Spring, Grimm and Dietz, 2008). The literature also reveals that the community service activities in which students are engaged tackle a broad range of societal issues, including those concerning the environment, health, public safety, human needs, literacy and multiculturalism (Tapia, 2008). While these community service activities typically focus on local issues, they can also be national or global in scope. In implementing service-learning activities, students can address a societal issue either through **direct service** (*e.g.* serving food at a homeless shelter) or **indirect service** (*e.g.* producing a research report that provides recommendations to the homeless shelter for improving its food distribution). Regardless of the type or focus of the service activity, academic service-learning is designed to help students apply their academic content knowledge to act on authentic and often complex societal issues.

Although service-learning resembles other forms of community-based learning approaches, such as internships, field studies, or volunteerism, it is distinguished from these programmes by placing equal emphasis on both community service and academic learning, as well as its intention to benefit both the provider and recipient of the service (See Figure 10.1).

Academic service-learning also resembles the popular educational practice of project-based learning (see Barron and Darling-Hammond, this volume), a pedagogy that actively engages students in learning academic knowledge through the development of individual or group projects. However, as distinct from many such activities, academic service-learning learning projects are purposefully community-focused and community-based, are usually conducted in partnership with members of the community, and, most importantly, are designed with a community need in mind. In essence, like a textbook or laboratory, the community becomes a resource for learning whereby the environs outside school offer students authentic learning opportunities to use their academic knowledge and skills to construct and implement solutions to real-life social problems in the local community or broader society.

Figure 10.1. **Service-learning compared to other forms of
experiential learning**

FOCUS

←————————————————————————————→

Service   Learning

PRIMARY INTENDED BENEFICIARY

←————————————————————————————→

Recipient   Provider

	Service-Learning	
Community Service	Field Education	
Volunteerism		Internships

Source: Furco, A. (1996).

In addition to academic service-learning, other less academically intensive forms of service-learning have emerged in recent years. These forms,
sometimes referred to as **co-curricular service-learning**, are typically
practised outside the formal academic curriculum (*e.g.* in school-sponsored
after-school programmes) or in non-formal educational settings (*e.g.* boys and
girls clubs, Boy Scouts of America). While co-curricular service-learning
also contains an organising curriculum with intentional learning objectives,
this curriculum tends to emphasise non-academic goals, such as developing
participants' personal leadership development, social development, diversity
awareness and the like.

The essence of the pedagogy

The emphasis on community service and its use of the community as a
resource for academic study intentionally shifts the role that students play in
the learning process: they become producers rather than recipients of knowledge, active rather than passive learners, and providers rather than recipients
of assistance (Cairn and Kielsmeier, 1991). Unlike most other experiential
learning approaches, academic service-learning places students in situations
where they focus less on utilising resources for their own gain and more on
acting as a resource for the benefit of others. Service-learning creates an
educational atmosphere whereby learners confront real-life issues through
community-engaged experiences that call on them to develop meaningful,
academically-relevant actions that have real consequences for the community
and themselves. Therefore, the true value of academic service-learning lies

in its capacity to include and incorporate several effective teaching practices which enhance learning and promote positive youth development (Eccles and Gootman, 2002). As exemplified by the case of the Argentinian students in the introduction, service-learning combines several important building blocks that create the conditions for quality teaching and optimal learning (see Figure 10.2).

Each of these blocks has been found, through independent research studies to enhance student learning and engagement in school.

Figure 10.2. **Quality teaching elements present in service-learning**

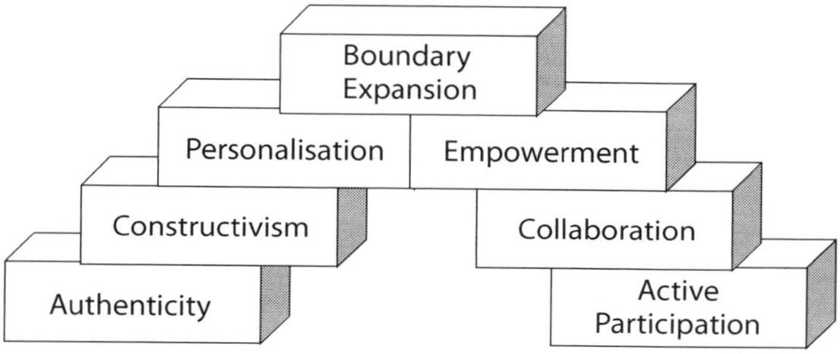

Source: Furco (2007).

Opportunities for authentic learning

In academic service-learning, students are confronted with real-life issues: the problem-solving is not about pre-fabricated questions at the end of a textbook chapter or hypothetical scenarios. Rather, the students are challenged to study real problems in real time for real people. In the case of the service-learning students in Argentina, the students explored an actual event and its consequences on the community in which they live. The students' work focused on identifying the best strategy to address an authentic problem that would have actual consequences for the people in their community. Authentic learning experiences help students create meaning and context in ways that can enhance their cognitive and emotional investment in the learning process (Slavkin, 2004).

Engaging students actively

Academic service-learning blends traditional classroom learning with hands-on application of academic content to real-life situations in the community. Like most experiential learning strategies, service-learning is inherently a student-centred pedagogy that conceives learning as a process in which students engage rather than as a set of products or outcomes that students have to produce (Kolb, 1984). The learning occurs in the journey students take to arrive at their intended outcomes (*e.g.* pass an examination, complete a research paper). For example, the quest to discover why their land was so barren today when it was fertile some years before put the students in the Argentine classroom on a learning journey in which they led the process of exploration and problem-solving. These students were active participants in the learning and their actions and ideas drove the curriculum. Moving students from being passive to active learners has been found to increase their investment in the learning tasks, raise their intrinsic motivation, and enhance their sense of ability to see the task through (Deci, 1984; Prince, 2004).

A constructivist approach

Through academic service-learning, students are asked to derive strategies that address messy and knotty societal issues through collaborative work with peers and adults in the community. Rather than focusing on finding the right answer, service-learning experiences engage students in exploring various options, perspectives and viable strategies. It also requires them to construct and implement the strategy (or strategies) that they believe will be most effective. As the students in Argentina sought to reclaim the water for their community, they considered and explored various approaches by consulting with peers and adults, and ultimately they built consensus on which approach would work best. Overall, service-learning relies on a constructivist philosophy of education which suggests that students internalise learning more fully when instruction is delivered through an active, discovery-focused process (Fosnot, 1996).

Forging co-operation, partnerships and collaboration

Learning is as much a social enterprise as it is a cognitive one. Many academic service-learning projects are built on co-operative group work whereby students learn to navigate and negotiate with peers and others as they develop and implement their community service plans. Co-operative and collaborative approaches to learning can enhance student engagement, and strengthen bonds among students from diverse backgrounds (Slavin, 1986; Erickson, 1990; Scheckley and Keeton, 1997; Johnson and Johnson, 2006). The concept of *solidaridad,* a central feature of the academic service-learning programmes in Argentina, is built on this collaborative approach to service and community-building. Young people join forces in challenging, transformational experiences that engender strong bonds and often produce long-lasting relationships (Tapia, 2007). As the students in the history class constructed the aqueducts, they worked with professionals and other adults who assisted and guided them throughout the process. This partnership played an important role in keeping the students committed as they felt their work was being validated by adult members of the community. Service-learning encourages students to work in partnership with community agency representatives who, as co-educators, often become important mentors to the students. Engagement with these and other adult role models can promote healthy adolescent development and young people's overall success in school (Eccles and Gootman, 2002).

Meeting individual needs and interests

Academic service-learning is centred on engaging students in community service projects that matter to them. High quality service-learning experiences tap students' individual talents and abilities in ways that allow all of them to make a contribution to the issue(s) at hand regardless of age, ability, or ambition. The history students embarked on their learning journey because **they** were curious about the state of their land. The work mattered to them personally, and consequently they invested themselves fully in the learning process. Highly personalised curricula have been found to increase students' time on task and overall engagement with learning (Jaros and Deakin-Crick, 2007).

Empowering learners

Student voice in academic service-learning is considered to be an important part of the pedagogy. Service-learners need to work out plans of action and are given the responsibility to decide how those actions will be enacted. Putting students in charge of the activities can help them to hone their decision-making skills, learn how to take responsibility for successes and failures, and build self-confidence and leadership capacities (Clark, 1988). Adolescents in particular need a lot of experience exercising these skills before they can apply them fully and efficiently. The students in Argentina were in charge of the project, and thus felt ownership and took responsibility for it. The work provided opportunities for them to develop the skills of analysis, development, planning, implementation, and evaluation that promote higher-order thinking. Community-based learning experiences like service-learning, in which students play a role in the programme design and implementation, can engage students in exercising these important and necessary skills (Eccles and Gootman, 2002).

Moving out of the comfort zone

In service-learning, students often are asked to venture into unfamiliar territory and interact with populations and in communities with which they may be unfamiliar. In these new environments, students are encouraged to reassess their assumptions and preconceived notions about issues and populations. The history students in Argentina had to confront officials in the nearby province to present their case for reclaiming the water. The students in this service-learning experience had to muster the courage to venture to a new location, make their case to sceptical adults, and then assume the responsibility for following through on a commitment on which many hopes rested. Boundary-crossing activities that challenge young people cognitively, physically, and emotionally to move out of their comfort zones have been shown to enhance the development of expert cognition (Engestrom, Engestrom and Merja, 1995).

It is the combination of these pedagogical factors that characterises the essence of service-learning. Each factor has the potential to enhance student learning and promote healthy youth development. Academic service-learning can help to create a favourable learning environment for students and mitigate some of the student disaffection that many schools are facing. Through engagement in the community, students can begin to see how the content they are learning in the classroom has meaning and relevance to their lives outside school. Academic service-learning can also offer students new vistas onto communities and issues with which they may be unfamiliar. For many students, their worlds are circumscribed within the social networks and physical spaces with which they are most accustomed and comfortable. Service-learning can provide opportunities for students to venture into new communities and social circles to address issues to which they have not been previously exposed. Thus, by using the community as a resource for learning, academic service-learning extends the education of students beyond the confines of the school building while keeping learning anchored in the academic subject areas that all young people should master.

With academic service-learning, teachers should be prepared to give up some control over their classrooms as they empower their students to play an active role in the learning process. Teachers need also to take time to develop relationships with community agency representatives who will be important partners in the service-learning enterprise. These community agency representatives will often serve as co-educators, supervising and guiding students through various service and learning tasks, as well as assisting with assessments of student learning and development. For academic service-learning to be effective, teachers must see the classroom activities and the community service projects as inextricably linked. What students learn in the classroom prepares them to do high quality service in the community. In turn, the service activities that students conduct in the community help them gain a better understanding of the academic content to be learned in class.

As an instructional strategy, therefore, academic service-learning should be applied at opportune points in the curriculum when community-based experiences can add value to learning, development and overall educational experiences. Much of how service-learning is implemented depends ultimately on the cultural norms and educational structures present within the systems in question. As service-learning becomes more prevalent in more countries, its character will evolve as national educational priorities and cultural contexts shape the ways in which it is applied in primary and secondary education.

The impacts of service-learning on students

Overall, the research on academic service-learning suggests that it can enhance students' academic, civic, personal, social, ethical and career development. In practice, academic service-learning has certain special features that are not offered through other active learning strategies. However, the extant research suggests that, by and large, these positive impacts may not be qualitatively different than those offered by other experientially-based pedagogies.

The first (English-language) research studies of service-learning published in the early 1980s were stimulated by the emergence of such practice within primary, secondary and higher education. Most such research has been and continues to be conducted in the United States, driven by the presence of research centres, funding and professional networks supporting the study of academic service-learning. The research agenda was originally focused on exploring service-learning's impact on participating students (or service-learners). Over the years, the agenda has gradually expanded to explore the impact on participating teachers, schools and communities, as well as factors that promote high quality service-learning practice and programme sustainability.

Most of the studies assessing the impacts on students have focused mostly on service-learning practice in tertiary or higher education, with more than 250 published studies now available. In contrast, there are fewer than 70 published service-learning impact studies on students enrolled in primary and secondary schools. (This review includes only those studies that have appeared in English-language publications.) Generally, however, the impacts reported from studies of higher education service-learning are parallel to those observed in studies conducted in primary and secondary school settings.

Over the years, sceptics and proponents alike have raised questions about the rigour and overall quality of service-learning research (Furco and Billig, 2002; Bailis and Melchior, 2003; Ziegert and McGoldrick, 2004; Reeb, 2006). For the most part, the body of research has not followed a logical line of inquiry. Rather, it can be best characterised as a mass of disparate studies which are not well-connected with each other or with previous research. Calls for more and better research that meets the standards of scientific inquiry have prompted the development of several research agendas, which have helped to build cogency in the conclusions of different investigations and have led to some important advances in the field (Giles and Eyler, 1998; Billig and Furco, 2002; *Service-Learning in Teacher Education International Research Affinity Group*, 2006).

Compared with the early studies in the field, today's investigations tend to employ more rigorous designs, make clearer ties to related research and prior service-learning studies, use more valid and reliable instruments, and employ more advanced and sophisticated analyses. Much more needs to be done, however, to raise the quality and quantity of service-learning research. Of the 67 published student impact studies based in primary and secondary education, fewer than half employed an experimental or quasi-experimental design with the others being outcome assessments in non-experimental conditions, analyses of existing data, or assessments from secondary data sources (*e.g.* teachers' reports of student outcomes). In many cases, the quality of the study is difficult to ascertain due to the lack of detail about the conceptual framework, research design, instrumentation and/or methodology. Such limitations notwithstanding and while more research is needed to confirm conclusions about the impacts of service-learning, the available evidence is allowing the picture of the potential impact on students to begin to come into focus.

Given that the practice of service-learning is built on classroom-based academic activities and civic-oriented community service, much of the research has focused on assessing impact on students' academic and civic development. The research summary presented below is based on a review of 55 investigations, most of which were conducted in primary and secondary schools.* As academic service-learning tends to be applied broadly as both an educational initiative and a community service programme in the United States, the primary outcomes from these studies are likely to have some relevance and generalisability to service-learning practices in other countries.

Academic Achievement and Educational Success

Much of the research on student impacts has centred on investigating the ways in which service-learning advances students' academic achievement and overall educational success. Akujobi and Simmons (1997), Klute and Billig (2002) and Kraft and Wheeler (2003) all found significantly higher improvements in reading and language arts among service-learning participants when compared to a comparable group of students not engaged in service-learning. In other quasi-experimental studies, researchers have noted similar positive academic impacts from service-learning participation in the areas of mathematics (Melchior, 1998; Melchior and Bailis, 2002; Davila and Mora, 2007), science (Klute and Billig; 2002; Davila and Mora, 2007) and

---

* The primary sources for 12 of the 67 studies cited in the service-learning literature were not accessible; the findings for these studies are not included in this research summary. The author wishes to acknowledge the contributions of Dr. Susan Root and Ms. Lisa Burton for their assistance in identifying and locating studies for this review.

social studies (Meyer, Billig and Hofschire, 2004; Davila and Mora, 2007). However, while the overall effect is statistically significant in all of these cases, the size of the effects has been generally small.

More robust outcomes have been found, however, in other areas of students' academic development. Several studies have revealed that, when compared with comparable students not engaged in such programmes, service-learning students maintain higher levels of motivation for learning (Conrad and Hedin, 1981; Melchior, 1995; Melchior, 1998; Scales *et al.*, 2000; Furco, 2002b; Hecht, 2002; Brown, Kim and Pinhas, 2005; Scales *et al.*, 2006), have improved student attendance (Follman and Muldoon, 1997; Melchior, 1998; Scales *et al.*, 2006), and have fewer disciplinary problems in the classroom (Calabrese and Schumer, 1986). Other studies reveal that service-learners maintain a stronger pursuit of good grades compared with students non-participants (Scales *et al.*, 2000; Ammon *et al.*, 2002), and have larger improvements in their academic marks and grade point averages (Laird and Black, 1999). Participants in these programmes have also reported learning more in service-learning classes than their other classes at school (Weiler *et al.*, 1998).

Beyond the classroom, several studies have found that students who participate in service-learning show stronger interest and engagement in school than comparable non-participating students (Melchior, 1995; Melchior, 1998), and are less likely to drop out of school (Bridgeland, Dilulio and Morison, 2006). In addition, students reported having a deeper commitment and connectedness to school work (Scales *et al.*, 2000; Scales *et al.*, 2006) because of their participation in service-learning. According to Scales *et al.* (2000), the number of hours of service-learning (31 hours or more), along with the amount and type of reflection and motivation to engage in community service and service-learning, predicted this outcome.

Although the research to date suggests that service-learning can have positive effects on a variety of academic areas, more research is needed to draw firmer conclusions. More experimental studies that include high quality service-learning programmes should produce additional insights into the various ways students learn and develop through such programmes. Moreover, we need trans-national studies conducted within and across different national contexts are needed to understand better how the local culture and social attitudes toward community involvement shape the service-learning experience and its impact on students.

Civic and citizenship development

Perhaps more than any other experiential or community-engaged learning pedagogy, academic service-learning has a strong civic dimension at its core. Its emphasis on community service establishes an inherent civic dimension that promotes social responsibility and citizenship among participants. Findings from the handful of civic-focused research studies available suggest that participating in academic service-learning and related community-based learning experiences can enhance: students' political knowledge and efficacy (Hamilton and Zeldin, 1987); political engagement (Morgan and Streb, 2001); self-efficacy for volunteering (Hamilton and Fenzel, 1988); attitudes towards government (Hamilton and Zeldin, 1987); participation in civic issues (Kahne and Sporte, 2008); likelihood to vote in the future (Hart, Donnelly, Youniss and Atkins, 2007); and likelihood to volunteer in the future (Hamilton and Fenzel, 1988).

Hart *et al.* (2007) assessed different types and levels of community service participation ("voluntary", "required", "mixed" and "no service") and found that all forms of community service were associated with elevated levels of voting. Their analyses revealed that while the frequency of community service in secondary school predicted future community service and engagement, the form this took (voluntary, required, mixed) did not. Voluntary community service in secondary school did predict future community involvement but mixed and required community service did not.

These results support those of a previous study which found that young adults who were required to participate in community service activities during their university studies were less likely to participate in community service five years after graduating than students who had participated voluntarily during their time at university (Stukas, Snyder and Clary, 1999). However, whether requiring community service or service-learning promotes positive civic (and academic) development remains to be seen. As some scholars have suggested, it is the overall quality and meaningful character of the experience that matters most (Billig, Root and Jesse, 2005). When students perceive service-learning as simply another school assignment to be completed, it can promote negative feelings for both the participating students and the members of the community (Covitt, 2002b).

Findings from in the Citizenship Education Longitudinal Study (CELS) – a national study of England's required citizenship education programme for secondary school students – are relevant to these issues (Benton, Cleaver, Featherstone, Kerr, Lopes and Whitby, 2008). Here, the citizenship education curriculum has sought to engage students in community-based activities, including service-learning, to develop their civic capacities and skills (Annette, 2000). As the only large-scale, longitudinal, national study on student citizenship development (and one of the few non-U.S. studies on youth service), Benton *et al.* (2008) measured the extent to which students' civic attitudes changed over a five-year period. The findings reveal that over time, students came to feel less attached to their communities, saw fewer opportunities to participate actively in lessons, were less trusting of authority figures and felt less empowered (Benton *et al.*, 2008). The researchers report that despite participating in the citizenship education curriculum, students maintain a narrow conception of civic engagement, focusing mostly on participation activities that require low levels of time (*e.g.* voting); there is no evidence that students have embraced broader notions of civic participation (*e.g.* volunteering or community service) that require more substantial commitments.

Programme quality has become an issue receiving some attention in recent studies. Not all service-learning is equal, and there are some elements that are fundamental to high quality service-learning practice. These elements include: sufficient duration and intensity of the experience, strong links between the service activities and the academic curriculum, collaborative and mutually beneficial partnerships with community members, meaningful service activities, student voice and choice, and ongoing reflection and analysis of the experience (Billig and Weah, 2008).

The importance of programme quality in service-learning was further addressed in a study by Billig, Root and Jesse (2005). The researchers used a battery of civic-focused measures that measure students' knowledge about government institutions and leaders, capacity to perform civic skills such as election campaigning, sense of belonging to the community, level of participation to meet community needs, feelings of making a difference and assuming adult roles, and current and future engagement in political discourse and activities. The researchers found that civic outcomes were generally more positive among students engaged in service-learning experiences of longer duration and whose teachers were more experienced with service-learning implementation. Students who participated in **direct service** (*e.g.* visiting seniors or tutoring) reported feeling more engaged with the community than did students participating in **indirect service** (*e.g.* fundraising). These findings support the results of an earlier study (Morgan and Streb, 2001) which found that service-learning is more likely to enhance self-concept, political engagement, and attitudes towards the elderly and the disabled when the experience contains a greater number of quality practice elements (*e.g.* service-learners perceive that they have real responsibilities, challenging tasks, as well as opportunities to plan the projects and make important decisions).

Other student outcomes

In addition to the academic and civic outcomes of academic service-learning, researchers have also explored various moral, vocational, personal, and social development outcomes. The findings from research in these areas suggest that service-learning as an instructional strategy can enhance the goals of other educational programmes, including values education, health promotion projects, drug abuse prevention initiatives, and youth leadership development activities. This research has helped to promote a broader range of service-learning forms beyond the core academic curriculum.

Several studies have found service-learning to be an effective instructional strategy for developing students' leadership capacity (Ladewig and Thomas, 1987; Weiler *et al.,* 1998; Boyd, 2001). In a study by Boyd (2001), students demonstrated significant increases in their capacity to make decisions and to engage in successful group work, based on a Leadership Life Skills Inventory. Boyd attributes these positive results to the principles of the community action programme, which involves students in assessing the needs of the community, planning the projects, practising decision-making and problem-solving, communicating with different audiences, and working in teams.

A number of recent studies have examined the relationship between service-learning and values development (Furco, Middaugh, Goss, Darche, Hwang and Tabernik, 2004; Berkowitz and Bier, 2005; Lovat and Toomey, 2007; Billig, Jesse, Brodersen and Grimley, 2008). Much of this research has grown out of concerns among proponents of values education that current approaches do not provide enough opportunities for students to practice in authentic settings the value traits they learn about from character education curricula (Lovat and Toomey, 2007). As Lovat and Toomey (2007) suggest, values education outcomes improve when the curriculum is tied to quality teaching practices, which include authentic, experiential learning opportunities.

Where national values education programmes are in operation, such as Australia and the United States, service-learning is being used to enhance the delivery of the values education curriculum. For example, Billig *et al.* (2008) assessed pre-post changes in values development among middle and secondary school students over a three-year period. The researchers compared the development of caring, altruism, citizenship, civic responsibility, persistence and respect (for self and others) between a group of students engaged in a character education curriculum that included service-learning activities and a group of students whose character education curriculum lacked this additional element. Their results support prior research findings that suggest that as young people mature, there is a gradual but steady diminution of values attainment (Furco *et al.*, 2004). Billig *et al.* (2008) found that over time, the students who participated in service-learning character education programmes had significantly less of a drop in value attainment than the students who did not. This suggests that service-learning helps students to retain their value (or character) assets as they mature.

Other research studies have found that service-learning and related community-engagement programmes can have positive impacts on students' self esteem (Yates and Youniss, 1996; Johnson and Notah, 1999; Martin, Neal, Kielsmeier and Crossley, 2006); sexual behaviour (Kirby, 2001; O'Donnell *et al.*, 2002); substance use (Tebes, *et al.*, 2007); preparation for the workforce

(Yamauchi, Billig, Meyer and Hofschire, 2006); transitions to adulthood (Martin, Neal, Kielsmeier and Crossley, 2006); and preparation for higher education (Furco, 2002a). In most of these investigations unfortunately the researchers did not extend the discussion beyond the classrooms or communities that were studied and their generalisability is limited. And, because few of the studies have yet to be replicated, strong assertions about service-learning's impacts in these areas cannot be made at this time.

Looking to the future

Overall, academic service-learning offers a way to rethink the ways in which education is delivered to primary and secondary students. Beyond the pedagogical issues, the practice of service-learning also has implications for how the curriculum is structured, student outcomes are assessed, teachers are trained and schools are managed. For example, the societal issues that students address through service-learning are inherently interdisciplinary in nature. A project about removing toxins from a polluted stream can require students to apply their knowledge and skills in science, mathematics, language arts and even history. As in the service-learning class in Argentina, the activities not only engaged students in learning history, but also mathematics, science, government, language arts and a host of career-related skills. The discipline-focused, subject-matter organisation of the curriculum in many school systems is often not conducive to facilitating inherently interdisciplinary learning activities. Therefore, even with a growing number of studies pointing to positive outcomes from service-learning participation, its practice may continue to struggle for academic legitimacy in educational systems until they evolve enough to make room for more innovative approaches like service-learning.

As academic service-learning comes of age in more countries, more and better research will be needed to determine to what extent it offers true value-added for students as well as for the communities served. As more nations adopt such initiatives and/or implement different forms of national service, there will likely be demand for cross-national assessment of service-learning. A growing number of efforts are underway to expand the global reach of service-learning, including international research conferences (*e.g.* the annual conference hosted by the International Association for Research on Service-Learning and Community Engagement); multi-language websites focused on service-learning and community engagement (*e.g. www.tufts.edu/talloiresnetwork*); and multi-national networks that support practitioners, such as *Centro Latinoamericano de Aprendizaje y Servicio Solidario* (CLAYSS) in South America and the new International Alliance for Academic Service-Learning. There are national and international efforts underway to prepare the next generation of primary and secondary school teachers with the skills they need to practice academic service-learning effectively. Much of this work is conducted through the International Association for Service-Learning in Teacher Education, which hosts an international biennial conference of prospective service-learning educators and scholars in teacher education. One of this Association's research projects is the development of a survey to assess the status of service-learning in teacher education across the globe (Anderson, Furco and Root, 2009).

The future research agenda for service-learning will call for studies that employ larger randomly-selected samples, more advanced analyses, and longitudinal designs to assess long-term impacts. The agenda should include more analysis of the specific programmatic features that have positive impacts on different areas of student development. The service-learning field could also benefit from targeted analysis of the unique effects of service-learning compared with related experientially-focused pedagogies that use the community as a resource for learning. Lastly, more in-depth international assessments and comparisons are needed to assess the true scale and scope of service-learning practice across the globe. Academic service-learning is likely to continue to gain attention in different educational systems especially given the growing evidence of its generally positive outcomes. More rigorous and refined investigations will further advance the evidence base and more precisely ascertain the true strengths and limitations of service-learning and related instructional pedagogies.

References

Akujobi, C. and R. Simmons (1997), "An Assessment of Elementary School Service-Learning Teaching Methods: Using Service-Learning Goals", *NSEE Quarterly*, Vol. 23, No 2, pp. 19-28.

Ammon, M.S., A. Furco, B. Chi and E. Middaugh (2002), *A Profile of California's Calserve Service-Learning Partnerships: 1997-2000*, California Department of Education, Sacramento, California.

Anderson, J., A. Furco and S. Root (2009), *Assessing the Status of Service-Learning in Teacher Education: International Perspectives*, International Association for Service-Learning in Teacher Education, Clemson, South Carolina.

Annette, J. (2000), "Education for Citizenship, Civic Participation and Experiential Learning and Service Learning in the Community", in D. Lawton, J. Cairns and R. Gardner (eds.), *Education for Citizenship*, Continuum, London, pp. 149-160.

Bailis, L. and A. Melchior (2003), "Practical Issues in the Conduct of Large-Scale, Multisite Research and Evaluation", in S.H. Billig and A.S. Waterman (eds.), *Studying Service-Learning: Innovations in Education Research Methodology*, Erlbaum Associates, Mahwah, pp. 125-147.

Benton, T., E. Cleaver, G. Featherstone, D. Kerr, J. Lopes and K. Whitby (2008), *Citizenship Education Longitudinal Study (CELS): Sixth Annual Report*, National Fourndation for Educational Research, Berkshire, England.

Berkowitz, M. and M. Bier (2005), *What Works in Character Education: A Report for Policy Makers and Opinion Leaders*, Character Education Partnership, Washington, DC.

Billig, S.H. and A. Furco (2002), "Research Agenda for K-12 Service-Learning: A Proposal to the Field", in A. Furco and S.H. Billig (eds.), *Service-Learning: The Essence of the Pedagogy*, Information Age Publishing, Greenwich, Connecticut: Information Age Publishing, pp. 271-280.

Billig, S.H., D. Jesse, R.M. Brodersen and M. Grimley (2008), "Promoting Secondary Students' Character Development in Schools through Service-Learning", in M.A. Bowdon, S.H. Billig and B.A. Holland (eds.), *Scholarship for Sustaining Service-Learning and Civic Engagement*, Information Age Publishing, Greenwich, CT, pp. 57-83.

Billig, S.H., S. Root and D. Jesse (2005), *The Impact of Participation in Service-Learning on High School Students' Civic Engagement,* The Center for Information and Research on Civic Learning and Engagement, College Park, Maryland.

Billig, S.H. and W. Weah (2008), "K-12 Service-Learning Standards for Quality Practice", in J. C. Kielsmeier, *et al.* (eds.), Growing to Greatness 2008: The State of Service-Learning Project, National Youth Leadership Council , St. Paul, MN, pp. 8-15.

Boyd, B. (2001), "Bringing Leadership Experiences to Inner-City Youth", *Journal of Extension,* Vol. 394, No. 4.

Boyd, B.L. (2001), "Bringing Leadership Experience to Inner-City Youth", *Journal of Extension*, Vol. 39, No.4.

Bridgeland, J.M., J.J. Dilulio and K.B. Morison (2006), *The Silent Epidemic: Perspectives of High School Dropouts,* Bill and Melinda Gates Foundation.

Brown, S., W. Kim and S. Pinhas (2005), *Texas Title IV Service-Learning Evaluation, 2004-2005, Interim Report,* RMC Denver Corporation, Denver, Colorado.

Cairn, R. and J. Kielsmeier (1991), *Growing Hope: A Sourcebook on Integrating Youth Service into the School Curriculum,* National Youth Leadership Council, St. Paul, Minnesota.

Calabrese, R.L. and H. Schumer (1986), "The Effects of Service Activities on Adolescent Alienation", *Adolescence,* Vol. 21, No. 83, pp. 675-687.

Clark, R.M. (1988), *Critical Factors in Why Disadvantaged Students Succeed or Fail in School,* Academy for Educational Development, New York.

Conrad, D. and D. Hedin (1981), *National Assessment of Experiential Education: A Final Report,* Center for Youth Development and Research, University of Minnesota, St. Paul, Minnesota.

Covitt, B.A. (2002a), *Middle School Students' Attitude Toward Required Chesapeake Bay Service-Learning,* Corporation for National and Community Service, Washington, DC.

Covitt, B.A. (2002b), Motivating Environmentally Responsible Behaviors through Service-Learning, Corporation for National Service, Washington, DC.

Davila, A. and M. Mora (2007), *Civic Engagement and High School Academic Progress: An Analysis Using NELS Data,* The Center for Information and Research on Civic Learning and Engaagement, College Park, Maryland.

Deci, E.L. (1984), "Quality of Learning with an Active Versus Passive Motivational Set", *American Educational Research Journal,* Vol. 21, No. 4, pp. 755-765.

Eccles, J. and J.A. Gootman (eds.) (2002), *Community Programs to Promote Youth Development,* National Academies Press, Washington, DC.

Engestrom, Y., R. Engestrom and K. Merja (1995), "Polycontextuality and Boundary Crossing in Expert Cognition: Learning and Problem Solving in Complex Work Activities", *Learning and Instruction,* Vol. 5, No. 4, pp. 319-336.

Erickson, F. (1990), "Going for the Zone: The Social and Cognitive Ecology of Teacher-Student Interaction in Classroom Conversations", in D. Hicks (ed.), *Discourse, Learning, and Schooling,* Cambridge University Press, Cambridge, pp. 29-62.

Eyler, J.S. and D.E. Giles (1999), *Where's the Learning in Service-Learning?,* Jossey-Bass, San Francisco.

Follman, J. and K. Muldoon (1997), "Florida Learn and Serve 1995-96: What Are the Outcomes?", *NASSP Bulletin*, Vol. 81, No. 591, pp. 29-36.

Fosnot, C.T. (ed.) (1996), *Constructivism, Theory, Perspectives, and Practice,* Teachers College Press, New York.

Furco, A. (1996), "Service-Learning: A Balanced Approach to Experiential Education", in B. Taylor (ed.), *Expanding Boundaries: Service and Learning,* Corporation for National and Community Service, Washington, DC, pp. 2-6.

Furco, A. (2002a), "High School Service-Learning and the Preparation of Students for College: An Overview of the Research", in E. Zlotkowski (ed.), *Service-learning and the First-year Experience: Preparing Students for Personal Success and Civic Responsibility,* University of South Carolina, National Resource Center for the First-Year Experience and Students in Transition, Columbia, South Carolina, pp. 3-14.

Furco, A. (2002b), "Is Service-Learning Really Better Than Community Service?: A Study of High School Service Program Outcomes", in A. Furco and S.H. Billig (eds.), *Service-Learning: The Essence of the pedagogy,* Information Age Publishing, Greenwich, Connecticut, pp. 23-50.

Furco, A. and S.H. Billig (2002), "Establishing Norms for Scientific Inquiry in Service-Learning", in S. H. Billig and A. Furco (eds.), *Service-Learning through a Multidisciplinary Lens,* Information Age Publishing, Greenwich, Connecticut, pp. 15-31.

Furco, A., E. Middaugh, M. Goss, S. Darche, J. Hwang and T. Tabernik (2004), *A Study of Character Development in Elementary School Students: Preliminary Findings,* U.S. Department of Education, Washington, DC.

Furco, A. (2007), "Experiential Education as a Pedaogy of Engagement", paper presented for the National Society for Experiential Education, Seattle, Washington.

Giles, D.E. and J. Eyler (1998), "A Service Learning Research Agenda for the Next Five Years", *New Directions in Teaching and Learning,* Vol. 73, No. 1, pp. 65-72.

Hamilton, S. and L.M Fenzel (1988), "The Impact of Volunteer Experience on Adolescent Social Development: Evidence of Program Effects", *Journal of Adolescent Research,* Vol. 3, No.1, pp. 65-80.

Hamilton, S. and R.S. Zeldin (1987), "Learning Civics in the Community", *Curriculum Inquiry,* Vol. 17, No. 4, pp. 407-420.

Hart, D., J. Youniss and R. Atkins (2007), "High School Community Service as a Predictor of Adult Voting and Volunteering", *American Educational Research Journal,* Vol. 44, No. 1, pp. 197-219.

Hecht, D. (2002), "The Missing Link: Exploring the Context of Learning in Service-Learning", paper presented at the 2nd Annual International Research Conference on Service-Learning, Nashville, Tennessee.

Jaros, M. and R. Deakin-Crick (2007), "Personalized Learning for the Post-Mechanical Age", *Journal of Curriculum Studies,* Vol. 39, No. 4, pp. 423-440.

Johnson, A. and D. Notah (1999), "Service-Learning: History, Literature, and a Pilot Study of Eighth Graders", *The Elementary School Journal,* Vol. 99, No. 5, pp. 453-467.

Johnson, D.W. and R.T. Johnson (2006), "Co-operative Learning and Social Interdependence Theory", in R.S. Tindale, *et al.* (eds.), *Theory and Research on Small Groups,* Springer, New York, pp. 9-35.

Kahne, J. and S. Sporte (2008), "Developing Citizens: The Impact of Civic Learning Opportunities on Students' Commitment to Civic Participation", *American Educational Research Journal*, Vol. 45, No. 3, pp. 738-766.

Kirby, D. (2001), *Emerging Answers: Research Findings on Programs to Reduce Teen Pregnancy,* National Campaign to Reduce Teen Pregnancy, Washington, DC.

Klute, M.M. and S.H. Billig (2002), *The Impact of Service-Learning on MEAP: A Large-Scale Study of Michigan Learn and Serve Grantees,* RMC Research, Denver, Colorado.

Kolb, D. (1984), *Experiential Learning: Experience As The Source of Learning and Development,* Prentice Hall, Englewood Cliffs, New Jersey.

Kraft, N. and J. Wheeler (2003), "Service-Learning and Resilience in Disaffected Youth: A Research Study", in J. Eyler and S.H. Billig (eds.), *Deconstructing Service-Learning: Research Exploring Context, Participation, and Impacts,* Information Age Publishing, Greenwich, Connecticut, pp. 213-238.

Ladewig, H. and J.K. Thomas (1987), *Assessing the Impact of 4-H on Former Members,* Texas A and M University, College Station.

Laird, M. and S. Black (1999), *Service-Learning Evaluation Project: Program Effects for at-Risk Students,* Quest International, San Francisco.

Lovat, T. and R. Toomey (2007), *Values Education and quality teaching: The double helix effect,* David Barlow Publishing, Sydney.

Martin, S., M. Neal, J. Kielsmeier and A. Crossley (2006), "The Impact of Service-Learning on Transitions to Adulthood", in J. Kielsmeier, M. Neal and A. Crossley (eds.), *Growing to Greatness: The State of Service-Learning Project*, National Youth Leadership Council, St. Paul, Minnesota, pp. 4-24.

Melchior, A. (1995), *National Evaluation of Serve-America: Final Report,* Center for Human Resources, Brandeis University, Waltham, Massachusetts.

Melchior, A. (1998), *National Evaluation of Learn and Serve America School and Community-Based Program,* Center for Human Resources, Brandeis University, Waltham, Massachusetts.

Melchior, A. and L. Bailis (2002), "Impact of Service-Learning on Civic Attitudes and Behaviors of Middle School and High School Youth: Findings from Three National Evaluations", in A. Furco and S.H. Billig (eds.), *Service-Learning: The Essence of the Pedagogy,* Information Age Publishing, Greenwich, Connecticut, pp. 201-222.

Meyer, S.J., S.H. Billig and L. Hofschire (2004), "The Impact of K-12 School-Based Service-Learning on Academic Achievement and Student Engagement in Michigan", in M. Welch and S.H. Billig (eds.), *Service-Learning: Research to Advance the Field,* Information Age Publishing, Greenwich, Connecticut, pp. 61-85.

Morgan, W. and M. Streb (2001), "Building Citizenship: How Student Voice in Service-Learning Develops Civic Values", *Social Science Quarterly,* Vol. 82, No. 1, pp. 154-169.

Newmann, F.M. and R.A. Rutter (1983), *The Effects of High School Community Service Programs on Students' Social Development,* Wisconsin Center for Education Research, University of Wisconsin, Madison, Wisconsin.

O'Donnell, L., A.Stueve, C. O'Donnell, R. Duran, A. San Doval, R. Wilson, D. Haber, E. Perry and J.H. Pleck (2002), "Long-Term Reductions in Sexual Initiation and Sexual Activity Among Urban Middle Schoolers in the Research for Health Service Learning Program", *Journal of Adolescent Health,* Vol. 31, No. 1, pp. 93-100.

Prince, M. (2004), "Does Active Learning Work? A Review of the Research", *Journal of Engineering Education,* Vol. 93, No. 3, pp. 223-231.

Reeb, R.N. (2006), "Community Service Self-efficacy: Research Review", *Academic Exchange Quarterly,* spring, pp 1-9.

Scales, P., D. Blythe, T. Berkas and J. Kielsmeier (2000), "The Effects of Service-Learning on Middle School Students' Social Responsibility and Academic Success", *Journal of Early Adolescence,* Vol. 20, No. 3, pp. 332-358.

Scales, P.C., E.C. Roehlkepartain, M. Neal, J.C. Kielsmeir and P.L. Benson (2006), "Reducing Academic Achievement Gaps: The Role of Community Service and Service-Learning", *Journal of Experiential Education,* Vol. 29, No. 1, pp. 38-60.

Scheckley, B.G. and M.T. Keeton (1997), "Service Learning: A Theoretical Model", in J. Schine (ed.), *Service learning: Ninety-Sixth Yearbook of the National Society for the Study of Education, Part I,* University of Chicago Press, Chicago, pp. 32-55.

Service-Learning in Teacher Education International Research Affinity Group (2006), "A Research Agenda for Advancing Service-Learning in Teacher Education", paper presented at the International Research Conference on Service-Learning and Community Engagement, Portland, Oregon.

Slavin, R. (1986), *Using Student Team Learning* (3rd edition.), Johns Hopkins University, Baltimore, Maryland.

Slavkin, M.L. (2004), *Authentic Learning: How Learning About the Brain Can Shape the Development of Students,* Scarecrow Education, Lanham, Maryland.

Spring, K., R. Grimm and N. Dietz (2008), *Community Service and Service-Learning in America's Schools,* Corporation for National and Community Service, Washington, DC.

Stukas, A.A., M. Snyder and E.G. Clary (1999), "The Effects of 'Mandatory Volunteerism' on Intentions to Volunteer, *Psychological Science,* Vol. 10, No. 1, pp. 59-64.

Tapia, M.N. (2007), "The Potential Effects of Service-Learning and Community Service in Educational Settings in Latin America", in A.M. McBride and M. Sherraden (eds.), *Civic Service Worldwide,* M.E. Sharpe, London, pp. 133-156.

Tapia, M.N. (2008), *Service-Learning Research in Argentina,* Centro Latinoamericano de Aprendizaje y Servicio Solidario (CLAYSS), Buenos Aires.

Tebes, J.K., R. Feinn, J.J. Vanderploeg, M.J. Chinman, J. Shepard, T. Brabham, M. Genovese and C. Connell (2007), "Impact of a Positive Youth Development Program in Urban After-School Settings on the Prevention of Adolescent Substance Use", *Journal of Adolescent Health,* Vol. 41, No. 3, pp. 239-247.

Weiler, D., A. LaGoy, E. Crane and A. Rovner (1998), *An Evaluation of K-12 Service-Learning in California: Phase II Final Report,* RPP International, Emeryville, California.

Yamauchi, L.A., S.H. Billig, S. Meyer and L. Hofschire (2006), "Student Outcomes Associated with Service-Learning in a Culturally Relevant High School Program", *Journal of Prevention and Intervention in the Community,* Vol. 32, No. 1, pp. 149-164.

Yates, M. and J. Youniss (1996), "A Developmental Perspective on Community Service in Adolescence, *Social Development,* Vol. 5, No. 1, pp. 85-111.

Ziegert, A.L. and K. McGoldrick (2004), "Adding Rigor to Service-Learning Research: An Armchair Economists' Approach", in M. Welch and S.H. Billig (eds.), *Service-Learning: Research to Advance the Field,* Information Age Publishing, Greenwich, Connecticut, pp. 23-36.

Chapter 11

The effects of family on children's learning and socialisation

Barbara Schneider, Venessa Keesler and Larissa Morlock
Michigan State University

Barbara Schneider, Venessa Keesler and Larissa Morlock address (a) how families influence children's learning development, (b) what families influence and (c) when this influence takes place. Socio-economic status exercises a profound influence on student learning yet is not simply deterministic as individual families play a key role, arguably a more important one than schools in shaping educational expectations, occupational aspirations and academic performance. Research shows how children's well-being and development are influenced by the engagement of both mothers and fathers. Children are more likely to learn when they have structured home environments with clear expectations about learning but adapted to child-specific needs and personalities. The socialisation received at home is critical to the development of ambition and perceived self-efficacy. Engaging in extra-curricular activities and parental involvement in schooling both show positive results, but they are beneficial particularly when they are consistent with the goals and activities of the school.

Introduction

The family is the first and primary social system in which young children begin to acquire fundamental cognitive and social skills that shape their motivation and early preparation for the challenges of schooling (Machida, Taylor and Kim, 2002). In the beginning stages of child development, parenting quality has been commonly measured by maternal supportiveness, sensitivity and responsiveness. These characteristics have been shown to be related to children's language skills, problem-solving, early number concept acquisition, classification abilities and interpersonal skills (Lugo-Gil and Tamis-LeMonda, 2008). Through familial relationships, children learn the fundamentals of communication, organisational skills and delegation of roles and responsibilities, as well as the family's educational expectations for their futures (Smith *et al.*, 2001). This chapter addresses **how** families influence children's learning development, **what** families influence and **when** this influence takes place.

How families influence their children's learning development

Parental impacts on learning: genetic factors

To understand how families influence their children's learning, one must consider both the biological and the environmental conditions critical in the developmental process. Disentangling some of the direct biological effects from those in the environment is a matter that continues to attract research from both social and biological sciences. Some researchers with a genetic perspective have argued that the relationship between children's development and environmental factors, such as parenting practices, has been overestimated in developmental research (Harris, 1995, 1998; Rowe, 1994; Scarr, 1992). Others take a more encompassing approach, arguing that individual differences in cognitive development and psychological dispositions are a function of both genetics and socialisation (Bouchard and McGue, 2003).

The case for paying closer attention to genetics is that when it is ignored, it limits the types of questions that can be investigated as well as the types of explanations that can be provided. Recent neuro-scientific studies examining the structure and functioning of the brain as it relates to learning and memory have focused on functions of the human brain as it interacts with the environment (Goswami, 2004). Increasingly, consensus is emerging in neuro-scientific research that the brain is malleable to experience throughout the lifespan (Baltes, Reuter-Lorenz and Rösler, 2006; Doyon and Benali, 2005; Geary and Huffman, 2002; Huttenlocher, 2002; Jenkins, Merzenich and Recanzone, 1990; OECD, 2007; Thelen and Smith, 1994). For example, researchers have shown that severe deprivation of social interaction in early childhood can alter one's neurochemistry and the production of oxytocin; this is a hormone implicated in social behaviour that influences bonding as well as protection against stress and pycho-pathology, such as anxiety and depression (Fries *et al.*, 2005; Heim *et al.*, 2008; Meinlschmidt and Heim, 2007).

These findings from neuroscience are consistent with the social science research that has emphasised the dynamic interactive relationship between genes and the environment (Maccoby, 2000). Supporting this position, Duyme, Dumaret and Tomkiewicz (1999) showed significant influences of both genes and the environment in a study of adopted children. Prior to adoption, the IQ scores of children who had been abused or neglected as infants were at least one standard deviation below the mean (<86). By 13 years of age, those children adopted by families with higher socio-economic status (SES) had significantly higher IQ scores (average IQ = 98) than those adopted by families with lower SES (average IQ = 85). However, they also found hereditary effects: the children's IQ scores at age 13 were significantly correlated with those of their biological parents, regardless of the SES of their adoptive family.

This study and several others (Dickens and Flynn, 2001; Kendler and Greenspan, 2006; Rutter, 2008; Uher, 2008) highlight the importance of the interactive influence of biology and environmental factors on children's cognitive and social development. Bronfenbrenner and Ceci's bio-ecological model (1994) provides a framework for interpreting the findings of Duyme and colleagues, proposing that all people have genetic potential which is actualised through interaction with the environment in what they refer to as a "proximal process". Similarly, Rutter (2008) argues that environmental risk and protective factors can impede or facilitate the realisation of genetic potential.

What seems most important about the links between genes and the environment is that humans and the social contexts they inhabit are fluid and permeable. The brain makes modifications **and** the environment matters. However, the environment appears to matter more for those who are economically and socially disadvantaged. Recent research on black and white children's test scores suggest that differences in cognitive performance among individuals in advantaged environments are influenced more by genetic factors, whereas differences in cognitive performance among those in less advantaged environments are more closely related to environmental conditions (Turkheimer *et al.*, 2003).

Parental impacts on learning: status variables

We now turn to those conditions in the household that have also been shown to affect learning. Social science, and educational research specifically, have focused on the impact that so-called "status variables" such as socioeconomic background and family structure have on the learning process.

Socio-economic background

Certain household characteristics have been shown to influence student learning profoundly. These characteristics generally include the human, financial, and social resources in the family, usually referred to as socio-economic status (SES). This multidimensional construct is typically measured with several indicators, including household income, parental education, occupation and family structure and relationships of individuals in the household (Entwisle and Astone, 1994). Social status – one indicator of SES – can be understood as the rank on a societal hierarchy that is conferred through education, income and social ties, reflecting differential access to, and control of, desirable resources (Mueller and Parcel, 1981). One's position on this social hierarchy imbues particular values and orientations toward work, school, and towards other individuals and social groups. These orientations are transmitted to children, often over generations, socialising them into a particular set of behaviours and motivations.

Decades of research have shown a strong relationship between SES and student achievement. Among the components of SES, the strongest effects are found with parental education (*e.g.* Baker, Riordan and Schaub, 1995; Boyle *et al.*, 2007; Zhou, Moen and Tuma, 1998). One of the earliest classic studies of SES and its influence was conducted by Blau and Duncan in 1967 in which they analysed survey data from over 20 000 participants, finding a direct link between parent education and the occupations their children pursued as adults. Coleman *et al.* (1966) and others also showed a significant relationship between family SES and achievement. More recently, results from the 2004 National Assessment of Educational Progress (NAEP) confirmed that students whose parents completed higher levels of education tend to perform better academically (Perie, Moran and Lutkus, 2005).

Not only are the effects of SES considerable, they are also enduring. Children with lower SES are at increased risk of repeating a grade (Bianchi, 1984; Byrd and Weitzman, 1994; Dawson, 1991; Entwisle *et al.*, 1988) and dropping out of high school (Alexander, Entwisle and Kabbani, 2001; Haveman, Wolfe and Spaulding, 1991; Laird, DeBell and Chapman, 2006; Rumberger, 1983, 1987). Research has linked both of these educational events to subsequent lower levels of educational attainment, less stable employment and higher incidences of family disruption (Chen and Kaplan, 2003; Hout, 1988). The sustaining effects of SES are also evident in post-secondary education. In a nationally-representative longitudinal study, Goldrick-Rab (2006) found that, even after controlling for the effect of prior achievement, students from lower SES backgrounds experienced more interruptions in their college education than their higher SES peers.

The relationship between SES and achievement is partly due to educational expectations, which are higher in families with greater economic and social resources. Sewell and Hauser (1972, 1980) investigated the causal path between parental background characteristics and student achievement by including in their models students' educational expectations – that is, what degrees the students expected to attain after high school. They showed that through interactions with significant others, primarily their parents, students develop educational expectations which subsequently affect their achievement.

Today, we continue to view parental educational expectations as part of a larger value system, transmitted by parents to their children. Research has consistently shown that the educational expectations that parents have for their children represent one of key mechanisms through which parents influence their children's schooling careers. As noted by Bourdieu (1984), it is the inter-action of families and friends that influence children's patterns of behaviour – from the foods they prefer, the style of clothes they wear, to their manner of speaking. Culturally transmitted norms and behaviours can have profoundly enduring effects and some of this transmission occurs in classrooms between students and teachers. In addition to these expectations, parents also hold expectations regarding their adolescents' performance in courses critical for post-secondary prospects, such as advanced-level high school mathemat-ics and science. Frome and Eccles (1998) showed that parents' expectations regarding their children's mathematics ability had more influence on the chil-dren's own perception of their abilities than their grades did.

Family structure

Family structure also plays a role in children's learning. Children from single-parent families are more likely to experience negative developmental outcomes (*e.g.* Park, 2007; Pong, Dronkers and Hampden-Thompson, 2003; Pong and Ju, 2000). Family size and parent responsibilities are also likely to influence children's learning and social skills as these factors are associated with the amount of time parents have to devote to interactions with their children. However, as noted by Weinraub, Horvath and Gringlas (2002), there is significant variation among families of different household configura-tions that may mediate some effects of structure. Duncan, Brooks-Gunn and Klebanov (1994) found that while ability scores were higher for children from dual-parent households, nearly all of this association could be explained by family income and poverty status.

The occupational experiences of parents are also an important factor in children's learning although the effects are less direct than those of parental education. Parents' work characteristics and attitudes can shape adolescents' work values, specifically the characteristics of occupations that adolescents see as viable choices for themselves (Galambos and Sears, 1998; Jodl *et al.*, 2001; Kracke, 2002; Mortimer, 1976; Rathunde, Carroll and Huang, 2000). Children can obtain knowledge about their parents' jobs directly, through conversations, or visiting their places of employment. Recent studies demonstrate a link between parents' job characteristics and teenagers' expressed preferences to find work like that of their parents when they "grow up" (Kalil, Levine and Ziol-Guest, 2005; Weinshenker, 2005). This is the case especially regarding fathers: adolescents are less likely to desire the occupations of their mothers even when they hold high status, well-paying jobs. Parents' jobs can serve as important "laboratories" for children's developing views of the occupational system and their future place within it.

Schools play a less important role than families in shaping educational expectations, occupational aspirations and academic performance. This is particularly the case for young children, for whom differences in test scores among various racial and ethnic groups are strongly related to economic and social inequalities in families. These effects are compounded by the environments in which young people live. Evans, Hout and Mayer (2004) argue that children's views of their family's income and social standing relative to other families in their neighbourhood may exert considerable influence on their learning and achievement. When economic inequalities increase, students whose families have fewer resources may feel less empowered to do well in school and consequently put less effort into their school work.

Parents' impacts on learning: process variables

Status variables do not fully explain the relationship between family background and academic achievement – attention needs to be directed at the processes and mechanisms through which parents can strengthen their children's learning. Some of these processes and mechanisms include the ways in which parents interact with their children, monitor their children's behaviour, help with homework and engage in discussions about future schooling opportunities.

Attachment and responsiveness

Although SES is a major factor in children's learning, parental actions – regardless of the economic and social constraints they face – can make a difference in their children's cognitive and social development. Beginning in infancy, the degree of responsiveness and sensitivity of a caregiver to a child's needs influence whether or not that child develops a **secure** attachment pattern, that is, an enduring connection to another human being (Ainsworth *et al.*, 1978; Belsky and Fearon, 2002; Isabella, 1993; Kivijärvi *et al.*, 2001). Infants who are securely attached to their caregiver feel comfortable exploring their environment because they can rely on their caregiver for security. Abusive or neglectful parenting, on the other hand, can lead children to develop avoidant or ambivalent attachment patterns. Children with "ambivalent attachment" tend to cling to their caregiver rather than exploring their surroundings independently and exhibit distress when a caregiver leaves, unsure of their return. Children with "avoidant attachment" tend to show little or no preference for their caregiver over a stranger.

Maternal sensitivity and responsiveness have also been shown to lead to positive developmental outcomes for children (Burchinal *et al.*, 1997; Ginsburg, 2007; Tamis-LeMonda, Bornstein and Baumwell, 2001). It is not only the mothers' roles that are important; there is accumulating evidence that the father-child relationship has an important influence on children's developmental outcomes (Cabrera *et al.*, 2000; Flouri and Buchanan, 2003; Lamb, 2004; Tamis-LeMonda and Cabrera, 2002). Increasingly, research is demonstrating that children's emotional regulation, well-being and cognitive development are related to the emotional involvement of both mothers and fathers and time spent together (Amato and Rivera, 1999; van Wel, Linssen and Abma, 2000; Williams and Kelly, 2005).

Parenting styles

Parents have different styles in the ways they interact with their children. Researchers have sought to characterise these relationships, often providing labels for different styles of family decision-making, usually focused on monitoring and other social control mechanisms. One commonly-used typology distinguishes between "authoritarian", "permissive" and "authoritative" parenting styles (Baumrind, 1966, 1967; Steinberg, 1996). Authoritarian parents are regarded as the most firm with respect to discipline and are viewed as exercising several different types of social control, including psychological ones, to encourage their children to behave in desired ways. Permissive parents, in contrast, are inclined to be more accepting of different behaviours, allowing their adolescent child more freedom in making their own decisions. These parents tend not to engage in disciplinary actions and instead focus on ensuring that their adolescents are "happy." Authoritative parents impose a disciplinary structure with established rules but these rules are typically made with the adolescent's' involvement and are constructive and caring when executed. These types of parents are likely to encourage their adolescents to exercise autonomy within the limits they provide.

Authoritative parenting has been linked to many positive adolescent outcomes including cognitive and social skills and emotional well-being. Adolescents whose parents practise more authoritative styles of parenting are more likely to have better performance in school, stronger self-esteem, higher levels of educational attainment, and decreased instances of delinquency and other social problems than others (Lamborn *et al.*, 1991; McBride-Chang and Chang, 1998; Steinberg, 2001; Steinberg *et al.*, 1992). In contrast to other parenting styles, authoritative parents are more likely to value goal-setting and hard work, and to instil a sense of self-efficacy in their teenage children. These parents are more likely to have their children see the connection between hard work and academic success. These children are more likely to be equipped to face challenging tasks and to work to overcome them since they have a greater sense of confidence and understanding that they can potentially affect the outcome through perseverance and hard work (Purdie, Carroll and Roche, 2004; Steinberg, 1996).

Developing agency

Despite agreement in the literature that certain parenting techniques are related to positive outcomes, there is also a body of evidence that suggests that we need to be concerned with how parents understand and comprehend their children's agency, as well as how children understand their parents' agency. In this context, "agency" refers to "the meanings [that parents and children] construct of each others' behaviour, in their capacity for strategic action, and in their ability to behave 'as if' the other is also an agent" (Grusec, Goodnow and Kuczynski, 2000, p. 205). This parent-child relationship requires parents to be cognisant of their child's moods, goals and methods, and to adapt accordingly. There is not necessarily a set of "preferred behaviours" for parents but instead overarching goals, which are then translated into specific interactions with their children. This perspective advocates that parents change their methods as a function of the child and the situation. Children are viewed as competent to make their own decisions as agents regarding their evaluations of fairness and parental intention. Parents are expected to develop socialisation goals for their children, choosing when the goals are "non-negotiable" and when there is room for partial compliance (Grusec, Goodnow and Kuczynski, 2000).

Increased agency among older children can be observed in a shift in their thinking to be more centred on independence and sense of self, and an increased social importance given to peers relative to parents. Parental influence during this period shifts away from the school and social life and rests more within the home, as shown by declining formal parental participation in school activities such as homework (Crosnoe, 2001; Eccles and Harold, 1996). During the teenage years, familial influence on learning is located primarily in the types of behaviours and activities that are sanctioned by family norms and values, with parent involvement taking more the form of supportive educational activities than those which directly involve parental action.

Agency can be understood through examination of how parents shift agency to their children (Lerner and Steinberg, 2004), how parents translate values about school to their children (Hektner and Asakawa, 2000; Rathunde, Carroll and Huang, 2000; Steinberg, 1996), and how parents equip their children to strategise about their educational goals. Schneider and Stevenson (1999) argue that only focusing on parent involvement in schools, discipline and participation in extra-curricular participation ignores critical aspects of how parents may provide opportunities to shift agency to their adolescents so that teenagers feel more entitled and responsible for planning their own futures. Optimal learning for adolescents includes a shift of agency, but this should be accompanied by sound information and a series of safety nets that ease the transition to adulthood. These steps include helping adolescents pursue their own interests, acquiring information regarding post-secondary opportunities, engaging in frequent communication about future plans, and making available realistic opportunities to learn about careers and the educational requirements to achieve them.

Mediating the influence of peers

A related way in which families are involved in the learning process is through the mediating influence of peers. Family environments can either serve as a protection against harmful associations with peers and other adults or potentially as a risk factor, depending on how the family dynamic is structured. Parents can be an especially strong influence in determining children's friendship patterns (Coleman, 1988): they can deter their children from forming relationships with peers whom they perceive as problematic by learning about their children's friends and whether they share similar values and aspirations (Crosnoe, Erickson and Dornbusch, 2002; de Kemp *et al.*, 2006; Offer and Schneider, 2007). These actions by parents tend to be effective only when families are part of whole community who share child-rearing ideologies and practices (Furstenberg *et al.*, 1999; Harris, 1995).

Parental involvement in school learning

Parents may be involved in schools during a child's formative years in different ways: by being physically present in the school, attending parent-teacher conferences and school activities, and volunteering for classroom work. Many studies seeking to link these specific parental school-based activities with student achievement have found small or non-significant effects. However, it is generally viewed that such parent actions, while having a minimal effect on performance, help to build a collective sense of community in the school that may indirectly affect student educational goals (Driessen, Smit and Sleegers, 2005; Schneider and Coleman, 1988; see the chapter by Kerbow and Bernhardt). More recent research suggests that parent involvement in school is linked to lower rates of dropping out in high school and increased on-time high school completion (Anguiano, 2004; Barnard, 2004). It would seem that while these types of activities do not significantly change academic performance at the time, they reinforce subjective messages about the importance and value of education which have enduring effects on educational attainment.

Successful collaboration between schools and parents may also enhance children's learning and adjustment when such collaborations involve parents undertaking specific actions at home (such as monitoring homework), thus supporting school goals. Parent academic involvement is largely about parents working with the school on activities and reinforcing values that directly benefit their children's educational outcomes and future success, including communication between parents and teachers and encouragement of academic work in the home (Hill *et al.* 2004). These factors are commonly associated with the academic achievement of elementary school students (Driessen, Smit and Sleegers, 2005; Eccles and Harold, 1996; Epstein and Sanders, 2002; Hill *et al.*, 2004; Kohl *et al.*, 2000; Steinberg *et al.*, 1992). This type of relationship between parental involvement in schooling influences children's academic achievement indirectly by increasing their motivation to succeed in school (Hill, Ramirez and Dumka, 2003; Young and Friesen, 1990), which is associated with increased academic achievement (Abu-Hilal, 2000; Trusty *et al.*, 2000).

Where direct parental involvement appears to matter most is in electing to send one's child to pre-school. Research has shown that children's participation in formal pre-school early childhood programmes is linked to higher levels of verbal and mathematics achievement, greater success at school, better health outcomes, less welfare dependency, and higher employment and earnings than similar children who do not participate in such programmes (Lynch, 2004; Melhuish *et al.*, 2008; Schweinhart, 2007). The body of evidence on formal early childhood education is clear – there are definite and pronounced benefits for exposure to high-quality pre-school education, both in terms of achievement as well as economic benefits (Cunha and Heckman, 2006; Sylva *et al.*, 2007). Using economic models to organise the evidence from studies of the Abecedarian Project, the Perry Pre-school Program, the Chicago Child-Parent Centre Program, and other interventions that target both early childhood and later childhood and adolescence, Cunha and Heckman (2006) found that "ability gaps in both cognitive and non-cognitive skills across individuals and across socio-economic groups open up at early ages" (p. 68) and that "it is possible to partially compensate for adverse family environments. Evidence from randomised trials conducted on intervention programs targeted at disadvantaged children who are followed into adulthood, suggests that it is possible to eliminate some of the gaps due to early disadvantage" (p. 69). They also found that, "the economic returns to initial investments at early ages are high. Early investment in cognitive and non-cognitive skills lowers the cost of later investment by making learning at later ages more efficient" (p. 69).

The key policy implication here is that the impact of the family on the learning process can and should be supported by well-structured, multi-faceted formal learning environments, and this is particularly the case for less advantaged children. Structured pre-school learning experiences are an important factor in helping to negate some of the well-documented negative impacts of growing up in less-resourced families. Attention should be paid to helping parents to identify pre-school programmes and services that are available and which of these are of quality, and providing them with educational and health resources to ensure access and success.

What school outcomes do families influence?

The discussion thus far has examined how the influence of parents has been measured both in terms of characteristics of the household and parent interaction styles and behaviours. We now turn to different school outcomes that have been shown to be influenced by parent characteristics and actions.

Cognitive development

Beginning with vocabulary development, children's learning is highly dependent on family influences, with clear differences in vocabulary acquisition by family socio-economic status and maternal speech patterns. Differences in maternal child-directed speech have been attributed to socio-economic status and in turn related to differences in language use (Hoff, 2003; Keown, Woodward and Field, 2001; Zhang *et al.*, 2008). Young children in families rich in resources are more likely to have larger vocabularies than children in families with fewer resources and these differences tend to increase over time. By three years old, the vocabularies of children from disadvantaged families are half the size of those whose families are more advantaged (Biemiller, 2006; Brooks-Gunn and Markman, 2005; Hart and Risley, 1995, 1999). Hart and Risley's (1995) study included transcriptions of parent-child interactions and monthly observations with 42 children, studied from the time they first began to say words (approximately one year old) until they were three years old. Children born into homes with fewer economic resources learn fewer words, have less frequent experiences with words in interactions with others, and acquire their vocabulary more slowly.

There is evidence that income is more highly related to cognitive than to behavioural outcomes (Duncan *et al.*, 1998; Kohen *et al.*, 2002) or to health outcomes (Burgess, Propper and Rigg, 2004; Korenman and Miller, 1997). Policies that increase parental income and employment may thus increase children's academic engagement, achievement, as well as educational and occupational aspirations (Gennetian *et al.*, 2002; Gennetian and Miller, 2002; Huston *et al.*, 2001; Kagitcibasi, Sunar and Bekman, 2001; Morris, Duncan and Clark-Kauffman, 2005; Soares and Collares, 2006). Morris *et al.* (2005) examined the effects of seven anti-poverty and welfare programme evaluations, which all employed random assignment to conditions. They found that programmes that increased parental employment and income led to significant increases in the cognitive performance of pre-school-aged children.

The mechanisms underlying the relationship between SES and children's development include family instability, social support, the parent-child relationship, parenting style and the characteristics of the home environment (Evans, 2004; McCulloch and Joshi, 2001; Pittman and Chase-Lansdale, 2001). In families where parents spend more time interacting with their children, encouraging them to speak, mimic words and identify objects, the children tend to acquire words sooner and more easily than in households where there is little communication. Research has shown that when parents model vocabulary, speech and logic through their daily interactions with their children in "real life" situations they are more likely to learn to speak and use words (Berger, 2000; Downey, 2002; National Research Council, 1998; Sénéchal and LeFevre, 2002; Weems and Rogers, 2007).

Parents' attitudes toward reading have a significant impact on children's views of reading and their engagement with the literacy process (Baker, Scher and Mackler, 1997; Hewison and Tizard, 2004). Studies conclude that parental involvement in reading should include (a) teaching letters, sounds and letter-sound relationships to children; (b) sharing conversations with children to stimulate vocabulary development; and (c) modelling good habits of reading and writing, reading together every day and visiting libraries and museums (National Reading Panel, 2000). Reading should be seen by children as an enjoyable experience, and for parents this often translates into making story time a positive interaction, where children are asked to participate in the telling of the story. Positive interactions with books help children to learn about the pleasure and satisfaction of reading, and such feelings are often linked with children's increased motivation to read (Baker, Serpell and Sonnenschein, 1995; McKenna, 1994; Snow and Tabors, 1996; Torr, 2004).

Families can also play an important role in creating an environment that promotes early exposure to numeracy skills. One of the major predictors of future academic success in school is the acquisition of early math skills – the types of numeracy skills that children learn prior to entering kindergarten (Duncan et al., 2007; Kaufmann et al., 2005). Neuro-imaging research shows strong links between brain activity involving numerical and spatial reasoning (Dehaene et al., 1999). These findings provide support for the use of concrete representations of abstract mathematical principles when interacting with young children including the use of manipulatives such as blocks, rods and board games (Case et al., 1996; Zhou et al., 2006). For children to acquire numeracy skills, families need to pay particular attention to providing explicit tools that aid the development of mathematical knowledge and reasoning.

Non-cognitive development: motivation, engagement and social support

Children are more likely to learn when they have structured home environments where parents indicate both expectations about learning and adapt these expectations given child-specific needs and personality (Downey, 2002; Maccoby and Martin, 1983; Neuenschwander *et al.*, 2007; Steinberg, 1996). While these parenting practices generally seem to be associated with academic achievement, there are other emotional states emphasised by researchers – such as competition, individuality and independence, and endurance – that may also be promoted by parents, particularly middle- and upper-class parents (Abu-Hilal, 2001; Kohn, 1986; Kusserow, 2004; Lareau, 2003; Robbins, 2006). For children to learn optimally it may not be enough for them to be "cultivated" – they may also need to be encouraged to learn to compete with others in healthy ways, pursuing goals even when they are difficult, and developing themselves as individuals with distinct personalities that operate outside the purview of their parents.

The relationship of parents and their children changes substantially in the adolescent years when teenagers begin to assume more independence and most parents refrain from directly supervising their activities in- and out-of-school. It is during this stage when adolescents are more aware of their parent's actions as well as their motivations and value orientations. Parental actions and attitudes are thus reviewed and interpreted by the teenagers, creating an environment where they come to react positively or negatively to positions and decisions taken by their parents. The "stage-environment fit" perspective outlined by Eccles *et al.* (1993) suggests that it is in the adolescent years when it is most important to achieve a good match between the structures of a given setting (in this case family environment) and the teenager's perceived needs (Eccles *et al.*, 1993, 1997; Goldstein, Davis-Kean and Eccles, 2005; Gutman and Eccles, 2007).

While much formal subject-based learning takes place in schools, families can be instrumental in developing the values and attitudes that encourage student engagement, motivation and success with learning. Helping with homework is one such modelling behaviour where parents not only reinforce lessons and concepts learned in schools (Hoover-Dempsey *et al.*, 2001; Xu and Yuan, 2003), but the parents also demonstrate attitudes and behaviours associated with success in school (Desforges, 2003; Hoover-Dempsey and Sandler, 1995). Given the positive benefits of parental involvement with homework, schools should seek to encourage interaction between teachers and parents in ways that articulate explicit guidelines on how parents can help with homework. Such guidelines can usefully include: (a) finding an appropriate place to study; (b) devoting sufficient time to the homework task; (c) being available to assist their children with their assignments but not completing them for their children; and (d) conveying messages about the value of homework and particularly its relationship to children's educational goals and those of the school.

Parental expectations are a strong force in developing children's perceived self-efficacy and abilities, which in turn relate to actual academic achievement. This becomes particularly relevant in adolescence. Just as their parents have expectations about their futures, adolescents also develop educational expectations and occupational aspirations but they are not always aware of the steps necessary for achieving them. One way to assist adolescents in developing a realistic plan for the future is through aligning ambitions with educational expectations consistent with the type of work they wanted to pursue as adults. In a study of adolescent orientations toward work, Schneider and Stevenson (1999) showed that adolescents who had aligned ambitions were more likely to achieve their goals following high school graduation. Parents can assist the alignment process by introducing their adolescent children to people who are employed in jobs similar to those the adolescents aspire to, supplying them with information about their college choices and majors and how such choices can influence career plans, as well as by engaging with them in strategic decision-making regarding future goals.

Families are an important conveyor of information regarding the labour market, providing a forum for discussing the training and preparation necessary for certain jobs, how one goes about obtaining such jobs, and what the chances are of finding such employment given the adolescent's talents and skills. Parents need to offer advice on navigating choices and decisions and identifying resources: even though they are influential in helping adolescents to develop study skills and subject-specific knowledge, a still more critical function is transmitting information and strategic planning to their teenage children.

One way of developing aligned ambitions is by creating a parent-adolescent dynamic that promotes academic performance yet at the same time offers emotional support. Such emotional closeness between parents and adolescents can facilitate the transmission of expectations regarding performance and social behaviours (Crosnoe, 2004). One model of the parent dynamic that affords both challenge and support has been developed by Csikszentmihalyi, Rathunde and Whalen (1993). In families that emphasise challenge, parents value teenagers taking responsibility, organising their actions in an adult manner, and feeling enabled to face difficult personal situations. Teenagers in families high on challenge are more likely to have a sense of goal direction and they are more likely to do more homework and recognise homework as a means to future growth and success.

In families that emphasise support, parents value making the adolescent feel loved and supported: teenagers in these families report feeling more optimistic and have more positive attitudes toward school. There are families that are high on both challenge and support; in these, adolescents report higher self-esteem and a greater sense of future goal orientation. Finding a balance between challenge and support is critical for creating an environment that promotes optimal learning conditions and social development opportunities in which adolescents feel empowered, optimistic, motivated and goal-directed (Rathunde, Carroll and Huang, 2000).

Adolescents with clear plans for their future spend a significant amount of time discussing actions and strategies with their parents to help them reach their educational and occupational goals, and do so in an environment that is also loving, caring and supportive (Schneider and Stevenson, 1999). Adolescents whose parents allow them considerable agency in school-related matters yet hold high expectations for them are more likely to engage in strategising behaviours with their families (Jones and Schneider, 2009). Adolescents whose parents took time to strategise with them were more likely to have higher expectations. Only focusing on high challenge by setting strict boundaries regarding the monitoring of homework and time spent with friends can dampen educational expectations and negatively affect emotional well-being.

Conclusion – strengthening home-school relationships

This chapter has focused primarily on the influence that family – not teachers or other school staff – has on children's learning but of course significant amounts of learning take place in formal schooling environments. When parents participate in formal schooling environments, the results are not uniformly positive. For example, if parental involvement places teachers and parents in opposition to each other, it is difficult to establish trusting relationships placing the welfare of the children first. Learning is adversely affected when schools lack these trusting relationships (Bryk and Schneider, 2002). This raises the question, "how can policies be structured to engage parents in ways that are meaningful and supportive of achievement, creating a true partnership?"

It is important to take into account potential barriers to effective home-school partnerships, such as low parental sense of self-efficacy and resource constraints (Hoover-Dempsey and Sandler, 1997). Esler, Godber and Christenson (2008) recommend that schools proactively and systematically identify families who are not yet involved in their children's schooling and extend to them personalised invitations to become involved. This should occur when the child is performing well in school as well as when he or she is struggling, since this sends the message to parents that the school genuinely values the child and does not see him or her as an administrative problem.

When parents are unwilling to engage in the learning process, what should the role of schools be? Schools need to function not only as a venue for formal academic learning, but also to provide many of the supplementary services that are traditionally the province of families. These initiatives include free lunch and breakfast programmes, which help to reduce nutritional deficits that are also linked to lower concentration levels (Gunderson, 2008). Another solution has been to transform schools into community centres through initiatives such as the 21st Century Community Learning Center Program (U.S. Department of Education, 2008). In these instances, schools provide extracurricular structure and stimulation as well as supplementary instruction in reading, and use teachers and volunteers as role models. While these programmes play an important role in providing additional services to many children, it is nevertheless difficult for schools to replicate the influence of families.

Another way that schools can be involved in providing some of the additional academic support that children require but may not receive at home is through after-school programmes. While these have had varied effects (*e.g.* see James-Burdumy *et al.*, 2005), research suggests that structured academic instruction, particularly in mathematics, leads to significant academic improvement for students who participate (Black *et al.*, 2008; Bray, 2006; Ireson, 2004; Rahm and Ash, 2008). Key features of successful after-school programmes are a broad range of enrichment opportunities, skill-building and mastery activities for academic work, intentional relationship building, strong leadership from programme staff, and strong fiscal and administrative support from the sponsoring organisation (Birmingham *et al.*, 2005; Fordham, 2004).

Lareau (2003), like other scholars, suggests that participation in extracurricular activities helps to develop well-rounded children, particularly when starting in the elementary grades and continuing into adolescence, and have been shown to be associated with a variety of positive outcomes in later adolescence, including reduced delinquency, reduced absenteeism and reduced drug and alcohol use (Derous and Ryan, 2008; Eccles and Barber, 1999; Marsh, 1992; Persson, Kerr and Stattin, 2007; Raymore *et al.*, 1999; Werner, 1993) and increased college matriculation (Schneider, 2003; Swanson, 2002). Structured extra-curricular participation often sparks interest and identifies talents in such areas as sports, music and the arts, through which children can learn firsthand about the need for effort and perseverance. Additionally, such activities can reinforce skills such as commitment, co-operation and interpersonal relationships. Hence, it is important to support extracurricular activities and make them available to children from all income levels, given that participation in these activities is often quite costly. Yet, extra-curricular activities should not overwhelm the family schedule or replace time for families to engage in activities together. Multiple extracurricular activities can leave children and parents weary and stressed, with limited family time together (Ochs and Shohet, 2006; Schneider, 2003).

Programmes can also be structured to support and encourage parents to take more of an active role in the learning activities of their children. The Parents as Teachers Program (Parents as Teachers National Center, 2008) recognises parents as the primary teachers of children, and brings resources to parents in order to help them to develop into effective parent-teachers. Parents who elect to participate in this programme receive social supports such as regular personal visits from programme staff, parent group meetings, periodic screening and monitoring of educational and sensory development by programme staff, and access to a parent resource centre (National Diffusion Network, 1996). Participation in the programme has been linked to improved school readiness through better parenting practices, such as increased time reading to children, and a greater likelihood that parents enrol their children in pre-school programmes (Zigler, Pfannenstiel and Seitz, 2008). The home visitation component of Parents as Teachers underscores the importance of social support for parents as they learn about the activities that will best involve themselves and their children in promoting literacy and school readiness (Zigler, Pfannenstiel and Seitz, 2008).

Another literacy programme in the U.S. involves paediatricians providing books and informational materials to parents during children's normal check-ups with their physicians (High *et al.*, 2000). In an evaluative study, families in the intervention group received children's books and educational materials that were developmentally appropriate for their children at their regular check-ups. For this group, there was a 40% increase in "child-centred literacy orientation" (a measure of a family's ability and willingness to engage in literacy-promoting activities with young children), as well as greater frequency of parents reading to toddlers and increased vocabulary scores in toddlers. These effects were mediated by increased shared reading to toddlers, suggesting that the intervention contributed to increased parent-child reading and vocabulary acquisition (High *et al.*, 2000).

While educational policy and funding decisions should obviously support school-based initiatives, it is also important to support family-based programmes, in order to continue to develop and encourage families to function as a key educational agent for their children. Altering family dynamics – particularly in the area of parenting – is difficult and the formal role of the government in this area is blurred, but supporting schools alone is not enough. For families which are struggling to promote learning, additional support is essential.

References

Abu-Hilal, M.M. (2000), "A Structural Model of Attitudes towards School Subjects, Academic Aspiration and Achievement", *Educational Psychology*, Vol. 20, No. 1, pp. 75-84.

Abu-Hilal, M.M. (2001), "Correlates of Achievement in the United Arab Emirates: A Sociocultural Study", in D.M. McInerney and S. Van Etten (eds.), *Research on Sociocultural Influences on Motivation and Learning*, Vol. 1, Information Age Publishing, Greenwich, CT, pp. 205-230.

Ainsworth, M.D.S, M.C. Blehar, E. Waters and S. Wall (1978), *Patterns of Attachment: A Psychological Study of the Strange Situation*, Lawrence Erlbaum Associates, Mahwah, NJ.

Alexander, K., D. Entwistle and N. Kabbani (2001), "The Dropout Process in Life Course Perspective: Early Risk Factors at Home and School", *Teachers College Record*, Vol. 103, No. 3, pp. 760-822.

Amato, P.R. and F. Rivera (1999), "Paternal Involvement and Children's Behavior Problems," *Journal of Marriage and Family*, Vol. 61, No. 2, pp. 375-384.

Anguiano, R.P.V. (2004), "Families and Schools: The Effect of Parental Involvement on High School Completion", *Journal of Family Issues*, Vol. 25, No. 1, pp. 61-85.

Baker, D., C. Riordan and M. Schaub (1995), "The Effect of Sex-Grouped Schooling on Achievement: The Role of National Context", *Comparative Education Review*, Vol. 34, No. 4, pp. 468-482.

Baker, L., D. Scher and K. Mackler (1997), "Home and Family Influences on Motivations for Reading," *Educational Psychologist*, Vol. 32, No. 2, pp. 69-82.

Baker, L., R. Serpell and S. Sonnenschein (1995), "Opportunities for Literacy Learning in the Homes of Urban Pre-schoolers," in L.M. Morrow (ed.), *Family Literacy: Connections in Schools and Communities*, International Reading Association, Newark, DE, pp. 236-252.

Baltes, P.B., P.A. Reuter-Lorenz and F. Rösler (2006), *Lifespan Development and the Brain*, Cambridge University Press, Cambridge, UK.

Barnard, W.M. (2004), "Parent Involvement in Elementary School and Educational Attainment," *Children and Youth Services Review*, Vol. 26, No. 1, pp. 39-62.

Baumrind, D. (1966), "Effects of Authoritative Parental Control on Child's Behavior," *Child Development*, Vol. 37, No. 4, pp. 887-907.

Baumrind, D. (1967), "Child Care Practices Anteceding Three Patterns of Pre-school Behavior", *Genetic Psychology Monographs*, Vol. 75, No. 1, pp. 43-88.

Belsky, J. and R.M.P. Fearon (2002), "Early Attachment Security, Subsequent Maternal Sensitivity, and Later Child Development: Does Continuity in Development Depend upon Continuity of Caregiving?", *Attachment and Human Development,* Vol. 4, No. 3, pp. 361-387.

Berger, E.H. (2000), *Parents as Partners in Education: Families and Schools Working Together*, Merrill Publishing, Upper Saddle River, NJ.

Bianchi, S.M. (1984), "Children's Progress through School: A Research Note", *Sociology of Education*, Vol. 57, No. 3, pp. 184-192.

Biemiller, A. (2006), "Vocabulary Development and Instruction: A Prerequisite for School Learning", in D.K. Dickinson and S.B. Neuman (eds.), *Handbook of Early Literacy Research, Vol. 2*, Guilford Press, New York, pp. 41-51.

Birmingham, J., E.M. Pechman, C.A. Russell, M. Mielke (2005), *Shared Features of High-Performing After-School Programs: A Follow-Up to the TASC Evaluation,* prepared for The After-School Corporation and Southwest Educational Development Laboratory, New York.

Black, A.R., F. Doolittle, P. Zhu, R. Unterman and J.B. Grossman (2008), *The Evaluation of Enhanced Academic Instruction in After-School Programs: Findings After the First Year of Implementation* (NCEE 2008-4021), National Center for Education Evaluation and Regional Assistance, Institute of Education Sciences, U.S. Department of Education, Washington, DC.

Blau, P.M. and O.D. Duncan (1967), *The American Occupational Structure*, John Wiley & Sons, New York.

Bouchard, T.J. and M. McGue (2003), "Genetic and Environmental Influences on Human Psychological Differences", *Journal of Neurobiology,* Vol. 54, No. 1, pp. 4-45.

Bourdieu, P. (1984), *Distinction: A Social Critique of the Judgement of Taste*, Harvard University Press, Cambridge, MA.

Boyle, M.H., K. Georgiades, Y. Racine and C. Mustard (2007), "Neighbourhood and Family Influences on Educational Attainment: Results from the Ontario Child Health Study Follow-Up 2001", *Child Development*, Vol. 78, No. 1, pp. 168-189.

Bray, M. (2006), "Private Supplementary Tutoring: Comparative Perspectives on Patterns and Implications", *Compare: A Journal of Comparative and International Education*, Vol. 36, No. 4, pp. 515-530.

Bronfenbrenner, U. and S.J. Ceci (1994), "Nature-Nuture Reconceptualized in Developmental Perspective: A Bioecological Model", *Psychological Review*, Vol. 101, No. 4, pp. 568-586.

Brooks-Gunn J. and L.B. Markman (2005), "The Contribution of Parenting to Ethnic and Racial Gaps in School Readiness", *The Future of Children / Center for the Future of Children, the David and Lucile Packard Foundation*, Vol. 15, No. 1, pp. 139-168.

Bryk, A.S. and B. Schneider (2002), *Trust in Schools: A Core Resource for Improvement*, Russell Sage Foundation, New York.

Burchinal, M.R., F.A. Campbell, D.M. Bryant, B.H. Wasik and C.T. Ramey (1997), "Early Intervention and Mediating Processes in Cognitive Performance of Children of Low-Income, African American Families", *Child Development*, Vol. 68, No. 5, pp. 935-954.

Burgess, S.M., C. Propper and J. Rigg (2004), *The Impact of Low Income on Child Health: Evidence from a Birth Cohort Study* (LSE STICERD Research Paper No. CASE085), University of Bristol, Department of Economics, UK, May.

Byrd, R.S. and M.L. Weitzman (1994), "Predictors of Early Grade Retention Among Children in the United States", *Pediatrics*, Vol. 93, No. 3, pp. 481-487.

Cabrera, N.J., C.S. Tamis-LeMonda, R.H. Bradley, S. Hofferith and M.E. Lamb (2000), "Fatherhood in the Twenty-First Century," *Child Development*, Vol. 71, No. 1, pp. 127-136.

Case, R. and M. Okamoto (1996), "The Role of Central Conceptual Structures in the Development of Children's Thought", *Monographs of the Society for Research in Child Development*, Vol. 61, No. 1-2, pp. 1-295.

Chen, Z-Y. and H.B. Kaplan (2003), "School Failure in Early Adolescence and Status Attainment in Middle Adulthood: A Longitudinal Study", *Sociology of Education*, Vol. 76, No. 2, pp. 110-127.

Coleman, J. (1988), "Social Capital in the Creation of Human Capital", *American Journal of Sociology*, Vol. 94, Supplement, pp. S95-S120.

Coleman, J., E. Campbell, C. Hobson, J. McPartland, A. Mood, F. Weinfeld and R. York (1966), *Equality of Educational Opportunity*, U.S. Government Printing Office, Washington, DC.

Crosnoe, R. (2001), "Academic Orientation and Parental Involvement in Education during High School", *Sociology of Education*, Vol. 74, No. 3, pp. 210-230.

Crosnoe, R. (2004), "Social Capital and the Interplay of Families and Schools", *Journal of Marriage and Family*, Vol. 66, No. 2, pp. 267-280.

Crosnoe, R., K.G. Erickson and S.M. Dornbusch (2002), "Protective Functions of Family Relationships and School Factors on the Deviant Behavior of Adolescent Boys and Girls", *Youth and Society*, Vol. 33, No. 4, pp. 515-544.

Csikzentmihalyi, M., K.R. Rathunde and S. Whalen (1993), *Talented Teenagers: The Roots of Success and Failure*, Cambridge University Press, New York.

Cunha, F. and J.J. Heckman (2006), "Investing in our Young People", unpublished manuscript, Department of Economics, University of Chicago.

Dawson, D.A. (1991), "Family Structure and Children's Health and Well-Being: Data from the 1988 National Health Interview Survey on Child Health", *Journal of Marriage and the Family*, Vol. 53, No. 3, pp. 573-584.

Dehaene, S., E. Spelke, P. Pinel, R. Stanescu and S. Tsivkin (1999), "Sources of Mathematical Thinking: Behavioral and Brain-Imaging Evidence", *Science*, Vol. 284, No. 5416, pp. 970-974.

Derous, E. and A.M. Ryan (2008), "When Earning is Beneficial for Learning: The Relation of Employment and Leisure Activities to Academic Outcomes", *Journal of Vocational Behavior*, Vol. 73, No. 1, pp. 118-131.

Desforges, C. (2003), *The Impact of Parental Involvement, Parental Support and Family Education on Pupil Achievements and Adjustment: A Literature Review* (Research Report RR433), DfES Publications, Nottingham, UK.

Dickens, W.T. and J.R. Flynn (2001), "Heritability Estimates versus Large Environmental Effects: The IQ Paradox Resolved", *Psychological Review*, Vol. 108, No. 2, pp. 346-369.

Downey, D. (2002), "Parental and Family Involvement in Education", in A. Molnar (ed.), *School Reform Proposals: The Research Evidence*, Information Age Publishing, Greenwich, CT, pp. 113-134.

Doyon, J. and H. Benali (2005), "Reorganization and Plasticity in the Adult Brain during Learning of Motor Skills", *Current Opinion in Neurobiology,* Vol. 15, No. 2, pp. 161-167.

Driessen, G., F. Smit and P. Sleegers (2005), "Parental Involvement and Educational Achievement", *British Educational Research Journal,* Vol. 31, No. 4, pp. 509-532.

Duncan, G.J., J. Brooks-Gunn and P.K. Klebanov (1994), "Economic Deprivation and Early Childhood Development", *Child Development,* Vol. 65, No. 2, pp. 296-318.

Duncan, G.J., C.J. Dowsett, A. Claessens, K. Magnuson, A.C. Huston, P. Klebanov, L. Pagani, L. Feinstein, M. Engel, J. Brooks-Gunn, H. Sexton, K. Duckworth and C. Japel (2007), "School Readiness and Later Achievement", *Developmental Psychology,* Vol. 43, No. 6, pp. 1428-1446.

Duncan, G.J., W.J. Yeung, J. Brooks-Gunn and J. Smith (1998), "How Much Does Childhood Poverty Affect the Life Chances of Children?", *American Sociological Review,* Vol. 63, No. 3, pp. 406-423.

Duyme, M., A-C. Dumaret and S. Tomkiewicz (1999), "How Can We Boost IQs of 'Dull Children'?: A Late Adoption Study", *PNAS,* Vol. 96, No. 15, pp. 8790-8794.

Eccles, J.S. and B.L. Barber (1999), "Student Council, Volunteering, Basketball, or Marching Band: What kind of Extracurricular Involvement Really Matters?", *Journal of Adolescent Research,* Vol. 14, No. 1, pp. 10-43.

Eccles, J., C. Midgley, A. Wigfield, C. Buchanan, D. Reuman, C. Flanagan and D. Mac Iver (1993), "Development during Adolescence: The Impact of Stage-Environment Fit on Adolescents' Experiences in Schools and Families", *American Psychologist,* Vol. 48, No. 2, pp. 90-101.

Eccles, J.S., D. Early, K. Frasier, E. Belansky and K. McKarthy (1997), "The Relation of Connection, Regulation, and Support for Autonomy to Adolescents' Functioning", *Journal of Adolescent Research,* Vol. 12, No. 2, pp. 263-286.

Eccles, J.S. and R.D. Harold (1996), "Family Involvement in Children's and Adolescent Years," in A. Booth and J.F. Dunn (eds.), *Family-School Links: How do they Affect Educational Outcomes?,* Lawrence Erlbaum Associates, Mahwah, NJ, pp. 3-34.

Entwisle, D.R. and N.M. Astone (1994), "Some Practical Guidelines for Measuring Youth's Race/Ethnicity and Socioeconomic Status", *Child Development,* Vol. 65, No. 6, pp. 1521-1540.

Entwisle, D.R., K. Alexander, A. Pallas and D. Cadigan (1988), "A Social Psychological Model of the Schooling Process over First Grade", *Social Psychology Quarterly*, Vol. 51, No. 3, pp. 173-189.

Epstein, J.L. and M.G. Sanders (2002), "Family, School, and Community Partnerships", in M.H. Bornstein (ed.), *Handbook of Parenting: Being and Becoming a Parent*, Lawrence Erlbaum Associates, Mahwah, NJ, pp. 407-438.

Esler, A.N., Y. Godber and S.L. Christenson (2008), "Best Practices in Supporting Home-School Collaboration", in A. Thomas and J. Grimes (eds.), *Best Practices in School Psychology V* (5th edition), NASP Publications, Bethesda, MD, pp. 917-926.

Evans, G.W. (2004), "The Environment of Childhood Poverty", *American Psychologist*, Vol. 59, No. 2, pp. 77-92.

Evans, W., M. Hout and S. Mayer (2004), "Assessing the Effect of Economics Inequality", in K. M. Neckerman (ed.), *Social Inequality*, Russell Sage Foundation, New York, pp. 933-968.

Flouri, E. and A. Buchanan (2003), "The Role of Father Involvement in Children's Later Mental Health", *Journal of Adolescence*, Vol. 26, No. 1, pp. 63-78.

Fordham, I. (2004), "Out-of-School-Hours learning in the United Kingdom", *New Directions for Youth Development*, Vol. 2004, No. 101, pp. 43-74.

Fries, A.B., T.E. Ziegler, J.R. Kurian, S. Jacoris and S.D. Pollak (2005), "Early Experience in Humans is Associated with Changes in Neuropeptides Critical for Regulating Social Behavior", *PNAS*, Vol. 102, No. 47, pp. 17237-17240.

Frome, P.M. and J.S. Eccles (1998), "Parents' Influence on Children's Achievement-Related Perceptions", *Journal of Personality and Social Psychology*, Vol. 74, No. 2, pp. 435-452.

Furstenberg, F.F., T.D. Cook, J. Eccles, G.H. Elder and A. Sameroff (1999), *Managing to Make It: Urban Families and Adolescent Success*, University of Chicago Press, Chicago.

Galambos, N.L. and H.A. Sears (1998), "Adolescents' Perceptions of Parents' Work and Adolescents' Work Values in Two-Earner Families", *The Journal of Early Adolescence*, Vol. 18, No. 4, pp. 397-420.

Geary, D.C. and K.J. Huffman (2002), "Brain and Cognitive Evolution: Forms of Modularity and Functions of Mind", *Psychological Bulletin*, Vol. 128, No. 5, pp. 667-698.

Gennetian, L., G. Duncan, V. Knox, W. Vargas, E. Clark-Kauffman and A. London (2002), *How Welfare and Work Policies for Parents Affect Adolescents: A Synthesis of Research*, Manpower Demonstration Research Corporation, New York.

Gennetian, L. and C. Miller (2002), "Children and Welfare Reform: A View from an Experimental Welfare Program in Minnesota", *Child Development*, Vol. 73, No. 2, pp. 601-620.

Ginsburg, K.R. (2007), "The Importance of Play in Promoting Healthy Child Development and Maintaining Strong Parent-Child Bonds", *Pediatrics*, Vol. 119, No. 1, pp. 182-191.

Goldrick-Rab, S. (2006), "Following Their Every Move: An Investigation of Social-Class Differences in College Pathways", *Sociology of Education*, Vol. 79, No. 1, pp. 61-79.

Goldstein, S.E., P.E. Davis-Kean and J.S. Eccles (2005), "Parents, Peers, and Problem Behavior: A Longitudinal Investigation of the Impact of Relationship Perceptions and Characteristics on the Development of Adolescent Problem Behavior", *Developmental Psychology,* Vol. 41, No. 2, pp. 401-413.

Goswami, U. (2004), "Neuroscience and Education", *British Journal of Educational Psychology*, Vol. 74, No. 1, pp. 1-14.

Grusec, J.E., J.J. Goodnow and L. Kuczynski (2000), "New Directions in Analyses of Parenting Contributions to Children's Acquisition of Values", *Child Development*, Vol. 71, No. 1, pp. 205-211.

Gunderson, G.W. (2008), *National School Lunch Program: Background and development*, New York.

Gutman, L.M. and J.S. Eccles (2007), "Stage-Environment Fit during Adolescence: Trajectories of Family Relations and Adolescent Outcomes", *Developmental Psychology,* Vol. 43, No. 2, pp. 522-537.

Harris, J.R. (1995), "Where is the Child's Environment? A Group Socialization Theory of Development", *Psychological Review*, Vol. 102, No. 3, pp. 458-489.

Harris, J.R. (1998), "The Trouble with Assumptions", *Psychological Inquiry*, Vol. 9, No. 4, pp. 294-297.

Hart, B. and T. Risley (1995), *Meaningful Differences in the Everyday Experience of Young American Children*, Paul Brookes Publishing, Baltimore.

Hart, B. and T. Risley (1999), *The Social World of Children Learning to Talk,* Paul Brooks Publishing, Baltimore.

Haveman, R., B. Wolfe and J. Spaulding (1991), "Childhood Events and Circumstances Influencing High School Completion", *Demography*, Vol. 28, No. 1, pp. 133-157.

Heim, C, J.D. Newport, T. Mletzko, A.H. Miller and C.B. Nemeroff (2008), "The Link between Childhood Trauma and Depression: Insights from HPA axis Studies in Humans", *Psychoneuroendocrinology*, Vol. 33, No. 6, pp. 693-710.

Hektner, J. and K. Asakawa (2000), "Learning to like Challenges", in M. Czikszentmihalyi and B. Schneider (eds.), *Becoming Adult: How Teenagers Prepare for the World of Work*, Basic Books, New York, pp. 95-112.

Hewison, J. and J. Tizard (2004), "Parental Involvement and Reading Attainment," in D. Wray (ed.), *Literacy: Major Themes in Education*, Routledge, London, pp. 208-217.

High, P.C., L. LaGasse, S. Becker, I. Ahlgren and A. Gardner (2000), "Literacy Promotion in Primary Care Pediatrics: Can we Make a Difference?", *Pediatrics,* Vol. 105, No. 4, pp. 927-934.

Hill, N.E., D.R. Castellino, J.E. Lansford, P. Nowlin, K.A. Dodge, J.E. Bates, G.S. Pettit (2004), "Parent Academic Involvement as Related to School Behavior, Achievement, and Aspirations: Demographic Variations across Adolescence", *Child Development*, Vol. 75, No. 5, pp. 1491-1509.

Hill, N.E., C. Ramirez and L.E. Dumka (2003), "Early Adolescents' Career Aspirations: A Qualitative Study of Perceived Barriers and Family Support among Low-Income, Ethnically Diverse Adolescents", *Journal of Family Issues*, Vol. 24, No. 7, pp. 934-959.

Hoff, E. (2003), "The Specificity of Environmental Influence: Socioeconomic Status Affects Early Vocabulary Development via Maternal Speech", *Child Development*, Vol. 74, No. 5, pp. 1368-1378.

Hoover-Dempsey, K.V., A.C. Battiato, J.M.T. Walker, R.P. Reed, J.M. Dejong and K.P. Jones (2001), "Parental Involvement in Homework", *Educational Psychologist,* Vol. 36, No. 3, pp. 195-209.

Hoover-Dempsey, K.V. and H.M. Sandler (1995), "Parental Involvement in Children's Education: Why Does it make a Difference?", *Teachers College Record*, Vol. 95, No. 2, pp. 310-331.

Hoover-Dempsey, K.V. and H.M. Sandler (1997), "Why do Parents become Involved in their Children's Education?", *Review of Educational Research*, Vol. 67, No. 1, pp. 3-42.

Hout, M. (1988), "More Universalism, Less Structural Mobility: The American Occupational Structure in the 1980s", *The American Journal of Sociology*, Vol. 93, No. 6, pp. 1358-1400.

Huston, A.C., G.J. Duncan, R. Granger, J. Bos, V. McLoyd, R. Mistry, D. Crosby, C. Gibson, K. Magnuson, J. Romich, A. Ventura (2001), "Work-Based Antipoverty Programs for Parents Can Enhance the School Performance and Social Behavior of Children", *Child Development*, Vol. 72, No. 1, pp. 318-336.

Huttenlocher, P.R. (2002), *Neural Plasticity: The Effects of Environment on the Development of the Cerebral Cortex*, Harvard University Press, Cambridge, MA.

Ireson, J. (2004), "Private Tutoring: How Prevalent and Effective is it?", *London Review of Education,* Vol. 2, No. 2, pp. 109-122.

Isabella, R.A. (1993), "Origins of Attachment: Maternal Interactive Behavior across the First Year", *Child Development*, Vol. 64, No. 2, pp. 605-621.

James-Burdumy, S., M. Dynarski, M. Moore, J. Deke, W. Mansfield and C. Pistorino (2005), *When Schools Stay Open Late: The National Evaluation of the 21st Century Community Learning Centers Program: Final Report,* U.S. Department of Education, Institute of Education Sciences, National Center for Education Evaluation and Regional Assistance, Washington, DC.

Jenkins, W.M., M.M. Merzenich and G. Recanzone (1990), "Neocortical Representational Dynamics in Adult Primates: Implications for Neuropsychology", *Neuropsychologia,* Vol. 28, No. 6, pp. 573-584.

Jodl, K.M., A. Michael, O. Malanchuk, J.S. Eccles and A. Sameroff (2001), "Parents' Roles in Shaping Early Adolescents' Occupational Aspirations", *Child Development,* Vol. 72, No. 4, pp. 1247-1265.

Jones, N. and B. Schneider (2009), "Rethinking the Role of Parenting for Adolescents", in N.E. Hill and R.K. Chao (eds.), *Family-School Relations during Adolescence: Linking Interdisciplinary Research, Policy, and Practice*, Teachers College Press, New York.

Kagitcibasi, C., D. Sunar and S. Bekman (2001), "Long-Term Effects of Early Intervention: Turkish Low-Income Mothers and Children", *Journal of Applied Developmental Psychology*, Vol. 22, No. 4, pp. 333-361.

Kalil, A., J.A. Levine and K.M. Ziol-Guest (2005), "Following in their Parents' Footsteps: How Characteristics of Parental Work Predict Adolescents' Interest in Parents' Jobs", in B. Schneider and L. Waite (eds.), *Being Together Working Apart*, Cambridge University Press, Cambridge, UK, pp. 422-442.

Kaufmann, L., M. Delazer, R. Pohl, C. Semenza, A. Dowker (2005), "Effects of a Specific Numeracy Educational Program in Kindergarten Children: A Pilot Study", *Educational Research and Evaluation,* Vol. 11, pp. 405-431.

Kemp, R.A.T. de, *et al.* (2006), "Early Adolescent Delinquency: The Role of Parents and Best Friends", *Criminal Justice and Behavior,* Vol. 33, No. 4, pp. 488-510.

Kendler, K.S. and R.J. Greenspan (2006), "The Nature of Genetic Influences on Behavior: Lessons from "Simpler" Organisms", *American Journal of Psychiatry,* Vol. 163, No. 10, pp. 1683-1694.

Keown, L.J., L.J. Woodward and J. Field (2001), "Language Development of Pre-School Children Born to Teenage Mothers", *Infant and Child Development,* Vol. 10, No. 3, pp. 129-145.

Kerbow, D., & Bernhardt, A. (1988), "Parent intervention in the school: The context of minority involvement" in B. Schneider and J. Coleman (Eds.), *Parents, their Children, and Schools,* Westview Press, San Francisco, pp. 115-146.

Kivijarvi, M., J. Oeten, H. Raiha, A. Kaljonen, T. Tamminen and J. Piha (2001), "Maternal Sensitivity Behavior and Infant Behavior in Early Interaction", *Infant Mental Health Journal,* Vol. 22, No. 6, pp. 627-640.

Kohen, D.E., J. Brooks-Gunn, T. Leventhal and C. Hertzman (2002), "Neighborhood Income and Physical and Social Disorder in Canada: Associations with Young Children's Competencies", *Child Development,* Vol. 73, No. 6, pp. 1844-1860.

Kohl, G.O., L.J. Lengua, R.J. McMahon and Conduct Problems Prevention Research Group (2000), "Parent Involvement in School Conceptualizing Multiple Dimensions and Their Relations with Family and Demographic Risk Factors", *Journal of School Psychology,* Vol. 38, No. 6, pp. 501-523.

Kohn, A. (1986), *No Contest: The Case against Competition,* Houghton Mifflin, Boston.

Korenman, S. and J.E. Miller (1997), "Effects of Long-Term Poverty on Physical Health of Children in the National Longitudinal Survey of Youth", in G.J. Duncan and J. Brooks-Gunn (eds.), *Consequence of Growing up Poor,* Russell Sage Foundation, New York, pp. 70-99.

Kracke, B. (2002), "The Role of Personality, Parents and Peers in Adolescents' Career Exploration", *Journal of Adolescence,* Vol. 25, No. 1, pp. 19-30.

Kusserow, A. (2004), *American Individualisms: Child Rearing and Social Class in Three Neighborhoods,* Palgrave, London.

Laird, J., M. DeBell and C. Chapman (2006), *Dropout rates in the United States: 2004* (NCES 2007-024), U.S. Department of Education, National Center for Education Statistics, Washington, DC.

Lamb, M.E. (ed.) (2004), *The Role of the Father in Child Development* (4th edition), Wiley, Hoboken, NJ.

Lamborn, S.D., N.S. Mants, L. Steinberg and S.M. Dornbusch (1991), "Patterns of Competence and Adjustment among Adolescents from Authoritative, Authoritarian, Indulgent, and Neglectful Families", *Child Development,* Vol. 62, No. 5, pp. 1049-1065.

Lareau, A. (2003), *Unequal Childhoods: Class, Race, and Family Life,* University of California Press, Berkeley, CA.

Lerner, R. and L. Steinberg (2004), *Handbook of Adolescent Psychology: Contextual Influences on Adolescent Development,* John Wiley: Hoboken, NJ.

Lugo-Gil, J. and C.S. Tamis-LeMonda (2008), "Family Resources and Parenting Quality: Links to Children's Cognitive Development across the First 3 Years", *Child Development,* Vol. 79, No. 4, pp. 1065-1085.

Lynch, R.G. (2004), *Exceptional Returns: Economic, Fiscal, and Social Benefits of Investment in Early Childhood Development,* Economic Policy Institute, Washington, DC.

Maccoby, E.E. (2000), "Parenting and its Effects on Children: On Reading and Misreading Behavior Genetics," *Annual Review of Psychology,* Vol. 51, No. 1, pp. 1-27.

Maccoby, E.E. and J. Martin (1983), "Socialization in the Context of the Family: Parent-Child Interaction", in E.M. Hetherington (ed.) P.H. Mussen (Series Ed.), *Handbook of Child Psychology: Vol. 4, Socialization, Personality, and social development,* Wiley, New York, pp. 1-101.

Machida, S., A.R. Taylor and J. Kim (2002), "The Role of Maternal Beliefs in Predicting Home Learning Activities in Head Start Families", *Family Relations,* Vol. 51, No. 2, pp. 176-184.

Marsh, H.W. (1992), "Extracurricular Activities: Beneficial Extension of the Traditional Curriculum or Subversion of Academic Goals?", *Journal of Educational Psychology,* Vol. 84, No. 4, pp. 553-562.

McBride-Chang, C. and L. Chang. (1998), "Adolescent-Parent Relations in Hong Kong: Parenting Styles, Emotional Autonomy, and School Achievement", *Journal of Genetic Psychology,* Vol. 159, No. 4, pp. 421-436.

McCulloch, A. and H.E. Joshi (2001), "Neighbourhood and Family Influences on the Cognitive Ability of Children in the British National

Child Development Study", *Social Science and Medicine*, Vol. 53, No. 5, pp. 579-591.

McKenna, M.C. (1994), "Toward a Model of Reading Attitude Acquisition", in E.H. Cramer and M. Castle (eds.), *Fostering the Life-Long Love of Reading: The Affective Domain in Reading Education,* International Reading Association, Newark, DE, pp. 18-40.

Meinlschmidt, G. and C. Heim (2007), "Sensitivity to Intranasal Oxytocin in Adult Men with Early Parental Separation", *Biological Psychiatry*, Vol. 61, No. 9, pp. 1109-1111.

Melhuish, E.C., K. Sylva, P. Sammons, I. Siraj-Blatchford, B. Taggart, M.B. Phan and A. Malin (2008), "The Early Years: Pre-school Influences on Mathematics Achievement", *Science,* Vol. 321, No. 5893, pp. 1161-1162.

Morris, P., G.J. Duncan and E. Clark-Kauffman (2005), "Child Well-Being in an Era of Welfare Reform: The Sensitivity of Transitions in Development to Policy Change", *Developmental Psychology*, Vol. 41, No. 6, pp. 919-932.

Mortimer, J. (1976), "Social Class, Work, and the Family: Some Implications of the Father's Occupation for Familial Relations and Sons' Career Decisions", *Journal of Marriage and the Family,* Vol. 38, No. 2, pp. 241-256.

Mueller, C.W. and T.L. Parcel (1981), "Measures of Socioeconomic Status: Alternatives and Recommendations", *Child Development*, Vol. 52, No. 1, pp. 13-30.

National Diffusion Network (1996), *Educational Programs that Work* (22nd Edition), Sopris West, Longmont, CO.

National Reading Panel (2000), *Put Reading First: Helping Your Child Learn to Read, A Parent Guide,* National Institute for Literacy at ED Pubs, Jessup, MD.

National Research Council (1998), *Preventing Reading Difficulties in Young Children*, National Academy Press, Washington, DC.

Neuenschwander, M.P., M. Vida, J.L. Garrett and J.S. Eccles (2007), "Parents' Expectations and Students' Achievement in Two Western Nations", *International Journal of Behavioral Development*, Vol. 31, No. 6, pp. 594-602.

Ochs, E. and M. Shohet (2006), "The Cultural Structuring of Mealtime Socialization", *New Directions for Child and Adolescent Development,* Vol. 2006, No.111, pp. 35-49.

OECD (2007), *Understanding the Brain: The Birth of a Learning Science*, OECD Publishing, Paris.

Offer, S. and B. Schneider (2007), "Children's Role in Generating Social Capital", *Social Forces,* Vol. 85, No. 3, pp. 1125-1142.

Parents as Teachers National Center (2008), "What is Parents as Teachers", *www.parentsasteachers.org/site/pp.asp?c = ekIRLcMZJxEandb = 272093*

Park, H. (2007), "Single Parenthood and Children's Reading Performance in Asia", *Journal of Marriage and Family,* Vol. 69, pp. 863-877.

Perie, M., R. Moran and A.D. Lutkus (2005), *NAEP 2004, Trends in Academic Progress: Three Decades of Student Performance in Reading and Mathematics*, National Center for Education Statistics, Washington, DC.

Persson, A., M. Kerr and H. Stattin (2007), "Staying in or Moving away from Structured Activities: Explanations Involving Parents and Peers", *Developmental Psychology,* Vol. 43, No. 1, pp. 197-207.

Pittman, L.D. and P.L. Chase-Lansdale (2001), "African American Adolescent Girls in Impoverished Communities: Parenting Style and Adolescent Outcomes", *Journal of Research on Adolescence*, Vol. 11, No. 2, pp. 199-224.

Pong, S.L., J. Dronkers and G. Hampden-Thompson (2003), "Family Policies and Children's School Achievement in Single-Versus Two-Parent Families", *Journal of Marriage and the Family*, Vol. 65, No. 3, pp. 681-699.

Pong, S.L. and D.B. Ju (2000), "The Effects of Change in Family Structure and Income on Dropping Out of Middle and High School", *Journal of Family Issues,* Vol. 21, No. 2, pp. 147-169.

Purdie, N., A. Carroll and L. Roche (2004), "Parenting and Adolescent Self-Regulation", *Journal of Adolescence,* Vol. 27, No. 6, pp. 663-676.

Rahm, J. and D. Ash (2008), "Learning Environments at the Margin: Case Studies of Disenfranchised Youth Doing Science in an Aquarium and an After-School Program", *Learning Environments Research*, Vol. 11, No. 1, pp. 49-62.

Rathunde, K.R., M.E. Carroll and M.P. Huang (2000), "Families and the Forming of Children's Occupational Future", in M. Csikszentmihalyi and B. Schneider (eds.), *Becoming Adult: How Teenagers Prepare for the World of Work*, Basic Books, New York, pp. 113-139.

Raymore, L.A., B.L. Barber, J.S. Eccles, G.C. Godbey (1999), "Leisure Behavior Pattern Stability during the Transition from Adolescence to

Young Adulthood", *Journal of Youth and Adolescence*, Vol. 28, No. 1, pp. 79-103.

Robbins, A. (2006), *The Overachievers: The Secret Lives of Driven Kids*, Hyperion, New York.

Rowe, D.C. (1994), *The Limits of Family Influence: Genes, Experience, and Behavior*, Guilford Press, New York.

Rumberger, R.W. (1983), "Dropping out of High School: The Influence of Race, Sex and Family Background", *American Educational Research Journal*, Vol. 20, No. 2, pp. 199-220.

Rumberger, R.W. (1987), "High School Dropouts: A Review of Issues and Evidence," *Review of Educational Research*, Vol. 57, No. 2, pp. 101-121.

Rutter, M. (2008), "Biological Implications of Gene-Environment Interaction", *Journal of Abnormal Child Psychology*, Vol. 36, No. 7, pp. 969-975.

Scarr, S. (1992), "Developmental Theories for the 1990s: Development and Individual Differences", *Child Development*, Vol. 63, No. 1, pp. 1-19.

Schneider, B. (2003), "Strategies for Success: High School and Beyond", in D. Ravitch (ed.), *Brookings Papers on Educational Policy 2003*, Brookings Institution Press, Washington, DC, pp. 55-79.

Schneider, B. and J. Coleman (1988), *Parents, Their Children, and Schools*, Westview Press, Boulder, CO.

Schneider, B. and D. Stevenson (1999), *The Ambitious Generation: America's Teenagers, Motivated but Directionless*, Yale University Press, New Haven, CT.

Schweinhart, L.J. (2007), "Outcomes of the High/Scope Perry Pre-school Study and Michigan School Readiness Program", in M.E. Young and L.M. Richardson (eds.), *Early Child Development from Measurement to Action: A Priority for Growth and Equity*, World Bank Publications, Washington, DC, pp. 87-102.

Sénéchal, M. and J-A. LeFevre (2002), "Parental Involvement in the Development of Children's Reading Skill: A Five-Year Longitudinal Study", *Child Development*, Vol. 73, No. 2, pp. 445-460.

Sewell, W.H. and R.M. Hauser (1972), "Causes and Consequences of Higher Education: Models of the Status Attainment Process", *American Journal of Agricultural Economics*, Vol. 54, No. 5, pp. 851-861.

Sewell, W.H. and R.M. Hauser (1980), "The Wisconsin Longitudinal Study of Social and Psychological Factors in Aspirations and Achievements", *Research in Sociology of Education and Socialization*, Vol. 1, pp. 59-99.

Smith, E.P., R.J. Prinz, J.E. Dumas and J.E. Laughlin (2001), "Latent Models of Family Processes in African American Families: Relationships to Child Competence Achievement, and Problem Behavior", *Journal of Marriage and the Family*, Vol. 63, No. 4, pp. 967-980.

Snow, C. and P. Tabors (1996), "Intergenerational Transfer of Literacy", in L.A. Benjamin and J. Lord (eds.), *Family Literacy: Directions in Research and Implications for Practice*, Office of Educational Research and Improvement, U.S. Department of Education, Washington, DC.

Soares, J.F. and A.C.M. Collares (2006), "Ressources des Familles et Performance Cognitive des Élèves de l'enseignement Primaire et Secondaire au Brésil" (Family Resources and Cognitive Performance by Primary School Students in Brazil), *Dados*, Vol. 49, No. 3, pp. 615-650.

Steinberg, L. (1996), *Beyond the Classroom: Why School Reform has Failed and What Parents Need to Do*, Simon and Schuster, New York.

Steinberg, L. (2001), "We Know Some Things: Parent-Adolescent Relationships in Retrospect and Prospect", *Journal of Research on Adolescence*, Vol. 11, No. 1, pp. 1-19.

Steinberg, L., S.D. Lamborn, S.M. Dornbusch, N. Darling (1992), "Impact of Parenting Practices on Adolescent Achievement: Authoritative Parenting, School Involvement, and Encouragement to Succeed", *Child Development*, Vol. 63, No. 5, pp. 1266-1281.

Swanson, C. (2002), "Spending Time or Investing Time? Involvement in High School Curricular and Extracurricular Activities as Strategic Action", *Rationality and Society*, Vol. 14, No. 4, pp. 431-471.

Sylva, K., B. Taggart, L. Siraj-Blatchford, V. Totsika, K. Ereky-Stevens, R. Gilden and D. Bell (2007), "Curricular Quality and Day-to-Day Learning Activities in Pre-School", *International Journal of Early Years Education*, Vol. 15, No. 1, pp. 49-65.

Tamis-LeMonda, C.S., M.H. Bornstein and L. Baumwell (2001), "Maternal Responsiveness and Children's Achievement of Language Milestones", *Child Development*, Vol. 72, No. 3, pp. 748-767.

Tamis-LeMonda, C.S. and N. Cabrera (eds.) (2002), *Handbook of Father Involvement: Multidisciplinary Perspectives*, Erlbaum, Mahwah, NJ.

Thelen, E. and L.B. Smith (1994), *A Dynamic Systems Approach to the Development of Cognition and Action*, MIT Press, Cambridge, MA.

Torr, J. (2004), "Talking about Picture Books: The Influence of Maternal Education on Four-Year-Old Children's Talk with Mothers and Pre-School Teachers", *Journal of Early Childhood Literacy*, Vol. 4, pp. 181-210.

Trusty, J., C.R. Robinson, M. Plata and K.M. Ng (2000), "Effects of Gender, Socioeconomic Status, and Early Academic Performance on Postsecondary Education Choice", *Journal of Counseling and Development*, Vol. 78, No. 4, pp. 463-472.

Turkheimer, E., A. Haley, M. Waldron, B. D'Onofrio and I.I. Gottes- man (2003), "Socioeconomic Status Modifies Heritability of IQ in Young Children", *Psychological Science*, Vol. 14, No. 6, pp. 623-628.

Uher, R. (2008), "Forum: The Case for Gene-Environment Interactions in Psychiatry", *Current Opinion in Psychiatry*, Vol. 21, No. 4, pp. 318-321.

U.S. Department of Education (2008), *Guide to U.S. Department of Education Programs 2008*, U.S. Department of Education, Washington, DC, *www.ed.gov/programs/gtep/gtep.pdf*

Van Wel, F., H. Linssen and R. Abma (2000), "The Parental Bond and the Well-Being of Adolescents and Young Adults", *Journal of Youth and Adolescence,* Vol. 29, No. 3, pp. 307-308.

Weems, D.M. and C. Rogers (2007), "America's Next Top Model: Parent Behaviors that Promote Reading", *Childhood Education,* Vol. 84, No. 2, pp. 105-106.

Weinraub, M., D.L. Horvath and M.B. Gringlas (2002), "Single Parenthood", in M.H. Bornstein (ed.), *Handbook of Parenting: Being and Becoming a Parent*, Lawrence Erlbaum Associates, Mahwah, NJ, pp. 109-140.

Weinshenker, M. (2005), "Imagining Family Roles: Parental Influences on the Expectations of Adolescents in Dual-Earner Families", in B. Schneider and L. Waite (eds.), *Being Together, Working Apart,* Cambridge University Press, Cambridge, UK, pp. 365-388.

Werner, E.E. (1993), "Risk, Resilience, and Recovery: Perspectives from the Kauai Longitudinal Study", *Developmental Psychopathology,* Vol. 5, No. 4, pp. 503-515.

Williams, S.K. and F.D. Kelly (2005), "Relationships among Involvement, Attachment, and Behavioral Problems in Adolescence: Examining Father's Influence", *The Journal of Early Adolescence,* Vol. 25, No. 2, pp. 168-196.

Xu, J. and R. Yuan (2003), "Doing Homework: Listening to Students', Parents', And Teachers' Voices in One Urban Middle School Community", *The School Community Journal,* Vol. 13, No. 2, pp. 25-44.

Young, R.A. and J.D. Friesen (1990), "Parental Influences on Career Development: A Research Perspective" in R.A. Young and W.A. Borgen (eds.), *Methodological Approaches to the Study of Career*, Greenwood Publishing Group, Santa Barbara, CA, pp. 147-162.

Zhang, Y., X. Jin, X. Shen, J. Zhang and E. Hoff (2008), "Correlates of Early Language Development in Chinese Children", *International Journal of Behavioral Development*, Vol. 32, No. 3, pp. 145-151.

Zhou, X., J. Huang, Z. Wang, B. Wang, Z. Zhao, L. Yang and Y. Zhengzheng (2006), "Parent-Child Interaction and Children's Number Learning", *Early Child Development and Care*, Vol. 176, No. 7, pp. 763-775.

Zhou, X., P. Moen and N.B. Tuma (1998), "Educational Stratification in Urban China: 1949-94", *Sociology of Education*, Vol. 71, No. 3, pp. 199-222.

Zigler, E., J.C. Pfannenstiel and V. Seitz (2008), "The Parents as Teachers Program and School Success: a Replication and Extension", *The Journal of Primary Prevention*, Vol. 29, No. 2, pp. 103-120.

Chapter 12

Implementing innovation: from visionary models to everyday practice

Lauren B. Resnick, James P. Spillane, Pam Goldman and Elizabeth S. Rangel
University of Pittsburgh and Northwestern University

Lauren Resnick, James Spillane, Pam Goldman and Elizabeth Rangel observe the lack of impact of the learning sciences on teachers' practice, identifying the reliance on "telling" as professional development and overly individualised perspectives as at cause. They also note the in-built conservatism and resistance to innovation of schools and school systems, and the gap between classroom practice, on the one hand, and the policies of organisations and systems, on the other. The authors argue for much greater attention to be given to the sociological understanding of organisations, organisational routines, and the role of professional learning communities. To enable change to happen, they identify the importance of "kernel routines" for seeding and propagating change focused on teaching and learning. Resnick et al. present and discuss two such routines. The first develops instructionally-focused leadership teams in schools and the second aims at direct improvement of teaching and learning through content-focused professional development.

Introduction

As evidence and enthusiasm for innovative forms of learning, teaching and schooling grow, the difficulties of changing practice in established institutions and organisations become clearer and more urgent. No-where is the challenge of innovation greater than in the education sector, where centuries-old practices of teaching are embedded in political and organisational structures which are resistant to new ideas – even in the face of growing evidence that traditional ways of working are not "paying off."

To meet this challenge and to overcome resistance to change, we argue in this chapter for serious attention to be given to the school organisation and its role for developing school practice. Our focus on organisational development does not simply stop with the building of new structures (*e.g.* formal positions, organisational routines). Rather, it is also fundamentally about implementing new structures such as the "kernel routines" that contribute to changing school practice as discussed in detail in this chapter. These shifts in school practice are designed to enable improvement in classroom practice *i.e.* teaching and learning. In this way, we use the fruits of research to craft school structures that enable certain social practices and constrain others. We present and discuss two such routines, implemented through the Institute for Learning at the Learning Research and Development Center, University of Pittsburgh, which confirm the promise of this approach.

The challenge of innovation in education

Why is the problem for innovation to take root and be sustained in education so marked? Several possibilities may be put forward. Most often cited is the fact that education has a relatively weak knowledge base compared with other service delivery organisations (especially those of the health professions). Although there exist a small number of practices that have been research-tested and shown to support student learning and development, most policy makers and practitioners are not deeply aware of the research base that might support (and sometimes challenge) their actions. Worse, there is no established way of incorporating new knowledge into institutional practices in a way that would improve professional practice and student learning outcomes. Education has a relatively undifferentiated set of roles for actors within the system, few required protocols systematically to incorporate "best practices" for managing school organisation and classroom activities, and there is little systematic in how new members are initiated into practice. As a result, education tends to be very conservative. By and large, the best way to predict which practices will predominate in five to ten years in most countries is to describe what is going on now.

Over the past several decades, the beginning of a science of learning and instruction has emerged (Anderson, 1983; Glaser, 1984; Glaser and Bassock, 1989; Resnick, 1987). The science of learning has grown mostly out of psychology and cognitive science, with the core focus on individuals – teachers and students. Efforts to put this new scientific knowledge of learning and instruction into practice have encountered difficulties associated with the organisational, institutional and political environments within which schools work. Learning scientists seeking to build a practically useful science of instruction have recognised again and again that "context" – the environment, organisation and general beliefs that surround any particular designed intervention in learning – matters a great deal. A few have redirected their careers to focus on issues formerly viewed as contextual nuisance (Bryk, Gomez Cobb, Stein and Resnick are among the U.S. scholars who have prominently emphasised context in their educational research). By and large, however, the creators of learning science have left contextual issues to others.

Not only has a focus on context been absent but a conspicuous reliance on canonical ways of imparting knowledge still predominates, that is, relying on an expert to tell others what they have found. Telling what is known via research articles and conference presentations is the method of sharing knowledge at which learning scholars are most adept. For the most part, however, presentations at professional meetings are aimed at "the choir" *i.e.* other researchers and scholars and a few "early adopters" among practitioners. Only through books and articles written specifically for practitioners and policymakers – of which this book is an example – do researchers engage in activities that are designed to make language and concepts accessible to audiences who are not specialists.

In the field of education, future practitioners experience a training process in which they read a specified set of texts – sometimes in the original scholarly versions, more often in adaptations intended for practitioners – that represent a canon of readings on learning and instruction. Most practitioners in the field can remember the names and claims of a few major theorists but the links between research-based prescriptions and what educators actually do in their work are thin. An unannounced visitor to a random school or classroom would encounter very little practice that matches the principles of learning and instruction being taught in teacher preparation programmes. The same goes for principles of educational leadership: the vocabulary of distributed leadership, or "professional learning communities", can be heard at professional meetings but is more rarely found in practice.

This limited impact of research on education practice is not for lack of sophisticated attempts to improve the communication process. To mention just one case, the cognitive research community in the United States has worked over the past fifteen years to communicate the most important findings of cognitive science research to policy makers and practitioners. The

National Research Council (NRC) Committee on Learning in 1996 produced a book entitled *How People Learn* (Bransford, Brown and Cocking, 1999), which quickly became the point of reference for scholars in the U.S. and other countries. Within a few months a more accessible version for educators appeared (Donovan, Bransford and Pellegrino, 1999). Through workshops and meetings with practitioners, the NRC launched a serious effort to carry the principles of *How People Learn* into classroom use. Most recently, a new volume has been published which includes detailed examples of how to apply the principles in teaching history, science and mathematics (Donovan and Bransford, 2005). These are sophisticated attempts by leading cognitive researchers to tell education practitioners what the research says and to craft the telling so that it relates to practice.

Yet even when they accept new programmes, educators' attempts to make sense of new information may lead them to fit the programmes into their existing scripts for instruction. For example, they may teach a math concept at greater length than the programme designers intended – so that all children seem to master it – and then skip the conceptual revisiting and extension that is built into a recommended teaching plan.

Teachers may also have strong beliefs about which students can learn what kinds of material and which students are "ready" for investments in learning. Beliefs about who can learn what run deep in our schooling systems and our societies. Despite substantial research showing that ability to learn can be acquired (Resnick and Nelson-LeGall, 1997; Greeno, Collins and Resnick, 1996), educators in most Western countries continue to believe that intelligence and aptitude set limits on learning, and we invest heavily in tests to detect that aptitude. The response of many psychologists to belief blockages is to try to intervene directly on the belief systems of students and teachers, instructing them to attribute success and failure more to their efforts than to their abilities (Dweck, 2003). They use group investigation strategies in an effort to enhance motivation (Shachar and Fischer, 2004) or focus on developing student self-regulated learning (Boekaerts, 2002). An alternative or supplementary approach might adjust institutional arrangements – for example, basing access to Advanced Placement and other high-level courses on students' willingness to do the work involved rather than on grades and aptitude test scores – but not call for any field-created change in practice.

Participatory structures for innovation

Telling can begin the process of delivering knowledge but it can never complete it, especially when the new knowledge departs significantly from existing understandings. Indeed, telling as a strategy has serious limitations because, when faced with new knowledge, human sense-making tends to conserve existing understanding. Something more than even sophisticated and audience-friendly reporting is needed; something that fits into what is now understood about the role of **learning in communities** as a crucial aspect of how people can change their practices. A powerful possibility and one only just beginning to be systematically explored is to develop and support professional learning communities for working educators.

The movement toward professional learning communities has a set of intellectual roots that lies in the discipline of anthropology and its offshoot, socio-cultural theory (Cole, Yrjo and Olga, 1997; Lave and Wenger, 1991) or, in its variant termed "situated learning" (Greeno, Collins and Resnick, 1996). In the 1970s, the work of Vygotsky (1978) was rediscovered and there were fruitful collaborations between learning, developmental and instructional psychologists with anthropologists. Partly as a result, a new way of thinking about learning began to develop (Hutchins, 1995; Resnick, 1987; Resnick, Levine and Teasley, 1991; Rogoff, Goodman-Turkanis and Bartlett, 2001). The new theories of situated cognition treat learning as not simply a matter of individual brains at work acquiring new knowledge or skills, but as persons coming to function effectively in specific, socially-defined situations. Cognition is viewed as a social activity, "stretched over" individuals, tasks and tools. Mind and motivation, skills and self-concepts are linked in an essentially socio-cognitive theory of learning and development.

One application of socio-cultural theory to the broader framework of education is "distributed leadership" (Spillane, 2005). A distributed perspective presses us to re-think leadership and management in organisations. Rather than focusing only on those with formal leadership positions, the distributed perspective allows for the possibility that all individuals have a hand in leading and managing, whether or not they are formally designated leaders. At the same time, it brings the interactional and situational aspects of leadership and management to the fore: the ways in which practice unfolds in interactions among leaders and followers as enabled and constrained by different aspects of their situation.

The concept of distributed leadership has sometimes been misunderstood as simply delegating leadership and management functions to individuals within an organisation, thus missing the crucial interactive or practice element. There are various ways in which distributed leadership can help frame ways of building new organisational processes (Spillane, 2005). However, there is no simple prescription for developing a high performing leadership organisation. For example, there are likely to be optimal numbers of participants for any particular leadership or management practice. Involving more people may result in diminishing returns, but at this time we do not know how to establish the parameters for optimal involvement. Further, distributing leadership beyond those at the top of the organisation is no guarantee for building social capital. While distributing leadership can increase opportunities for individuals in the organisation to be networked with one another and potentially with individuals beyond the organisation, whether it will build social trust among individuals ultimately depends on the nature of the interactions that make up day-to-day practice. Moreover, we cannot design practice; we can only design **for** practice (Spillane and Diamond, 2007). Designing for practice necessitates we attend to the organisation.

Strategies for organisational design: sociology and organisational theories

With only rare exceptions (Engeström and Middleton, 1999), socio-cultural analyses are largely silent on the organisations within which groups interact. It is as if the broad societal culture – long the purview of anthropology as a discipline – and formal organisational structure is carried by individuals into their group interactions without any institutional or organisational mediation. For more help in designing organisations, we have to turn to other fields of research rooted in sociology.

Finding powerful solutions to education and learning problems requires looking beyond individuals and even beyond the face-to-face social groups that individuals participate in. In order to "cash in" on what has been discovered about the nature of learning, we will have to examine the organisations within which teaching and learning take place, with special attention given to whether and how deep shifts in organisational practice might be induced. This means joining the growing knowledge about how individuals (and small groups) learn with theories of organisational performance and, especially, organisational change (Choo, 1998; Mabey and Iles, 1994; Senge, 1994; Sparrow, 1998).

Beginning with Max Weber in the 19th century, sociologists have sought to understand how formal organisations work and why they come into being. Weber sought to explain how bureaucratic structures (governmental and private) were efforts to rationalise and make more efficient the work and accountability of large organisations, where personal relationships could not sufficiently govern actions (Weber, 1947). Weber's theories were taken up by students and colleagues worldwide; variants of this rationalist theory dominated social science thinking about organisations throughout the first half of the 20th century. They were used to prescribe organisational designs in both public agencies and private businesses. In the United States, bureaucratic principles travelled from business into education along with the general principles of scientific management that were applied to industrial production (Tyack, 1974). In other countries, similar principles of rational management entered educational practice through governmental agencies.

For multiple reasons the Weberian rationalist analysis lost favour among sociologists in the 1960s and 1970s. More recently, however, a "new institutionalism" theory has developed (Meyer and Rowan, 1977; Powell and DiMaggio, 1991). This work tells us that organisations operate within a set of taken-for-granted (institutionalised) beliefs, practices and structures. Organisations mostly conform to these constraints, adopting ritualistic forms and structures for the purpose of legitimacy that often compete with efficiency; thus enabling survival over time. Organisations can also challenge these ritualised practices, becoming more effective in meeting reform goals but reducing the odds of survival. Indeed, some influential commentators suggest that true innovation can rarely happen in an established organisation, but instead will require the formation of new breakaway institutions (*e.g.* Christiansen, Horn and Johnson, 2008).

Among the institutionalised practices of public service organisations that make innovation difficult, including in education, are professional associations which control entry and advancement, labour agreements, expectations for transparency and consultation outside the organisation. In education, the traditional "decoupling" or "loose coupling" of the technical core (*i.e.* classroom teaching) from the formal organisation and from the policy environment slows innovation down. Of particular note is the way in which new instructional initiatives can be treated as experimental field trials, allowing the organisational leaders to inject multiple, sometimes conflicting, new programmes and leave for later (often for a new administration) the task of deciding whether to continue them and of figuring out how to spread them among teachers who were not among the "early adopters." In this way, education organisations can appear progressive while in fact maintaining institutionalised practices that prevent new programmes from penetrating the technical core (the majority of classrooms) beyond the few experimental sites.

Recent research on reform initiatives suggests that certain forms of institutional redesign can overcome some of the expected resistance to new practices (see, for example, Rowan, 2002; Rowan, Correnti, Miller and Camburn, 2009; Spillane and Burch, 2006). A decade or more of educational reforms involving systemic, standards-based curricula and intensified instructional guidance for local schools in Britain and the United States shows that policy reform focused directly on curriculum and backed by testing and accountability can shape, for better and worse, the technical core in schools – although not always in precisely the ways intended by the reformers (Firestone Mayrowetz and Fairman, 1998; Resnick and Zurawsky, 2005). Variants arise because policy implementation is also shaped by the sense-making interpretations of educators (Spillane, 2004). In addition, institutionalised norms linked to specific subject matter sub-cultures in, for instance, mathematics or history contribute to distinct patterns of tight and loose coupling. Some dimensions of instruction, such as the topics covered in a mathematics course, respond more quickly to policy prescriptions than others, such as the nature of classroom discourse or the mathematics representations used in teaching (Spillane and Burch, 2006). Recent work suggests that school leaders deploy organisational routines in an effort to connect external policy initiatives to classroom teaching and learning (Spillane, Mesler, Croegaert and Sherer, 2007).

School routines and bounded rationality

Schools function, as do all organisations, through a set of more or less interconnecting routines – "repetitive, recognisable patterns of interdependent actions, involving multiple actors" (Feldman and Pentland, 2003, p. 311). These routines are critical for any organisation to function because they provide stability and continuity over time (Feldman, 2000; Feldman and Pentland, 2003; March, 1981; March and Simon, 1958; 1993), and they structure action in the organisation (Allison, 1971; Gersick and Hackman, 1990). Theorists March and Simon argued (1958; 1993) that individuals cannot routinely use fully rational decision-making because of inherent limits in information-processing capacity. Instead, people "satisfice" *i.e.* find a workable but not necessarily perfect solution rather than attempting continually to optimise. Organisations, they maintained, do the same. Groups and individuals in the organisation develop routines that constitute the normal ways in which work gets done. These routines are not always in the official manuals, but they allow members to perform satisfactorily, in the judgment of clients and supervisors and for their own self-satisfaction. Such routines often involve adaptation to internal and external institutional constraints and may also recruit the power of informal "below the radar" work groups, as documented by socio-cognitive research (Orr, 1996; Suchman, 1996; Brown and Duguid, 2000; Resnick, Saljo, Pontecorvo and Burge, 1997).

Research has documented how formal and informal organisational routines frame and enable interactions, provide stability across time, and assist in socialising new organisational members (Feldman and Pentland, 2003; Cohen and Bacdayan, 1994; Sherer and Spillane, in press; Spillane, Mesler, Croegaert and Sherer, 2007). Their very pervasiveness and efficiency, however, together with the fact that they often function without official or explicit recognition, can result in routines acting as inhibitors of innovation (Hannan and Freeman, 1984). People in organisations often resist disruption of their ongoing practice, which is understandable in light of the significant personal and group costs that changing established practice entails (Hallet, 2010Marris, 1974). The more complex the organisation, the more stable the personnel, the more demanding the external demands – the more members resist changes in routines. Just as existing routines work to stabilise organisations, sometimes to the extent of inhibiting much-needed innovation, so too new routines can serve as sources of change (Feldman and Pentland, 2003; Sherer and Spillane, in press; Spillane, *et al.*, 2007). Responding to a shifting policy environment that presses attention to classroom teaching and student learning, school leaders designed and redesigned organisational routines in efforts at re-coupling government regulation with classroom teaching (Spillane, *et al.*, 2007).

Redesigning school practice: "kernel routines" for organisational change

When chosen purposefully and implemented well, new organisational routines can function as powerful instruments for transforming school practice. Resnick and Spillane (2006) used the term "kernel routine" to denote an organisational routine that has the potential for transforming school practice by "seeding" and "propagating" new forms of practice in schools. The idea is to introduce a routine that – because it is highly specified and supported by well-defined tools and strategies – can be implemented quickly at a reasonable level of quality under the guidance of the principal or other school leader. The routine has to be visibly focused on teaching and learning and responsive to established standards of accountability in the school.

Kernel routines serve two core goals. First, they link school management functions to classroom practice, thus helping to reverse the loose coupling between classroom practice and policy that has hindered progress in education. The kernel routine strategy does not simply impose a new process on teachers but rather provides sets of structured opportunities for teachers to understand and embrace new forms of teaching. Kernel routines work by connecting and weaving together other organisational routines in the organisation. Rather than attempting to drive out current practices, the kernel routine recruits and "re-purposes" the familiar ways of doing things.

This is not a simple process, and it cannot be simply announced by education policy makers or managers. For kernel routines eventually to supplant less productive existing ones, they must be sufficiently specified, developed and scaffolded so as to change the way people work. By "sufficiently specified" we mean clear articulation of the steps in the routine, the rationale for these steps and the requirements of each one. This calls for training procedures and a set of tools and artefacts for performing the routine.

Although initially to be enacted as specified, successful kernel routines are not strict scripts that actors in schools are expected to follow indefinitely. To function as a kernel for organisational change, the routine must be designed to encourage a process of appropriation (Wenger, 1998), in which users adapt the routine to their particular conditions and capabilities. The appropriation is accomplished by developing new forms of the routine and related routines over time. It is this designed openness to local, even individual, variants that makes the routine a **kernel** for organisational change. Hence, although kernel routines have to be well specified and developed to ensure implementation at the outset, they must also enable appropriation and adaptation if they are to seed and propagate new school practice.

In the first phase of implementation, kernel routines are introduced for faithful high-fidelity implementation with their original design. Through training and scaffolded performance of the routine, school leaders and then wider groups of classroom teachers learn to perform it in ways consistent with its designed intent. The first phase "seeds" by building social, human and physical capital. This allows propagation in the second phase, in which a release occurs from the performance of the specifics of the original kernel routine and allows for the generation and evolution of new routines as well as the re-design of existing ones in the school. In order to seed and propagate work in schools, a kernel routine must meet the following six criteria:

- First, it must be centred on the technical core – teaching and student learning.

- Second, it must be anchored both in the official curriculum of the district **and** the enacted curriculum of the classroom – what is actually delivered to students.

- Third, it must build common understanding about teaching and learning among district and school staff members.

- Fourth, it must build trust and mutual access among school staff members.

- Fifth, it must provide routes by which new knowledge can enter the school's community of practice.

- Sixth, it must be open to transformation over time without loss of its core designed elements.

We will describe two kernel routines developed by the Institute for Learning at the Learning Research and Development Center, University of Pittsburgh that meet these criteria. The first, *The Learning Walk®* routine, aims at developing an instructionally-focused leadership team within a school. The second, the "Pedagogy and Content Routine", focuses on direct improvement of teaching and learning through content-focused professional development within core school subjects.

"Learning Walks" as kernel routines for educational change

Imagine a group of school staff visiting classrooms in their own building. Their classroom visits are part of an initiative adopted to transform the school based on *The Learning Walk®* routine (LWR). A team composed of the principal, a coach and three teachers enters a fourth-grade classroom. This kind of visit is by now so routine that it evokes only a nod from the teacher. Students continue their work without interruption. A read-aloud of *The Upside Down Boy* by Juan Felipe Herrera (2006) is in progress. Students are discussing the main character in the book, an immigrant who feels "upside down" because he doesn't understand or speak English yet and is confused about school routines such as recess and lunchtime in the cafeteria.

The students (with teacher guidance) discuss the symbolism of borders in this book and identify those that they want to traverse in their own lives. On the wall is a large chart listing four books by Herrera and across the top are written schema categories for an author study: what the books are about, range of genres, elements of style and craft, and significance of the author in the world of literature. A visitor notices samples of student writing from another unit posted on the wall, with written feedback from the teacher and a criteria chart for good writing posted next to the work. A second visitor concentrates on the teacher's talk, trying to understand whether the teacher is reading this book to the class for the first time or whether this is a re-reading with the intent of comparing it to other texts by this author. A third visitor examines students' writing in reader response journals. The last two visitors talk with students and ask questions such as, "What are you learning today?" "What are you working on?" or "How will you know if your work is good?" After ten minutes, the team moves to the hall where they briefly describe their observations and raise questions about what they observed. After a few minutes, they move to another classroom and repeat the process.

At the end of the day, the team meets with the teachers whose classrooms were observed. The team describes what they observed and the questions that emerged during hallway conversations. The classroom teachers make comments, take notes and raise additional questions. The literacy coach wonders what might be heard from students if they were internalising the schema for an author study. Teachers talk about the schema categories on the wall chart and ask if there was evidence in student journals of themes the author writes about or references to web resources about the author by others. One of the participants (a "walker") notes that several students in the classroom could name barriers that they or their families had encountered similar to those in *The Upside Down Boy*. The coach presses walkers to articulate the question asked by the teacher to elicit this discussion. Hearing the exchange a teacher says, "I'm going to try that" and another teacher agrees. But the second teacher wonders how students will transfer what they learn from talking about these complex ideas to writing about them. A lively discussion follows and both teachers ask the coach to help them to plan an arc of lessons with writing assignments on authors they are studying. The group then plans the date and focus of the next round of learning walks, which will occur a couple of weeks ahead, with three of the teachers who were observed this time being the observers.

Figure 12.1 summarises the routine. It consists of the eight components shown in Column 2 that are intended to be practised in a continuous cycle of observation and professional learning.

Figure 12.1. **The Learning Walk® as a Kernel Routine**

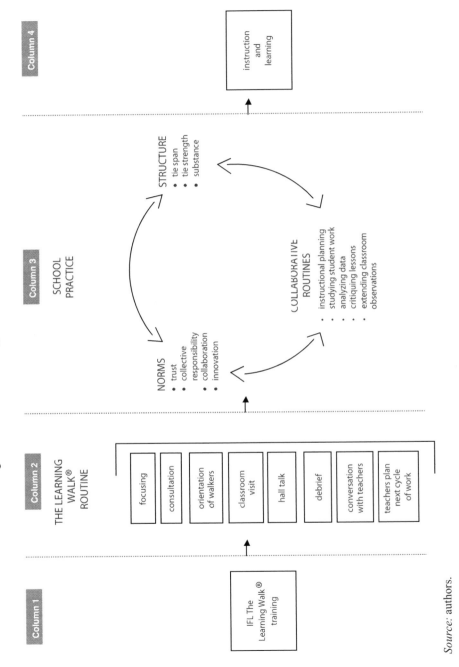

Source: authors.

Focusing

The LWR leader or team uses the "classroom instruction and learning observation" tool to specify an instruction and learning focus for its classroom observations. They plan the classrooms to be visited and who will be participants. The focus is based on current professional learning of the classroom teachers to be visited. Often, this professional learning has been planned in response to observations from a previous LWR visit.

Consultation

Once the focus for the walk has been set, the leader informs teachers who will be visited of its date and focus and asks for their guidance on what to observe within the chosen focus.

Orientation of walkers

Immediately before the walk, participants receive updated information about the focus of the walk, including relevant data and materials provided by the teachers to be visited. At this step, walkers plan questions they might ask students that they believe will yield information pertinent to the focus.

Classroom visit

The LWR school visit consists of three to five classroom visits, typically for about ten minutes each. Different walkers make different observations, individually or in pairs. These include talking with students, examining classroom artefacts on the walls or boards or in student notebooks or portfolios, listening to teacher-student interactions and listening to student-student interactions.

Hall Talk

After each classroom visit, the walkers have a brief conversation in the hall. The purpose is to check the accuracy of observations and ensure that all participants are adhering to the focus and the frame for that particular walk. In addition to piecing together the evidence, walkers help each other to **understand** what they have observed.

Figure 12.2. **The Pedagogy and Content Kernel**

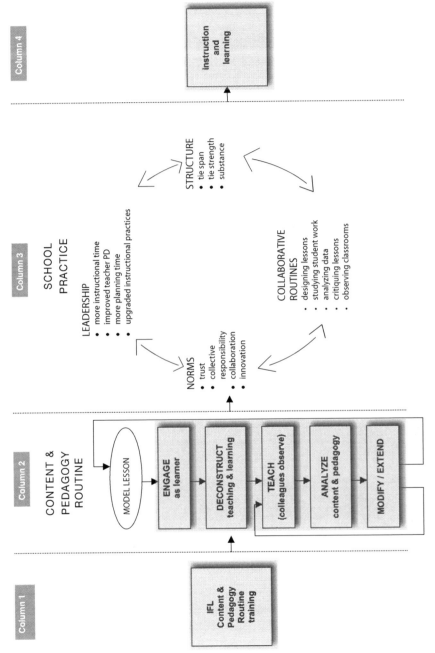

Source: authors.

Debrief

After all visits are completed and in preparation for discussing The Learning Walk® observations with the teachers whose rooms were visited, walkers meet to consolidate their observations and questions, looking for patterns across classrooms.

Conversation with teachers

Walkers discuss their observations and questions with teachers. They discuss possible next steps in professional learning and may consider a focus for a subsequent LWR school visit.

Teachers' planning

Teachers who have been visited discuss plans for their next step in collaborative learning. The principals, a coach and/or a lead teacher are included in these planning sessions.

As a kernel, the LWR routine is designed to be implemented initially with the specific sequence of steps taught, but also to generate new routines and transform existing ones in the school (see Figure 12.1, Column 3).

Curriculum-based teacher development: the Pedagogy and Content Routine

Another of the Pittsburgh kernel routines – the Pedagogy and Content Routine (PCR) (see Figure 12.2) – focuses on direct improvement of teaching and learning through content-based professional development within school subjects (McConachie and Petrosky, 2010). Designed as a direct route to implementation of innovative instruction, the Pedagogy and Content routine is a highly participatory training routine for teachers and coaches that is specific to the demanding programmes they are expected to teach. Like the Learning Walk® routine, it begins by engaging teachers in a tightly constructed routine consisting of a specific set of training practices. The training routine is expected, through the kernelling process, to produce new local school and classroom practices that are "propagated" from the training routine, but not direct copies of it.

Training and practice of the Content and Pedagogy routine occur separately within each content area but if this routine is introduced in several curricula, there can be "cross seeding" and the development of a larger institutional change within a school or clusters of schools. Teachers, coaches and lead teachers experience the following sequence.

Model lesson

The keystone component of the PCR is a set of content-specific units and model lessons. Each unit or set of individual lessons is designed to support the teaching of important concepts in a discipline. Units are thoughtfully designed to provide a coherent arc of lessons with subject matter, disciplinary thinking and reasoning skills and disciplinary pedagogy.

The lessons are academically rigorous, engaging and accessible to students, and include systematic supports for students who are not fluent in academic English. Importantly, the lessons include assessments on facts and on the conceptual frameworks that connect them (McConachie and Petrosky, 2010).

Educators engage as learners

Because a primary purpose of these units is to support the kinds of changes in teacher practice that support student learning and that educators may never have experienced themselves as students, educators engage as learners in a carefully chosen selection of one or more lessons from the unit and experience the classroom practice that will be expected when they teach the model lessons.

Deconstruct teaching and learning

The facilitator helps teachers step back and analyse the content, the disciplinary reasoning required, and the pedagogy and the architecture of the lesson. They discuss what it would take for them to teach the lesson to their students, including: what the lesson assumes the learner knows ahead of time, whether their students know this, and, if not, how they can provide the background knowledge without watering down the lesson.

Teach with colleagues observing

Lead teachers or coaches provide teachers with a second model by teaching students and using the model lesson as their guide. Coaches and lead teachers invite their principals and teachers to observe and take notes on the process and on student responses. All then debrief the content, pedagogy and architecture of the lesson, and student responses for a second time. The same routine is followed again as teachers teach the units to students in their classes.

Analyse pedagogy and content

Collaborative analysis of the pedagogy and content of a lesson or unit, usually led by the coach or lead teacher, is the core of the work of the professional learning community. It is what helps them individually and as a community continually to refine their practice. Common language, common professional development and common experience in classroom practice focus the work of the community.

Modify and adapt

As teachers teach model units and deepen their understanding of the units' content, pedagogy and architecture, of their teaching, and of their students' learning (or lack of it), they build the capacity to understand the modifications that will improve teaching and learning, not just in these lessons but throughout their curriculum.

A research team headed by Joan Talbert of Stanford University evaluated the PCR in six urban high schools in Austin, Texas. The evaluation report (Talbert and David, 2008) suggests that the PCR provides an effective vehicle for developing teacher collaboration centred on instruction, as well as for increasing the academic rigour of teaching and learning. A similar study in Los Angeles yielded similar results (David and Greene, 2007), as did a study of a related Pittsburgh kernel routine (Content Focused Coaching) in Austin elementary schools (Matsumura, Garnier and Resnick, 2008).

Both The Learning Walk® routine and the Pedagogy and Content routine, meet the six criteria for a kernel routine elaborated above. First, they are centred on the technical core of teaching and learning – the Learning Walk® routine on observation and refinement, PCR on adoption and adaptation of model units and lessons. Second, both are anchored in the official curriculum of the school **and** the enacted curriculum of the classroom. Third, they both use research-based principles of learning (Resnick and Hall, 2003) and principles of disciplinary literacy (McConachie and Petrosky, 2010), and they use content-specific observation guides or research-based model lessons and units. All this creates understanding of teaching and learning among participants. Fourth, both routines build trust and mutual access among staff. Carefully-designed practices in each allow for predictability when enacting the new routine and provide safe venues for educators to try out and observe new practices. Fifth, both provide routes by which new knowledge can enter a school's community of practice through training, observation and discussion. Sixth, both facilitate tailoring by school staff and are open to transformation over time, the "kernelling" aspect of both routines which is discussed in the next section.

School practice and kernelling

Kernel routines generate new school practices (Column 3 in Figures 12.1 and 12.2) that build the human, social and leadership capacity that are the seeds for new social practices in schools. These kernel routines generate social practices and other school routines that contribute to the creation of strong learning communities and to teachers' knowledge base, professionalism, as well as their ability and motivation to act on what they learn (McLaughlin and Talbert, 2006). They do this by structuring the interactions among staff (*i.e.* practice) and the norms.

Kernel routines can generate and grow other school routines such as instructional planning, studying student work, designing lessons, analysing data, critiquing lessons and extending classroom observations. These other routines contribute to the knowledge base of teachers and leaders and their ability to act on what they learn. When teachers work together to explore concrete connections between practice and outcomes, they create a setting in which discussion and reflection on data results in new understanding and motivation for change (McLaughlin and Talbert, 2006). Through practice and exposure to expert personnel, leaders and teachers improve their ability to critique and design lessons, thus becoming more expert in the different capabilities associated with effective teaching.

Structure of practice

Organisational routines can structure or influence the interactions among staff – who talks to whom, how frequently they talk and what they talk about – and in this way change practice (Spillane, *et al.*, 2007; Spillane and Diamond, 2007). The component sub-routines of the LWR and PCR provide school staffs with focused opportunities to interact with colleagues more frequently about instruction and student learning. The architecture of these two kernel routines helps to ensure that these interactions remain focused on teaching and learning. These interactions can increasingly span grade levels to include teachers in different grades (in order to build sequential and vertical alignment). These interactions can involve school leaders and individuals beyond the immediate school organisation so that school staff can learn from successful implementers in other schools and build equity of opportunity and inter-school coherence. As a result, the strength of ties among staff increases over time and tie span changes in important ways. The strength and span of ties are important for innovation in organisations. Research suggests that strong ties are necessary for the transfer of tacit, complex and sensitive knowledge (Uzzi, 1997; Reagans and McEvily, 2003), which are the kinds of knowledge often critical for improving classroom teaching. Strong ties also support joint problem-solving among organisational members (Uzzi, 1997).

Recent research has examined the extent to which social capital* influences reform implementation (*e.g.* Frank, Zhao and Borman, 2004) and how access to reform "expertise" within social networks influences teachers' instructional practices (Penuel, Frank and Krause, 2006). With respect to tie span, interactions that span "multiple knowledge pools" (Reagans and McEvily, 2003, p 242) reaching beyond their immediate grade level, or even school, allow staff to access new information about instruction and avoids "group think". One recent study of 88 urban schools in the U.S., for example, concludes that a school's internal and external ties (social capital), predict student achievement (Leana and Pil, 2006). A recent study of 47 Dutch elementary schools suggests that the more dense the work and personal advice ties among teachers the greater a schools' innovative capacity (Moolenaar, Daly, Sleegers, in press).

Norms

Implementation of both kernel routines leads, by design, to improvements in norms of trust, collective responsibility for student learning, collaboration and openness of innovation among school staff. This takes place through agreements to schedule and support collaborative school-based study and through the joint enterprise of studying the subject matter routines.

These norms are recognised characteristics of strong professional communities (*e.g.* Newmann, Marks and Gamoran, 1996; Kruse, Louis and Bryk, 1995; Talbert and McLaughlin, 1999), and are consistent with the communities of practice developed through the Pedagogy and Content routine (David and Greene, 2007; Talbert and David, 2008). Researchers have examined variation in the degree to which teachers feel collectively responsible for student learning; have a shared commitment toward high academic standards; trust their leader and one another; are open to innovation; and are reflective about their own practice. Many of these factors within a school have been correlated with higher teacher satisfaction and retention, higher student

---

*"Social capital" refers to those resources for action that inhere in the relations or interactions among people – the opportunities that some people have, and that organisations can create, for acquiring knowledge and other resources through interactions with others (original formulations include Becker, 1964 and Coleman, 1988). It refers to social ties and trustful relationships (Adler and Kwon, 2002; Nahapiet and Ghoshal, 1998). Some have begun to document the links between social capital (e.g. groups of teachers professionally engaged with one another within a school) and the forms of knowledge-based constructivism that cognitive and socio-cognitive instructional theory recommends (*e.g.* Bryk and Schneider, 2002; Frank, Zho, and Borman, 2004; Gamoran, Anderson, Quiroz, Secada, Williams and Ashmann, 2003; McLaughlin and Talbert, 2001; Newman, 1996).

engagement, student commitment to learning and higher student achievement (Bryk and Schneider, 2005; Newmann and Wehlage, 1995; Louis and Marks, 1998; Talbert and McLaughlin, 1999; Leana and Pil, 2006). The professional community in which teachers work influences how they teach. High levels of social capital among teachers in a school or department are associated with improved classroom practices and the achievement levels of students (Leana and Pil, 2006).

Leading and managing the technical core

Implementation of kernel routines generates positive shifts in leadership and management practice. It promotes a view of leadership that goes beyond the school principal to include other formally designated leaders as well as individuals with no formal designation. It focuses on the practice of leading and managing, develops that practice *in situ*, and, most important, focuses it on classroom instruction. School leadership and management become focused on instruction and on planning for its improvement. The LWR itself provides a structure and guidance for such improvements in leadership and management practice. Routines such as PCR that are more directly focused on instruction serve to support improved leadership and management practice by providing school leaders with a focus within the cyclical routine of school practice. Kernel routines reflect those instructional leadership and management practices associated with facilitating change and improvement in student achievement (Gates, Ross and Brewer, 2000, Leithwood, Louis, Anderson and Wahlstrom, 2004; Purkey and Smith, 1983; Elmore, 2006; Leithwood and Riehl, 2003).

Summary conclusions

The education bazaar has no shortage of ideas, some good and some even well-tested, about how to improve student learning yet we do not see widespread use of these well-tested ideas. One reaction to this limited adoption of research findings in education is to call for further research and, usually, for research of the same kind about how people learn specific subject matters. Most of those who do this research pay very limited attention to the social situation in which these ideas might be eventually taken up – classrooms, schools and school systems. As several generations of implementation research makes clear – these organisational arrangements matter to whether instructional ideas get noticed, adopted, adapted and implemented for some period of time.

We have argued that the problem goes beyond the need for more detailed research on learning. We need to understand the social and organisational factors that inhibit the implementation of new and effective practices. In fact, we have argued what most learning scholars call "context" ought to be a much more central focus of research and of implementation.

When we study context, we come up against the need to understand organisations and this leads directly to the sociology of organisations. A first look makes one pessimistic about change because organisations are powerful in maintaining themselves by adopting ritualistic forms and structures for the purpose of legitimacy that often compete with efficiency. On the whole, organisations keep doing what they have been doing even when what they have been doing is not working. So what resources for organisational change exist short of walking away from existing organisations? Clues about how to address this lie within these same theories about how organisations work. It is through routines that organisations live. By introducing new routines that propel change, we can position organisations for more success.

We call those new routines with the capacity to change school practice "kernel routines". These combine high specificity with openness. At the outset, they require step-by-step fidelity in uptake. At the same time, training is designed to invite subsequent building of next-generation routines.

The notion of kernels comes from biology. Think about how a farmer sets aside some kernels from this year's crop of corn to seed next year's. When that time comes, the farmer prepares the soil, plants the kernels, and again gets the same broad category of plant – corn – but it will not be identical. Biology processes produce varieties in order to maintain genetic health. The farmer may work deliberately to create new varieties to accommodate changing goals such as greater yields or to confront changing circumstances such as persistent drought.

In the same kind of healthy process, kernel routines are re-used and re-planted for each cycle of school work. The next cycle will be recognisable but not identical. Or, with deliberate intervention, the next cycle may result in a hybrid. Either way, the kernel routine is built on a biological model of continuity and transformation. Kernel routines such as The Learning Walk® routine and the Pedagogy and Content routine offer a promising approach to forging a working link between visionary models of educational practice and the practice itself, and between researchers and practitioners. Kernel routines have the potential to connect research and practice in dynamic ways. They provide educators with structured professional training building human, social, and leadership capacity but deliberately encourage them then to appropriate and transform the routines to meet the needs of their own school communities.

The development and transfer of knowledge is at the core of the educational research and development enterprise. We have argued for serious attention to the school organisation for developing school practice. In other words, our focus on organisation development does not simply stop with the building of new structures (*e.g.* formal positions, organisational routines). Rather, it is also fundamentally about implementing new structures (*e.g.* kernel routines) that contribute to changing school practice. These shifts in school practice are designed to enable improvement in classroom practice – teaching and learning. In this way, we use the fruits of research to craft school structures that enable certain social practices and constrain others.

References

Abrutyn, L.S. (2006), "The Most Important Data", *Educational Leadership*, Vol. 63, No. 6, pp. 54-57.

Adler, P.S. and S. Kwon (2002), "Social capital: Prospects for a New Concept", *The Academy of Management Review*, Vol. 27, No. 1, pp. 17-40.

Albert, S., B. Ashforth and J. Dutton (2000), "Organizational identity and identification: Charting New Waters and Building New Bridges", *The Academy of Management Review*, Vol. *25*, No. 1, pp. 13-17.

Albert, S. and D. Whetten, D. (1985), "Organizational Identity" in L. L. Cummings and B. M. Straw (eds.), *Research in Organizational Behavior*, Greenwich, CT: JAI Press, pp. 63-295.

Allison, G.T. (1971), *Essence of Decision*, Little, Brown and Company, New York.

Anderson, J.R. (1983), *The Architecture of Cognition,* Harvard University Press, Cambridge, MA.

Ball, S. (1994). *Education Reform*, Open University Press, Philadelphia.

Barnes, F. and M. Miller (2001), "Data Analysis by Walking Around", *The School Administrator*. Vol. 58, No. 4.

Becker, G. (1964), *Human Capital: A Theoretical and Empirical Analysis, with Special Reference to Education,* Columbia University Press for the National Bureau of Economic Research, New York.

Blase, J. and J. Blase (1999), "Principals' Instructional Leadership and Teacher Development: Teachers' Perspectives", *Educational Administration Quarterly*, Vol. 35, No. 3, pp. 349-378.

Boekaerts, M. (2002), "Bringing about Change in the Classroom: Strengths and Weaknesses of the Self-regulated Learning Approach", *Learning and Instruction*, Vol.12, No. 6, pp. 589-604.

Bransford, J.D., A.L. Brown and R.R. Cocking (1999), *How People Learn: Brain, Mind, Experience, and School*, National Academy Press, Washington, DC. Available online at *www.nap.edu/html/howpeople1/*

Brown, J.S. and P. Duguid (2000), *The Social Life of Information*, Harvard Business School Press, Cambridge, MA.

Bruner, J. (1960), *The Process of Education*, Harvard University Press, Cambridge, MA.

Bruner, J. (1986), *Actual Minds, Possible Worlds*, Harvard University Press, Cambridge, MA.

Bryk, A.S. and B. Schneider (2002), *Trust in Schools: A Core Resource for Improvement*, Russell Sage, New York.

Choo, C. (1998), *The Knowing Organization: How Organizations Use Information to Construct Meaning, Create Knowledge, and make Decisions*, Oxford University Press, New York.

Christensen, C.M., M.B. Horn and C.W. Johnson (2008), *Disrupting Class: How Disruptive Innovation will Change the Way the World Learns*, McGraw-Hill, New York, NY.

Cohen, M.D. and P. Bacdayan (1994), "Organizational Routines are Stored as Procedural Memory: Evidence from a Laboratory Study", *Organizational Science*, Vol. 5, No. 4, pp. 554-568.

Cole, M., E. Yrjo and V. Olga (eds.) (1997), *Mind, Culture, and Activity*, Cambridge University Press, Cambridge.

Coleman, J. S. (1988), "Social Capital in the Creation of Human Capital", *The American Journal of Sociology*, Vol. 94, S95-S120.

David, J. (December 2007/January 2008), "What the Research says about... Classroom Walk-throughs", *Educational Leadership*, Vol. 65, No. 4, pp. 81-82.

David, J.D. and D. Greene (2007), *Improving Mathematics Instruction in Los Angeles High Schools: An Evaluation of the PRISMA Pilot Program*, Bay Area Research Group Report.

Donovan, S. and J. Bransford (2005), *How Students Learn: History, Mathematics, and Science in the Classroom*, National Academy Press, Washington, DC.

Donovan, S., J. Bransford and J. Pellegrino (1999), *How People Learn: Bridging Research and Practice*, National Academy Press, Washington, DC.

Dweck, C.S. (2003), "Ability Conceptions, Motivation and Development", *British Journal of Educational Psychology Monograph Series II, Part 2* (Development and Motivation), pp.13-27.

Elmore, R.F. (2000), *Building a New Structure for School Leadership*, Albert Shanker Institute, Washington, DC.

Engeström, Y. and D. Middleton (eds.) (1999), *Cognition and Communication at Work,* Cambridge University Press, Cambridge, UK.

Feldman, M.S. (2000), "Organizational Routines as a Source of Continuous Change", *Organization Science,* Vol. 11, No. 6, pp. 611-629.

Feldman, M.S. and B.T. Pentland (2003), "Reconceptualizing Organizational Routines as a Source of Flexibility and Change", *Administrative Science Quarterly*, Vol. 48, No. 1, pp. 94-118.

Firestone, W.A., D. Mayrowetz and J. Fairman (1998), "Performance-based Assessment and Instructional Change: The Effects of Testing in Maine and Maryland", *Educational Evaluation and Policy Analysis*, Vol. 20, No. 2, pp. 95-113.

Frank, K.A., Y. Zhao and K. Borman (2004), "Social Capital and the Diffusion of Innovations within Organizations: the Case of Computer Technology in Schools", *Sociology of Education,* Vol. 77, No. 2, pp.148-171.

Gamoran, A., C. W. Anderson, P. A. Quiroz, W. G. Secada, T. Williams and S. Ashmann (2003), *Transforming Teaching in Math and Science: How Schools and Districts can Support Change,* Teachers College Press, New York.

Gardner, H. (1995), *Leading Minds: An Anatomy of Leadership,* Basic Books, New York.

Gersick, G.J. and J.R. Hackman (1990), "Habitual Routines in Task-performing Groups", *Organizational Behavior and Human Decision Process,* Vol. 47, No. 1, pp. 65-97.

Ginsberg, M.B. (2001), "Data-in-a-Day Technique provides a Snapshot of Teaching that Motivates", *Journal of Staff Development,* Vol. 22, No. 2, pp. 44-47.

Glaser, R. (1984), "Education and Thinking: The Role of Knowledge", *American Psychologist,* Vol. 39, *pp.* 93-104.

Glaser, R. and M. Bassok (1989), "Learning Theory and the Study of Instruction", in *Annual Review of Psychology,* Annual Reviews, Inc., Palo Alto, CA.

Goldman, P., L. B. Resnick, V. Bill, J. Johnston, D. Micheaux and A. Seitz (2004), *LearningWalkSM Sourcebook* (Version 2.0), Available from the Institute for Learning, Learning Research and Development Center, University of Pittsburgh.

Greeno, J.G., A. Collins and L. B. Resnick (1996), "Cognition and Learning", in D. C. Berliner and R. C. Calfee (eds.), *Handbook of Educational Psychology*, Macmillan, New York, pp. 15-46.

Hallett, T. (2010), "The Myth Incarnate: Recoupling Processes, Turmoil, and Inhabited Institutions in an Urban Elementary School", *American Sociological Review*, Vol. 75, No. 1, pp. 52-74.

Hannan, M.T. and J. Freeman (1984), "Structural Inertia and Organizational Change", *American Sociological Review,* Vol. 49, No. 2, pp. 149-164.

Harbison, R. and E. Hanushek (1992), *Educational Performance for the Poor: Lesson from Rural Northeast Brazil*, Oxford University Press, Oxford.

Herrera, J.F. (2006), *The Upside Down Boy,* Children's Book Press, San Francisco.

Hill, H., B. Rowan and D. Ball (2005), "Effects of Teachers' Mathematic Knowledge for Teaching on Student Achievement", *American Educational Research Journal*, Vol. 42, No. 2, pp. 371-406.

Hopkins, G. (originally published 4/12/2005, links last updated 2/5/2007), "Walk-Throughs Are On the Move!", *www.education-world.com/a_ admin/admin/admin405.shtml*, retrieved 1 August 2007.

Hutchins, E. (1995). *Cognition in the Wild,* Cambridge, MA: MIT.

Kachur, D.S., J.A. Stout and C.L. Edwards (2010), *Classroom Walkthroughs to Improve Teaching and Learning*, Eye on Education, Larchmont, NY.

Keruskin, T. E. (2005), *The Perceptions of High School Principals on Student Achievement by Conducting Walkthroughs*, Unpublished Doctor of Education, University of Pittsburgh, Pittsburgh, PA.

Kruse, S. *et al.* (1995), "An Emerging Framework for Analyzing School-based Professional Community", in K. Louis and S. Kruse and Associates, *Professionalism and Community: Perspectives on Reforming Urban Schools,* Corwin Press, Inc., Thousand Oaks, CA, pp. 23-44

Lave, J. and E. Wenger (1991), *Situated Learning: Legitimate Peripheral Participation,* Cambridge University Press, Cambridge, UK/New York.

Leana, C.R. and F.K. Pil (2006), "Social Capital and Organizational Performance: Evidence from Urban Public Schools", *Organization Science,* Vol. 17, No. 3, pp. 353-366.

Leithwood, K., K.S. Louis, S. Anderson and Wahlstrom, K. (2004), *How Leadership Influences Student Learning. Review of Research,* The Wallace Foundation, New York, NY.

Leithwood, K. and R. Steinbach (1990), "Characteristics of Effective Secondary School Principals' Problem Solving", *Educational Administration and Foundations*, Vol. 5, No. 1, pp. 24-42.

Louis, K.S. and H.M. Marks (1998), "Does Professional Community Affect the Classroom? Teachers' Work and Student Experiences in Restructuring Schools", *American Journal of Education,* Vol. 106, No. 4, pp. 532-575.

Mabey, C. and P. Iles (eds.) (1994), *Managing Learning*, Routledge, London/ New York.

March, J.G. (1981), "Exploration and Exploitation in Organizational Learning", *Organizational Science,* Vol. 2, No. 1, pp.71-87.

March, J.G. and H. A. Simon (with the collaboration of H. Guetzkow) (1958), *Organizations.* Wiley, New York.

March, J.G. and H. A. Simon (with the collaboration of H. Guetzkow) (1993), *Organizations* (2nd ed.), Blackwell, Cambridge MA.

Marris, P. (1974), *Loss and Change*, Anchor Press/Doubleday, New York.

Matsumura, L.C., H. Garnier and L.B. Resnick, (2010), *Implementing Literacy Coaching: The Role of School Social Resources. Educational Evaluation and Policy Analysis*, OnlineFirst, published on 3 May, 2010.

McAdams, D. (1993), *The Stories We Live By: Personal Myths and the Making of the Self,* W. Morrow, New York.

McConachie, S.M. and A.R. Petrosky (eds.) (2010), *Content Matters: A Disciplinary Literacy Approach to Improving Student Learning,* Jossey-Bass, San Francisco.

McLaughlin, M.W. and J.E. Talbert (2001), *Professional Communities and the Work of High School Teaching,* University of Chicago Press, Chicago.

McLaughlin, M.W. and J.E. Talbert (2006), *Building School-based Teacher Learning Communities: Professional Strategies to Improve Student Achievement,* Teachers College Press, New York NY.

Meyer, J. and B. Rowan (1977), "Institutional Organizations: Formal Structure as Myth and Ceremony", *American Journal of Sociology,* Vol. 83, No. 2, pp. 340-63.

Michaels, S., M.C. O'Connor and M.W. Hall (with L.B. Resnick) (2002), *Accountable TalkSM: Classroom Conversation that Works* [CD-ROM Set, Beta version 2.0]. Available from the Institute for Learning, Learning Research and Development Center, University of Pittsburgh.

Moolenaar, N., A. Daly, P. Sleegers (in press), "Ties with Potential: Social Network Structure and Organizational Innovative Capacity in Dutch Schools", *Teachers College Record.*

Nahapiet, J. and S. Ghoshal (1998), "Social Capital, Intellectual Capital and the Organizational Advantage", *Academy of Management Review",* Vol. 23, No. 2, pp. 242-266.

Newman, F.M. (1996), *Authentic Achievement: Restructuring Schools for Intellectual Quality,* San Francisco, CA: Jossey-Bass.

Newmann, F., H. Marks and A. Gamoran (1996), "Authentic Pedagogy and Student Performance", *American Journal of Education*, Vol. 104, No. 4, pp. 280-312.

Newmann, F.M. and G.G. Wehlage (1995), *Successful School Restructuring: A Report to the Public and Educators by The Center on Organization and Restructuring of Schools.* University of Wisconsin-Madison, Madison WI.

Orr, J. (1996), *Talking about Machines,* Cornell University Press, Ithaca NY.

Penuel, W.R., K.A. Frank and A. Krause (2006), "The Distribution of Resources and Expertise and the Implementation of Schoolwide Reform Initiatives", *Proceedings of the 7th International Conference on Learning Sciences,* International Society of the Learning Sciences, Bloomington, IN.

Powell, W.W. and P.J. DiMaggio (eds.) (1991), *The New Institutionalism in Organizational Analysis*, The University of Chicago Press, Chicago/ London.

Purkey, S.C. and M.S. Smith (1983), "Effective Schools: A Review". *The Elementary School Journal,* Vol. 83, No. 4, pp. 426-452.

Reagans, R. and W. McEvily (2003), "Network structure and Knowledge Transfer: The Effects of Cohesion and Range", *Administrative Science Quarterly*, Vol. 48, No. 2, pp. 240-267.

Resnick, L.B. (1987), *Education and Learning to Think,* National Academy Press, Washington, DC.

Resnick, L.B. and V.L. Bill (2001), *Clear Expectations: Putting Standards to Work in the Classroom* [CD-ROM, Beta version 1.0], available from the Institute for Learning, Learning Research and Development Center, University of Pittsburgh.

Resnick, L.B. and T.K. Glennan (2002), "Leadership for Learning: A Theory of Action for Urban School Districts", in A.M. Hightower, M.S. Knapp, J.A. Marsh and M.W. McLaughlin (eds.), *School Districts and Instructional Renewal,* Teachers College Press, New York.

Resnick, L.B., M.W. Hall and Fellows of the Institute for Learning (2001), *Principles of Learning: Study Tools for Educators* [CD-ROM], Institute for Learning, Learning Research and Development Center, University of Pittsburgh, Pittsburgh, PA.

Resnick, L.B., M.W. Hall and Fellows of the Institute for Learning (2003), *Principles of Learning for Effort-based Education,* [abridged version of E-book excerpted from CD-ROM], University of Pittsburgh, Pittsburgh PA.

Resnick, L.B., J.M. Levine and S.D. Teasley (eds.) (1991), *Perspectives on Socially Shared Cognition,* American Psychological Association, Washington, DC.

Resnick, L.B. and S. Nelson-Le Gall (1997), "Socializing Intelligence", in L. Smith, J. Dockrell and P. Tomlinson (eds.), *Piaget, Vygotsky and Beyond,* Routledge, London/New York, pp. 145-158.

Resnick, L.B., R. Saljo, C. Pontecorvo and B. Burge (eds.) (1997), *Discourse, Tools, and Reasoning: Essays on Situated Cognition,* Springer-Verlag, Berlin.

Resnick, L.B. and J. Spillane (2006), "From Individual Learning to Organizational Designs for Learning", in L. Verschaffel, F. Dochy, M. Boekaerts and S. Vosniadou (eds.), *Instructional Psychology: Past, Present and Future Trends. Sixteen Essays in Honor of Erik De Corte* (Advances in Learning and Instruction Series), Pergamon, Oxford.

Resnick, L.B. and C. Zurawsky (2005), "Getting Back on Course: Fixing Standards-based Reform and Accountability", *American Educator,* Vol. 29, No. 1, pp. 8-46.

Rogoff, B., C.G. Goodman-Turkanis and L. Bartlett (2001), *Learning Together: Children and Adults in a School Community,* Oxford University Press, New York, NY.

Rowan, B. (2002), "The Ecology of School Improvement: Notes on the School Improvement Industry in the United States", *Journal of Educational Change,* Vol. 3, Vol. 3-4, pp. 283-314.

Rowan, B., R. Correnti, R. Miller and E. Camburn (2009), "School Improvement by Design: Lessons from a Study of Comprehensive School Reform Programs" in B. Schneider and D. Sykes (eds.), *AERA Handbook on Education Policy Research.*

Schon, D. (1987), *Educating the Reflective Practitioner,* Jossey-Bass, San Francisco.

Senge, P. (1994), *The Fifth Discipline Fieldbook: Strategies for Building a Learning Organization*, Currency Doubleday, New York.

Shachar, H. and S. Fischer (2004), "Cooperative Learning and the Achievement of Motivation and Perceptions of Students in 11th Grade Chemistry Classes", *Learning and Instruction*, Vol. 14, No. 1, pp. 69-87.

Sherer, J.Z. and J.P. Spillane (in press), "Constancy and Change in Work Practice in Schools: The Role of Organizational Routines", *Teachers College Record*.

Sparrow, J. (1998), *Knowledge in Organizations: Access to Thinking at Work*. Sage, London.

Spillane, J. (2004), *Standards Deviation: How Local Schools Misunderstand Policy*, Harvard University Press, Cambridge, MA.

Spillane, J. (2005), *Distributed Leadership*, Jossey-Bass, San Francisco.

Spillane, J., E. Benz and E. Mandel (2004), *Organizational Identity: The Stories Schools Live By*, paper presented at the Annual Meeting of the American Educational Research Association, April, New Orleans.

Spillane, J. and P. Burch (2006), "The Institutional Environment and Instructional Practice: Changing Patterns of Guidance and Control in Public Schools", in H. Meir and B. Rowan (eds.) *The New Institutionalism in Education*, SUNY Press, Albany, NY.

Spillane, J.P. and J.B. Diamond (eds.) (2007), *Distributed Leadership in Practice*, Teachers College Press, New York NY.

Spillane, J.P., L. Mesler, C. Croegaert and J. Sherer Zoltners (2007), "Organizational Routines and School-level Efforts to Establish Tight Coupling: Changing Policy, Changing Work Practice?", working paper, Northwestern University.

Staub, F.C. and E. Stern (2002), "The Nature of Teachers' Pedagogical Content Beliefs Matters for Students' Achievement Gains: Quasi-experimental Evidence from Elementary Mathematics", *Journal of Educational Psychology*, Vol. 94, No. 2, pp. 344-355.

Strauss, S. and T. Shilony (1994), "Teachers' Models of Children's Minds and Learning" in L. A. Hirschfeld and S. A. Gelman (eds.), *Mapping the Mind*, Cambridge University Press, New York.

Suchman, L. (1996), "Constituting Shared Workspaces" in Y. Engeström and D. Middleton (eds.), *Cognition and Communication at Work*, Cambridge University Press, Cambridge, UK.

Talbert, J.E. and J.L. David (with W. Lin) (2008), *Evaluation of the Disciplinary Literacy-Professional Learning Community (DL-PLC) Initiative in Austin Independent School District*, Final Report, Center for Research on the Context of Teaching, Stanford University.

Talbert, J. and M. McLaughlin (1999), "Assessing the School Environment: Embedded Contexts and Bottom-up Research Strategies", in S. Friedman and T. Wachs (eds.), *Measuring Environment across the Life Span,* American Psychological Association, Washington, DC

Tyack, D. (1974), *The One Best System: A History of American Urban Education,* Harvard University Press, Cambridge, MA.

Uzzi, B. (1997), "Social Structure and Competition in Inter-firm Networks", *Administrative Science Quarterly*, Vol. 42, No. 1, pp. 35-67.

Vygotsky, L. (1978), *Mind in Society,* Harvard University Press, Boston.

Weber, M. (1947), *The Theory of Social and Economic Organization,* Free Press, London.

Wenger, E. (1998), *Communities of Practice: Learning Meaning and Identity,* Cambridge University Press, New York.

Chapter 13

Future directions for learning environments in the 21ˢᵗ century

David Istance and Hanna Dumont
OECD and University of Tuebingen, Germany

David Istance and Hanna Dumont summarise the key conclusions that emerge from the different chapters taken together. Learning research strongly suggests that an effective learning environment is one that:

- *Makes learning central, encourages engagement, and in which learners come to understand themselves as learners.*

- *Is where learning is social and often collaborative.*

- *Is highly attuned to learners' motivations and the importance of emotions.*

- *Is acutely sensitive to individual differences including in prior knowledge.*

- *Is demanding for each learner but without excessive overload*

- *Uses assessments consistent with its aims, with strong emphasis on formative feedback.*

- *Promotes horizontal connectedness across activities and subjects, in- and out-of-school.*

The chapter presents the educational agenda – learner-centred, structured, personalised, social and inclusive – consistent with these conclusions, before discussing some of the tricky issues related to implementation.

Introduction

This volume has presented a wealth of findings and discussion about learning. In this final chapter, we summarise a selection of the key conclusions about optimising learning* particularly with practitioners and decision makers in mind. Without such summary transversal conclusions or "principles", this rich vein of knowledge risks to remain fragmented and hard to apply by those looking for clear directions for practice from the research. We then show how the learning sciences give particular substance and interpretation to familiar terms on the educational agenda. We finally but briefly broach the tough issues of implementation, both through the priorities suggested by the authors and through discussion of making change happen.

Key transversal conclusions

The hundreds of studies reviewed in the preceding chapters were conducted under many different terms and conditions and have analysed the nature of learning in a very wide range of different contexts. While the fact that learning always is "contextualised" (De Corte) may inherently limit the comparability of the studies reviewed, when particular findings are repeated time and again they become the more compelling, despite the diversity of learners and settings. We interpret the situational nature of learning less as ruling out any generalisation about the dynamics of learning because of the infinite number of different contexts – though this does mean that no generalisation will ever fit perfectly – but as underlining the fundamental importance of the social, cultural and educational contexts in which learning develops and plays out.

The focus on learning environments, in preference to summary conclusions about different facets of individuals' learning, responds directly to this contextual reality. We suggest that a good deal of the research needs to be interpreted and "translated" into a more holistic perspective as this is precisely the one relevant for many practitioners and decision makers. Their guiding questions are less of the sort "how can I improve this particular aspect of learning of this particular individual?" and more "how can we organise matters to optimise conditions for learning for all those for whom we are responsible?". Answering the first question may provide invaluable information for addressing the second, but they are not identical.

---

* For the most part, this discussion is based on the different preceding chapters, indicating a particular chapter by the author's name – *e.g.* (De Corte) or "De Corte notes…" – rather than as a conventional reference. Naturally, where additional references have been added they are cited in the normal fashion with a publication year and are included in the bibliography at the end.

In fact, despite acknowledgement of the importance of learning contexts or environments, many working in the learning sciences have tended to focus on individual students or teachers and have left contextual issues to others (Resnick, Spillane, Goldman and Rangel). Resnick and her colleagues see a corollary regarding change: as well as seeking change via the skills and capabilities of individual professionals, they place great store by the development and support of "professional learning communities for working educators".

The conclusions presented below have recast the evidence reviewed in this volume into this more holistic perspective. In our view, this renders them immediately more relevant for shaping the nature of learning and education. More inter-disciplinary research within the holistic perspective, that combines the micro understanding of the "black box" with the study of learning environments in all their cultural and social richness, will serve to flesh out these broad conclusions.

Core "principles" for designing learning environments

> The learning environment recognises the learners as its core participants, encourages their active engagement and develops in them an understanding of their own activity as learners.

The learning environment recognises that the learners in them are the core participants, because knowledge is always actively constructed by the learner. "[Learning is] the mindful and effortful involvement of students in the process of knowledge and skill acquisition in interaction with the environment" (De Corte); for Schneider and Stern, students are **the** central players as ultimately the learning takes place in their heads. This is further confirmed by neuro-science showing that the brain is not a passive recipient of stimuli and information but actively constructs and interprets (Hinton and Fischer).

Recognising this central characteristic of construction implies that it is important actively to engage the individual in the learning; at least as important, engagement is needed by all in the environment not just by the quickest or most motivated. Making learning more active is a key rationale for different approaches as described in this volume, whether this be co-operative learning where the young people collaborate to advance their knowledge (Slavin), inquiry-based learning (Barron and Darling-Hammond), or as service learning (Furco). And as Wiliam summarises from extensive research on the benefits of feedback, just giving students feedback about current achievement produces relatively little benefit, but where feedback engages students in mindful activity, the effects on learning can be profound.

A learning environment oriented around the centrality of the activity of learning pays particular attention to fostering a keen and well-developed sense of what is being done when learning is engaged – *i.e.* it encourages students to become "self-regulated learners". This means developing the "meta-cognitive skills" to monitor, evaluate and optimise their acquisition and use of knowledge (Schneider and Stern). It also means to be able to regulate one's emotions and motivations during the learning process; for instance, using one's emotions as a source of energy or to maintain attention and motivation in the face of taxing problems (Boekaerts; De Corte).

Self-regulated learners "manage study time well, set higher specific and proximal goals, monitor more frequently and accurately, set a higher standard for satisfaction, are more self-efficacious, and persist despite obstacles" (De Corte). "Self-regulation" is not a separate set of learning skills from knowledge acquisition but an integral part of it.

When learning is recognised as the core activity in the learning environment, the gap between what goes on at the "technical core" (the classroom or wherever is the teaching/learning interface) and the priorities of the organisation in which it is located is significantly reduced. Resnick, Spillane, Goldman and Rangel identify such gaps ("decoupling" or "loose coupling" as they term it) as a critical factor explaining why change is often so difficult in education and why innovations and reforms are not sustained.

> The learning environment is founded on the social nature of learning and actively encourages well-organised co-operative learning.

"Effective learning is not purely a 'solo' activity but essentially a 'distributed' one: individual knowledge construction occurs throughout processes of interaction, negotiation, and co-operation" (De Corte). Neuroscience has also shown that the human brain is primed for interaction (Hinton and Fischer). Interaction and co-operation do not just mean face-to-face interaction but will nowadays often involve learners working together at a distance in co-operative projects using the possibilities opened up by ICT and digital resources.

Co-operative group work, appropriately organised and structured, can be enormously beneficial for achievement as well as for behavioural and affective outcomes (Slavin; Barron and Darling-Hammond). Slavin notes, however, that too many teachers regard co-operative methods as essentially unstructured, a misunderstanding which helps to explain why good co-operative learning approaches remain on the margins of much school activity despite the robust evidence base in their favour.

Wiliam proposes "activating students as instructional resources for one another" as one of the five key strategies that define formative assessment, which has been demonstrated to be integral to good teaching. The positive impact of co-operation in strengthening bonds among students from diverse backgrounds is also one of the arguments in favour of service learning in the community (Furco).

The ability to co-operate is a valuable outcome in its own right and needs to be fostered, quite apart from its impact on measured outcomes. Co-operation features prominently in the 21st century competences we discussed in Chapter 1 and referred to by other of the authors (*e.g.* Barron and Darling-Hammond). When co-operation takes the form of, say, collective problem-solving or project work it mirrors the situations that the young person will meet throughout his or her life. If school learning is dominated entirely by individuals working "with their hands round their copy" they will be poorly prepared for contemporary economic and social life. This is particularly challenging for assessment regimes as they need both to recognise and report individual achievement and to promote rather than impede positive learning and innovation (Looney, 2009).

The importance of co-operative learning, however, does not downgrade autonomous work, personal research and self-study. These have key roles to play especially as individuals approach and reach the teenage years. One benefit of adopting the learning environments perspective is to bring to the fore how effective learning will involve different pedagogies and modes of study over the course of the learning day, week, or month, not depend on a single approach. Hence, the well-researched benefits of collaborative learning are perfectly compatible with the need for individual study as each has its place.

> The learning professionals within the learning environment are highly attuned to the learners' motivations and the key role of emotions in achievement.

Learning results from a dynamic interplay of emotion, motivation and cognition. The emotional and cognitive dimensions of learning are inextricably entwined (Boekaerts; Hinton and Fischer; Schneider and Stern). It is therefore important to understand not just learners' cognitive development but their motivations and emotional characteristics as well. One of the five key components for developing deep understanding and "adaptive competence" for De Corte is positive beliefs about oneself as a learner in general and in a particular subject, and other components include self-regulatory skills and meta-knowledge regarding one's motivations as well as one's cognitive processes.

Yet, this interplay is much easier to acknowledge in theory than it is truly to absorb and act upon; attention to learner beliefs and motivations is much further away from standard educational thinking, even in teacher education, than goals framed in terms of cognitive development (Boekaerts).

Teachers need to be aware of students' motivational beliefs and emotional responses to guide the learning process and students need to become attuned to their own emotions and motivations if they are to become effective, self-regulated learners (Boekaerts). Being "highly attuned to learners' motivations and the key role of emotions in achievement" is not an exhortation to be "nice" for the sake of it and indeed misplaced encouragement will do more harm than good. Schneider and Stern address the common idea that learning should be fun by drawing a comparison with climbing a mountain: the fun of learning is like a testing ascent to the summit, not sitting up at the top with a digital camera taking snapshots of the view. So, attention to motivations – by all involved in learning, including students – is about making learning first and foremost more effective, not more enjoyable. At the same time, if learners do not get satisfaction [experience "positive emotions" (Boekaerts)] from the challenge it will ultimately have a detrimental effect on their performance.

Powerful reasons for the success of many approaches using technology (Mayer), co-operative learning (Slavin), inquiry-based learning (Barron and Darling-Hammond) and service learning (Furco) reside in their capacity to motivate and engage learners. That is, the child or young person is motivated to learn because the mode of learning using technology is appealing, or because the process and content are meaningful – as in many inquiry-based or community-based approaches – or because the learner is stimulated by contact with others outside the conventional educational community. Such examples show that the choice need not be between approaches that are stimulating and interesting, on the one hand, and those which result in measured learning gains, on the other, but instead of deploying meaningful, stimulating approaches precisely to promote learning.

> The learning environment is acutely sensitive to the individual differences among the learners in it, including their prior knowledge.

Students differ in many ways fundamental to learning: prior knowledge, ability, conceptions of learning, learning styles and strategies, interest, motivation, self-efficacy beliefs and emotion, as well in socio-environmental terms such as linguistic, cultural and social background. Hence, a fundamental challenge for learning environments is to cope with fundamental individual differences, while at the same time ensuring that young people learn together within frameworks of a shared education and culture. There is a constant and complex interaction between inherited capacity and experience in shaping learning (Hinton and Fischer; Schneider, Keesler and Morlock). Neuroscience confirms that people follow different learning pathways and it is increasingly able to chart how this is mirrored in the brain.

A fundamental characteristic of all human thinking is that people try to make sense of new information by linking it to what they already know and can do (De Corte; Schneider and Stern). Contrariwise, learners unable to make such connections will be seriously handicapped in addressing a new and challenging learning task. Prior knowledge thus substantially influences the learning process. It is one of the most important resources on which to build current learning as well as one of the most marked individual differences among learners (Mayer).

Such knowledge is built up from different sources and experiences, formal and informal – everyday life observations, hobbies, media, friends, parents and previous school experiences (Schneider and Stern). Schneider, Keesler and Morlock emphasise the importance of family in shaping educational expectations, occupational aspirations and academic performance.

Hence, understanding the different backgrounds and starting points that young people bring with them to the learning environment is an integral element of understanding the strengths and limitations of individuals and groups of learners, as well as the motivations and aspirations that so shape the learning process. Learning environments should thus be able to adapt activities and pacing to reflect these individual differences and preferences in ways that are sustainable both for individual learners and for the work of the group as a whole (Boekaerts, De Corte). Connecting very strongly with the prior knowledge of the learners thus makes the learning more meaningful and it serves to construct bridges between formal and informal learning.

> The learning environment devises programmes that demand hard work and challenge from all without excessive overload.

That learning environments are more effective when they are sensitive to individual differences stems also from the findings stressed by several authors that each needs to be sufficiently challenged to reach just above their existing level and capacity. The corollary is that no-one should be allowed to coast for any significant amounts of time on work that does not stretch them.

For Schneider and Stern, one of their fundamental cornerstones is that "learning is constrained by capacity limitations of the human information-processing architecture". Similarly, Mayer makes central to his chapter on learning through technology the notion of "limited capacity" (people can process only small amounts of material at any one time), and the need to attend to the distinction between each person's limited working memory regarding learning at any one time and the unlimited storehouse of long-term memory.

Boekaerts identifies as her first "key principle" that students are more motivated when they feel competent to do what is expected of them – hence, expectations do not wildly exceed perceptions of capability – and that students with "well-calibrated" judgments (*i.e.* in line with actual performance) are much more effective at regulating their learning. She also reports how, ideally, self-efficacy judgments should slightly exceed actual performance, raising effort and persistence without too many disappointments – repeated failure despite high self-efficacy judgments decreases persistence.

Slavin reports how evaluations show that co-operative learning methods tend to work equally well for all types of students. This counters the concern of some teachers or parents that such approaches will hold back high-achievers whereas the research suggests that high-achievers gain from co-operative learning (relative to high achievers in traditional classes) as much as do low and average achievers. This is partly because the effective group methods push learners of all abilities; it is partly that the high-achieving students learn through supporting the learning of their weaker classmates. Well-designed group methods can thus be an important way of realising this principle of stretching each learner.

Hence, the learning environment should demand hard work and effort from all involved, pushing them constantly to excel. But the findings reported in this volume also underscore the need to avoid overload and de-motivating regimes based on grind, fear and excessive pressure, not just for humanistic reasons but because these are not consistent with either the cognitive or the motivational evidence on what constitutes effective learning. Both this principle and the preceding one argue for "personalised" learning environments as they will need to cater both for substantial individual differences and be able to stretch each learner just beyond what they would normally think themselves capable of.

> The learning environment operates with clarity of expectations and deploys assessment strategies consistent with these expectations; there is strong emphasis on formative feedback to support learning.

The learning environment should clearly state what is expected, so that students know what they are doing and fit discrete learning activities into larger frameworks. If learners don't know what they are doing and why they are doing it, their learning will at best be haphazard and they will not become self-regulated learners.

More generally, assessment strategies have enormous implications for what is taught, and how effectively. Barron and Darling-Hammond express it as: "the nature of assessments defines the cognitive demands of the work students are asked to undertake". Wiliam similarly places assessment to the fore as "the bridge between teaching and learning", especially given the different capabilities and speeds of the learners.

Therefore, performance assessments should be authentic and intellectually ambitious and based on multidimensional criteria. The assessment strategies need to be consistent with the learning objectives and be appropriate for the learners involved. Assessment can be very positive for learning when it is well designed. Inappropriate assessments, however, including those that inordinately favour only a very narrow range of outcomes or that do not serve to progress the learning (the key element of Wiliam's definition of "formative assessment"), can have a corresponding negative influence.

Formative assessment is a central feature of the learning environment of the 21st century (Wiliam; Barron and Darling-Hammond; Schneider and Stern; Hinton and Fischer). Learners need substantial, regular and meaningful feedback that they can use to revise their understanding and their work. This kind of feedback supports students' motivation and helps them to sustain confidence in their own ability to learn. Formative assessment has to be integrated into classroom practice in order to be effective: the on-going assessment of students' learning should be used constantly to shape organisation and practice in the learning environment and to adapt instruction to student's needs (Wiliam).

> The learning environment strongly promotes "horizontal connectedness" across areas of knowledge and subjects as well as to the community and the wider world..

A key feature of learning is that complex knowledge structures are built up by organising more basic pieces of knowledge in a hierarchical way. Another of the "cornerstone" findings outlined by Schneider and Stern is that optimal learning builds up transferable knowledge structures – that is, discrete objects of learning are integrated into larger frameworks, understandings and concepts so that that learning can be transferred to new situations. In other words, an effective learning environment strongly promotes "horizontal connectedness".

Such connectedness – the ability to develop the larger frameworks and then to transfer and use knowledge across different contexts, including to address unfamiliar problems – is one of the defining features of the 21st competences that excite so much interest in contemporary educational discourse. But evidence shows that often students are unable to transfer understanding of the same idea or relationship in one domain to another, and even that changes in the illustrative examples of the same maths problem can make a marked difference to getting it right. What from a teacher's viewpoint might be obviously related will often be highly fragmented and chaotic from their students' point of view (Schneider and Stern). Helping students gradually to become more expert by successively linking more and more pieces of knowledge in the students' minds is thus a major aim of teaching.

The horizontal connections extend well beyond the learning environment itself as it is important for learners to see connections between the learning that goes on in formal learning environments and the wider environment and society as this helps to create meaning (De Corte; Furco). Students learn more deeply through "authentic learning" (Barron and Darling-Hammond). Thus, meaningful real-life problems have a key role to play in bolstering the relevance of the learning being undertaken: inquiry-based and service learning offer extensive examples of how this can be done.

Students only spend a minority part of their time in formal learning settings: interactions with parents, peers and media provide a raft of other opportunities and sources for learning. "[It is of] the utmost importance to look for and enhance cross-fertilisation between formal learning environments and students' informal learning" (De Corte). The most important influence and setting, especially in the younger years, is the family. "Families serve as the major conduit by which young children acquire fundamental cognitive and social skills." (Schneider, Keesler and Morlock) An effective learning environment will at the least not be at odds with the influences and expectations from home; better still, it will work in tandem with them.

A demanding educational agenda

It might be tempting to respond to the above conclusions and "principles" that they offer little that is new. In that the chapters have reviewed decades of research there is inevitably familiarity with many of the findings and proposals taken individually. Their force and relevance do not lie in each one taken in isolation from the others, however, nor whether they are formulated in an unfamiliar way. Instead, they derive from what they add up to taken as a whole.

We can go further to assert that **all the principles should be present in a learning environment for it to be judged truly effective**. Cast in this light, the agenda defined by these principles is in fact a demanding one and scarcely typical of many schools and classrooms. The conclusions and principles are highly flexible in the sense that they will not be realised in the same way in different learning environments nor in the same learning environment at different times; they are compatible with different educational models and approaches. However, if one of them is absent – robust formative feedback evaporates, or the awareness of the motivational drivers disappears, or the learners cease to learn together, or wider relevance or transfer is lost, or many learners disengage for extended periods – then effectiveness will not be maintained via greater emphasis on one of the other principles. They are all needed.

To be relevant to educational leaders and wider publics, the directions proposed by the learning sciences and synthesised above can usefully be translated into more familiar educational terms.

Learner-centred environments but with teachers in a central role

The principles identified through the chapters of this volume and presented in the previous section can be characterised as "learner-centred": an effective learning environment needs to be highly focused on learning as the principal activity. This is not as an alternative to the critical role of teachers and other learning professionals and indeed those responsible for implementing these principles will need high levels of professionalism and commitment. The focus of this strand of OECD work on learning environments is precisely to emphasise that learning is not something that takes place just "inside individuals" but is about their structured interactions with the content, with the learning professionals, and with the resources, facilities and technologies. The key players for designing and orchestrating learning environments are the teaching professionals and those in leadership positions.

For instance, Barron and Darling-Hammond note the demands of inquiry-based approaches: "it takes significant pedagogical sophistication to manage extended projects in classrooms so as to maintain a focus on 'doing with understanding' rather than 'doing for the sake of doing'". For Mayer, the distinction between the disappointing technology-centred approaches and the promising learner-centred technology approaches is in the way that the technology is adapted to the needs of learners – an altogether more sophisticated and demanding enterprise than simply generating access to computers and other digital resources. Wiliam discusses the importance of "regulating" classroom activity, not in terms of adherence to rules but as creating and adjusting conditions conducive to learning. He notes that many have called for a shift in the role of the teacher from the "sage on the stage" to the "guide on the side." The danger with such a characterisation is when it is interpreted as relieving the teacher of responsibility for ensuring that learning takes place: he sees the teacher instead as responsible for "engineering" a learning environment, both in its design and its operation.

Hence, it is quite misleading to contrast or oppose "learner-centred" with recognition of the work and professionalism of teachers. It **is** in contrast with "teacher-centred" when this means to dilute the core mission of engaging students in learning.

Structured and professionally-designed learning environments

These principles also imply an agenda of learning through structured and professionally-designed learning environments. They allow for inquiry and autonomous learning and with differing degrees of non-formal components, but they are not predicated on simply leaving learners to discover their own interests, tasks and talents in unstructured, unguided or unsupervised ways. The different chapters report the benefits both of teacher-initiated and autonomous learning, but these are neither accidental nor unstructured. The conclusions reached by Barron and Darling-Hammond, Slavin and Mayer as referred to above point in the same direction.

Hence, the conclusions emerging from the learning sciences reject an image of learning environments as primarily hoping that young people will discover interests and knowledge on their own, still more as something done as a solitary activity, even though all these should be possible. Learning professionals bring "value-added" with their expertise and the appropriate design and engineering of learning situations. In any event, young people often do not bring the requisite motivation with them for unguided discovery to work as the core approach (Boekaerts; Schneider, Keesler and Morlock). De Corte refers to an earlier Mayer study (2004) on the measured learning benefits of guided discovery ahead of both direct instruction and unguided discovery methods.

The focus on learning environments as patterned mixes of different learning activities that take place in context over time facilitates the insight that the learners need to experience a range not a single method or pedagogy. This insight can be overlooked when the unit of analysis is the single class-room or learning episode. In a well-designed environment, there may well be plenty of occasion for direct instruction as one of the range of methods for introducing and pacing content, to be used in combination with other, less directed approaches. Hence, this holistic focus invites the question of what mixes of approaches are most effective and innovative for particular aims and groups of learners, not whether any one of them is definitively superior to the rest.

Personalised learning environments

The above principles are fundamentally about personalisation (OECD, 2006). The term "personalisation" and approaches associated with it have their advocates and detractors, and it risks being just another "isation" with-out substantive content. The conclusions and evidence of the learning sci-ences as reviewed in this volume, however, give a particular endorsement of personalisation. We have described learning environments ideally organised so that they are highly sensitive to what the different learners within them already know and can do, and they actively build on this sensitivity and knowledge, *i.e.* they are highly adapted to individual differences. They give tailored and detailed feedback and they both challenge the quick learners and support those facing difficulties. This describes in effect a profoundly personalised learning environment, not as a uniform presence or as a par-ticular pedagogical or curriculum approach but instead imbuing the learning environment in manifold ways.

If a learning environment makes the activity of learning central and is to reflect the rich diversity of individual differences, it needs to be information-rich especially for the learning professionals working within it. This raises the importance of knowledge management and the use of information technologies, not only to stimulate learning but to manage information about learners (OECD, 2000; 2004). The more personalised becomes the learning environment, the greater this potential application.

Social and inclusive

Some take issue with "personalisation" when it is assumed to suggest either the solitary individual learning in isolation or choosing a curriculum for himself or herself from a *smorgasbord* menu on offer. In contrast, the principles outlined above are social – they stress that learning is effective when it takes place in group settings, when learners collaborate as an explicit part of the learning environment, and when there is a connection to community. Indeed, as we have seen, well-designed group methods can be an important way of stretching each learner.

Moreover, the principles have inclusion at their heart. Put negatively, a learning environment that is not motivating and does not engage most of its learners, does not give personalised and systematic feedback to all and especially those who are struggling, and that does not engage all learners in work leading to higher-order competence – *i.e.* is not profoundly inclusive – cannot be described as meeting the core conclusions and "principles" outlined in this chapter.

In summary, this educational agenda may be characterised as: i) learner-centred but with a central role for teachers; ii) with structured and professionally-designed learning environments albeit giving ample room for inquiry and autonomous learning; iii) personalised in being sensitive to individual differences including through different pacing and tailored feedback; iv) fundamentally inclusive and social in nature.

Outcomes

The different chapters in this volume report a wealth of analyses and meta-analyses showing the positive, as well as the sometimes negative, effects of different practices and arrangements. It cannot be assumed, however, that desired outcomes are agreed by all. It is important to ask what kinds of learning effects and outcomes are most valuable – a study demonstrating improved short-term capacity to recall nonsense words is clearly not worthy of the same attention by practitioners as one showing promise in promoting the sustained mastery of complex conceptual material.

The authors in different ways acknowledge how the demands of the "knowledge society" inform the underlying learning goals, cutting across their different perspectives and recommendations. The importance of establishing the foundations for lifelong competence and capacity to learn is repeatedly underscored, whether defined as "adaptive competence" or "meaningful learning" or "deep learning" or "generative processing" – all of which are understood to enable critical thinking, flexible problem-solving, and the transfer of skills and use of knowledge acquired in one situation to address problems arising in new situations. It calls for the capacity to grasp the parallels between superficially different problems or routines or pieces of knowledge – something which even learners that seem to have mastered an area often find difficult.

At the same time, developing adaptive competence should not be understood as something at odds with learning routines; mastery of content and routines indeed facilitates it. "Well-practiced procedures help students to solve routine problems efficiently and with minimal cognitive resources. These resources can then be used to solve newer and complex problems on the basis of deeper conceptual understanding" (Schneider and Stern). This is especially true for those students who experience difficulties developing higher-order thinking skills.

In addition to "adaptive competence", we noted above that the ability to co-operate is a valuable outcome in its own right and needs to be fostered, quite apart from its impact on measured achievement outcomes. We might observe the same thing about creativity, or willingness to take risks, or indeed the capacity for diligent persistence. These are not simply capacities and attitudes to promote as a route to higher test scores – though they may certainly be that too – but are important in their own right.

If an excessively narrow understanding of effects or outcomes is used, however, it will define an impoverished educational agenda. There is a common temptation to favour any approach associated with higher measurable scores, but if an alternative raises scores **and** improves motivation, interest, problem-solving ability and creativity this is essential information to know. Assessment design is thus a critical issue for revealing the benefits of different approaches to learning, as well as for promoting learning. As Barron and Darling-Hammond argue in their chapter, if one only looks at traditional learning outcomes, inquiry-based and traditional methods of instruction appear to yield similar results. The benefits for inquiry learning are found when the assessments require application of knowledge and measure quality of reasoning.

While many of these "softer" and long-term outcomes will by their nature be difficult to measure, we should not hide behind the difficulty of measurement to avoid evaluation. If new and innovative approaches deserve closer attention, it is only natural that the supportive evidence should be marshalled or gathered, so far as this is possible.

The challenge of implementation

The obvious question posed by any review of research that has sought to identify promising ways forward is: "but how do we get there?" We begin with the variety of proposals contained within the preceding chapters. The chapter that most explicitly addresses implementation is that by Resnick, Spillane, Goldman and Rangel as they take as their subject the challenge of moving from visionary isolated cases of innovation to widespread routine practice. We conclude the chapter with some observations of our own and from related OECD work about the thorny issue of implementation.

Identified priorities for change

The ideas for change emerging from the above chapters do not add up to a single or elaborated set of reform proposals: this was neither part of the authors' brief nor would they necessarily agree on reform priorities even if it had been. The ideas for change formulated in sharpest relief revolve around teacher professional development.

De Corte argues for intensive teacher and leadership professional development aiming at "high fidelity" applications of innovative learning environments, supported by initiatives to change teacher (and student) beliefs about learning. Boekaerts calls for wide-ranging review of teacher education programmes to ensure that teachers arrive at more comprehensive understandings of how cognition, motivation, teaching and learning work together, together with training in applications that put such understanding into practice. The chapters on demanding applications – co-operative learning (Slavin), inquiry-based approaches (Barron and Darling-Hammond), formative assessment (Wiliam; Barron and Darling-Hammond) and service learning (Furco) – all stress the high levels of professional demands they make, arguing equally for intensive teacher professional development.

For Slavin, new professional knowledge needs to be adopted and applied in a sustained way in different learning environments, so that teacher education programmes can usefully be supplemented through follow-up such as knowledgeable coaches giving feedback, demonstrations and providing support to teachers. Barron and Darling-Hammond suggest in their chapter that appropriate resources can help to scaffold both teacher and student learning using such means as models, public forums, tools, books, films and fieldtrips. Hence, a broad understanding of professional development is needed. And as Wiliam points out, it is natural that the teacher should be identified first in the front line of change as this is where the responsibility for "engineering" the teaching-learning interface ultimately lies.

However, in our view it is far from clear that the complexity and profundity of change implied by the transversal conclusions will be realised simply through a new teacher skills set, still less that this can be effected through appropriate teacher education programmes. There clearly is a major project of teacher learning to address but while this may be a necessary condition of widespread change, it is far from sufficient.

The authors themselves are not only concerned with teacher education as the mechanism of change. Other suggestions contained in the chapters revolve around different means of creating stronger links between the learning environments of schools and the wider community beyond. An important part of this relates to the links between schools, families and households.

Hinton and Fischer, for instance, argue to enhance the community orientation of learning environments to make more explicit the links between formal learning and the wider world beyond schools; Furco similarly proposes different forms of service learning as a means of widening the horizons and relevance of learning. Schneider, Keesler and Morlock advocate giving direct support to families as key loci of learning, particularly the less advantaged, rather than leaving the responsibility entirely to the school, albeit that this can and should be supported by well-structured, multi-faceted formal learning environments. They suggest – in line with the personalisation agenda identified earlier in the chapter – that there is need to personalise relationships with learners' families as well as with the learners themselves. At a more general level, De Corte proposes to foster communication with the wider community so as to elicit the support of stakeholders who may well hold traditional goals and expectations and hence impede change. This assumes, of course, that the learning environment itself is persuaded about, and well advanced on, a "non-traditional" course.

The third set of suggestions made by the chapter authors recognises that this is not a realistic assumption in many cases. De Corte himself identifies student and teacher beliefs about learning as a serious obstacle for the implementation of the kinds of learning approaches outlined earlier, the more because of the deeply entrenched stability of teaching behaviour. As he puts it "… changing beliefs constitutes in itself a major challenge". This clearly goes much deeper than teacher knowledge or expertise that might be addressed through appropriate teacher education courses. Such beliefs have their source both in the wider culture of social expectations and in the cultures and "grammars" (*e.g.* Tyack and Tobin, 1994) of schools with deeply-entrenched structures and routines. Resnick, Spillane, Goldman and Rangel similarly locate deep-seated teacher beliefs as fundamental, and they analyse these within the organisational structures – "routines" – which are particularly powerful in education and in schools in particular.

A good illustration of the challenge of altering well-established "grammars" or "routines" is offered by Robert Slavin regarding co-operative learning. The evidence base on the beneficial effects of cooperative learning is robust, it features in many teacher education programmes, and student teachers and practising professionals largely endorse its value, yet still it remains on the margins of practice. Despite thirty years of experimentation and evaluative research showing positive results and widespread endorsement, co-operative learning still belongs in the category "innovation" having not managed to break into the routines and arrangements of many schools and classrooms. Much the same could be observed about inquiry-based learning and formative assessment. If these approaches which enjoy a strong measure of support from research evidence about their benefits struggle to make headway, the challenge facing innovations that are not so widely accepted is indeed imposing.

Resnick, Spillane, Goldman and Rangel succinctly summarise the limited impact of the aspects of teacher education most closely related to the subject of this volume to find their way through into everyday practice later on:

> Most practitioners in the field can remember the names and claims of a few major theorists but the links between research-based prescriptions and what educators actually do in their work are thin. An unannounced visitor to a random school or classroom would encounter very little practice that matches the principles of learning and instruction being taught in teacher preparation programmes. The same goes for principles of educational leadership: the vocabulary of distributed leadership, or "professional learning communities," can be heard at professional meetings but is more rarely found in practice.

While part of the problem might be ineffective teacher education, the causes are much more deep-seated within the routines and cultures of educational institutions. This is not specific to education; as expressed by Resnick and her colleagues it is about organisational behaviour in general: "The more complex the organisation, the more stable the personnel, the more demanding the external demands – the more members resist changes in routines".

Making change happen

The issue of introducing change into longstanding, highly structured "mass" school systems, and the organisations operating within them, enjoys an enormous literature and is a subject well beyond this volume. We can offer no more than some concluding thoughts, based both on this study and related OECD work.

One approach to change lies in developing organisational strategies such as those described by Resnick, Spillane, Goldman and Rangel as "kernel routines". A first phase builds social, human and physical capital that allows for the propagation of "kernelling" in the second phase, which is more generalised and promotes the generation and evolution of new routines as well as the re-design of existing ones in the school. The authors describe the conditions and prerequisites for this to work. These, and strategies like them that combine deep understanding of learning and of the organisational routines that can allow them to flourish, are an integral part of positively disrupting the powerful forces maintaining the *status quo*. They call for innovative forms of leadership (OECD, 2008a) and a strong focus on professional collaboration and communities of practice.

The reference to "physical capital" raises the design dimension often overlooked in the more general literature on educational innovation.** Flexible, adaptable spaces facilitate the introduction of new approaches by learning professionals working individually or collectively, while unsuitable ones impede their adoption except among the most highly motivated groups of teachers and learners. Formative assessment and co-operative and project-based learning are all facilitated in flexible spaces designed to accommodate them. For technology to make a decisive impact requires that thresholds of equipment and use are reached (see OECD, 2010a), with its implications for the design and flexibility of facilities (even if, as Mayer forcefully reminds us, access to technology itself is far from sufficient for good learning). The implications of more thorough-going versions of service-learning (Furco) alter the demands on and use of conventional facilities.

In addressing the aim of systemising innovation, a key role is to be played by improving knowledge management (OECD 2009a; 2009b). This characteristic of education systems has been identified as typically weak in education systems and in schools in particular (OECD 2000). They are conventionally poor at using the four key "pumps of innovation" – research knowledge, networking, modular restructuring, technological advance (OECD 2004). Increasingly, these different sources of dynamic change are being better understood and addressed, whether through networking (*e.g.* OECD, 2003), or knowledge brokerage, making research knowledge accessible to practitioners in diverse forms (OECD, 2007), while there is longstanding analysis of technology in education [most recently at OECD in work on digital resources (OECD 2009a) and technology use in schools (OECD, 2010a)].

Improving knowledge management arrangements in this context is especially about providing the structures, mechanisms and incentives so as to move away from individual teachers continually having to "rediscover

---

** It has long been the focus of OECD work through its section formerly known as the Programme on Educational Building (PEB) and more recently renamed as the "Centre for Effective Learning Environments" (CELE).

the wheel" for themselves but instead being well informed about already-implemented innovative practices and their strengths and weaknesses. The dual innovation challenge is to create more systemic innovation in education systems, on the one hand, and ensure that the competences underpinning innovation in the wider society and economy are more systematically developed through education, on the other (OECD 2010b). Why this is so relevant to the issues discussed in this volume, and the directions for change summarised in this chapter, is that they call for a fundamental innovation drive in most education systems.

This is not about simply encouraging innovation for its own sake – "letting a thousand flowers bloom" – but of fostering it in order to realise as the norm the demanding principles we have elaborated above. The "routines" described by Resnick, Spillane, Goldman and Rangel as a means of seeding and propagating innovation (using powerful biological metaphors), are distinctive in being so strongly focused on the nature of learning itself, as opposed to some other aspect of organisational functioning further removed from the learners and learning.

Much has been done to address the knowledge management weaknesses in education over recent years. It brings the discussion back to the often tenuous links between research on learning, on the one hand, and practice and policy, on the other, which is where this volume began (the "great disconnect" as referred to De Corte, citing Berliner [2008]). There remains much to be done to bring the three worlds together. Far too often, research is addressing problems or is produced in formats and language which cannot be applied by those working in education. But equally, in a world where increasingly policy and practice are meant to be "evidence-informed" (even if to be "evidence-based" may be largely out of reach given education's sheer complexity), there is need to take much more seriously the evidence on the nature of learning as covered in this volume. It should be used to help redesign learning environments and to inform policy programmes aimed at raising educational quality and equity.

Several of the authors suggest, more or less directly, that structures and practices that inhibit the possibility to take time to learn deeply, or inhibit inter-disciplinary practice, or discourage inquiry- and community-based approaches, need to be re-examined. This applies especially to the core areas of curriculum and assessment. We have focused much on assessment practices and policies ourselves in the opening chapter and in this one: assessment in particular provides the key signposts – to learners, teachers and parents – about what is valued and what is peripheral in education. If on balance assessment favours traditional approaches to learning, rather than fostering 21st century competences, it should not be surprising that learning environments resembling the conclusions introducing this chapter remain the exception rather than the rule (see *e.g.* Looney, 2009).

Therefore, while it is understandable that agendas for change regarding schools as learning organisations begin with teacher knowledge and skills and focus on teacher education and professional development, ensuring consistent and forward-looking assessment systems may well be at least as important to effect change. The more general policy role lies in the diffuse but essential one of framing and supporting positive climates, influencing positive general cultures within schools and in the wider society.

We conclude with a general concern about the demands required by the concluding principles of this volume, based on extensive learning science research. Many of the directions for change as suggested by the authors call for high levels of expertise and professionalism. The flexible use of well-resourced learning spaces assumes a level of investment that is out of reach in many corners of the world. Does this mean that such directions represent a privileged and unrealistic luxury? Clearly, ample resources well-spent can make a real difference to what learning environments can do. But education systems are already highly expensive and we believe that many of the proposals contained in this volume call for the re-direction of existing resources rather than the creation of significant new ones. The first "Innovative Learning Environments" publication (OECD, 2008b) showed what can be done with often low financial investments in poor communities given appropriate creativity and motivation (in that case in Mexico). Given the right stimulus and momentum, the conclusions outlined in this volume show the way for designing and sustaining learning environments for the 21st century.

References

Berliner, D. (2008), "Research, Policy, and Practice: The Great Disconnect" in S.D. Lapan and M.T. Quartaroli (eds.), *Research Essentials: An Introduction to Designs and Practices,* Jossey-Bass, Hoboken, NJ, pp. 295-325.

Looney, J. (2009), *Assessment and Innovation In Education,* OECD Education Working Paper No. 24, July, 61 pp.

Mayer, R.E. (2004), "Should There Be a Three-Strikes Rule against Pure Discovery Learning?", *American Psychologist,* Vol. 59, No. 1, pp. 14-19.

OECD (2000), *Knowledge Management in the Learning Society,* OECD Publishing, Paris.

OECD (2003), *Networks of Innovation: Towards New Models for Managing Schools and Systems,* OECD Publishing, Paris.

OECD (2004), *Innovation in the Knowledge Economy: Implications for Education and Learning,* OECD Publishing, Paris.

OECD (2006), *Personalising Education,* OECD Publishing, Paris.

OECD (2007), *Evidence in Education: Linking Research and Policy,* OECD Publishing, Paris.

OECD (2008a), *Improving School Leadership – Volume 2: Case Studies in System Leadership* (edited by Beatriz Pont, Deborah Nusche, and David Hopkins), OECD Publishing, Paris.

OECD (2008b), *Innovating to Learn, Learning to Innovate,* OECD Publishing, Paris.

OECD (2009a), *Beyond Textbooks: Digital Learning Resources as Systemic Innovation in the Nordic Countries,* OECD Publishing, Paris.

OECD (2009b), *Working out Change: Systemic Innovation in Vocational Education and Training,* OECD Publishing, Paris.

OECD (2010a), *Are the New Millennium Learners Making the Grade?: Technology Use and Educational Performance in PISA 2006*, OECD Publishing, Paris.

OECD (2010b), *The OECD Innovation Strategy: Getting a Head Start on Tomorrow,* OECD Publishing, Paris

Tyack, D. and W. Tobin (1994), "The "Grammar" of Schooling: Why Has it Been so Hard to Change?", *American Educational Research Journal*, Vol. 31, No. 3, 453-479.